Measures for Manufacturing Excellence

Harvard Business School
Series in Accounting and Control
Series Editor, Robert S. Kaplan

Board of Advisers

Rewarding Results
Motivating Profit Center Managers
by Kenneth A. Merchant

Measures for Manufacturing Excellence
Edited by Robert S. Kaplan

Measures for Manufacturing Excellence

Edited by
Robert S. Kaplan
Harvard Business School

Harvard Business School Press
Boston, Massachusetts

The paper used in this publication meets the requirements of the American National
Standard for Permanence of Paper for Printed Library Materials Z39.49–1984.

LIBRARY OF CONGRESS CATALOGING-IN-PUBLICATION DATA
Measures for manufacturing excellence / edited by Robert S. Kaplan,
    p.   cm. —(Harvard Business School series in accounting and
control)
    Includes bibliographical references.
    ISBN 0-87584-229-1 (alk. paper)
    1. Manufactures—Management—Congresses.   I. Kaplan, Robert S.
II. Series.
HD9720.5.M43   1990
658—dc20   88-77840
                                                       CIP

Contents

Measures for
Manufacturing Excellence

Introduction

Robert S. Kaplan

ON January 25–26, 1989, a colloquium was held at the Harvard Business School to discuss contemporary trends in measuring manufacturing performance.[1] Twelve papers, by a total of twenty-four professors from business schools around the world, were presented to and discussed by an audience of eighty-five manufacturing and finance executives, consultants, and academics.

The colloquium, held in the last year of the 1980s decade, was particularly timely and important. That decade shocked Western manufacturers into a new paradigm for competitive success. As inflationary demand subsided in the early 1980s, manufacturing firms saw how companies from East Asia, primarily Japan, were achieving enormous gains because of their ability to design high-performance, high-quality products that could be manufactured reliably and efficiently. Western companies realized they had to make fundamental changes in their design and manufacturing processes if they were to survive in the new global competition.

Many companies did make enormous strides during the 1980s to incorporate total quality management (TQM), just-in-time (JIT) manufacturing and distribution processes, design for manufacturability (DFM), and flexible manufacturing systems (FMS) into their operations. Many companies, however, were much slower to adapt their financial and managerial accounting systems to the new operating en-

1

vironment.[2] As a consequence, operating improvements, which were considerable, were not being tracked well by traditional financial performance-measurement systems. Existing systems for cost and performance measurement provided little motivation to support companies' attempts to incorporate TQM, JIT, DFM, and FMS concepts into ongoing, continuous improvement activities. In some instances, the traditional financial-performance measures actually inhibited the improvement activities. Several companies joined a consortium to document their frustration with existing performance-measurement systems and to attempt to establish a framework for a new generation of cost management systems.[3]

By the closing years of the decade, companies were starting to develop and implement new approaches for motivating manufacturing and design excellence. The colloquium documented the status of these approaches in leading organizations in the United States, Canada, Japan, and Europe. The contributors to the colloquium, all with prior field study experience, were asked to investigate important changes in measuring manufacturing performance at innovative companies. The authors represented both the accounting and operations management areas, and several papers were co-authored by faculty from the two areas. Thus, the colloquium highlighted the value of multi- and interdisciplinary research in addressing the important questions that arise as companies attempt to attain manufacturing excellence.

The companies studied are leading manufacturers in North America, Europe, and Japan. Many are in the electronics industry (including semiconductor, instrument, and computer manufacturers) or in the automobile industry—a representation that is not surprising given the technology changes and vigorous global competition taking place in both industries.

The twelve papers presented at the colloquium have been grouped into four categories for this volume:

1. Measures of Organizational Improvement
2. Measures to Facilitate Organizational Learning
3. Measures for Product Design Improvements
4. Measures for Production Planning and Evaluation

Papers in the first category document the new measures being used by organizations to motivate and evaluate their continuous improvement activities. These papers examine the appropriate roles for traditional financial measures—standard costs and variances, and labor and machine efficiency measures—and for operational measures of quality, delivery time, and flexibility.

In the second category, the papers study measures used for motivating organizational learning. In this role, information is not used to control operations but to improve operations. The locus of information shifts from summarizing shop-floor performance for higher-level managers (the traditional role for manufacturing performance measurement) to summarizing local (shop-floor) performance and reporting it back to the local managers and employees to guide their learning and improvement activities.

Attempts to achieve manufacturing efficiencies after products have been designed and large-scale production is already underway may provide only limited opportunity for cost and productivity improvements. The third set of papers explores how companies use activity-based cost systems to provide product designers with more accurate information on the manufacturing cost consequences of their decisions.

In the fourth category, the papers investigate the interaction between production-planning models and systems of performance measurement and evaluation. Historically, production planning and performance measurement have been treated as separate and independent tasks. The papers in the last category highlight the value of treating these two tasks in a more systemic and integrated fashion.

MEASURES OF ORGANIZATIONAL IMPROVEMENT

The paper by Kaplan reports on a study of performance measures in the printed circuit board departments of three electronics companies. All three departments had instituted programs to improve quality and to reduce total cycle time and inventory. To a considerable extent, all had made substantial progress along these dimensions. Yet, despite improvements in operating performance, the financial summaries of each department's operations revealed level, or higher, costs. More-detailed investigation revealed that the cost summaries had been adversely affected by the failure to adjust departmental performance for decreased volume of activity and for increased complexity in the activity mix, and by the somewhat arbitrary allocation of plant-level costs. Kaplan concludes by questioning whether the variances reported by even a well-functioning standard cost model are meaningful when direct measures of operating performance are available. He suggests that relegating cost reports to a more analytic role and relying on timely and frequent reports on actual trends in operating performance can assess the success of departments' continuous improvement activities.

The Sakurai paper contrasts U.S. and Japanese management accounting systems. Sakurai points out that Japanese systems do not differ greatly from those found in Western companies, which is not surprising since many of the systems were derived from those of Western firms. Japanese companies, however, have been quicker to abandon standard cost systems for variance analysis and control in the new manufacturing environment. They have also been reluctant to embrace some of the more complex (activity-based) cost systems now being adopted by several U.S. companies, preferring simple and easy-to-understand overhead allocation systems, even at the expense of accuracy. Sakurai describes innovative Japanese practices in three areas. *Target costing* develops product cost information by working back from market-based pricing and subtracting a standard return-on-sales percentage to yield an allowable cost for new products. This allowable cost then establishes a cost reduction target for engineers, stimulating them to reduce costs by improved cost designs, value engineering, and perhaps trade-offs on functionality. As Japanese companies introduce more *factory automation* (their term for robots, flexible manufacturing systems, and computer-integrated manufacturing), a higher percentage of capital costs must be devoted to developing sophisticated software. Consequently, new procedures have been instituted for measuring the costs of software development projects. A final innovation is really not a new idea at all. Japanese companies prefer, for a variety of reasons, to use *return on sales* rather than return on investment (ROI) for measuring divisional and product performance. They want a simple, relatively unambiguous measure of profitability that neither encourages companies to underinvest in new technology nor requires allocations of fixed capital to departments or products. Investments in fixed capital are controlled directly by formal capital-budgeting procedures, not by ex post ROI measures. Investment in working capital is minimized by commitment to just-in-time (JIT) production procedures and direct measures of success in achieving JIT goals.

Tom Johnson studies two innovating divisions of large U.S. com-

panies. Both divisions were committed to achieving world-class manufacturing capability and had successfully implemented considerable
improvements in their quality and cycle time performance. They relied on direct operating measures of performance but were still using
traditional cost accounting systems to evaluate their continuous improvement activities. Johnson believes that in the future there will be
a greatly reduced reliance on financial summary measures as managers
rely on direct operating measures of actual performance to guide their
continuous improvement activities.

Armitage and Atkinson study the productivity measurement
programs of seven Canadian companies that had been singled out for
distinguished accomplishment in productivity improvement. None of
the seven companies used comprehensive productivity measurement
programs; none found its financial or cost accounting system useful
in the productivity-enhancing program. Each company had identified
one or more key activities that it had to perform well in order to produce substantial improvements in productivity. And each company
had chosen to measure the performance of that key activity (or activities) and highlight improvement along that particular measure. This
paper concludes, as does Tom Johnson's, that traditional financial
summary measures play a small role in companies attempting to improve performance.

This group of four papers, each of which differs in several respects, nevertheless yields some important common insights. Primarily, the authors find that variances from standard cost systems are not
an effective tool for motivating improvements in operations. They
notice an increased trend for direct, operational measures of process
improvements—in quality, delivery time, and productivity—to motivate and evaluate process improvements. Still to be resolved by future experience and research is the appropriate balance between financial and operational measures of performance.

MEASURES TO FACILITATE
ORGANIZATIONAL LEARNING

The paper by Chew, Bresnahan, and Clark examines productivity variation across 40 similar plants in a food-preparation organization. Despite the similarity of operation, productivity differences among the plants ranged as high as 3:1. These differences,
however, were obscured by the financial system, which tracked only

profitability and failed to distinguish profitability caused by higher selling prices from that caused by higher productivity. The differences were significant, since merely raising the below-average plants to the average level of productivity would have increased overall profits by more than 20%.

Despite the incentives for disseminating innovations from high-productivity sites to low- or average-productivity ones, the various plants shared virtually no information. Strong cultural forces, embedded in the beliefs and values of the managers, precluded the organization from capturing the benefits from its innovative sites. The paper raises several extremely important questions about managing complex organizations. First, it demonstrates that managers of multiplant organizations need to concentrate on leveraging local innovations to all plants in the network and need to manage knowledge and information flows, not just materials flows. Second, it demonstrates the tension between rewarding local plant performance (thereby encouraging local efforts and innovation) and rewarding overall divisional performance to encourage sharing and dissemination of knowledge throughout the network. Resolving this tension requires fundamental decisions on how a general manager sets the degree of competition and cooperation among various plants and on which functions in the information flow management should be centralized or decentralized.

The Grönlund and Jönsson paper studies organizational learning at a micro level through clinical observations over extended periods at manufacturing work stations. The paper provides vivid examples of how continuous improvement activities are actually carried out by local production teams. Flexible and responsive information systems played a vital role for the successful teams. The information systems for the less successful teams were too complex and may have precluded the teams from getting timely, accurate feedback on their experimental activities. Grönlund and Jonssön agree with the observations of Chew, Bresnahan, and Clark that local innovation is best done by independent production units and that active centralized management of the process can inhibit the development of new ideas. Interestingly, as in the study by Chew, Bresnahan, and Clark, employees felt that conditions at each site were unique and that they had unique informational needs that precluded sharing of ideas or information systems across organizational units.

Jaikumar's paper provides powerful insights on the role of financial information in guiding and setting priorities for organizational learning and improvement activities. He presents a six-epoch model of manufacturing process control, starting with the English system that introduced machine tools and mechanization in the early 1800s and culminating with today's world of intelligent systems and computer-integrated manufacturing (CIM). The present epoch enables a manager to have complete information about production processes. (Jaikumar considers the manager an *omniscient* observer.) The manager in this environment needs cost information to determine which contingencies are most expensive to the organization so that projects to determine how to alleviate or avoid these events can be given the highest priority. The information system, as the other papers in this section state, is also needed to provide rapid, accurate feedback on the consequences of local process-improving experimental activities. The concepts are illustrated by activities currently underway in a technologically advanced wire-drawing factory.

The three papers in this section point to the use of cost-based information to provide feedback to employees and managers about the consequences of their activities for process improvement. The settings and analyses of the papers are radically different: a statistical cross-sectional analysis of kitchen productivity; a three-year clinical observation in an automobile components factory; and a conceptual theorizing of manufacturing development, over a 200-year period, applied to a computer-controlled wire-drawing facility. This diversity only makes the commonality of the message from the three papers all the more striking: cost-based information can play a powerful role to motivate, guide, and implement process-improvement activities. But none of the organizations' existing financial systems normally produced the appropriate cost-based information.

MEASURES FOR PRODUCT DESIGN IMPROVEMENTS

The three papers in this section present how companies have developed more accurate cost models of products in order to guide engineers' product design activities. Historically, engineers in Western companies have designed products for functionality and product performance. Little attention was paid to the manufacturing consequences of product design decisions. In technologically advanced companies, product design engineers and marketing experts were dominant, with the manufacturing function relegated to merely producing the products, however complex, that emerged from the lengthy design process. The use of activity-based cost systems has enabled companies to better inform engineers about the manufacturing cost consequences of their product design decisions.

Foster and Gupta describe the implementation of a comprehensive activity accounting system in a division of an electronics instruments company. In addition to obtaining better information for product designers, the division felt it needed to get more accurate information about the relative costs of low- versus high-volume products and about the actual drivers of the costs of individual production and support departments. The new system incorporated cost drivers based on the *complexity* of products (e.g., number of part numbers) and on the *efficiency* of the product's production process (e.g., cycle time and setup time variables). It produced dramatically different product costs—with complex, low-volume products experiencing the largest cost increases. Despite the increased complexity of the activity accounting system, it had been widely accepted by engineers and managers. Product designers, recognizing the complexity of their task, no longer trusted numbers produced by a cost system that used only a few simple drivers. Marketing personnel preferred seeing the explicit trade-offs among functionality, complexity, cost, and hence price.

Banker, Datar, Kekre, and Mukhopadhyay describe ongoing research in estimating an activity-based cost model in the lamp division of an automobile company. The division produced a huge variety of lamps that made widely different demands on the plant's critical resource—the injection-molding process. The existing cost system, based on direct labor and machine-processing times, failed to signal the great differences between simple and complex lamps in the resources required for setup, quality control, and supervision. Statistical analysis of resource requirements indicated that design parameters such as the number of moving parts in a mold, the number of functions for the lamp, and the use of two different colors contributed significantly to the indirect manufacturing resources required to mold a lamp. The costs of these complexity factors could now be signaled to help product engineers to make trade-offs among cost, functionality, commonality, and esthetics.

Cooper and Turney describe the experiences of three electronics companies attempting to gain control of their product design and manufacturing processes. Traditional cost systems had led the firms to great proliferation of parts counts and products and to complex manufacturing processes. Rather than conduct a detailed study of the primary drivers of materials and manufacturing overhead costs (as described in the Foster and Gupta and Banker et al. papers), the three companies had loaded many overhead costs directly on to the two cost drivers that they knew would get the immediate attention of product designers: number of unique parts and cycle time. Cooper and Turney discuss the circumstances that cause companies to use cost drivers that will influence behavior in a desired way rather than estimate a more accurate model so that their strategy can be influenced by the model's results.

MEASURES FOR PRODUCTION PLANNING AND EVALUATION

The final section contains two papers that explicitly recognize the interaction between performance measurement and production planning. Harrison, Holloway, and Patell study the production-scheduling process of a large semiconductor company. They provide a model of three interacting organizational units—sales, manufacturing, and production control—and the three information systems—order entry, inventory tracking, and production scheduling—that link the three units' functions. The model shows the complexity introduced to the order quotation process by statistical variation in order arrival and processing times, scheduling algorithms, and local performance evaluation and incentive systems. The paper is a fascinating exercise in explicating the interactive roles of information systems, performance measures, and scheduling rules in producing difficult-to-anticipate consequences. Previous attempts to model complex production settings have typically focused on only one of the three determining factors (information, incentives, or algorithms). This paper highlights the difficulty (perhaps the impossibility) of obtaining an "optimal" systems design. It encourages researchers and managers to confront the highly interactive nature of production systems design.

Karmarkar, Lederer, and Zimmerman perform a cross-sectional statistical analysis to determine whether they can explain why individual companies use particular production control and cost accounting systems. They find weak correlations between production control systems and the production environment—materials requirement planning (MRP) systems are more likely found in batch than continuous production processes—but, in general, they do not find associations among the adoption of particular costing and production control systems and characteristics of the firms' environment and production processes. The study indicates the difficulty of studying cross-sectionally the match between a firm's environment and its management practices in a situation in which environmental change is rapid but significant lags may exist between the need for and the actual adoption of new procedures.

SUMMARY

These twelve papers present an excellent summary of performance measurement in manufacturing organizations in the late 1980s. Clearly, by this time, companies had recognized the limitations of traditional cost accounting systems for measuring, motivating, and evaluating manufacturing performance. Emphasis had shifted from controlling operations to providing timely, relevant information to local workers, managers, and engineers for their continuous improvement activities. The papers capture companies at a relatively early stage of transition: problems with the old measurement system had been recognized and a vision for improvement adopted, but only preliminary steps had been taken to implement a new set of measurement procedures.

Physical, operational measures were playing a much more important role and were starting to replace cost system variance reports as a source of information for managers and employees. But increased use of physical measures leads to new problems. No longer can performance measured at a local level be aggregated into the performance measures of the plant, the division, and the company. Just how to design a hierarchical, comprehensive system of local shop-floor measures, departmental and plant measures, and divisional performance measures remains a task for future research and experimentation. Companies that have abandoned or greatly reduced their reliance on local financial measures are asking their higher-level managers to deemphasize traditional short-run financial controls—by allowing plants to be guided by measures on quality, throughput, cycle times, and on-time delivery—and to accept, perhaps on faith, that long-run financial success will follow improvements in these operational performance measures. Whether such faith is well placed will be answered by the experiences of innovating companies in the years ahead.

A second set of unresolved issues concerns the design of incentives for managers that will support continuous improvement activities within organizations. Two papers, one by Chew, Bresnahan, and Clark and one by Harrison, Holloway, and Patell, explicitly note difficulties that arise when managers are rewarded on incentives that may not be compatible with improving the overall performance of their entities. Most of the remaining papers assume implicitly that managers are motivated to do the right things; thus, the main task is to provide information to them and to their employees that will point them in the right direction. Will managers emphasize continuous improvement activities when their personal evaluation depends upon traditional profit center measures, such as earnings, earnings growth, and return on assets? Much research remains to be done concerning the design of managerial incentive and reward systems that support and sustain activities to achieve manufacturing excellence.

Both unresolved issues—the appropriate mix at each level of the organizational hierarchy between financial and nonfinancial measures, and the design of incentive systems for manufacturing managers—are linked. If we had complete confidence in a set of operational measures, knowing that they supported long-run competitive success, then we could certainly use them to define appropriate incentive contracts for managers of manufacturing organizations. But we are at an early stage in our understanding of how to integrate local plant-floor measures of continuous improvement and manufacturing excellence into the long-run measures of competitive success for the entire organization. Companies, at present, are unsure about the factors that they want to incorporate into the annual performance targets for managers. As more organizations gain experience with actions and measures that contribute to long-run manufacturing excellence, we can expect that the measures used to motivate and evaluate managers will give less weight to the currently used measures of short-run financial profitability. Undoubtedly, a colloquium on performance measurement in manufacturing organizations held in 1995 will incorporate knowledge and insight on these issues well beyond that captured in the papers in this volume. But these papers indicate the direction and magnitude of changes already underway and show the great opportunities that lie ahead for innovating companies striving for manufacturing excellence.

Boston, Massachusetts   Robert S. Kaplan
August 1989

NOTES

1. The colloquium was the successor to a colloquium on field studies in accounting and control held at Harvard in June 1986. Papers from the first colloquium were published in William J. Bruns, Jr., and Robert S. Kaplan, *Accounting & Management: Field Study Perspectives* (Boston: Harvard Business School Press, 1987).

2. This lag has been widely reported and recognized; see, for example, Robert S. Kaplan, "Yesterday's Accounting Undermines Production," *Harvard Business Review* (July–August 1984), 95–101; and H. Thomas Johnson and Robert S. Kaplan, *Relevance Lost: The Rise and Fall of Management Accounting* (Boston: Harvard Business School Press, 1987).

3. See Callie Berliner and James A. Brimson, eds., *Cost Management for Today's Advanced Manufacturing: The CAM-I Conceptual Design* (Boston: Harvard Business School Press, 1987).

PART I

Measures of Organizational Improvement

CHAPTER 1

Limitations of Cost Accounting in Advanced Manufacturing Environments

Robert S. Kaplan

DURING 1986, the Harvard Business School rearranged its curriculum, moving the first-year accounting course (called "control") from the fall to the spring semester and the production/operations management (POM) course from spring to fall. The stated goal was for students to start their business studies with courses on how to make products and how to sell them (in the POM and marketing courses), deferring to the second semester the details on how to finance and account for them. One unexpected consequence occurred in the first year of teaching control with the new calendar: students seemed to resist, even more than usual, the presentation of the standard cost model and the analysis of variances from this model. After several frustrating sessions, one section was finally able to articulate its concerns. An intrepid spokesperson asserted:

What you're teaching doesn't square with what we learned last semester in POM. If there was one message that was drilled over and over, it was the need for continuous improvement and learning. Being as good as you were last year is no longer sufficient.

Now we get to the cost accounting material, and you measure results against static budgets and historically determined standards. Where's the drive for improvement? How can we encourage workers and managers to do better and better, if their performance is deemed adequate as long as they meet standards that were in force last year and in years prior to that?

This episode is at the heart of this paper and, indeed, the motivation for all the papers presented in this volume. The cost accounting model of standard costs and the periodic analysis of variances from standard costs had their origins in the scientific management movement of 80 to 100 years ago.[1] That environment, and the environment of the next half-century, featured mass production of standardized products, wherein the key to efficiency was maximizing the output produced by direct labor and the machines operated by the workers. Thus, accounting systems emerged that developed standards for, and subsequently closely tracked, individual worker and machine efficiencies.

The current environment, however, has led many manufacturers to attempt to achieve the goals of total quality control, just-in-time production, and the rapid introduction of new products that can be efficiently produced in low volumes. Numerous articles and books (and several first-year control sections), however, have claimed that the traditional cost accounting model has become a major stumbling block to companies' efforts to become high-quality, responsive, flexible manufacturers.

This study was motivated by comments, frequently heard from managers and manufacturing engineers, that the considerable operating improvements they had achieved were going unrecognized in their financial results. Unit costs and financial efficiency measures had not improved—in some cases, had even deteriorated—during periods when operational measures showed lower part-per-million (PPM) defect rates and reduced product throughput times. Such a phenomenon was difficult to explain. Even though traditional cost accounting measures may not actively encourage the continuous improvement activities required for leading-edge manufacturing today, any operational improvements achieved should translate into improved financial results. For this study, I visited three companies who had improved their operating performance but had experienced little or no improvement in their measured financial results. The plants had similar production processes: integrated circuit (IC) printed circuit board assembly and test. In the case studies, I describe the situation in each company and analyze the factors that led to operational and financial measures moving in opposite directions. Then, I present a general analysis of the findings and pose several questions concerning the design of future operational control systems. The primary, still unanswered, question is whether a significant role exists for a standard cost approach in advanced manufacturing environments.[2]

COMPANY D

Company D, a broad-line producer of information-processing equipment, had a strategy of offering the lowest price-to-performance ratio in the industry. My visit focused on the printed circuit board (PCB) assembly operation, with particular emphasis on the IC (integrated circuit) Test department. The IC Test facility had responsibility for testing and improving the quality and reliability of semiconductors and discrete components.

During the 1986–1988 period, IC Test methods had evolved rapidly to reflect the latest thinking in total quality control management. The 1986 methods emphasized inspecting-in quality: 62% of the items were tested and 35% were subjected to "burn-in" procedures (48-hour operation under high temperatures to simulate conditions that cause devices to fail early). The 1986 goals also emphasized meeting production targets and always having enough inventory on hand to keep production well stocked.

During 1987, a preferred vendor program was initiated, testing was reduced, and an active inventory reduction plan started. By 1988, sophisticated software diagnosis tools were being used to detect failure trends in items tested. By year-end, only 20% of incoming items were to be tested and just 5% subjected to burn-in. Active vendor partnerships had been established and inventory levels and through-put times greatly reduced. Summary statistics of the improved operating performance (some disguised to protect confidentiality) are shown in Table 1-1.

Senior management relied more on financial, not operating, summaries of the performance of the IC Test department (and indeed of the entire PCB assembly facility). Weekly summaries were prepared of direct labor efficiency and utilization, headcount, overtime, and scrap by individual cost center and business unit. At the PCB assembly facility, direct labor represented less than 20% of operating expenses (excluding materials purchases) but was the basis of departmental and managerial performance measures. Overhead was assigned to products based on direct labor hours (DLH), and the ratio of overhead to DLH was monitored closely. Total expenses were split into three broad cost behavior categories—variable, step-fixed, and fixed—with costs collected in up to 40 finer accounts among these broad categories.

Apart from the weekly, monthly, and annual financial reports, which emphasized traditional variance analysis from standards,

Table 1-1 Summary of IC Test Performance: 1986–1988

	1986	1987	1988
Defects (PPM)	1,000	500	270
Throughput (days)	35	9	3
Schedule Performance	85%	89%	99%
Inventory (000 units)	2,000	288	120
Scrap ($000)	600	171	74

simple summary financial measures were used to evaluate the efficiency of local operating units. Unfortunately, for IC Test, the dramatic improvement in operating performance shown in Table 1-1 was not reflected in its financial performance. Table 1-2 shows (disguised) financial summaries of the IC Test department.

Despite the considerable reduction in testing, the decline in inventory, and greatly improved responsiveness and quality, the cost per IC processed had increased 10% from 1986 to 1988, and the cost per incurred DLH had more than doubled. The IC Test department had already experienced adverse consequences from its failure to reduce costs: testing of simple dynamic random access memories (DRAMs) had been shifted to a lower-cost Southeast Asian facility ($0.30 per unit, compared to the $0.50 at IC Test), and some sourcing was being done directly with a Korean supplier (bypassing IC Test) for components where burn-in procedures were not required. The puzzle was how the improvements of the past two years had failed to translate into lower testing costs.

The engineers and local accounting staff had recently been able to identify the solutions to the puzzle. Significant changes in the volume, mix, and nature of the tested items had occurred, which masked the benefits from the operating improvements. In addition, the accounting system failed to recognize some costs and benefits that related to the operations of IC Test (and other departments) and inappropriately classified other cost components in ways that distorted the efficiency measures being used to evaluate departmental performance.

The Volume Story

The first distortion arose from allocating capacity-related costs on the basis of actual volumes rather than practical capacity. Because of sales decreases in the parent company, the number of units processed by

Table 1-2 Financial Summary of IC Test: 1986–1988

	1986	1987	1988
Cost/IC	0.50	0.52	0.55
Cost/Incurred hour	50.00	54.86	101.642

IC Test had declined from 16 million in 1986 to around 14 million in 1987 and 1988. Since the majority of costs were in the semifixed and fixed categories and had not declined with the short-term volume decrease, the unit costs in IC Test had risen by 14% due to this volume effect alone.

Reinforcing this trend were the activities to certify vendors so that none of their incoming devices would have to be tested. As more vendor parts were certified to be "free of test," the cost per incurred DLH would increase.

The application of capacity-related costs to actual volumes was having an even more deleterious impact in another area of the plant, the printed circuit board (PCB) assembly department. Three types of assembly technologies were being used: manual, automatic dual inline package (DIP), and, recently introduced, surface mount devices (SMD). The SMDs offered increased insertion speed and higher board density and functional performance. To date, only a few products had been designed to exploit SMDs. As a consequence, the volume on the expensive, recently purchased SMD insertion machine was only a small fraction of its capacity. Based on forecasted 1988 volumes, the costs per DL incurred hour for the three types of insertion machines were

Type of Insertion Technology	Cost per DLH ($)
Manual	30.00
Automatic DIP	133.59
Surface Mount	362.43

The cost per incurred DLH measure was appropriate when all insertions were done manually and devices could have different amounts of time required per insertion. By the time automatic insertions technology was introduced, a cost per insertion would have likely provided a better basis for measuring insertion costs. The DLH-based cost system required the accountants to estimate the average number of machines supervised by each operator in order to compute a cost per DLH. But even aside from delays in shifting from

DLH to a machine-hour or unit-of-production cost base, the under-utilization of the SMD process was sending incorrect signals to product designers. As engineers developed new products that used the SMD technology, they saw quite high processing costs relative to using traditional devices that could be inserted on the already heavily used (and, therefore, lower unit cost) automatic machines. Consequently, the load on the SMD insertion machine was well below forecast, and the company was not encouraging the use of the higher density and simpler-to-insert SMDs in their new product designs.

The Mix Story

The second cost distortion arose from the considerable diversity in the mix of products IC Test was processing. Originally, the department was likely to test homogeneous items such as 16K DRAMs. In this environment, a simple measure like testing cost per device was reasonable and appropriate. By 1988, however, many different IC devices were being inserted onto the PCBs. A special study had revealed that unit testing costs (shown below, disguised) varied enormously across these different devices.

Device	Cost/Unit
Memory	$0.23
TTL	0.28
Linear	0.55
PAL/PROM	1.92
EPROM	3.97
Average	$0.55

Not unexpectedly, the mix of devices in recent years had shifted from simple dynamic memory devices to the far more complex ICs such as programmable read only memory (PROM) and erasable programmable read only memory (EPROM) devices that required, in addition to testing, the programming of appropriate instructions into the devices (a mission that had been assigned to the IC Test department). In fact, the IC Test department's mission had also expanded to include some testing of passive components, an activity that was not counted in its output volume measure.

The changing mix of work being performed by IC Test had several obvious implications. First, as product variety increased, simple measures of cost per unit processed no longer provided adequate summaries of departmental performance. The need to adjust the performance measure for mix changes is, as with the volume story, a simple point. But the point is frequently overlooked in organizations that start out with a narrow product range, design systems appropriate for that narrow range, and then produce products with a wide range of complexity.

Second, the decision to outsource much of the testing of simple DRAMs to a Southeast Asian facility no longer seemed sensible. Although the overseas facility offered lower testing cost than the $0.50–0.55 unit cost of IC Test, its unit cost of around $0.30 was still above the actual $0.23 unit cost in IC Test for DRAMs, even before accounting for the longer lead times and higher inventory levels required for overseas testing. By failing to control for the greater diversity and complexity demanded of IC Test, the company had outsourced an operation to a higher-cost facility.

The Overhead Allocation Story

The shift in costs from direct labor to process automation, through hardware and software investments, had caused the cost per incurred DLH in IC Test to double over a two-year period (see Table 1-2). The change in technology had made obsolete this formerly useful summary measure of the cost and efficiency of the department. Prior to 1988, however, DLH remained as the primary basis for allocating overhead to departments and to products. For example, in 1986 and 1987, IC Test's actual incurred hours were higher than budgeted, whereas the remainder of the plant's operating departments' incurred hours were lower than budgeted. With the allocation of administrative expenses based on actual DLH, IC Test received 12% of administrative costs rather than the budgeted amount of 6%. A new system, in which administrative costs would be allocated based on departmental spending, not DLH, was being introduced in 1988.

The Omission of Actual Cost Savings Story

Several important cost savings had been realized from the operational improvements noted in Table 1-1, but the savings were not captured by the company's traditional cost accounting system. The benefits from the 90% reduction in inventory were not measured because inventory holding costs were not included in operating costs or financial summary of operations. Floor-space reductions because of the lower inventory were also substantial but unmeasured.

Many savings were omitted from the departmental performance summary because they occurred in other organizational units. The more than 50% reduction in defect rates (see Table 1-1) represented measurements made by the **customers** of IC Test; i.e., PCB assembly and test areas. These units were experiencing much lower scrap and rework costs because of the improved performance of IC Test. In addition, the higher compliance with scheduled delivery performance of IC Test permitted lower inventory, less disruption, and more orderly production schedules in PCB assembly.

As part of the quality improvement effort, IC Test had added a person to serve as a liaison with product designers. In the past, especially with its large-batch production philosophy, the department had tested and programmed many PROMs that subsequently had to be scrapped because they did not contain the latest code revisions. The new person eliminated the test and release of obsolete PROMs. Thus, operating expense had increased—a cost that was easily tracked by the cost system. But the benefit—the major reduction in scrap of obsolete devices—was not tracked back to the department that had produced the savings. In fact, by reducing the volume of obsolete devices tested, IC Test had lowered the activity basis over which its costs were spread (the volume story), thereby raising its unit testing cost.

Summary

The operations and accounting staff at Company D's plant had eventually recognized all the problems described in this case study. The plant's programs to improve quality, reduce inventory, and shorten throughput times had been so beneficial that the continuous improvement efforts were now sustainable even without an accurate management accounting system to report on the financial consequences from the actions. When the lower cost of testing DRAMs in the United States versus Southeast Asia was discovered, the Asian plant was scheduled for shutdown, and the work moved back to IC Test. Currently, efforts are being taken to reduce senior management's focus on overly aggregated financial summaries and to encourage reliance on the operational measures shown in Table 1-1. Also, a more accurate management accounting system based on the actual activities being performed in each operating department is being developed. In early 1989, labor reporting, now viewed as a fundamental stumbling block to the plant's continuous improvement activities, will be eliminated entirely.

In fact, the quality improvement programs at IC Test have been so successful that the department may soon be eliminated entirely. The quality assurance function will be shifted to vendors who will deliver ICs directly to all of Company D's PCB assembly plants, on time and in the correct quantities, without any need for incoming inspection. Apart from the significant savings realized by eliminating in-house testing, the cost of funnelling all incoming materials to IC Test and from there to the assembly facilities in the company will be avoided.

COMPANY V

Company V, a leading supplier of computer-based, information-processing systems, operated for many years with a traditional batch manufacturing philosophy. The major production facility contained a large department that assembled printed circuit boards (PCBs) for a full range of products. The PCBs were processed in large batches (100, 500, 1,000) through functionally oriented shops. The goal was to keep people and machines busy. Thus, many batches of boards would frequently be started into production without having all the component parts in-house. If the parts had not shown up by the time the boards were ready to be shipped, the parts would be cannibalized from other boards already built. Also, with the goal of keeping machines busy stuffing components, no attempt was made to determine whether parts currently being inserted might be needed for other boards with more stringent delivery dates. With large numbers of boards being built for inventory, the risk of an engineering change order (ECO) making a recently assembled batch obsolete was always present.

What factors contributed to this emphasis on large-batch production that created constant confusion in the manufacturing area? First, measuring individual machine efficiency promoted a policy of build, build, build. Each machine had its own utilization chart, based on direct labor hours earned. The earned hours were based on standards for each board, calculated at the time the PCB was released into production. For each period, managers were evaluated on their ratio of earned to actual DLH (in Company V, called hours applied to hours paid).[3] Setup standards had been established based on preset lot sizes, but actual setup times and batch sizes were not monitored closely. Since setup hours were not counted as "earned hours," managers were motivated to produce in large-lot sizes.

Reacting to the emphasis on keeping earned DLH high, operations managers attempted to keep the insertion machines and personnel fully loaded. Boards were produced for inventory 30 days in advance of probable need. This speculative building of boards frequently led to parts shortages for boards subsequently processed, huge amounts of rework if defective components had been used or if an ECO was issued, and high amounts of scrap. Scrap, however, was recorded in a material usage account—perhaps at a subsequent stage—and not charged back as an effective decrease in utilization.

The materials function was evaluated by its kit fill rate—the proportion of parts that was available when a batch of boards was started into processing. Kit fill rates had improved to 80–95%, but any percentage below 100% would cause problems subsequently in the production process.

The Purchasing department was evaluated by a traditional cost accounting measure: the purchase price variance (PPV). This measure had occasionally led the department to choose suppliers who could not deliver parts with zero defects. Consequently, quality was a constant problem. At one time, the facility had one inspector for every two operators, or a total of 150 inspectors.[4] Even though the quality was not very good, the quantities were also incorrect. To reduce purchase costs (and thereby show favorable PPVs), much sourcing was being done in the Far East. Overseas sourcing, while lowering purchase prices, led to long delivery lead times and uncertain arrival patterns. If the production schedule changed, due to shifts in sales mix and volumes, the purchase order could not be adjusted. So the facility accumulated much obsolete inventory at favorable purchase prices, yet the correct parts were not available when a group of boards was to be started into production. Purchasing could report good progress in meeting cost and scheduled delivery goals, but the actual costs of its policies were shifted onto indirect manufacturing costs.

Perhaps the most overriding plant-level measure was delivery shipment performance: "Ship them critters," especially near the end of a fiscal quarter. This emphasis led to kits being released for assembly even with significant parts missing, to critical boards being expedited through the facility (occasionally interrupting a batch that had just been set up on the insertion machines), to much overtime work, to cannibalization of boards and parts from already built machines, and even to shipments of products with missing boards or components. The report for that period might show favorable delivery performance but also showed spending variances (such as on overtime) that also had to be explained.

Manufacturing managers' frustration with the performance measurement system included the following problems:

- The measures produced irrelevant or misleading information, or worse, provoked behavior that undermined the achievement of strategic objectives.
- Measures that tracked each dimension of performance in isolation were distorting management's understanding of how effectively the organization as a whole was implementing the company's strategy.
- Traditional performance measures did not take into account the requirements and perspective of *customers,* both internal and external.
- Bottom-line financial measures came too late (monthly) for mid-course corrections and remedial actions.[5]

During the past two years, a new production philosophy had been successfully introduced into the PCB assembly area. Production was now organized by group technology, using U-shaped cells and sophisticated production control software to maximize throughput (not individual machine utilization) of successfully completed items. Bottlenecks were identified and production released only at a rate that could be accommodated by the bottleneck resource. Boards were now processed one at a time, in batches of no more than 15–20. Frequently, defects were detected before most of the batch had been produced. Highly specialized job classifications for direct labor had been eliminated. Workers were cross-trained to perform a variety of functions, including being redeployed to relieve unexpected bottlenecks when they occurred.

The quality focus shifted from inspecting-in quality to preventing defects from occurring in the first place. The success of this program can be seen in the steady, dramatic improvement in first pass yields:

First Pass Yields

FY 1987	Q1	43%	FY 1988	Q1	80%
	Q2	60		Q2	85
	Q3	72		Q3	86
	Q4	76		Q4	87
			FY 1989	Q1	91

Charts of first pass yields were prominently displayed in production areas. All employees could see the importance of maintaining continuous improvement against this measure.

Inventory had dropped enormously, and the next goal was to eliminate the stock room. An operating rule had been established that no board would be started without a complete kit. This discipline had helped reduce throughput times from 14–18 days (under the old system) to 1 1/2 days.

The new manufacturing policies had produced dramatically improved quality and had reduced throughput times. Yet the traditional financial measures of efficiency and unit cost were not showing any improvements. Machine utilization had decreased and reported productivity was flat. Machines were less busy because less rework was being performed and less scrap was being produced. But the overall load on the factory was also decreasing, first, because of a downturn in final product sales and, second, because of technology. As more functionality was imbedded into individual ICs, fewer PCBs were needed to accomplish the same function. Again, the traditional cost accounting measures failed to control well for volume effects so that real efficiency gains were being masked by declines in activity levels.

At present, an innovative measurement approach is being introduced to track better the improvements in manufacturing performance.[6] The approach is hierarchical in nature, starting with department and work center measures on quality, delivery, process time, and cost. At the next level, each business operating system (e.g., production, order management, and new product development) has three driving forces: 1) customer satisfaction, 2) flexibility, and 3) productivity. The three sets of measures at the business operating system-level are linked upward into aggregate business unit measures of market and financial performance.

The new philosophy defines performance measures from the viewpoint of the final customers and works back from them to the upstream production and supply departments. Previously, each department defined its own quality measure but did not relate it to the

Exhibit 1-1   Monthly Performance Measures: Company V, 1985

Shipments	**Labor Performance** (*continued*)
Actual	Productivity
Performance-to-Build Plan	Overhead %
Current Backlog	Overtime
	Absenteeism
Inventories	Indirect:Direct Ratio
Total (weeks and $)	
Scrap	**Capital**
Excess	Appropriations
Obsolete	Expenditures
Variances	**Spending**
Purchase Price	Salaries and Benefits
Production Burden	Controllable Expenses
Materials Acquisition	Noncontrollable Expenses
Materials Burden	
Materials Usage	**Headcount**
Labor	Direct
	Indirect
Labor Performance	Total
Efficiency	By Functional Areas
Utilization	

needs or the measurement system of its customers. Now, measures on quality and delivery performance are defined by the customer. These measures are then calculated and reported by the supplying departments.

The evolution of the measurement philosophy can be tracked by the new measures introduced during the past three years. The standard monthly performance report in 1985 presented data in the categories shown in Exhibit 1-1. The categories reflect the system's aggregate measurement of output, personnel count, and the full array of standard cost accounting variances.

During 1986, a system of plant-level critical success factors had been identified to provide improved measures of plant performance (see Exhibit 1-2). These measures retained many of the traditional financial measures of Exhibit 1-1 but were starting to introduce operational measures of delivery performance, reliability, quality, and human resources. By 1988, a shop-floor (or departmental) measurement system had been tried in a pilot site, the PCB assembly area. The measures used at this site (see Exhibit 1-3) implemented the phi-

Exhibit 1-2 Critical Success Factors: Plant XYZ of Company V, 1986

Customer Satisfaction
  On-time Deliveries
  Order Completeness Index
  Current Order Index
  Aging of Past-due Orders
  Work Order Accuracy
  Product Performance (Plug and Play) Index
  Manufacturing Quality Index (actual to required inspections)

Production Schedule Achievement
  Factory Performance-to-Build Plan
  Total Output-to-Build Plan
  Performance-to-Field Service Demands
  Repair Performance

Materials Management
  Inventory Levels
  Inventory Turnover
  Obsolete Inventory
  Excess Inventory
  Records Accuracy

Cost Effectiveness
  Spending Variances
  Cost per Value-added DLH
  Production Variances
  Purchase Price Variances
  Product Cost Improvement
  Projected Annual Spending

Human Resources
  Employee Turnover
  Affirmative Action
  Lost Workdays/100 Employees
  Absenteeism

Systems Development
  Applications Availability Index
  Manpower Utilization
  Systems Implementation Effectiveness

losophy of customer-defined measures of quality, cost, and delivery performance. The new measurement philosophy of Company V was soon to be implemented in its entire factory and domestic distribution system. After this implementation, observers will have an opportunity to determine the feasibility and value of shifting from traditional cost accounting measures to a well-defined set of operating performance measures that emphasize customer service and quality.

COMPANY L

Company L produces sophisticated communications equipment. My visit encompassed the printed circuit board (PCB) assembly area, a facility comparable to those of Companies D and V. PCB assembly inserted one to one and a half million parts per week, with manufacturing processes encompassing manual insertions as well as highly automated insertion of IC components (the surface mount devices described for Company D). Discrete hand insertion required hand-picked components and an entirely manual process that included component preparation (cutting and forming), staking, eyelet insertion, hand soldering, and inspection. The surface mounted devices, in contrast, required virtually no transactions—whether for receiving and inspecting, stock room, or component preparation. Despite this wide range of processes, engineers were still attempting to design products that minimized bill-of-material cost, with little regard to the impact that alternative component choices made on the manufacturing process.

Company L had a major ongoing education program on the new manufacturing environment. General managers and operations managers throughout the company had attended two-week seminars that described the opportunities to be gained by implementing total quality control (TQC), just-in-time (JIT), and computer-integrated manufacturing (CIM). The operations manager of the PCB assembly area had recently been successfully implementing many of these TQC and JIT concepts and had realized immediate benefits. Over a 15-month period, defects per hundred units had dropped nearly 70%, from 2.45 to 0.80, with an additional 70% reduction to 0.25 planned for the next 12 months. Cycle time reductions of 50% had also been achieved. Despite these local operating improvements, no corresponding improvement in the department's cost performance had occurred.

The company operated with an extensive system to track labor

Exhibit 1-3   PCB Assembly Measures: Company V, 1988

Customer Defined
  Plug and Play: Final Assembly and Test
  Plug and Play: Field
  % On-time to Schedule
  % On-time to Specials

Internal (Departmental) Defined
  Process Time
  Waste Rate

Supplier Relationships
  Schedule Change Index
  Kit Integrity
  NPI Package

costs and total manufacturing costs. A weekly labor report was prepared for each department and group of departments. The reporting categories are shown in Exhibit 1-4. Monthly profit and loss statements were prepared for each product line. These reports were the primary focus of senior management. The key measure of manufacturing performance was manufacturing cost as a percentage of net sales. Since PCBs were used in all the division's final products, the costs incurred in PCB assembly were spread across dozens of P&L statements.

While the reasons for the lack of correspondence between manufacturing cost and the realized improvements in quality and cycle time reductions were still not completely clear, several explanatory factors had already emerged. First, volume and mix stories, similar to those already encountered in the other two sites, were present. When measuring the cost per earned hour, efficiency gains were being offset by decreases in earned hours. Part of this decrease was caused by overall sales trends, but part was also due to increased functionality per board (or per component) and because fewer defective boards were being produced.

The mix story was more interesting. The division was selling more of its sophisticated equipment, but it turned out that many of the most recently designed, sophisticated products were using some of the oldest boards and components. While the mix had shifted to more recently designed, complex products, the demands on the manufacturing process had increased for older boards, requiring a higher

Exhibit 1-4   Weekly Labor Reporting Categories: Company L

Direct Labor	Lost Time (*continued*)
Earned Standard DL	Rework and Repair
Specialty Earned DL	Pilot Run
Customer Parts Orders	Rework due to Engineering
	Total as % of Total Direct Labor
Burden	
Analyzers	**Other Overhead**
Handling	Supervisors
Repair	Overtime Premium
Retest	Shift Bonus
Inspection	
Total as % of Total Direct Labor	**Direct Labor Variation** (Efficiency)
Lost Time	**Total DL Overhead and Variation**
Training	
Factory Management	

percentage of hand-inserted components; little use was being made of the most efficient, surface-mounted IC devices. Thus, the aggregate cost per insertion, or per earned hour, was increasing because of an unfavorable mix shift to older process technology. The initial failure to recognize the discrepancy between product and process technology perhaps indicated that manufacturing considerations had yet to become embedded in decisions on product design.

The constant (rather than improving) percentage of manufacturing cost to sales could also be explained by a downward trend in unit selling prices due to competitive pressures. Thus, reduced manufacturing costs were being passed on to customers by lower selling prices, keeping the ratio of costs to sales relatively constant during a period when significant cost improvements were actually occurring.

Within the department itself, several additional factors were at work to limit the amount of cost improvement reported. PCB assembly was committing resources for the prototyping of new boards so that bugs could be worked out in the design phase. This effort required more direct labor to perform work that would be classified as "unearned hours," but with the expectation that future engineering and direct labor costs would be lower because fewer engineering change orders would be required to modify already released product designs.

PCB assembly had also expanded its quality assurance function and had acquired better test equipment to reduce the number of defective boards produced for the final assembly departments. Thus, higher costs were being incurred in PCB assembly, with the savings realized in other departments as they encountered less scrap, rework, and incoming testing. The failure to measure costs and savings across organizational units prevented some of the benefits of higher quality from being recognized. The assembly departments had recognized the improved quality and responsiveness from PCB assembly, but they had yet to translate these improvements into measurable operating savings.

Though many manufacturing managers had been indoctrinated into the joys of just-in-time production, the philosophy had yet to be fully incorporated into the company's operations. Production schedules changed in the middle of the month as customer requirements and orders became firm. Frequently, marketing accelerated orders originally scheduled to be produced in the following month in order to achieve the financial goals established for the current month. Manufacturing managers were expected to do everything possible to meet customer shipments by the end of each month, including expediting from suppliers and using extensive overtime work. As the manufacturing operations manager explained:

We attempt to build to schedule, based on forecasts, and then tweak the system based on actual orders. Sometimes we anticipate the following month's orders and build this month in order to meet the financial plan. We scramble to acquire materials so that we can build one to two weeks early. The last two to three days of the month are pretty hectic, taking care of end-of-month exceptions.

I would say we have about 70% accuracy between the monthly forecast and what turns out to be actually requested, but we often get a 10:1 actual-to-forecast differential. We have the capacity in a month to build 400 units, yet we may be only forecasting 40 units of a particular PC board. When the actual orders arrive, we are asked for 400 boards that had not been previously scheduled. We then have to expedite material for the new boards and make production capacity available to complete an additional 360 units in the short time remaining before the end of the month. These schedule changes create under- and overutilized capacity problems that are difficult to manage. Last year, we kept trying to catch up, but we could never compensate for the higher expediting and overtime costs caused by schedule changes.

In this type of environment, local (departmental) improvements in quality and cycle time may have little significant impact on overall cost reduction. Both the overall operating philosophy and the measurement system have to recognize the systemic nature of the role for manufacturing in the company's product design, sales, and marketing activities.

ANALYSIS

Several issues are reasonably clear from these three descriptions. None of the cost accounting systems encountered represented an "ideal" design. Many of the measurement problems could have been due to implementation errors rather than to a fatal flaw with standard cost systems in advanced manufacturing environments.

In all three sites, level-to-increased unit costs, during a period when quality and throughput times were improving, could be traced to inadequate treatment of **volume and mix** shifts. Avoiding cost shifts because of fluctuations in capacity utilization does not require new cost accounting developments. The cost of capacity resources can be applied based on practical (not actual) utilization of capacity. Of course, when demand is below practical capacity, not all capacity costs will then be absorbed by products actually produced. The solution is not to apply the cost of excess or idle capacity to the products that were produced, but to treat the unabsorbed cost as an expense of the period—in effect, a cost of products that were not produced— and have it appear as a line item in the departmental income/expense statement. Managers have a variety of actions they can take with respect to idle or excess capacity. I cannot, however, discover any useful purpose served by allocating the idle-capacity costs to items actually produced. This is not a new insight. Donaldson Brown, for one, implemented a system of charging for capacity resources over a standard (80%) measure of utilization more than 60 years ago at General Motors.[7]

Distortions introduced by **mix** shifts occur when the organization fails to recognize the increasingly diverse nature of its output. As significant variation arises in the demand that products make on organizational resources, simple summary measures of cost per unit produced are no longer meaningful. Either product complexity indices can be developed—so that a cost per equivalent unit can be computed—or else the unit cost summary can be eliminated, with efficiency measured relative to a flexible budget for the volume and mix actually produced. Again, these ideas are well known and have been implemented in several organizations.

It is surprising, however, how few U.S. organizations operate well-functioning standard cost systems that accurately capture short-run cost behavior as a function of volume and mix. Thus, watching how U.S. company cost systems fail in advanced manufacturing environments may not be a fair test for judging the adequacy of standard cost systems. German companies, in contrast, have systems with hundreds and thousands of cost centers and have thought carefully about the variables that best explain the short-run variation in cost in each of the cost centers. These sites may provide a much better test environment for how standard cost systems perform as companies implement TQC, JIT, and CIM innovations in their factories.

In addition, the emphasis on **direct labor expenses** and **direct labor efficiency** causes companies to focus on a relatively unimportant factor of production. Instead, if the systems had focused on materials utilization—for example, closely monitoring reductions in inventory levels, rework, scrap, obsolescence, and throughput times—and not on labor utilization, the financial measures would likely have supported, not conflicted with, the fundamental operating improvements. Again, nothing in the standard cost model, at least as taught in U.S. cost accounting courses, features the local measures of direct labor and machine efficiencies so prevalent in U.S. industry. My current belief is that the practice of emphasizing direct labor utilization measures, with ratios such as *earned to actual hours* and *indirect to direct labor* was a mutation of the standard cost model; a mutation that has survived for decades without being adequately recognized in academic teaching and research, but a mutation that no longer matches current environmental conditions and hence one that will likely soon become extinct.[8]

Unquestionably, then, considerable improvements can be made to the standard cost systems used by discrete parts manufacturing companies. The appropriate question is whether such improvements are worth making. The alternative view would eliminate the periodic reporting of financial summaries of manufacturing operations against standards and replace these financial summaries with physical and operational measures: e.g., quality measures—PPM defect rates, first pass yields, scrap, rework, obsolescence; throughput measures—ratio of processing time to lead time, linearity of production, actual versus planned production line item by line item; and delivery performance measures—percentage delivery commitments met within ± 1 day and percentage deviation between customer requested delivery and committed delivery. In this view, manufacturing costs are the results of underlying activities. If we want to reduce costs, then we should measure the activities that create costs and attempt to make improvements directly on the underlying activities.[9] Improving quality, throughput, and delivery performance should automatically produce reduced costs and higher profits. Thus, the financial summaries should follow, and be the results of, the underlying activities (as opposed to the current practice wherein financial summaries are presented first, and then operating managers are asked to determine which activities explain the financial summaries).

The extreme form of this view has been articulated by Eli Goldratt, who advocates that all manufacturing expenses other than materials purchases be treated as fixed operating expenses of the period.[10] Goldratt wants to report all actual expenses, other than materials costs, as operating expenses and to subtract these from throughput—measured as sales revenue of items sold less materials expenses—to obtain the actual operating profit each period. Operating managers are then motivated to increase throughput (sales revenue less materials purchases), while controlling all other fixed expenses and maintaining or reducing inventory levels.

CONCLUSIONS: A NEW ROLE FOR ACCOUNTING IN PERFORMANCE EVALUATION?

I have some clear and some tentative thoughts about cost accounting trends in advanced manufacturing environments. My clear thoughts are, first, that traditional summary measures of local performance—purchase price variances, direct labor and machine efficiencies, ratios of indirect to direct labor, absorption ratios, and volume variances—are harmful and probably should be eliminated, since they conflict with attempts to improve quality, reduce inventories and throughput times, and increase flexibility.

Second, direct measurement is needed of quality, process times, delivery performance, and any other operating performance criterion that companies want to improve. For departmental managers and for plant managers, these direct measures will be much more useful than the monthly financial summaries they now receive. Conceptual thinking must still be developed to aggregate the daily or batch-by-batch operating measures at local departments, cost centers, and machines into appropriate periodic (weekly, monthly) measures of plantwide performance.

Third, financial summaries should exploit available information-processing technologies to capture the actual consumption of resources by individual batches or processing lines. The actual consumed quantity of resources, such as materials, energy, labor, and machine time, can be priced using standard or budgeted unit costs to obtain an aggregate cost figure. And the actual resource consumption and aggregated cost figures should be compared not to cost standards but to trends of past actuals. That is, the standards for today's production should require improvement from the levels established by production in previous batches, days, or months. If any comparison to a standard is performed, it should be done against the performance of the company's best worldwide competitor. Graphical presentation of the trends in unit, batch, and production-line resource consumption, and comparisons with ideal and "stretch" targets, can replace the myriad of numbers currently reported in aggregate monthly financial summaries.

My less clear thoughts concern the appropriate interplay between financial and operating measures. In measuring the performance of the purchasing department, I, and others, clearly want to de-emphasize a purchase price variance measure. Yet purchase cost is still a relevant variable when it can be combined with other attributes of the purchase decision. Some companies are attempting to evaluate purchasers and vendors not merely by the purchase price but by the **total cost of ownership** of materials, a cost that includes

the purchase price of the materials

plus the associated costs of
 ordering and paying,
 scheduling delivery,
 receiving, inspecting, handling and storing,
 scrap, rework, and obsolescence, and
 schedule disruptions (value of lost output) from incorrect delivery

of the purchased materials.

With this measurement, a supplier might have a higher unit price than alternative vendors but nonetheless offer a much lower cost because it can supply defect-free products, requiring no incoming handling or inspection, in exactly the right quantities, directly to the machine, minutes before the materials are needed, with ordering, invoicing, and payment handled automatically and electronically. Such a concept was clearly behind Company D's ability to have its vendors supply ICs directly to each of its plants' assembly departments, enabling it to close the IC Test department.

Developing a cost-of-ownership measure would be comparable to computing the **cost of quality**—a financial, systemwide measure of the costs associated with preventing, testing for, or correcting defective items.[11] Both the cost of ownership and the cost of quality provide an overall financial summary (cutting across organizational boundaries) of all the expenses associated with two important activities: purchasing materials and eliminating defects. What other organizational activities would warrant computing aggregate cost summaries—a cost of customer responsiveness, a cost of product design (including prototype, startup, and engineering change order expenses)?

Advanced manufacturing environments are characterized by much tighter linkages across organizational units, both within and external to the company. Traditional cost accounting measures fail when they focus on small, local (but not systemwide) measures of efficiency and productivity. Thus, the new role for aggregate cost measures would seem to require financial summaries that cut across machines, cost centers, and other organizational units. The measures would attempt to incorporate the cost consequences from performance in all areas. Financial summaries—such as cost of quality or cost of ownership—would, however, not be the primary focus of near-term managerial activities. The financial summaries would be informational, not control, measures. They would be attention-directing and aggregate score-keeping in nature, perhaps computed only semiannually or annually, to provide a comprehensive, interorganizational measure of financial performance for key activities. The short-term, operational feedback needed for control (and learning) would be provided by direct physical measures—actual outputs coupled with the actual quantities of labor, materials, machine time, and energy consumed, or yields, defect rates, throughput times, adherence to production and delivery schedules, and so forth. Each of these operational measures would be compared, not against standard, but to the trend of actual performance of prior batches or deliveries.

Admittedly, these ideas are tentative and speculative. In this paper, I have attempted to document conflicts between traditional cost accounting measures and the operating improvements required for the new manufacturing environment and have proposed remedies for eliminating such conflicts. Collaborative arrangements between company experimentation and academic research during the next several years should provide a clearer picture on the appropriate roles and interplay for operational and financial measurements and help promote the productivity, efficiency, and continuous improvement activities necessary for long-term success in global competition.

NOTES

1. See "Efficiency, Profit, and Scientific Management: 1880–1910," in H. Thomas Johnson and Robert S. Kaplan, *Relevance Lost: The Rise and Fall of Management Accounting* (Boston: Harvard Business School Press, 1987), chap. 3, 47–59.

2. This study focuses solely on the use of cost accounting systems for operational control and performance measurement. The role for cost systems to estimate product costs and to measure the profitability of an organization's diverse activities (see Robin Cooper and Robert S. Kaplan, "Measure Costs Right: Make the Right Decisions," *Harvard Business Review* [September–October 1988], 96–103) is not considered. On the different roles for operational control and product costing, see Robert S. Kaplan, "One Cost System Isn't Enough," *Harvard Business Review* (January–February 1988), 61–66.

3. Direct labor, in 1985, was about 5% of total costs in the PCB assembly function. By 1988, the percentage was down to 1–2%.

4. Currently, after an intensive total quality control program, inspectors have been replaced by audit teams performing random inspections, equipment calibration, and documentation with visual aids and schematics. The 150 inspectors have been replaced by 17 persons on the quality audit teams.

5. Kelvin Cross and Richard L. Lynch, "A SMART Way to Define and Sustain Success," *National Productivity Review* (Winter 1989).

6. Cross and Lynch, "Sustain Success," and "Accounting for Competitive Performance," *Journal of Cost Management* (Spring 1989), 20–29.

7. Johnson and Kaplan, *Relevance Lost*, 103–107.

8. Determining the origin of labor and machine efficiency ratios would be a highly worthwhile investigation for an accounting historian.

9. See H. Thomas Johnson, "Activity-Based Information: A Blueprint for World-Class Manufacturing Accounting," *Management Accounting* (June 1988), 23–30.

10. Eliyahu M. Goldratt and Jeff Cox, *The Goal:* A Process of Ongoing Improvement; and Robert Fox and Eliyahu M. Goldratt, *The Race* (Croton-on-Hudson, NY: North River Press, 1986).

11. See Chris Ittner and Robert S. Kaplan, "Texas Instruments: Cost of Quality (A) and (B)," #9–189–029 and #9–189–112. Boston: Harvard Business School, 1989.

CHAPTER 2

The Influence of Factory Automation on Management Accounting Practices: A Study of Japanese Companies

Michiharu Sakurai

INTRODUCTION

THIS paper summarizes Japanese management accounting practices, using several interview and mail surveys. (See the Appendix for details of my study.) I will first describe changes in traditional management accounting concepts and techniques and then describe the new management accounting tools and target-profit concepts used in typical Japanese assembly-oriented companies. The characteristics of Japanese management accounting concepts and techniques in advanced manufacturing environments are presented as a conclusion.

Factory automation (FA) has stimulated the major changes in management accounting concepts and techniques. Two underlying forces, demand and supply, have caused the changes.

As the income of the average Japanese citizen increased dramatically during the 1960s and early 1970s, the demand for durable consumer goods increased greatly. With a much higher standard of living, most Japanese consumers became dissatisfied with mass-produced products and sought high-quality, specialized products, customized to their needs.

I gratefully acknowledge the helpful comments on a previous draft made by Larry N. Killough and Philip Y. Huang, both at Virginia Polytechnic Institute and State University.

39

Numerous Japanese companies focused on supplying a variety of high-quality products in lower production volumes, especially in assembly-oriented industries. However, the companies needed to overcome the high cost of producing lower volumes and a wider variety of products. FA solved this problem by making it possible to provide flexibility to the production processes of assembly-oriented industries at low cost (see the insert "What is Factory Automation (FA)?" for details). Companies that have introduced FA have achieved both low cost and high quality due to several important changes.

What is Factory Automation (FA)?

The phrase factory automation (FA) is used often in Japan. FA can be defined as the automation of a factory through the usage of a flexible manufacturing system (FMS), computer-aided design/computer-aided manufacturing (CAD/CAM), and office automation (OA). Among these three basic elements, FMS is the core of FA. Typically designed for midrange volume and midrange variety production, FMS integrates industrial robots, numerical control (NC) machines, and automated materials-handling systems using the concept of cellular manufacturing. At the end of 1987, Japanese companies used 141,000 industrial robots, 67% of the world's robot population, compared with the 29,000 units (14%) in American companies (Robotics Society of Japan 1988).

According to the results of our 1988 mail survey, integrated FA or computer-integrated manufacturing (CIM) is not well advanced in Japanese companies. Only 4% of all respondents (279 companies) apply CIM as an integrated system of development, production, finance, sales, and personnel; 22% of them apply it as an automated system of order receipt, design, production, and shipment; 30% are in the planning stage; 44% use no CIM (Sakurai and Huang 1988). Thus, I use the acronym FA instead of CIM here.

First, manual production has been replaced by automated machines, reducing direct labor content dramatically. On the other hand, indirect labor in the areas of design, monitoring, and R&D has increased sharply. Plant and equipment have also increased because of the large amount of capital required for FA facilities.

Second, product life cycles have declined. Many Japanese products have life cycles of 2–3 years (Nakane et al. 1985). Assembly-oriented companies must frequently redesign manufacturing flow lines to meet this shortened life cycle. The planning and designing stages (upstream of production stages) have become much more important for cost management than the manufacturing process.

Third, software development lies at the heart of the increasingly information-intensive manufacturing process. Software and information-processing costs have risen sharply, amounting to 40% or more of FA facility costs. Consequently, Japanese companies have created management systems to control software costs.

Does this change in the manufacturing environment create a need for a parallel change in management accounting? I believe it does. Thus, with the above background in mind, I will discuss changes in management accounting in the next section.

CHANGES IN MANAGEMENT ACCOUNTING SYSTEMS CAUSED BY THE CHANGES IN MANUFACTURING ENVIRONMENT

The major trends in the manufacturing environment have brought about changes in the management accounting systems of Japanese companies. The decrease in direct labor has forced management accountants to reassess the traditional basis of overhead allocation. Large investment in plant and equipment having a short product life cycle has also made companies change their investment appraisal method from discounted cash flow (DCF) to the payback method. Decreased direct labor content and increased process reliability have forced management accountants to give up labor efficiency-oriented performance measures such as standard costing.

Overhead Allocation

The concept of direct labor hours (DLH) has been widely used as a sound basis for allocating overhead cost. For example, in 1978, DLH was used by 41% of the companies surveyed (175 public companies), while only 9% used the machine-hour (MH) concept (Yoshikawa 1979). However, DLH allocation is only appropriate when products are produced by labor-paced processes. As automation increases, and labor is replaced by machines, the importance of using DLH as an allocation basis diminishes and the importance of an MH basis increases. Therefore, it is only natural for companies introducing FA to eliminate the use of DLH as a basis for allocating overhead cost.

Implementation problems arise, however, when introducing an MH basis into an automated factory. Some companies do not fully utilize their capacities. In that case, a problem of allocating idle capacity cost arises. Automation is not uniformly applied to all processes, only to a few processes. Therefore, a single overhead machine rate may not be adequate for FA companies. Even in an FA environment, cost management by DLH is still important, not only for field work, but also for indirect labor such as maintenance and supervising.

For example, a big electric company producing car telephones did not use MH because the rate of production fluctuated widely. A giant automobile company did not use MH because robots were installed only in certain processes: robots were used in 98% of the body-assembly process but in only 8% of the final assembly process.

Due to the difficulty of solving these problems, the number of advanced FA companies that had switched to a single plantwide machine rate was not as large as I had expected in my 1983 and 1984 surveys (Sakurai 1984). Even in the 1987 interviews and 1988 mail surveys, when FA and its management control systems were better organized, we found that very few companies used MH; only 6% of the companies in the 1988 survey were using a single machine rate basis, while 42% were still using DLH, as shown in Table 2-1 (Sakurai and Huang 1988).

Interestingly, about 44% of the companies surveyed used both DLH and MH for each work center or group of work centers, as Table 2-1 indicates. Why, then, do Japanese companies prefer to apply MH only in certain processes? An example may best explain the reason.

The semiconductor industry is well known as a "money-gobbling industry." In order to produce chips, companies must invest heavily in capital equipment. Due to the large capital invested in FA facilities, the ratio of depreciation to labor cost increased dramatically in the semiconductor industry. To cope with this new phenomenon, Oki Electric, for example, decided to change the overhead rate basis from the DLH to the MH method in the two work centers, wafer fabrication and testing, that used expensive machines. Direct labor methods continued to be used in the more manual assembly process (Kaneko 1988).

Table 2-1 Allocation Basis of Overhead

Application Basis	Number of Companies	Percentage
Direct Labor Hour (DLH) Only	111	41.7%
Machine Hour (MH) Only	17	6.4
Both DLH and MH	116	43.6
Others	22	8.3
Total	266	100.0%

Japanese managers and academics actually prefer simple methods for allocating overhead to the more complex activity accounting allocation methods advocated by several U.S. academics (Cooper 1987–1988; Cooper and Kaplan 1988; Johnson 1988).

Certainly, Japanese companies have been trying to connect costs directly to cost drivers. For example, most Japanese manufacturing companies treat setup cost as a direct cost. They think it better, for cost control, to identify setup cost with its product. Design cost is also identified as direct when it is used for specific products. But when it is treated as indirect, some companies use a cost accounting system with different overhead rates applied to products. For example, one heavy industry company separates overhead into two parts: design cost and other overhead costs. Design cost is allocated to low-volume products using high overhead rates and to high-volume products with low overhead rates. The remaining overhead cost is allocated by the usual allocation procedure.

One Japanese executive, in charge of R&D, expressed concern that an activity-based system would hinder the development of new products by allocating more cost to new, low-volume products. The controller of a leading maker of car audio equipment alleged that the company might not meet the needs of consumers if the company were to introduce the system because the firm's profitable products are varied, and production volume is low. The executives may be confusing the accounting method with marketing policy. However, the lack of use of the more complex activity-based accounting schemes stems from most Japanese managers' belief that for overhead allocation, "simple is beautiful."

Investment Justification

Since FA needs a large amount of capital investment, careful investment appraisal is critical for investment justification. Investment justification for R&D and software has also become indispensable in the new manufacturing environment.

While discounted cash flow (DCF) is the most popular method of investment justification in the United States, Japanese companies typically use payback to justify investments. Surveys by Tsumagari and Matsumoto (1971) and Shibata and Kumada (1988) on the investment appraisal policies of the same companies indicated that payback was used by more than 60% of companies. Internal rate of return (IRR) and net present value (NPV) were used by only 12–13% of the companies surveyed by Shibata and Kumada (1988).

Some companies use a combined payback and DCF method to account for the magnitude or timing of cash flow during the payback period. For example, Furukawa Electric, one of the Big Two in the Japanese electric wire and cable industry, discounts cash flow for a new investment, but payback is also computed and used as the decisive criterion for economic justification of new investment.

Why do Japanese managers prefer to use the payback method in spite of its well-known shortcomings? Some may suspect that its simplicity and ease of use is the explanation. Currently, low interest rates may also be a contributing reason.

Akira Koike, an executive of NEC and recognized as one of the most knowledgeable management practitioners in Japan, uses a two-year payback period. He believes that the capital invested in high-tech products must be recovered as soon as possible since the products soon become obsolete. At NEC, at least, payback is used not because it is simple but because of the stringent requirements for early recovery.

Our 1988 FA survey suggests that the nearly 20% of respondents that actually had installed FA changed their appraisal method when evaluating the investment needed for FA facilities. Almost 75% of these respondents used payback when they evaluated FA facilities. Table 2–2 shows the overall results.

It may be surprising to see that although Japanese managers are believed to take a long-term perspective, many actually use the payback method, which focuses on the short term. Indeed, projects with faster payback have more favorable short-term effects on earnings per share. This is quite contrary to the general understanding of Japanese management style.

The inferences from our survey and interviews are as follows:

1. In an era of striking technological innovation such as FA, it is too risky to invest capital for an extended period. New technol-

Table 2-2 Appraisal Method Used for Investment Justification

Investment Appraisal	General Purpose	FA Facilities
Payback Method	151 (65.4%)	34 (73.9%)
IRR	14 (6.0%)	4 (8.7%)
NPV	24 (10.4%)	4 (8.7%)
Combination	36 (15.6%)	4 (8.7%)
Others	6 (2.6%)	0 (0.0%)
Total	231 (100.0%)	46 (100.0%)

Source: Mail survey of January 1988, conducted with Prof. Huang. All 277 respondents were Japanese companies (general purpose, 231; FA facilities, 46).

ogy may change before the company can recover its earlier capital expenditures. Existing equipment may be soon rendered obsolete.

2. The life cycle of assembly products has become much shorter. Because of a high risk of obsolescence of these products, it becomes more difficult for companies to recover capital with long payback periods.

3. Facility life cycle has also become shorter. Table 2-3 indicates how short is the life cycle for FA facilities in Japanese companies. Among the respondents that used the payback method, approximately 41% adopted a payback period threshold of three years or less, and 84% used five years or less. These results conform with the short-term orientation of the investments being made.

4. Japanese managers find it difficult to predict sales volume accurately for highly advanced products, such as semiconductors. Furthermore, the statistical techniques for sales forecasting are rather unsophisticated. So, if sales volume cannot be predicted accurately, it is meaningless for managers to compute future profitability in much detail.

Japanese companies do evaluate investment not only by economic performance but also by other quantitative and qualitative measures. Only a small number of companies, however, have established comprehensive models to justify investment for FA facilities such as suggested by several researchers (Kaplan 1986; Primrose and Leonard 1987; Howell and Soucy 1987). In addition to some of the cited intangible benefits from FA, Japanese executives often mention

Table 2-3   Payback Period of Japanese Facilities

Payback Period	Number of Companies	Percentage
2 Years	12	6.3%
3 Years	67	34.9
4 Years	19	9.9
5 Years	64	33.3
10 Years	26	13.5
Others	4	2.1
Total	192	100.0%

elimination of dirty work and accident prevention. According to my October 1988 mail survey on FA and management accounting, 72% of the respondents (196 companies) evaluate their investment by overall measures, while 22% justify investment by economic performance alone. When Japanese companies quantify such tangible and intangible benefits as high quality (reduction of defective units), reduced inventory, reduced lead time, and avoidance of dangerous or dirty work, some do build DCF models, but most still use the payback method.

Standard Costing

Standard costing variance analysis has been viewed as the most effective tool for cost control, being an effective basis for problem identification and performance evaluation. In theory, standard cost variance analysis can pinpoint a diverse range of activities and summarize them in a way that clarifies factory operations. The question is whether standard costing remains an effective tool in an FA environment.

When I visited Japanese assembly-oriented companies in 1984–1985, their cost accountants never failed to point out that standard costing was no longer an effective tool for cost control. For example, the controller of Atsugi Motor Parts (an affiliate of Nissan) told me that he had performed detailed variance analysis when he joined the company 25 years ago but no longer allowed his men to do variance analysis. In another company, affiliated with Toyota, standard costing is no longer the main tool for cost control or cost reduction. Cost reduction at the upstream production processes has become much more important in these companies. Thus, we need to explore the possible reasons for the declining role of standard costing as a cost control tool and whether the decline is caused by FA.

First, standard costing was developed as a cost control tool for improving factory efficiency. In order to improve workers' efficiency, standard costing focuses on the control of direct labor. The variance analysis of the direct labor is, therefore, believed to be the most important of the manufacturing cost variance analyses. Since the ultimate goal of FA is to achieve an unmanned factory, it is meaningless to set standard costs or analyze cost variances of direct labor for highly automated factories.

Second, with advanced technology, the stability of the production process, one of the most important conditions for implementing standard costing, has been reduced.

Third, because of shortened product life cycles, it has become too time-consuming to set standard costs for all the new products. For example, it takes two months to set standard costs in a certain giant automobile company. Worse still, standard costs have to be recalculated whenever new products are introduced.

As a result of introducing FA, manufacturing support staff, in such areas as product planning, design, R&D, software development, supervision, and maintenance has increased. While traditional standard costing is still used by some companies for controlling production costs, the method is not suitable for controlling indirect labor. As Kobayashi (1988) points out, business budgeting with motivation control plays a much larger role in these factories. My October 1988 mail survey supports this conclusion: out of 178 respondents, 67 companies (38%) replied that the role of budgeting had increased as a result of automation; only 1 company (0.6%) replied negatively.

In summary, the development of FA has reduced the importance of standard costing as an efficiency control device. Nevertheless, many Japanese companies still use standard costing, perhaps for two reasons. First, costs can still be reduced by 2–5% at production stage. Since no other tool exists for effectively controlling cost at the production stage, standard costing is used for this purpose. Second, standard costing is still important for furnishing data for financial statements and for simplifying and speeding up computational procedures.

As the rate of technological innovation and FA speeds up, the focus of cost management will be switched from the production stage to the upstream, that is, the product planning and product design, stages.

EMERGING COST MANAGEMENT TECHNIQUES

Since World War II, Japanese academics and management practitioners have concentrated on introducing American management accounting concepts and techniques into Japan. They had few management tools of their own during the 1950s and the early 1960s. In the late 1960s, some Japanese companies began to create their own cost management systems in order to reduce product costs and improve quality. Today, most Japanese practitioners believe that they must develop innovative management accounting concepts and techniques to fit their new manufacturing environment.

Several management accounting concepts and techniques have been developed in major Japanese companies, especially since the 1970s. The increasing importance of the design stage has given rise to new techniques, such as target costing, and to new engineering tools. In addition, the sharply increased use of information technology has prompted Japanese managers and researchers to create new cost accounting systems for software.

Target Costing

The cost management tool named target costing (*genkakikaku* or *mokuhyou genka*) has been widely used (since the early 1970s) in prominent Japanese assembly-oriented industries such as automobiles, semiconductors, household appliances, and precision machinery. This tool is especially popular among high-tech companies, which need to achieve high productivity and strong competitiveness (Sakurai and Huang 1988).

Target costing, also called cost planning or cost project, is a cost management tool for reducing the overall cost of a product over its entire life cycle. It requires extensive interactions among the production, engineering, R&D, marketing, and accounting departments. The main purpose of target costing is to reduce cost at the planning and design stages of the product life cycle, i.e., at the upstream stages of the production processes.

Target costing typically uses three steps (see Figure 2-1):

1. Planning and designing products of high quality that best meet customers' needs

Figure 2-1 The Target Costing Procedure

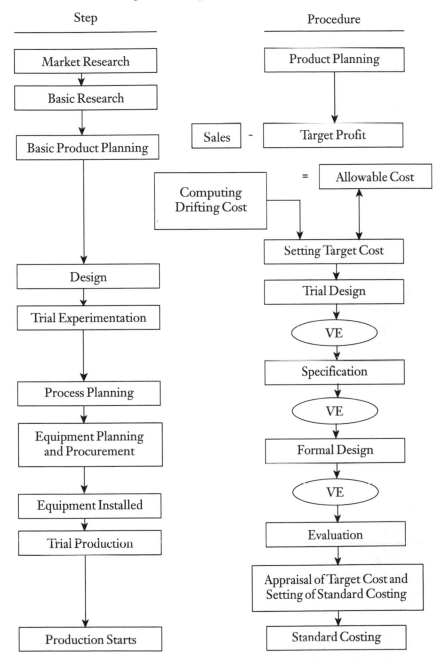

2. Setting the target cost for the products and then establishing the target by applying value engineering (VE)

3. Attaining the target cost at the production stage, using standard costing

Once a company determines the needs and preferences of its customers, a project is clearly defined at the product-planning stage. Marketability is confirmed at the first stage. A tentative project is prepared after evaluating the results of market research.

In the second step, a target cost is established. Although various methods can be used to establish target costs, costs are typically set based on engineering planning and profit planning. Before establishing a target cost, an allowable cost is computed as the "allowable utmost cost for the production cost" (Tanaka 1979) and calculated by deducting the target profit from the selling price. Return on sales (ROS) is used to determine the target profit percentage. The drifting cost is computed as the estimated cost based on current cost projections. After checking drifting costs of parts one by one and then trying to reduce them toward the allowable cost, the gap between allowable cost and drifting cost can be decreased. Value engineering (VE) is applied at this stage. The allowable cost is the one desired by top management; consequently, it tends to be rather tight. On the other hand, the drifting cost is only an estimated cost and has no target. The target cost represents an attainable cost—but attainable only after considerable effort.

Between the design and production stages of the product life cycle, trial experimentation is performed, followed by process and equipment planning. After making a trial design, VE activities are applied again in order to reduce further the cost of the new products.

The third step, specifying the actual activities after establishing the target cost, is the responsibility of the factory foreman. Generally speaking, target costs are utilized to set standard costs. However, in budgeting, some companies use the target cost instead of standard costing. Japan Conveyer Corporation, a small company with about 300 employees, is one such example (Kumagaya 1977). The challenge of attempting to attain the target cost with standard costing or budgeting starts with production activities.

In setting standard costs from target costs, many companies usually add new cost reduction targets to standard costs. The cost reduction targets reflect effects due to the learning curve and to increased volume production. While target costing is driven by both technology and market, standard costing is primarily driven by technology (see Figure 2-2).

Cost Accounting for Software

Expanded use of robots requires extensive, expert software systems. It is widely recognized among Japanese managers that the most important aspect of operating industrial robots is having sophisticated, reliable software. Japanese managers prefer custom-made software rather than commercial software packages. For example, sales of software packages are only 8% of total annual software sales in Japan (Japan Information Service Industry Association 1987), compared to about 60% in the United States. Thus, software development cost is typically 40% or more of FA facility cost in Japanese companies. This shows how important it is to control software costs in FA production facilities and why cost management in Japan is gradually shifting its emphasis from measuring hardware costs to software costs.

Automation software is produced mainly by user-firms and software houses. Japanese user-firms are now introducing cost accounting systems for software. According to my October 1988 mail survey, 36 companies (24%) out of 148 have cost accounting systems for software development, and 15 companies (10%) are planning to introduce cost accounting systems for software.

The cost concepts for software are quite different from those for hardware. First, work-in-process cost is intangible, so it is physically harder to control software costs. For cost control, it is important to measure accurately the time spent developing software (Koike 1987). Second, the software industry is a typical labor-intensive industry. The average labor cost of 422 Japanese software houses was 58% of total manufacturing costs for software in 1985 (Information Processing Promoting Business Association 1985), compared to an average 11% for all Japanese public manufacturing companies (Bank of Japan 1985). The production cost report in Table 2-4 suggests that the labor portion of software development cost is extremely high compared to the cost structure of typical manufacturing companies.

Third, because of the high possibility of failure when writing code and because of the considerable skill differences among software engineers, input-output relationships in software production are difficult to determine. This makes the use of standard costing inappro-

Figure 2-2   The Relationship between Target Costing and Standard Costing

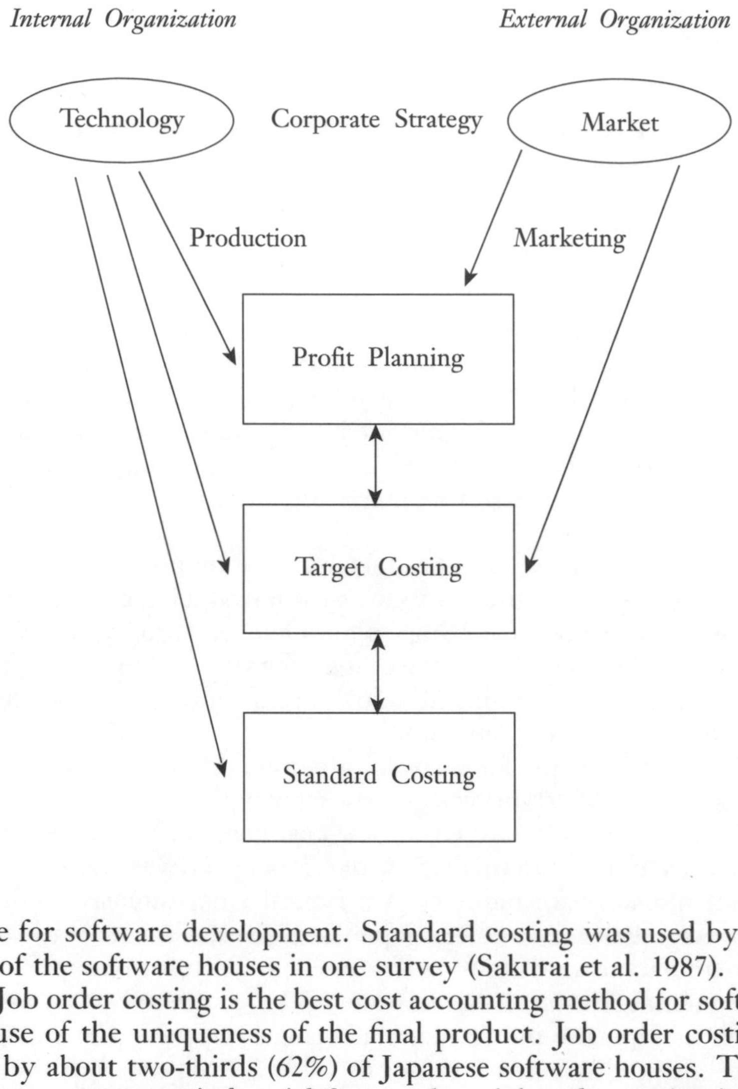

Internal Organization   *External Organization*

priate for software development. Standard costing was used by only 13% of the software houses in one survey (Sakurai et al. 1987).

Job order costing is the best cost accounting method for software because of the uniqueness of the final product. Job order costing is used by about two-thirds (62%) of Japanese software houses. This is in sharp contrast to industrial firms, where job order costing is used by only one-third (32%, 286 companies) of 889 public companies for costing industrial products (Sakurai 1982). In cost accounting for software, process costing was used by only 12% of the software houses surveyed. Another quarter (26%) of the companies used "departmental income costing," a unique costing method originally developed by Japanese software developers.

Table 2-4   Sample CSK Production Cost Report
(September 21, 1986 to September 20, 1987)

Cost Item	Amount (¥ 1,000)	Percentage
Labor	¥ 16,032,179	81.1%
Contract	1,980,529	10.0
Overhead	1,757,984	8.9
Computer Rental	89,633	
Depreciation	71,729	
Welfare Expense	227,016	
Travel Expense	421,197	
Rent	397,902	
Miscellaneous	550,504	
Total Production Cost	¥ 21,528,673	100.0%

Note: Job order costing by project has been used as the cost accounting system.

Though job order costing is accurate, and therefore desirable, it takes time and increases clerical cost. Small software developers need a simpler but equally effective cost accounting method. Departmental income costing meets this need. Table 2-5 illustrates the departmental income statement used by Chuo Computer Systems, a small software house with about 400 employees.

Department income costing is not process costing because software is not mass-produced. It could be called project costing for software. With departmental income costing, costs are not assigned to work-in-process because a job order is not issued. This has not become a critical problem, however, because Japanese companies do not have to value software work-in-process for tax and public reporting.

ROS AS A TARGET PROFIT FOR FA

One of the most controversial topics in management accounting has been the choice between return on investment (ROI) and residual income (RI) to evaluate divisional performance. In the United States, many managers continue to use ROI even though its use has been criticized by several academics for its tendency to encourage division managers to avoid active investment (Solomons 1965; Mauriel and Anthony 1969; Reece and Cool 1978).

In Japan, some influential researchers (Moori 1962; Itami 1982) have advocated wider use of ROI by Japanese management. In spite of the advocacy for ROI, many practitioners have continued to use the absolute amount of profit, such as ordinary income, because

Table 2-5   Departmental Income Statement
(¥ 1,000)

Items	Total	Project A	Project B	Project C	Project C
Sales					
Cost of Sales					
Machine					
Contract					
Part-time Labor					
Full-time Labor					
Equipment					
Supplies					
Miscellaneous					
Distributed Cost					
Beginning WIP					
Ending WIP					
Total Cost of Sales					
Gross Income					
Common Costs					
Marketing Cost					
Administrative Cost					
Operating Income					
Nonoperating Income					
Nonoperating Expense					
Ordinary Income					
Extraordinary Items					
Income Tax					
Net Income after Tax					

1. there is little or no pressure from stockholders to increase dividend or ROI, and

2. high economic growth coupled with the high rate of inflation between 1950 and the early 1970s convinced most Japanese executives that rapid expansion of production capacity was the best way of ensuring business survival. With expansion in the overall economy, capital gains were available if management actively invested resources into land, equipment, and machines. Low-cost bank loans practically ensured that companies would expand their production capacity. In addition, Japanese companies tend to invest in new markets even if the investments

Table 2-6 Corporate Goals and Their Trends

Measures	Past	Present	Future[2]
Operating Profit	6.7%	5.5%	3.8%
Ordinary Income (EBT)	38.7	47.3	35.4
Net Profit after Tax	17.9	17.4	13.5
Periodic Profit Subtotal	63.3	70.2	52.7
Return on Total Assets	12.4	13.9	28.3
Return on Owners' Equity	0.6	0.8	2.9
Return on Paid-in Capital	1.1	1.1	1.6
ROI Subtotal	14.1	15.8	32.8
Return on Sales	20.5	12.6	11.8
Internal Rate of Return	1.2	0.7	1.8
Others	0.9	0.7	0.8
Total Company (Percentage)[1]	1,000(100)	996(100)	992(100)

Notes: 1. "Total Company" is the number of companies that responded.
2. "Future" does not mean any definite year but usually is within five or ten years.
Source: The Economic Planning Agency, 1976.

have an adverse effect on short-run profitability. Consequently, most Japanese managers think that the maximization of earnings before taxes is the best corporate goal and performance measure (Sakurai, Killough, and Brown 1985).

The use of the periodic profit as a performance measure was consequently quite popular in the 1960s and early 1970s in Japan. Table 2-6 presents the results of a mail survey conducted by the Economic Planning Agency (1976).

Since the late 1970s, however, the number of companies using the absolute amount of profit has been decreasing, year by year, especially among those assembly-oriented companies producing a variety of products. In my interview survey of 1984, the absolute amount of profit was used by only 5 of 32 companies (16%), while ROS was used by 23 (72%) companies (Sakurai 1984). In my mail survey on pricing in 1986, ROS was also found to be used widely. Surprisingly, 143 (46%) of 309 Japanese public companies used ROS, while ROI was used by only 12 (4%) companies (Sakurai 1986).

My October 1988 mail survey shows the increase of ROS as a goal for profit planning, especially in assembly-oriented companies producing a variety of products. Although absolute amount of profit is still used by 53 companies (45%) of 117 respondent companies,

Table 2-7   Measures for Profit Planning

Type of Industry	Periodic Profit		ROI		ROS		Total of Firms
	No. of Firms	%	No. of Firms	%	No. of Firms	%	
Electrical Equipment	29	44.7	12	18.5	24	36.9	65
Transportation Equip.	24	46.2	9	17.3	19	36.5	52
Subtotal	53	45.3	21	17.9	43	36.8	117
Chemicals	40	57.1	10	14.3	20	28.6	70
Iron and Steel	9	34.6	6	23.1	11	42.3	26
Subtotal	49	51.0	16	16.7	31	32.3	96
Total	102	47.9	37	17.4	74	34.7	213

Source: My October 1988 mail survey on FA and management accounting.

ROS is used by as many as 43 companies (37%), as shown in Table 2-7.

Why do Japanese assembly-oriented companies prefer to use ROS?

1. ROS can clearly reveal the profitability of each product in an environment of high product variety. It is almost impossible for companies producing high-variety, low-volume products to compute ROI for each product. On the other hand, it is easy to compute ROS for each product.

2. It is easy to set prices for various products using target costing. (In the process of computing the target cost, the target profit is easy to set by using ROS; see Figure 2-3.)

3. ROI cannot be computed reasonably in high-tech companies because the amount of capital investment fluctuates frequently.

4. Since the capital investment required for producing profitable products will be quite large in the future, ROI can make a promising business look unattractive.

5. ROI can be effectively applied when there is a stable demand and little or no anxiety about the drop in sales volume. In the case of high-tech products, these conditions do not exist.

6. There is little or no pressure from the stockholders.

The critical problem in using ROS arises from its failure to recognize asset turnover or the effective use of capital, as the following equation indicates:

Figure 2-3 Setting Target Profit in Target Costing
(¥ 1,000)

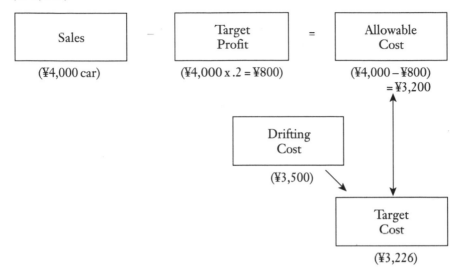

Note: Target profit (800) is computed by multiplying sales (4,000) by ROS (.2). Details presented in my paper, "The Concept of Target Costing and How to Use It," *Journal of Cost Management for the Manufacturing Industry* 3 (Spring 1989): 39–50.

$$\text{ROI} \quad = \quad \text{ROS} \quad \times \quad \text{TURNOVER}$$

$$\frac{\text{Income}}{\text{Investment}} = \frac{\text{Income}}{\text{Sales}} \times \frac{\text{Sales}}{\text{Investment}}$$

Are excellent companies such as Toyota, Epson, or Fanuc really not paying attention to capital utilization? I think not. Why then do they use ROS and not ROI? I suspect they have other, more effective tools for increasing asset turnover.

On the debit side of the balance sheet, assets are roughly divided into three parts: 1) cash and accounts receivable, 2) inventory, and 3) plant and equipment. Japanese companies cannot expedite the recovery of accounts receivable without the risk of losing sales because terms of payment are customarily determined. Reducing plant and equipment may help stockholders receive a higher immediate dividend, but it is sure to hurt the future growth of the company. Thus, the critical asset among the three to reduce is inventory.

Toyota uses JIT and ROS together. Why did Toyota create JIT?

Why did Toyota create target costing? I suspect that JIT and target costing are closely related to the use of ROS as a profit goal. We should remember that a goal for JIT is to have zero inventory. If JIT is realized in the entire firm, "the ratio of capital turnover will be increased" (Monden 1983). Since inventory is the only promising candidate for reducing assets and thus increasing asset turnover, a company must use additional tools besides ROS to reduce inventory. NEC, Epson, Fanuc, and other excellent Japanese companies, which focus on ROS as a target profit, use both JIT and target costing to effectively utilize capital.

The essence of the Japanese approach lies in separating ROI into two parts: ROS and turnover. By doing so, they manage to obtain separate measures and thus avoid the two inherent weaknesses of ROI: a negative attitude toward investing large sums of capital resources in FA, and in the problem of measuring the investment denominator (whether a company should choose fixed assets at cost, net book value, or appraised value).

CONCLUSION

I can categorize the characteristics of Japanese management accounting practice into three areas.

First, Japanese managers prefer simple systems, especially in overhead allocation. They do not wish to use sophisticated methods such as activity costing. Similarly, they prefer to use the payback method to justify investments. Also, JIT is a much simpler concept than economic order quantity (EOQ) analysis. Japanese managers often talk about ease of understanding as the main reason for using ROS. Most Japanese practitioners and academics believe that good management tools must be fully understood by all managers and field workers. Therefore, management accounting tools must be simple and easy to understand.

Second, the emphasis of cost management in Japanese companies has shifted from cost control in the manufacturing process to cost reduction at the product planning and design stages. Most Japanese managers believe that few significant opportunities exist to reduce product costs once manufacturing activities have been started. Target costing is the best tool for cost reduction in the design stage. As a contrast to standard costing, target costing can reduce cost without compromising the quality of the product.

Third, Japanese management accountants have actively been trying to integrate such engineering tools as total quality control

(TQC), total preventive maintenance (TPM), value engineering (VE), and just-in-time (JIT) into their management accounting systems. As a result, they try to cooperate with managers in such departments as engineering and marketing. For example, at one company, most of the 50 staff members in the target costing department are VE engineers. The controller at a large automobile company indicated that target costing requires keeping good relations with marketing people. In the new FA manufacturing environment, accountants must learn to co-operate with other department managers.

APPENDIX

Interview and Mail Surveys Used

1. Interview survey in 1984 of 32 companies producing a variety of products (Sakurai 1984). The industries of the companies sur-veyed were Electrical Equipment, 10 companies; Transporta-tion Equipment, 6; Other Manufacturing, 3; Machinery, 4; Chemicals, 3; Foodstuffs, 2; Precision, 2; Metal Products, 1; and Glass, 1. Half of the persons interviewed were controllers, 8 were in planning departments, 4 in cost accounting depart-ments, and 4 in accounting.

2. Interview survey of 8 public companies in 1985, conducted to supplement the 1984 survey and to compare assembly- and process-oriented industries. (Sakurai 1985; Sakurai and Huang 1986). The assembly-oriented companies in the survey were Nissan, NEC, Daihatsu, Aisan, Hitachi, Mitsubishi Electric, and Panasonic; the process-oriented companies were Nippon Steel, NKK (Nippon Kokan), Topy Industries, Mitsubishi Chemical, and Kawasaki Chemical.

3. Mail survey on pricing (Sakurai 1986). The 394 respondent companies represented 53.2% of 740 public manufacturing com-panies listed on the Toyko, Osaka, and Nagoya stock exchanges.

4. Mail survey of 1986 on software cost accounting (Sakurai et al. 1987). The survey was conducted by the Cost Accounting Com-mittee for Software, JISA (Japan Information Service Industry Association), where the author serves as committee chairman. The 176 respondent companies represented 44% of the 398 member companies of JISA.

5. Interview survey of 18 companies, 1987, with Professor Huang (Huang and Sakurai unpublished). The companies surveyed

were in Transportation, 5; Electrical and Precision, 6; Process-oriented, 5; and Software Houses, 2.

6. Mail survey on FA, January 1988, with Professor Huang (Huang and Sakurai 1988). The companies were in the following six industries: Precision, Electrical Equipment, Transportation, Machinery, Metal, and Miscellaneous Manufacturing. All were public companies listed on the Tokyo, Osaka, and Nagoya stock exchanges. Of 573 companies queried, 300 (52.4%) responded, but 16 companies did not use FA. Therefore, useful responses totaled 286.

7. My October 1988 mail survey on automation and management accounting. The companies were in the following four industries: Electrical Equipment, Transportation, Chemical, and Iron and Steel. All were public companies listed on the Tokyo, Osaka, and Nagoya stock exchanges. Of 493 companies queried, 225 (45.6%) responded. Since 26 companies did not answer because of insufficient automation, useful responses totaled 199; almost all respondents were controllers.

References

Bank of Japan, Research Statistic Bureau. *Syuyou kiggyou keiei bunseki* (Financial statement analysis of major business). Tokyo, 1985: 4. In that year, materials cost 68.8%, labor 11.3%, and overhead 19.8%.

Cooper, Robin. "Cost Management Concepts and Principles." *Journal of Cost Management for the Manufacturing Industry* (Spring 1987): 45–49; (Summer 1987): 43–51; (Fall 1987): 39–48; (Summer 1988): 45–54.

Cooper, Robin, and Robert S. Kaplan. "How Cost Accounting Distorts Product Costs." *Management Accounting* (April 1988): 21–25.

———. "Measure Costs Right: Make the Right Decision." *Harvard Business Review* (September–October 1988): 302–339.

Dearden, John. "The Case Against ROI Control." *Harvard Business Review* (May–June 1969): 124.

Economic Planning Agency. *Survey on Searching Business Behavior.* Tokyo: Ministry of Finance, Printing Office, 1976.

Hayes, Robert H., and Kim B. Clark. "Why Some Factories Are More Productive Than Others." *Harvard Business Review* (September–October 1986): 68.

Howell, A. Robert, and Stephen R. Soucy. "The Manufacturing Environment: Major Trends for Management Accounting." *Management Accounting* (July 1987): 25.

Huang, Philip, and Michiharu Sakurai. "Factory Automation in Japan." Senshu University, 1989. Information Processing Promoting Business Association. *Jyouhou syori sangyou keiei jittaicyousa houkokusyo* (Survey report on information processing industry, 1983). Tokyo, 1985: 60.

Itami, Hiroyuki. *Nihonteki keieiwo koete* (Beyond Japanese management: comparison of business power between US and Japan). Touyoukeizai, 1982: 31–32.

Jaikumar, Ramchandran. "Postindustrial Manufacturing." *Harvard Business Review* (November–December 1986): 69–76.

Japan Information Service Industry Association. *Review and Forecast of the Japanese Information Service Industry.* ALPHACOM, 1987: 8.

Johnson, H. Thomas. "Activity-Based Information: A Blueprint for World-Class Manufacturing Accounting." *Management Accounting* (June 1988): 23–30.

Johnson, H. Thomas and Robert S. Kaplan. *Relevance Lost: The Rise and Fall of Management Accounting.* Boston: Harvard Business School Press, 1987: 1.

Kaneko, Kimio. "Cost Accounting for IC Factories." In *High-tech Kaikei* (High-tech accounting), edited by Kiyoshi Okamoto, Masaaki Miyamoto, and Michiharu Sakurai. Tokyo: Douyuukan, 1988: 267.

Kaplan, Robert S. "Must CIM be Justified by Faith Alone?" *Harvard Business Review* (March–April 1986): 87–93.

Kobayashi, Kengo. "Cost Accounting in the High-tech Manufacturing Environment." *Aoyama Business Review* (March 1988): 14.

Koike, Akira. *Soft Jidaino genkakannri no hanashi* (A story on cost control in the age of software). Tokyo: NEC Culture Center, 1987: 110–116.

Kumagaya, Tokuhichi. "The Important Points of Cost Management in Custom-made Industries." *Genka keisan* (Cost accounting) (August 1977): 31.

Mauriel, John S., and Robert N. Anthony. "Misevaluation of Investment Center Performance." *Harvard Business Review* (March–April 1966): 100–102.

Monden, Yahuhiro. *Toyota Production System,* Tokyo: Industrial Engineering and Management Press Institute of Industrial Engineers, 1983: 4.

Moori, Shigetada. *Keiei gaku no kiso* (The foundation of business administration). Tokyo: Moriyama Syobou, 1962: 287.

Nakane, Jinichiro et al. *FA ka no shinten to kongo no kadai* (The development of FA and its future). Tokyo: Japan Society for the Promotion of Machine Industry, May 1985: 11–12. For example, in 1985, product life cycle of the electric industry was 2–3 years, 29.0%; over 5 years, 21.0%; 3–4 years, 16.1%; and 1–1.5 years, 19.3%. In the precision machinery industry, 3–5 and over 5 years are 30.8%; 1–1.5 years, 23.90%; 1.5–2 and 0.5–1 years are 15.4%, respectively.

Primrose, P. L., and R. Leonard. "Performing Investment Appraisals for Advanced Manufacturing Technology." *Journal of Cost Management* (Summer 1987): 34–40.

Reece, James S., and William R. Cool. "Measuring Investment Center Performance." *Harvard Business Review* (May–June 1978): 20–30. Out of the 1976 *Fortune* 1,000 companies, 62% responded.

Robotics Society of Japan. *Sangyouyou Robot no genjyou to tenbou* (Present and future of industrial robot). Tokyo: Robotics Society of Japan, October 1988: 18.

Sakurai, Michiharu. "Cost Accounting Systems in Japan." *Genkakeisan* (Cost accounting) (1982): 33–34.

———. "Cost Accounting in Varied Production." *Genkakeisan* (Cost accounting) Special Edition of the *Journal of Japan Cost Accounting Association*, no. 278 (1984): 94–105.

———. "FMS and New Development of Management Accounting." *Kigyoukaikei* (Business accounting) 37, no. 2 (February 1985): 25–35.

———. "How FA Changes Control Systems." *Diamond Harvard Business* (Japanese version of *Harvard Business Review*) (February–March 1986): 67–76.

———. "Pricing Practices in Japanese Companies, in Comparison with American and Canadian Companies." *Kigyoukaikei* (Business accounting) 38, no. 11 (November 1986): 41–52.

———. "Change of Management Accounting Systems Caused by the Introduction of FA." *Diamond Harvard Business* (Japanese version of *Harvard Business Review* (April–May, 1988): 63.

———. "Target Costing and How to Use It." *Journal of Cost Management* (Summer 1989): 39–50.

Sakurai, Michiharu, and Philip Y. Huang. "Factory Automation and Its Impact on Management Control Systems: A Japanese Survey." *Bulletin of the Institute of Business Administration* 76 (February 1988): Senshu University.

———. "Factory Automation and its Management Accounting Systems." *Senshu keieigakuronshu* (Business review of the Senshu University) 46 (September 1988): 74.

Sakurai, Michiharu, Larry N. Killough, and Robert M. Brown. "Performance Measurement Techniques and Goal Setting . . . A Comparison of American and Japanese Practices." *Senshu keieigakuronshu* (Business review of the Senshu University) 39 (February 1985): 69–85.

Sakurai, Michiharu, et al. *Hakutou syobou* (Software cost accounting). Tokyo, 1987: 171–217.

Shibata, Norio, and Kumada Yasuhisa. "Budgeting System of Japanese Companies." *Kigyoukaikei* (Business accounting) (April 1988): 86.

Solomons, David. *Divisional Performance: Measurement and Control*. Financial Executive Research Foundation, The Wharton School of the University of Pennsylvania, 1965: 64.

Tanaka, Masayasu. "Cost Management by Target Cost." *Genkakeisan* (Cost accounting) (October 1987): 36.

Tsumagari, Mayumi, and Jyouji Matsumoto. *Nihonkigyou no yosanseido* (Budgeting system of Japanese companies: survey and subject to be discussed in the future). Japan Productivity Center, 1972: 95. The result was adjusted to meet the other survey.

Yoshikawa, Takeo. "Comments on Mail Survey of Cost Accounting Practices." *Keiei-jutsumu* (Business practice) (May 1979): 17. Others are direct labor cost, 7.4%; output, 16.0%; prime cost, 6.3%; others, 16.0%; and no answer, 4.0%.

CHAPTER 3

Performance Measurement for Competitive Excellence

H. Thomas Johnson

INTRODUCTION

FOR years American businesses have relied on accounting information to assess operating performance. They view the double-entry cost, revenue, asset, and liability accounts as an integrated data base containing all cause and effect relationships that determine the financial outcome of operating activities.

Over the past decade, however, there has been growing doubt about the efficacy of managing business operations with accounting-based information.[1] World-class businesses organize their operations quite differently today than they did before the 1970s. However, most modern American businesses use management accounting systems that had their origins in the early 1900s. Using information from these systems to evaluate operating performance unwittingly causes companies to make decisions that impair competitiveness in today's global economy.

Managing with information from financial accounting systems impedes performance because traditional cost accounting data do not track sources of competitiveness such as quality, flexibility, dependability, and service in the global economy. At best, costs are imperfect signals that a problem exists; they provide no clues as to what the problem is, or how to treat it.

Several years have passed since we first heard about the obsolescence and irrelevance of management accounting in today's global economy. Lately, almost everyone agrees that businesses must change their information systems as well as their operating systems if they are to achieve competitive excellence. But what effect has this growing chorus of opinion had on business practice? How has the process by which information is used to measure performance been altered, if at all, in leading-edge companies that have changed the way they do business to meet the global competitive challenge?

To answer that question, I visited sites in GE Company and in Allen-Bradley—two manufacturing organizations that were among the first in America to understand and meet the challenge posed by high-quality, low-cost foreign competition in the late 1970s. Both GE and Allen-Bradley have successfully adopted new manufacturing strategies aimed at eliminating waste and achieving continuous flow production processes. Consequently, both firms have maintained or increased profitable positions in world markets in the 1980s.

On visits to these companies in 1988, I expected to see two developments: the appearance of new, performance information systems focused on sources of competitiveness such as quality, flexibility, and dependability and the phasing out of management accounting systems that cost inventory or track direct labor. In both companies, I saw encouraging changes. But I was disappointed to see managers' attention still dominated by the accounting issues of the past.

The following two sections describe the current performance measurement systems in each company. A final section discusses the implications that my observations on these two companies have for the future of management accounting.

GE COMPANY

GE Company is a global manufacturer of industrial and consumer products, with nearly 300,000 employees making about 135,000 different products in over 350 locations worldwide. New competitive pressures in several of its markets prompted teams from GE to visit Japanese plants in 1980. GE financed the first English translations of classic works on Japanese management, such as Taiichi Ohno's monograph on the Toyota production system, and GE was among the first to initiate pilot projects to implement just-in-time (JIT) and computer automation concepts in American plants. By 1984, some of those pilot plants had radically transformed their production methods, achieving results touted in the national business press as a sign of American industrial recovery.

Some GE managers who adopted the new methods saw that their conventional accounting systems did not track the benefits from JIT and computer automation, benefits such as reduced inventory quantities, shorter lead times, higher final yields, and improved workers' skill portfolios. Moreover, they realized that GE's traditional performance measures, emphasizing variables such as direct labor and machine utilization, impeded progress in further implementation of JIT and automation. In 1985, GE began a concerted effort to design performance measures appropriate to the new manufacturing practices.

The task of designing measures for the new manufacturing environment was assigned to a team of corporate-level staff consultants who thoroughly understood new Japanese management ideas and who were familiar with the recent efforts to implement these ideas in GE's plants. The performance measures articulated by this team were based on a Japanese-inspired concept they referred to as "activity management."[2]

Activity management begins with the proposition that a competitive business must provide value to customers at a cost less than the price customers pay for that value. Therefore, being competitive entails managing sources of value and drivers of cost in resource-consuming activities. Activities that consume resources (and therefore cause costs) can add value or they can represent waste (i.e., nonvalue). The global competitor continuously attempts to eliminate nonvalue activities and to reduce resources consumed by value-adding activities.

The central theme of activity management can be summed up as follows: companies strive to be competitive by achieving a continuous and rapid flow of value-adding work from product design to final customer payment. To achieve continuous and rapid flow of value-adding activity means eliminating anything that causes delay, unevenness, or excess in the flow of value-adding work. Sources of delay, including lengthy machine setups, unscheduled maintenance, defective work, defective parts, and performance measures that encourage overproduction and cause wasteful (i.e., nonvalue) activities such as moving, storing, inspecting, waiting, scheduling, and expediting. By eliminating generators of nonvalue activities (such as lengthy setups), the company eliminates the "need" for wasteful activity (such as storing and inspecting) and thereby delivers value to customers faster (i.e., at lower cost). Achieving competitiveness, then, entails careful attention to activities and to the generators of waste that cause nonvalue activity.

GE's team recognized several implications for performance measurement in this concept of activity management.[3] First, companies need information about activities—about all work that consumes resources in a company. Second, they require information about the causes of waste that create nonvalue work. This includes information about setup times, defect rates, and unscheduled maintenance, among other things. Third, to motivate people to find and eliminate waste, they need information confirming success at achieving value and continuous flow. Such information might be product lead times, space utilized by operations, or total payroll dollars per unit of output.

Having formulated these ideas by 1986, the team then chose one of GE's plants in which to experiment with activity-based performance measures. The plant they chose manufactures a variety of technologically sophisticated electronic products. To keep the project manageable, the activity-based performance experiment, begun in early 1987, was limited at first to activities involved in assembling just one product. The experiment entailed charting activities, identifying generators of waste, redesigning the work to eliminate generators of waste, and designing measures to motivate and confirm their progress at eliminating waste.[4] Today it is inappropriate to call this project an "experiment," because the redesigned work practices and new performance measures are now the modus operandi for this product line and for several other lines in the plant (and in other GE plants as well). I visited the plant and observed this product line in late 1988, about 20 months after the start of the initial experiment with activity management.

When the activity management experiment began, the product was assembled in lots of sixteen at a time. Workers moved hundreds of different components from a central storeroom and from twenty-five different subassemblies, variously located in the plant, to sixteen separate "pads," where assemblers performed all steps required to complete a finished unit, except testing and inspection. Three specialists roved among the assembly pads to perform tests and inspection at designated stages in the assembly process. Inspectors often had no work to do, but at other times they were a bottleneck. Work stopped frequently on the pads to wait for inspectors to arrive and perform their function.

Components, materials, and subassemblies were carried to each pad, often over great distances. These items were released to the pads according to MRP schedules that had generous cushions for safety stock and lead time uncertainties. Nevertheless, it was not uncommon for work to halt because of shortages of parts or subassemblies. Total lead time to assemble one unit of the product was about 60 hours. When assembled, the product contained almost 400 separate parts and weighed nearly one ton.

Before the activity management team entered the picture in late 1986, GE's top management had already been pressuring managers of this product line to cut costs and to meet delivery schedules more promptly. The managers had cut carrying costs by reducing raw and in-process inventories and, following the advice of outside manufacturing consultants, had started a campaign to cut direct labor costs by outsourcing many components. By mid-1987, they had outsourced (mostly in the local area) a wide variety of component-making activities, ranging from circuit board fabrication to traditional metal-bending.

Meanwhile, the activity management team began experimenting with new management methods to reduce inventories and to improve delivery schedules. Top management accepted in principle the team's new management methods. But while encouraging these methods to deliver lower costs and faster deliveries, senior executives still held plant managers accountable for traditional performance measures. That expectation produced continual tension between production people at the plant level and cost accountants at the business level. I will discuss that tension after describing the new management methods and new performance measures GE's activity management team introduced to this special product assembly line in 1987.

The activity management team's work entailed three basic steps.

1. Identify externally focused measures of how the product gives value to the customer and how the product line supports the goals of the business.

Figure 3-1 relates key success factors for the customer and the business to specific measures of operating performance for the product assembly line. The activity management team selected the new product line performance measures shown in Figure 3-1 with two important conditions in mind: first, as plant-level performance measures improve, key success factors have to improve; second, the product line performance measures should improve whenever the plant eliminates nonvalue activities (more below). The team insisted on these two conditions to avoid the problem with traditional performance measures such as labor efficiency variances; namely, steps taken to improve performance measures can impair competitiveness (by diminishing quality and so forth) and diminish long-term profitability. It is worth noting that it was quite difficult to compile data for the new product line performance measures. GE's cost accounting department had virtually none of this information in its mainframe accounting data base. A financial analyst in the plant had to compile the data on a personal computer.

2. Identify activities that cause work on the product line and assess how each activity adds value or creates waste.

Figure 3-2 shows the equivalent number of full-time people who worked on the pilot-project line (63.0), how their time was distributed among various activities (about 30 in all), and which of those activities were judged to add value or not. Listing activities enables one to search for types of work that consume resources but add no value to customers. To be efficient, however, the GE activity management team did not search for waste in all activities at once. After determining the percentage of time any person in the plant spent on each activity for the pilot-project product line, the team identified the five most time-consuming nonvalue activities. In a Pareto sense, these activities were considered the largest sources of waste.

3. Identify and eliminate generators of the work that causes nonvalue activities.

The activity management team set out to eliminate waste by systematically eliminating the generators of the five most time-consuming nonvalue activities. Figure 3-3 contains a partial list of generators (drivers) of waste the activity management team associated with the five major nonvalue activities. They distinguished between generators that were immediately controllable in the product assembly area (internal drivers) and generators that could be eliminated only through joint action with units in other parts of the plant or company (external and semigiven drivers).

Defective parts from vendors and poor layout of the process were two frequently mentioned drivers of waste that seemed to contribute to each of the five major nonvalue activities: namely, accumulating materials, expediting, moving, testing, and reworking. The prevalence of those two drivers appears even in Figure 3-3's truncated list in terms such as stock layout, assembly sequence, supplier quality, layout, and quality problems. Focusing their efforts on those two generators of waste, the activity management team began efforts to reorganize the product assembly process and permit workers to contact vendors directly on quality problems.

Figure 3-1 Hierarchy of Measurements at GE

	Customer			Business

Key Success Factors	Quality	Dependability	Price	R O I

Internal Indicators	Defects	Schedule Realization	Cost	Inventory

New Product Line Performance Measures

Payroll $ / Units shipped per week

Material $ / Units shipped per week

Inventory in plant / Material $ in units shipped

shipments on time

Defects at final test / Units shipped per week

Field Repairs / Units in the field

Old Product Line Performance Measures

Percentage of total direct labor $ applied to inventory

Percentage of total overhead $ applied to inventory

Inventory turnover

Scrap and rework

It chose to lay out the assembly process as a classic JIT flow of linked processes. In the layout of the old plant, parts, people, and equipment moved as needed among the sixteen stationary pads at which products were assembled. In the new layout, equipment or people are more or less fixed in position and the product moves one at a time along a line where parts are called out of stock only as needed. To permit the product (a one-ton piece of machinery) to "flow" required an ingenious breakthrough—the design of an inflatable rubber pallet on which the product is easily moved from one

Figure 3-2   Work Force Activity Distribution

Activity	Equivalent People	Value-Added	Gray	Waste
Assemble	22.0	22.0		
Accumulate Materials	8.0			8.0
Expedite Materials	4.0			4.0
•				
•				
•				
Work Assignment	2.0		2.0	
Wait for Materials	1.0			1.0
•				
•				
•				
Implement ECNs	.5		.5	
Employee Communication	.5		.5	
MRB	.5			.5
Total	63.0	22.0	9.0	32.0
		35%	14%	51%

work station to the next. Developing the pallet took an outlay of $35,000, virtually the only investment needed to implement the change to a flow line. The change was completed during August 1987.

The results of redesigning the assembly process were immediate and dramatic. As efforts to eliminate generators of nonvalue activity progressed, the new performance measures listed on Figure 3-1 improved. Measured from the start of 1987 to September of that year, the major improvements were

- product lead time cut by 60%
- specialized inspection labor eliminated, except at final test
- defects in final test reduced by 50%
- total payroll cost per unit reduced 21%
- work-in-process inventory reduced 50%
- space utilized reduced 50%
- stockroom transactions reduced 57%
- number of orders delivered on time improved five percentage points
- number of units completed and shipped per week rose from six to ten
- improved opportunities for learning

Figure 3-3 Five Greatest Waste Activities

Activity	Accumulated Materials (floor)	Expedite Materials	Move Materials	Rework	Test/Verify	Total
Equivalent People	8.0	4.0	4.0	4.0	4.0	24.0
Internal Drivers	• Stock Location (Layout) • Stocking Procedures • Assembly Sequence	• Line Scrap • Make Work • Stock Balance Errors • Ordering Errors • MRP Lead Times	• Layout • Handling Equipment	• Ignoring Kanbans • Assembly Errors • Large Batches • Handling Damage • Methods/Procedures	• Interpretation of Design • Training • Quality Problems	
External Drivers		• ECNs • Schedule Changes • Supplier Delivery • Supplier Quality		• ECNs • Supplier Quality		
Semigiven	• Volume of Part Numbers		• Labor Classifications	• Quality of Design	• Design Regulations	

Of the new performance measures listed in Figure 3-1, plant management most closely watches weekly payroll dollars per unit shipped. Payroll, the largest nonmaterial cost charged to the product line, comprises direct labor and virtually all other personnel whose work impinges in any way on assembling the product, including people in stores, production control, materials control, and engineering. GE's traditional labor productivity measure (percentage of direct labor absorbed into inventory), still the performance measure most watched by top management, does not reflect the productivity of any nondirect labor nor any so-called "overhead" labor.

Plant personnel, including the local financial analysts, feel that payroll dollars per unit shipped gives them a better handle on the total resource implications of eliminating nonvalue activity than does the traditional direct labor productivity measure. And their dedication to performing well by the new measures causes them to shun overproducing (with the familiar end-of-period "hockey stick" production spurts) in order to make the old-style productivity measure look good. However, business-level cost accountants and top management still insist on measuring performance with the traditional direct labor productivity measure (percentage of direct labor cost absorbed into inventory).

Figure 3-4a and 3-4b show these new and old measures diverging at several points in fiscal 1987. The trends roughly represent three periods. The first period, running to about midyear, shows both measures improving. This was the early phase of the activity management experiment, before the product line was converted to continuous flow. Nevertheless, significant payroll reductions occurred in this period, largely because assemblers themselves took on much of the inspection work. That change not only eliminated indirect jobs, causing the new measure in Figure 3-4a to improve, it may have caused assemblers to report more direct hours, causing the old measure in Figure 3-4b also to improve.

The second period, running from about midyear to about week 35, saw two contrary events occur. One event, short-lived, was marked by disruptions caused by the arrival for the first time of newly outsourced component supplies. Accompanying this was a sharp increase in vendor quality problems as well as learning curve problems as workers who were displaced by outsourcing "bumped" regular workers on the production line. All this caused some severe shipment delays, dramatically impairing the new measure in Figure 3-4a and probably causing the old measure in Figure 3-4b to deteriorate at the same time (as lost time not charged to direct hours rose). The second

Figure 3-4a   Payroll/Shipments
(1987)

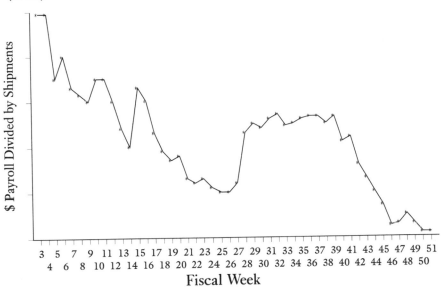

Figure 3-4b   Direct Labor Productivity
Year to Date
(1987)

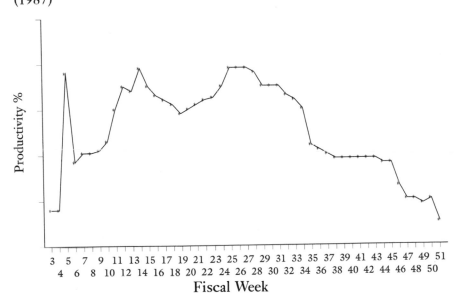

event in the second period was the conversion of production assembly to continuous flow, which was completed by about week 35.

The third period begins after week 35, when full JIT production and rapid elimination of both excess inventory and nonvalue activity caused the new measure to improve steadily and sharply while the old measure deteriorated to almost the same degree. I am told that the same divergence in these two measures continued more or less through 1988. At first, management attributed deterioration in the old measure to increased time spent in training (i.e., time not absorbed into inventory) on the new JIT line. Lately, however, they attribute the problem more to the difficulties workers have in tracking their hours, owing to the large number of different direct labor operations they perform under JIT.

GE's cost accounting system has over 300 distinct operation codes to which workers can charge their time. Under the old production regime, the average direct worker was usually assigned to no more than two or three operations per day—not an impediment to keeping track of chargeable direct hours. Now, a worker may spend time on ten or twenty different operations per day. The time spent tracking time is now an impediment to careful charging of direct hours. Hence, the portion of time workers charge en bloc to unassigned indirect codes grew steadily after the conversion to JIT.

To address top management's growing criticism of his "poor" productivity record, the manager of the JIT product line took control of weekly labor reporting late in 1988. Instead of having workers fill out their labor reports in the customary manner, he had a group leader from the product line take the cost accounting department's 300 or so operations control cards every Friday afternoon and "backflush" labor hours at standard for the number of units shipped in the week. That caused his productivity by the old measure to improve dramatically. The business-level cost accountants were quick to notice the productivity improvement, but when they learned about the change in reporting procedure they were irate.

On the day I visited GE's plant late in 1988, the plant's production and finance managers were stewing over a reprimand they had just received from the business-level cost accounting office. I was not able to discuss the matter at that time with the business-level accountants. Their offices are in another city, and, as plant personnel told me, they almost never visit the manufacturing sites. However, as I listened to the production manager of the JIT line, I was reminded of Alex Rogo, the hero in the best-selling book *The Goal*, who found himself in a similar predicament.[5] I left hoping that the real-life production managers I spoke to in GE would soon resolve the problems with their business-level accountants as happily as Alex Rogo had resolved his problems.

ALLEN-BRADLEY

Allen-Bradley is a large manufacturer and international supplier of controls used both for industrial automation systems and for industrial and commercial products. The company employs nearly 12,000 people worldwide; headquarters and about 40% of its manufacturing capacity are located in Milwaukee. Allen-Bradley was privately held until 1985, when Rockwell International purchased it for $1.6 billion in cash. Allen-Bradley's annual sales, currently around $1.3 billion, generate about 10% of Rockwell International's sales.

Like so many American manufacturers that had thrived for decades selling standardized products in the North American market, Allen-Bradley felt the pinch of high-quality, low-priced imports in the late 1970s. Its competition came largely from components used in foreign-made industrial machinery. As foreign competitors drove out American industrial machine makers, they drove out Allen-Bradley's principal customers. To survive, Allen-Bradley realized its products had to achieve global standards, not just traditional North American standards.

Allen-Bradley was among the first American manufacturers to recognize the strategic role of manufacturing in achieving global competitiveness. Visits to competitors' plants in France, West Germany, and Japan in 1983 caused Allen-Bradley's executives to consider new production methods aimed at drastically reducing product cycle times, lot sizes, defects, and costs. In the past five years, they have applied just-in-time (JIT) methods to existing production processes and have established automated, computer-integrated (CIM) processes in a new factory of the future. To achieve global standards of quality, dependability, flexibility, and cost, Allen-Bradley manages manufacturing activities quite differently today than it did before the mid-1980s.

Allen-Bradley introduced JIT practices among its existing production lines by adopting statistical process control, regrouping production activities into product line cells, promoting setup-time reduction, adopting preventive maintenance programs, working to reduce defects in vendors' shipments, and more. Starting from ground zero in 1983, the Milwaukee plant in 1989 will produce about 60% of its volume and 80% of its revenue on JIT lines.

Besides simplifying its existing production lines, Allen-Bradley's efforts to achieve global standards have also entailed building a new CIM plant to make world-class controls. Operating since 1985, the CIM plant currently makes to order over 800 varieties of about 12 basic types of controls. It makes those products in minutes and at mass production cost in lots of one, with zero defects, using no direct labor and minimal inventories of parts and raw materials. The company promises customers it will ship from this plant within 24 hours from the time an order is received.[6]

These new JIT and CIM methods have prompted Allen-Bradley's managers to adopt several new measurements of quality, dependability, and flexibility:

- In continuous flow production systems, managers view scrap and rework as disruptions to be eliminated, not as costs to be held to "acceptable" levels. To improve quality, therefore, Allen-Bradley has supplemented traditional standards for scrap and rework with data on test yields in final assembly. The yield is almost always 100% in the CIM plant, but on JIT lines the goal is to improve parts-per-million reject rates by a set annual percentage.
- To advance its quality control measures a step further than final test yield, which measures internal conformance, Allen-Bradley recently began compiling a "customer satisfaction index," an external, field-based measure of customer satisfaction.
- To promote greater dependability at meeting promised delivery schedules, production managers get a daily report showing the number and dollar value of past-due items per department (almost always zero for the CIM plant).
- To track determinants of flexibility in focused product cells, managers now compile data on setup times, product lead times, and number of skills mastered by each employee.

To monitor cost itself, Allen-Bradley still compiles information from the traditional cost accounts and allocates indirect costs over direct labor dollars (except in the CIM plant, where all expenses are considered period costs). Unlike many American manufacturing firms, however, the company has, for many years, used about 250 burden-center rates, not one plantwide burden rate, to allocate indirect costs to products. Each burden center handles one or more homogeneous tasks (or machines) identified with the routing for a particular product or component.

Some 20 department managers (other than the manager of the CIM plant, which has no direct labor) compile burden-center rates once a year, using data from the controller's office. That data contain two items: the past six months' indirect costs for the department (both "traceable" and allocated) as recorded in approximately 110 ledger accounts (divided into two categories—variable and fixed) and the past six months' direct labor dollars incurred in each of the department's burden centers.

Each department manager partitions indirect costs among burden centers according to his or her estimate of how the department's activities will generate cost in the next six months. Department managers partition indirect costs among burden centers using their own systems, in many cases a PC spreadsheet on which they periodically update historic data on burden-center overhead costs. The accounting system itself codes labor hours and dollars to the burden-center level but does not code overhead cost data below the departmental level.

The resulting standard burden rates provide input for two purposes. One is to compile each department's monthly "burden analysis," a traditional direct labor variance "efficiency" report prepared monthly by the controller's office (see Figure 3-5). The report uses only departmentwide average burden rates, not the detailed burden-center rates. Those rates range from about 500–1,200% in fabrication departments and are around 300% in assembly departments. Each department's monthly burden analysis culminates in a line showing the "efficiency percentage," a ratio of burden "earned" at standard to actual indirect costs for the month.

The other purpose served by these burden rates is to estimate long-run costs saved (or increased) by changing either product routings or production processes (e.g., how much is saved by reducing setup time on a particular machine). This is the primary use Allen-Bradley makes of the detailed burden-center rates. The company also uses these same burden-center rates, but for variable costs only, to compile information for make-buy decisions.

Allen-Bradley does not always rely on cost information to control performance in the new manufacturing settings. It also relies on intuition and visibility to control many critical success factors. In the CIM plant, for instance, flexibility is a key determinant of long-term profitability. No quantitative measure yet covers this dimension of competitiveness. But the vice president of operations, Larry Yost,

Figure 3-5

10/14/88

Allen-Bradley Burden Analysis
09/30/88

	Current Month			Year to Date		
Actual Burden Expense Summary	$ Actual	$ Plan	$ Variance	% Variance	$ Actual	$ Plan	$ Variance	% Variance
Salaried Compensation								
Production Indirect Labor								
Capital Labor—Net								
Premium Labor								
Employee Benefits								
Supplies								
Rework								
Recoveries								
Shipping Expense								
Tooling Expense								
Maintenance Expense								
Shop Experimental								
Utilities								
Rent—Occupancy								

Miscellaneous				
Transferred Burden and Allocation				
Total Budget Adjustments				
Spending % of Standard Direct Labor				
Burden Absorption Summary				
Standard Cost of Direct Labor Production				
Multiplied by Average Burden Rate				
Standard Cost of Burden Production				
Actual Burden Expense (Including/Expected Effect on Profits)				
Efficiency Percentage	97	92	95	92

views profitability in the CIM plant as largely a function of the speed with which manufacturing can respond to new marketing opportunities. Hence, he focuses on training people to cooperate across organizational functions, so they will turn new product ideas into new products as rapidly and as efficiently as possible. He sees cross-functional, customer-oriented organization, not quantitative measures, as a key driver of flexibility in the CIM environment.

Yost also expresses reservations about the value of quantitative measures to control performance in the JIT lines. While JIT lines measure a few critical factors such as setup times and cycle times, Yost believes it is more important to train people to understand the broad implications of reducing setup times, cutting lot sizes, and linking processes than it is to spend time measuring the results of these efforts. Given the way activities are linked in focused cells, he says results are readily visible in the form of reduced work-in-process, less space utilized, less distance travelled, and so on.

No evaluation of Allen-Bradley's performance measurement system would be complete without considering how astutely people in the organization comprehend drivers of performance that cost data and other quantitative measures do not reflect. Their comprehension of what determines global competitiveness extends far beyond the picture drawn by cost numbers and other financial measures. Larry Yost has probably shaped the company's understanding of this issue as much as anyone.

Yost, who began his career as a machinist apprentice, led Allen-Bradley's team to Japan in 1983. He was, of course, impressed by the usual things that impress Western visitors to Japanese companies—signs of team spirit, impeccable housekeeping, top-management regard for employees, and all the rest. Perhaps because manufacturing is his area, he was especially impressed by how rapidly the Japanese set up machines. In one case, he saw people change over in four minutes a molding die similar to one it took his people in Milwaukee two hours to change.

But Yost was not impressed merely by the speed of Japanese machine setups. He noticed fewer people in Japanese plants doing work that American plant managers associate with overhead cost, work such as moving, storing, and inspecting. He perceived that faster setups, by allowing processing to flow more continuously, eliminates work (the storing, waiting, and moving) that seem necessary when setups take a long time. His visit to Japan helped him see that the Japanese cut cost (and improve other sources of competitiveness as well) by redesigning the way they work to eliminate the need for work caused by delays attendant upon lengthy setups.

Yost has spent much of the past five years implementing that insight in Allen-Bradley's manufacturing operations. His effort has entailed, in part, educating people to understand how setup time reduction affects overhead activities. Specific examples of this training include videotaping setups and conducting seminars on continuous flow processes. He also spearheaded the development of systems to track setup time, something done infrequently in Allen-Bradley's shops before the 1980s. As I mentioned before, however, Yost prefers teaching people what they must do to be competitive, rather than tracking results. He believes that if people know the right thing to do, the desired results should follow as a matter of course.

Given these views, I was surprised, therefore, to hear Yost explain the importance he places on managing cost. Many consultants and practitioners today will argue that you can not manage costs, the dollar results of past resource consumption; they believe that you can manage only the activities that drive costs. Yost clearly understands that cost numbers do not identify cost drivers. His views on how setup time reduction affects overhead costs make that apparent. But he also believes cost is so important to competitive advantage that it is imperative for production people to understand "what things cost" and to "keep costs in control." He staunchly defends the company's use of burden-rate information and burden variances. Indeed, he requires his production people to complete a sixteen-week course on cost accounting, taught by faculty from a local university, so they can communicate with accountants and understand accountants' cost reports.

Yost's explanations of how he uses information from the monthly burden reports indicate that while he respects what cost accountants do, his use of cost information does not impair his vision of what Allen-Bradley must do to achieve global competitiveness. He uses the burden-center rates, for instance, to estimate where and by how much costs will fall if defects in a certain incoming part are reduced by x%. He emphasizes the cost-driver—incoming defects—and assumes that the only way to reduce cost is to eliminate the cost driver. Eventually he expects numbers in the monthly cost budget to reflect the results of reducing incoming defects. But he views numbers in the monthly overhead cost analysis quite differently than would someone trained in cost accounting. To Yost, it seems fair to say, those numbers confirm the results of efforts to manage drivers of competitiveness.

He does not see costs as numbers to be managed in their own right. Costs certainly must be kept in control. But he believes control is achieved by controlling cost drivers, not by curtailing spending or by controlling cost numbers.

Nevertheless, one wonders if the emphasis he places on monthly burden absorption and "efficiency percentages" impairs competitiveness. Department managers can manipulate such numbers by overproducing or by arbitrarily shifting workers between direct and indirect labor tasks. Either attempt to improve "efficiency" causes waste and diminished value, a result not shown by traditional accounting information. Allen-Bradley's MRP system tends to check the tendency of department managers to "game" the standard cost variance numbers by overproducing. Managers can not build components or products without authorization from a dispatch list or a manufacturing order. Attempts to build ahead of schedule will quickly generate shortages as the MRP system fails to release parts.

Moreover, efforts to increase direct labor efficiency by overproducing would show up rather promptly in the inventory information Allen-Bradley began to track a few years ago and in daily production reports. It compiles detailed data on number of days' inventory by product and by plant. For the company as a whole, this statistic at the end of 1988 was less than one-third what it was in late 1984. The downward trend has been steady over that period and is expected to continue indefinitely. It does not seem that the company's use of direct labor efficiency variances has prevented it from squeezing out a great deal of inventory.

There remains, of course, the question of whether the firm might reduce inventories even more if production managers did not have to consider the impact of burden absorption on net income. In the hands of managers trained in finance rather than in production, efforts to manage burden absorption can often impede efforts to find and eliminate waste. However, the instincts with which Larry Yost and his production managers approach their jobs seem to minimize the potential ill effects from overproducing to satisfy burden-absorption performance measurements.

CONCLUSION

In 1982 and 1983, Robert S. Kaplan visited several companies to discover if "firms making major changes in their manufacturing operations were developing and using [new] measures of quality, inventory reductions, manufacturing flexibility, employee morale and abilities, productivity, and new product effectiveness." He found that companies at the leading edge of new JIT and CIM developments still were using cost accounting systems developed seventy-five years ago to track costs/efficiencies of direct labor and inventory—two variables that were vanishing from the factory.[7] What I observed in GE and in Allen-Bradley indicates that "accounting lag" still exists in 1989.

American companies have changed their manufacturing practices enormously since 1982. GE and Allen-Bradley have perhaps advanced farther than most along the path to JIT and CIM, but they are not unique in placing high priority on these new manufacturing strategies. American companies today understand much better the contribution manufacturing makes to competitiveness than they did at the start of the 1980s.

But the evidence from GE and Allen-Bradley suggests today's manufacturers place as much importance as ever on accounting for direct labor and inventory. Moreover, a high percentage of managerial time, perhaps as much or more as in the early 1980s, is spent tracking and analyzing costs of resource-consuming activities that ought to disappear as companies eliminate waste and achieve continuous flow. I refer not just to activities related to direct labor and inventory, but to those related to moving, inspecting, scheduling, and expediting as well. American businesses still manage costs much more than they manage the resource-consuming activities that give rise to costs, and they still place a profound emphasis on information compiled primarily for external financial reporting.

That does not mean companies are not developing and using measures of quality, inventory reductions, manufacturing flexibility, employee morale and abilities, productivity, and new product effectiveness. Indeed, GE and Allen-Bradley have shown tremendous ingenuity in developing and using such measures. They now pay serious attention to nonaccounting measures of competitiveness that were seldom, if ever, compiled four or five years ago. But these measures seem to take a back seat to the direct labor, inventory, and standard cost budget measures that have dominated performance measurement in American business since the early 1900s.

Some writers use the metaphor "migrating along a path" to describe the changes companies should make as they move their manufacturing practices to JIT and CIM.[8] This metaphor aptly describes how global competitors, companies such as GE and Allen-Bradley, change their manufacturing strategies. They do not transform the entire company overnight. They start by simplifying and removing waste in selected parts of the firm, then they move on to automation, and finally they consider full-blown CIM. After change succeeds at one level, in one part of the company, they "migrate" to the next level, and to other parts of the company.

While "migration" seems a good term to describe changes in manufacturing systems, it does not describe well the changes we observe in performance measurement systems. As manufacturing changes, the new procedures replace the old. The old procedures and equipment disappear. With performance measurements, however, we observe the old persisting alongside, and in many cases even dominating, the new. Perhaps it is better to describe the change we observe in performance measurements as "ships passing silently in the night," not as "migration along a path." Financial performance measurement stays on its course, unaffected by—often oblivious to—the appearance of new nonaccounting performance measures. However, "passing silently in the night" does not seem to describe the tension between accountants and production people in GE. Nor does it describe the mutual harmony between those groups in Allen-Bradley. More research is needed to explain the tenacity with which businesses cling to accounting performance information. More empirical research into the consequences of managing with accounting information is also in order. But there already is much evidence that businesses impair their competitiveness and profitability by managing with the information found in standard cost variances, flexible budgets, product cost, return on investment, and other financial measures. Less well understood is why "world-class" manufacturing companies persist in using accounting-based financial performance measures.

My observations in several companies, including GE and Allen-Bradley, suggest that a certain mind-set concerning the capital markets is primarily responsible for the tenacious hold accounting-based performance measurement has on American managers. When one asks managers why they spend time managing accounting numbers, they usually answer, "Capital markets (or investors) ultimately judge us by the bottom line."

This answer seems to explain why the principal demand for "managing by the numbers" comes from top management. Most top managers see themselves as primarily driven by the capital markets' alleged insistence on short-term profit performance. This attitude characterizes almost all top managers, whether their backgrounds have been in finance, engineering, marketing, or production. Feeling driven by the bottom line, they view the controller's office as the company's logical information headquarters. The controller fulfills this expectation by "rolling" top-level financial targets down into the organization through flexible budgets, product costs, and other accounting controls. "Managing by the numbers" has been the American way of doing business at least since the 1950s.

I believe this habit will change as top managers develop a genuine commitment to doing what it takes to be competitive in today's global economy—giving primacy to the customer, eliminating waste, striving for continuous flow, and adopting the mind-set of continuous improvement. Managers who understand the imperatives of competitiveness realize that accounting information, especially information about costs, provides no clues to sources of value or drivers of waste. Other information must guide today's managers along the road to competitiveness.

Nevertheless, the global competitor does not simply take for granted that doing the right things will generate profits or prevent bankruptcy in the long run. Competitive businesses must still budget and still track accounting-based results. However, they will do these things to plan and to monitor, not to control, results. Denominating plans in accounting-based terms does not mean one must then delegate targets, in the same accounting terms, to subordinate managers and workers.

Thus, I do not advocate throwing out the general ledger. Companies years from now will report to third parties—the IRS if no one else—according to double-entry canons of GAAP. Accounting profit will be a fact of management life for a long time. But it is to be hoped that managers someday will regard financial statements as something they glance at over their shoulders as they race forward on a track to competitiveness that is marked by nonaccounting signposts. At that time, all managers will understand what so few seem to understand today, namely, that long-term profitability results from being competitive, not from managing accounting numbers.

Perhaps a glimpse of what that future may be like is available in information certain Japanese companies use to manage performance. Kenneth J. McGuire, a consultant who frequently visits companies in Japan, recently showed me an example of the summary management information used to measure and control performance in a well-known Japanese manufacturing firm—call it Company J. The information is reported in twelve graphs—"charts on the wall." Company

J apparently keeps a series of these charts for each major product or product line.

The "top" chart concerns total cost of product, which, like most American companies, Company J sees as a key determinant of profitability. But unlike American reports on product cost, Company J's graph reports only *percentage change* in cost from month to month. And the title of this graph is "Total Costs Down." On the graph I saw, for one year, cost fell each month. Interestingly, however, the line on this graph, and on all the other graphs, went up. To reinforce everyone's psychic commitment to continuous improvement, the "default direction" of lines on Company J's graphs is northeast.

According to McGuire, Company J's managers use information in the other graphs (not the "Total Costs Down" graph) to control operating activities. The other graphs depict such variables as average setup time per job by department, process times per minute, number of defect claims from customers (i.e., next users), downtime percentages, number of line stops per day (one worker oversees on average about 50 unattended devices in Company J's plant), and amount of inventory. Company J's managers seem to devote their primary attention to these variables that ultimately affect total product cost, not to the total cost statistic itself.

Nor does Company J appear to use any other accounting cost information to control operations, even though company accountants keep the usual double-entry books for external reporting purposes. In short, Company J's management information seems to focus on the control of activities that determine competitiveness, not on the financial results of being competitive. It does not ignore the financial results (indeed, Company J has an enviable record of long-run profitability). It reports cost information only so that managers can look over their shoulders to be sure costs are where they are supposed to be as everyone in the company races to do what it takes to be competitive.

Top managers in American companies must adopt the mind-set we observe in Company J. Until they do, the cost to them of clinging to traditional accounting performance measures grows larger all the time. Here are some examples of that cost.

- **The cost of systems to track direct labor and inventory cost.** Personnel devote enormous time to accounting for items that comprise smaller and smaller percentages of total company costs. It is no longer uncommon to hear about companies that spend more on accounting for direct labor than they spend on direct labor itself. And in companies that have slashed inventories by implementing JIT practices, one often hears that the accounting department still spends the same amount of time valuing inventory at the close of each fiscal year. That time is obviously driven by the excruciating detail of burden allocations designed to satisfy canons of GAAP, not by the amount of inventory.

- **The cost of opportunities missed and resources wasted because of decisions based on accounting costs.** In general, resources tend to be wasted (in overproduction, rework, and overtime) when managers strive to minimize standard cost variances. Moreover, opportunities can be missed by basing business decisions on accounting cost information. In one company, for instance, production managers turned a product assembly line around by adopting JIT manufacturing practices just as top management independently embarked on a major campaign to cut costs by outsourcing component production. It appears top management did not consider how JIT practices might reduce component-making costs. No doubt the decision to outsource much component production has caused the company to miss many opportunities for learning and for redeploying workers made redundant by JIT or CIM projects elsewhere in the company. The decision to outsource also causes difficulties for workers on the JIT lines who now must cope with more outside vendor quality problems.

- **The cost of shunning continuous improvement strategies because they will cut inventory.** There are two sides to this problem—one involving income taxes and the other involving net income per se. On the tax side, top managers of many companies still resist JIT because reducing inventory will increase tax payments by eliminating LIFO layers. These executives seem not to understand the **magnitude** of the *continuing* annual savings from JIT efficiencies (reduced lead times, space-saving plant layout changes, improved quality, and less inventory). They appear to place more weight on *one time* tax expenditures caused by liquidating inventory layers. Turning to the net income side of this problem, countless top managers seem to resist the idea of inventory reduction because it can cause deferred absorbed burden to have a serious one-time effect on reported net income. The pervasiveness of this concern among top executives in American manufacturing firms shows up every year in news stories about companies that boost reported earnings by overproducing at year-end.

- **The cost of failing to lower lot sizes for fear unit costs will rise.** Here the "scale economies" mind-set is at work. Traditional cost information fails to apprise managers of the competitive advantages that accrue from faster changeover and smaller lot sizes. Larry Yost and his production managers at Allen-Bradley are well aware of this. But they are exceptions. Not many American managers, seeing two plants with identical total setup costs or identical purchasing costs, would understand why performance is superior in the plant with faster setups or in the plant with more frequent deliveries from vendors. Managers who do not understand this will undoubtedly persist in trying to be profitable by making decisions that "minimize cost." They will be overtaken by more competitive companies whose managers control activities for value and continuous flow.

One hopes that as knowledge increases about the dysfunctional behavior induced by traditional accounting measurements, top managers of American companies will gradually reject the notion that they should control competitive operations with accounting measures of performance. This essential change in managers' thinking is not going to occur easily, because it must emanate from acceptance of a new paradigm. The old paradigm says profitability comes from optimizing within constraints (i.e., minimize costs and maximize profits) and from mass-producing to achieve economies of scale. The new paradigm says profitability comes from continuous improvement at eliminating waste, delivering quality, achieving dependability, and being flexible. Smart, profit-seeking business people are beginning to understand and follow the practices of companies that succeed in the global economy by continuously improving at achieving flexibility and quality. The only thing stopping a rush to abandon the old paradigm, in my opinion, is the faith some American managers (and many American investment analysts) seem to have in the efficacy of controlling business operations with accounting performance measures.

NOTES

1. H. Thomas Johnson and Robert S. Kaplan, *Relevance Lost: The Rise and Fall of Management Accounting* (Boston: Harvard Business School Press, 1987).

2. A member of the GE consulting team, Larry Utzig, contributed the key ideas on activity management (*not* to be confused with activity accounting) to the

CAM-I cost management system (CMS) conceptual design. A brief summary of Ut-zig's (and GE's) views on activity management is found in Callie Berliner and James A. Brimson, eds., *Cost Management for Today's Advanced Manufacturing: The CAM-I Conceptual Design* (Boston: Harvard Business School Press, 1988), 3–6 and 159–174.

3. These implications are explored in H. Thomas Johnson, "Activity-Based Information: A Blueprint for World-Class Management Accounting," *Management Accounting* (June 1988): 23–30; "Activity-Based Information: Accounting for Competitive Excellence," *Target* (Spring 1989): 4–9; and "Managing Costs: An Outmoded Philosophy," *Manufacturing Engineering* (May 1989): 42–46.

4. Thomas O'Brien, director of GE's manufacturing consulting unit, which ran this project, has described the experiment in "Measurements in the New Era of Manufacturing," *Cost Accounting for the '90s: Responding to Technological Change* (Montvale, NJ: National Association of Accountants, 1988): 63–80.

5. Eliyahu M. Goldratt and Jeff Cox, *The Goal: A Process of Ongoing Improvement* (Croton-on-Hudson, NY: North River Press, Inc., 1984).

6. The evolution and operation of Allen-Bradley's CIM plant are discussed in Sabra Goldstein and Janice Klein, "Allen-Bradley (A)," 9-687-073, and "Allen-Bradley (B)," 9-687-074. Boston: Harvard Business School Case Services, 1987.

7. Robert S. Kaplan, "Accounting Lag: The Obsolescence of Cost Accounting Systems," in *The Uneasy Alliance: Managing the Productivity-Technology Dilemma*, eds., Kim B. Clark, Robert H. Hayes, and Christopher Lorenz (Boston: Harvard Business School Press, 1985): 220.

8. C. J. McNair, William Mosconi, and Thomas Norris, *Meeting the Technology Challenge: Cost Accounting in a JIT Environment* (Montvale, NJ: National Association of Accountants, 1988): 30.

CHAPTER 4

The Choice of Productivity Measures in Organizations

Howard M. Armitage and Anthony A. Atkinson

SUMMARY

THIS paper summarizes how seven Canadian firms chose the productivity measures in their respective organizations.

The project was designed

- to understand how successful organizations defined productivity,
- to understand why, and how, these organizations developed their productivity measurement systems, and
- to develop tentative hypotheses to explain the observations.

The project consisted of four steps:

1. A review of the literature in accounting, economics, industrial engineering, psychology, and management to determine the nature of productivity systems that have been proposed for use in practice.

2. A mail survey of the *Financial Post 300*—the 300 largest (ranked by sales) firms operating in Canada—to determine the nature, and extent, of productivity systems in that population of firms.

3. A field study of seven firms located in Canada to determine the source, nature, focus, and scope of their respective productivity systems.

4. A study and synthesis of the information developed in the first three steps to develop hypotheses to explain the observations.

Our major conclusions are

1. The use of productivity measurement systems is widespread, and the number of systems in place appears to be growing.

2. Productivity is a term that is diversely interpreted, but, in practice, generally refers to the relationship between outputs and inputs. Based on our observations, we believe that output, in the most useful definition, focuses on the strategic dimensions of the goods or services produced as defined by each organization's key success factors. For example, McDonald's Corporation has identified quality, service, cleanliness, and value as the major dimensions of performance. The store manager's rating is based on a scoring system that weights each factor. Therefore, output is generally defined as a vector of attributes and not simply as units of production.

   On the input side, the observed organizations concentrated on key input resources that were crucial to achieving output objectives. Total factor productivity measures, often prescribed by researchers, were rejected by the practitioners as unnecessary.

3. Most of the productivity measures that we observed were based on nonfinancial data, such as production rates, yield rates, and defect rates rather than on financial measures such as profits or costs.

4. Based on our observations, we believe that effective organizations use productivity measures as strategic operational aids that keep track of what is required for the organization to achieve its long-run goals.

The balance of this chapter is organized as follows: a summary of the major perspectives on productivity found in the literature review; a summary of the results of the mail questionnaire; a summary of the empirical results of the field work involving seven firms; a discussion of the tentative hypotheses developed in the study to be tested in future field studies; a discussion of the relationship between organization success factors and measurement systems in the firms in our study; a comparison of the results of our study with those in a previous study of productivity systems; and a comparison of the results of our study with the focus of conventional management and cost accounting education.

LITERATURE REVIEW

This study was prompted by the lack of discussion of productivity in the accounting research literature. To develop the widest possible perspective of the scope and issues considered in the literature, we undertook a search using a computer-based bibliographic system. The search yielded approximately 150 articles drawn from journals in five disciplines: accounting, economics, general management, industrial engineering, and psychology. Approximately 70 papers were reviewed. A representative selection of the articles reviewed appears in Appendix 1.

From the literature review, two district methodologies emerge: the *aggregate* approach to measuring productivity, which, for the most part, fails to acknowledge both practice and managerial perspectives (a significant exception being Hayes and Clark 1986) and the *component* approach to measuring productivity, which describes practice and draws implications for the design of productivity systems from these observations. These two perspectives on productivity measures are evident in the following remarks by Mammone (1980):

Component productivity measures are designed to measure the performance of a single activity or a relatively small organizational unit. They assist first-line managers in improving productivity. . . . Goals are established for the productive use of resources, and actual performance is compared to the predetermined objectives.

Aggregate productivity measures are designed to evaluate the performance of a large collective body (a plant, division, company, or an industry) over an extended time frame. Generally, an aggregate measure is an index that relates current period performance to performance of a base period adjusted to real unit terms to facilitate comparison. The index, expressed in real unit terms, should be free of the distortions in units costs from the impact of inflation.

In retrospect, we feel that these two approaches reflect very different perspectives and objectives for productivity measures.

The aggregate approach, following the economics tradition of economywide productivity measures, focuses on the design of total corporate productivity measures using aggregated financial data.

These measures are thought, by their supporters, to be useful in developing long-run, strategic implications for an economy, industry, or organization.[1] Practice, however, seems to use, almost exclusively, individual, or component, measures of productivity to judge short-run effectiveness, efficiency, or competitiveness.[2]

The following calculus for choosing between aggregate and component productivity measures is suggested by Teague and Eilon (1973):

Guidelines as to how to measure productivity may be gained from an analysis of why we should wish to measure it. The reasons are fourfold:
  i. for strategic purposes, in order to compare the global performance of the firm with that of its competitors or related firms,
 ii. for tactical purposes, to enable management to control the performance of the firm via the performance of individual sectors of the firm, either functional or by product,
iii. for planning purposes, to compare the relative benefits accruing from the use of different inputs or varying proportions of the same inputs, and
 iv. for internal management purposes, such as collective bargaining with trade unions.

In a related vein, many authors describe the uses of productivity systems that they have observed. Aggarwal (1980) provides the following synthesis that we found repeated, in various forms, both in other articles and in our field work:

Most organizations and their managers are aware that they need to measure productivity for (1) comparing their own performance with that of their competitors, (2) knowing the relative performance of their individual departments, (3) comparing relative benefits of various inputs, and (4) collective bargaining purposes while dealing with trade unions.

Almost without exception, however, the prescriptions in the articles favoring the aggregate approach to productivity measurement are not carried out in practice. When asked about these prescriptions, practitioners refer to them as misdirected, irrelevant, or too complex to be understood and effective in motivating performance. The following cogent statement of this perspective is provided by Meadows (1980):

Businessmen see productivity through a wider lens than is customarily used by economic analysts. On the factory floor, almost any sort of improvement may be counted as a productivity booster. It isn't one, however, unless it increases output by more than the increase in inputs—or reduces the amount of inputs needed to produce the same amount of output. When outputs and inputs are counted in dollar terms, this latter technique becomes manifest as a cost reduction program. In fact, it is by way of cost reduction programs that most corporations tackle productivity.

Our questionnaire and field work confirm the observation by Meadows that business people use a wide lens to view the productivity issue. In sharp contrast with the cost perspective mentioned by Meadows, however, our survey of practice and field work found a decided preference for the use of operating data, such as yields, defect rates, throughput time, and rate of production per unit of the constraining factor of production. This preference is reflected in the following comment by Hayes and Clark (1986):

In none of these companies did the usual profit-and-loss statements—or the usual operating reports—provide adequate, up-to-date information about factory performance. Certainly, managers routinely evaluated such performance, but the metrics they used made their task like that of watching a distant activity through a thick, fogged window. Indeed the measurement systems in place at many factories obscure and even alter the details of their performance.

This observation was repeated, independently, by an executive in one of the firms we visited. This executive observed that the key to achieving success is to focus on, and control, the factors that create success rather than to focus on profit or cost—the often imperfect and clumsy artifacts of success or failure in controlling the activities critical to the survival of the firm. The executive likened the indirect aspect, of attempting to control performance by using profit or cost, to driving a vehicle blindfolded and relying on a passenger for instructions to turn right or left.

Interestingly, Tuttle (1983) describes a discipline bias in approaching productivity that might explain the lack of interest among management accounting researchers with the productivity measures found in practice and the lack of interest among practitioners with most accounting research on productivity:

Economist   Productivity is the relationship between output and its associated inputs when the outputs and inputs are expressed in real (physical volume) terms.

Engineer   Productivity is viewed as efficiency, the ratio of useful work divided by the energy applied. This measure can be applied to inputs and output separately or jointly.

Accountant　　Typically, financial ratios serve as the tools for monitoring financial performance.

Manager　　Surveys report that 8 out of 10 respondents would include efficiency, effectiveness, and quality in their productivity definition. Seven out of 10 would also include disruption, sabotage, absenteeism, and turnover as well as output-related factors, even if these are difficult to measure.

Psychologist　Psychologists and other organizational researchers have typically given more attention to organizational effectiveness and, more recently, quality of work life than to productivity. Although these concepts are related to productivity, the nature of the relationship is often implicit and unclear.

As suggested earlier, most productivity articles emphasize an aggregate/normative approach, an approach that is virtually ignored in practice. Examples of the aggregative/normative approach of the productivity literature are

1. The classical approach from economics using indices based on the ratio of weighted current production to weighted base period production (see Silver 1982).

2. The Craig and Harris (1973) productivity model using the ratio of output to a weighted index of the various input factors (labor, capital, raw materials and purchased parts, and other goods and services).

3. The Gold (1980) productivity model, which decomposes the return-on-investment number into constituent components consisting of output value, average costs, capacity usage, the productive yield of fixed costs, and the proportion of fixed investment to total investment.

4. Other approaches to productivity that involve comparing the aggregate value of total output to a weighted index of inputs (see Taylor and Davis 1977 and Mundel 1976).

5. The value-added approach to defining the output component in the productivity equation (see Coates 1980).

These aggregate, multifactor indices are not widely used in practice. Babson (1981) provides the following commentary:

For most industrial plants, however, there is no one valid index that captures the true essence of productivity. Instead a profile of productivity can be developed—a profile being a series of separate and distinct indices of trends, each of which is significant and important to watch as an indication of what is happening.

Aggarwal (1980) makes a similar observation:

There can be no single universal measure of productivity because various parties . . . will have different goals and, in turn, must use alternative sets of productivity measures. The chosen measures should apply not only to direct materials and direct labor but also to facilities, management efforts, and marketing inputs. . . . [They] should also be applicable to all activities of the organization in question and must be interpretable by all.

The importance of having measures that can be interpreted by all helps to explain the widespread use of operations-based, rather than finance-based, productivity measures. In fact, the productivity systems that we observed in many (but not all) organizations reflect the following point of view expressed by Schroeder, Anderson, and Scudder (1986):

. . . workers should be involved in deciding how to measure their own jobs. It was thought that this would not only result in better measures but in greater acceptance of the measures used. . . . The implication of this idea is that white-collar workers should understand the need for measurement as well as specific measurement techniques.

Observations of practice led Schroeder, Anderson, and Scudder to develop the following prescriptions for practice that had been independently developed in several of the firms in our field study:

1. Measurements should be understandable by all organization members.
2. Measurements should be accepted by the individual involved (which ordinarily means that the measurement should be developed jointly by worker and supervisor).
3. Rewards and measurements should be compatible.
4. Measurements should offer the minimal opportunity for manipulation.
5. Measures should be results oriented.

Babson (1981) argues that productivity measures should be developed for each of the key resources used in the manufacturing process: materials (focus on spoilage, procurement, and turnover), people (standardize for purchased outside labor content in purchased materials and equipment improvements and then use monthly output divided by labor input), equipment and facilities (measure equipment usage, and return on assets employed, and follow up, using post-implementation audits, on capital investment decisions), and money. Teague and Eilon (1973), commenting on the scope of the productivity measure, remark that

. . . an attempt to measure overall productivity immediately meets the problem of heterogeneous, and possibly intangible, inputs. . . . One means of relieving the problem of non-homogeneous inputs is to concentrate attention on the productivity of the input which most seriously limits the activities of the firm.

A related development is the use of an index approach to measuring productivity that combines performance on various facets of a job into an overall index of performance (Rowe 1981).

The idea of using several productivity measures in order to focus on the organization's key success factors was an approach that we found repeatedly in our field work. For example, Meadows (1980) makes the following observation:

A consistently hot Whopper, and ice in the drinks, mean more sales per hour, which, in the fast food industry, is how you measure higher productivity.

This quote captures two important messages. First, output is multifaceted and includes both extrinsic features (such as style and quantity) and intrinsic features (such as quality and timeliness). This multifaceted nature of output must be captured by the productivity measure. Second, the organizations in our field study focus either on the limiting factor of production or on the key controllable cost factor. Given constraints on raw materials, the use of yields is predominant in the natural resource and food-processing industries. The use of output per person is common in the steel (controllable cost) and service industries (limiting factor of production). This conclusion is reflected in the following comment by Aggarwal (1980) based on his field study of 27 organizations:

The following general comments summarize all the different measures used in various industries:

a. In machine-dominated operations . . . the increased productivity may have been generated by additional fixed capital and not by labor. . . . The productivity should be measured in terms of productivity of capital only.

b. In labor-dominated operations . . . the increase in the productivity of labor does not decrease the fixed capital requirements. . . . The productivity of operations must be measured by the productivity of direct labor alone.

c. In operations dominated by materials . . . increases in the productivity of labor or capital reduce their own respective requirements and do not affect the productivity of materials. On the other hand, an increase in materials productivity always results in an increase in labor and capital productivity. Therefore, the productivity of materials-dominated operations must be measured by materials productivity alone.

Mammone (1980), summarizing the results of his field study of six firms, concludes that

. . . a leading metal producer, calculates a partial productivity measure—output per employee hour. . . . The company maintains that its very tight control over capital expenditures and energy costs (the other major costs in the company), in combination with the partial measurement technique, produces better control over productivity than if it were to attempt to measure total factor productivity.

. . . before starting on the program of productivity measurement, the organization must be able to determine which productivity factors are relevant as indicators of performance and organizational success. . . . Furthermore, top management and the responsible management accountant must assure themselves that, within the organization, all concerned levels of management are focusing on a comparatively limited number of productivity relationships, which, in total, reflect organization success.

Our field work, in every sense, confirms this latter observation, which we think is one of the most important, and most misunderstood, issues in productivity measurement. We will return to this important issue after summarizing the results of the mail questionnaire.

MAIL QUESTIONNAIRE

A one-page questionnaire was distributed to the *Financial Post 300* firms, which are the largest 300 firms, ranked by sales, operating in Canada. The questionnaire was addressed to the chief executive officer of the firm, and a cover letter describing the project, as well as a prepaid reply envelope, were included in the mailing. Bilingual questionnaires were sent to firms in the province of Quebec.

Figure 4-1 presents the response rates to the questionnaire. A summary of the questions and the responses appears in Appendix 2.

We recognized that many of the addressees were holding companies for which the questionnaire might not be relevant. However, no attempt was made to edit the mailing list. A follow-up mailing was sent out six weeks after the initial one, reminding the respondents to return the questionnaire if it had not been returned already.

The questions were open-ended. Since this was an exploratory study, we wanted to avoid constraining the responses. From the summary of the responses in Appendix 2, it is evident that respondents interpreted the questions differently. In many cases, the respondents gave answers that, although different in form, constituted the same response to a given question. As a result, there are obvious opportunities to aggregate similar responses into larger groups. These opportunities were avoided to preserve the original form of the results.

Summary Comments on the Survey Results

The survey results are, in many ways, consistent with what we found in later field studies. Almost without exception, the questionnaires and the field work suggest that practitioners partial factor (component) productivity measures are used. Moreover, it is not surprising that in setting criteria for these productivity measures people specify that they should be comprehensive in describing all facets of the job, specified by the incumbent of the position (and therefore comprehensible to the person whose job is being evaluated by the measure), and measurable. In our field work, we found that, in general, as we moved higher in an organization, financial measures tended to be substituted for productivity measures. We feel that there are two plausible explanations for this phenomenon. First, the financial measure is used to assess aggregate performance in a way that is consistent with the manner in which the organization communicates with outsiders. Second, the financial measure is used because people at the middle- and upper-management levels, who come from differing backgrounds, do not have the individual or joint understanding of the operating implications of the productivity measures and, because of this, must manage the organization by aggregate financial numbers.

On the other hand, total factor productivity (aggregate) measures are recommended for use as a summary measure to assess the strategic

Figure 4-1   Productivity Measures in Organizations

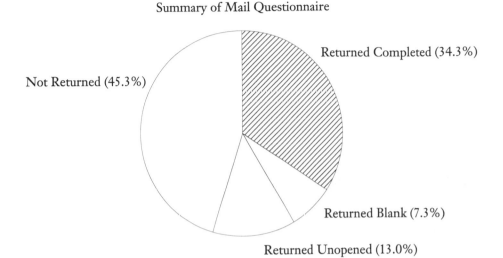

Summary of Mail Questionnaire

Returned Completed (34.3%)

Not Returned (45.3%)

Returned Blank (7.3%)

Returned Unopened (13.0%)

performance of the organization. These productivity measures are not recommended for operational control; they are used for management control—to summarize results and to determine whether the operational control systems are doing their job.

Therefore, we conclude that the total factor productivity measures recommended in the literature are often economic (or accounting) prescriptions intended to evaluate or summarize the performance of the entire organization. In practice, however, these aggregate measures do not seem useful. The measures actually used are inevitably partial (component) productivity measures based on operational, rather than financial, data.

These observations are tentative and preliminary. Despite the high rate of usable responses to the questionnaire (34%), the absolute rate of response is not high, and, therefore, our confidence in the results is low. A follow-up questionnaire, which anticipates the breadth of the responses, is required so that more precise responses can be elicited and firmer conclusions can be drawn. For our purposes, we merely observe the breadth of the responses and the general preoccupation with operating, rather than financial, numbers in extant productivity systems.

FIELD WORK

The field work for this project consisted of an on-site study of the productivity systems in seven firms. These firms were not chosen randomly; the profiles that follow are not representative of all firms. Rather, the firms chosen for this study either had won the Government of Canada–Department of Regional and Industrial Expansion's productivity award or were regarded, within their respective industries, as innovative firms.

The individual firms have quite different histories. Some have always been successful, but more than half had experienced serious adversity in the past. Therefore, we took the productivity systems that we found in the latter firms to be suggestive of the types of approaches and mechanisms that can be used to rescue a troubled firm.

Two of the seven firms requested that their identity be disguised. These two firms have been given the names Colt Steel and Modern Motors Company.

The firms chosen included three in the manufacturing sector, two in the natural resource/food sector, and two in the service sector. Appendix 3 describes the productivity system in each firm and a brief description of the company, the motivation for developing the system, the focus and scope of the productivity system, and the actual productivity measures used.

Table 4-1 summarizes the major empirical findings of the field work.

Guiding Principles Mentioned by the Field Study Firms

In our exploratory study, we can supply only tentative hypotheses to summarize the principles of developing effective productivity measures.

1. The objects of measurement must be comprehensive in terms of capturing the essence of the individual's job, what the individual controls, and how that job relates to the key result areas of the firm. In all our study firms, there are specific productivity measures developed either for each job or for each major process.

2. The objects of measurement must be comprehensible to the individual, reflecting how the individual thinks about the job. In

Table 4-1 Summary of the Major Empirical Findings in the Seven
Field Studies

The Firm	Major Focus of Measurement System	Reason for Major Focus of Measurement System	Compensation Tied to Productivity Performance
London Life Insurance Co.	output or activities per employee-hour	employee costs significant and, with fixed labor hours, output rate is correlated with service quality level	yes; but employee bonus based on aggregate corporate productivity improvement
Bell Canada	output or activities per employee-hour	employee costs significant and, with fixed labor hours, output rate correlated with service quality level	yes; rewards based on aggregate productivity improvement reflected in financial performance, and customer satisfaction index also used in performance review
Allen-Bradley Canada	contributed value per employee, throughput, and percentage on-time production	high investment in plant and criticality of on-time delivery	no; however, productivity results are published and groups vie for best performance
Colt Steel	output per employee-hour	employee work quality is the major strategic cost variable	no; however, there is an employee suggestion system that pays rewards for innovation
Modern Motors	quality, cost, responsiveness	the firm believes these are the key result areas in this industry	no; however, extra production is given to top-performing plants
J.M. Schneider Inc.	labor efficiency and materials yield	raw materials are the major cost of production, and efficiency reflects employee skill level	no; however, operations are monitored closely, and there is a corporate effort to improve yields and efficiency

Table 4-1   (*Continued*)

The Firm	Major Focus of Measurement System	Reason for Major Focus of Measurement System	Compensation Tied to Productivity Performance
Fishery Products International Ltd.	yield and pack-output	industry raw materials constrained by quotas, and pack-output reflects employee skill level	yes; however, bonus system was inherited by current management and is to be phased out

most firms in our study, the individual identified the appropriate objects of measurement for the job or process. Primarily for this reason, only one firm expresses productivity measures in financial terms, and all of the productivity measures we observed are single factor measures.

3. Managers in four firms feel that it is inappropriate or unnecessary to convert productivity assessments to financial measures because either the productivity measure is capable of signaling improvement (and there is no need to quantify this improvement further) or because use of a financial number might obscure performance on an activity that the productivity system is capable of measuring directly. In some firms, there is a specified or standard level for the productivity measure. In other firms, the goal is either to steadily improve the productivity measure or to become a world-class competitor.

4. Most firms are reluctant to tie performance, as measured by the productivity system, to bonuses. (The exceptions are London Life Insurance Co. and Bell Canada, the two service organizations in our field study.) The productivity measures in most firms are reported to the individuals as a matter of information and are not used as a management control device or as a basis for intrinsic compensation. In three organizations, all aspects of standards and piece work have been eliminated on the grounds that they were inconsistent with a positive program of employee relations.

5. In all cases, the introduction of the productivity program has been accompanied by a major employee relations program

stressing that employees will not be discharged as a result of productivity improvements and that employees are equal partners with management in deciding how their respective jobs are to be done.

6. In all cases, the members of the organization take productivity performance seriously and are committed to productivity performance improvement.

7. In four of the seven organizations, the productivity program was initiated following a major corporate reorganization resulting from management or financial problems.

Strategic Factors and Organization Measurement

We saw a reasonably consistent process in all seven firms that we visited.

1. Specifying What Matters in the Organization
   The responsibility of senior management is to select the watchwords that summarize the key success factors facing the organization. Modern Motors uses quality, cost, and responsiveness. Fishery Products International Ltd. uses yield, throughput, and quality. Corporate watchwords are used in many organizations; for example, Volvo Motors uses quality, delivery/reliability, flexibility, and productivity; the Department of Veterans Affairs in the Canadian government uses courtesy, responsiveness, and generosity; and Kodak uses quality, productivity, and delivery. The most enduring observation of the study is that effective firms choose a small number of watchwords to communicate throughout the organization. Although some organizations may use fewer words, it appears as if at least three items are needed to provide the requisite variety to capture the environment of the firm. On the other hand, having more than five items is likely to cause confusion and conflict in the organization.

2. Communicating What Matters to the Organization Members
   Considerable care is taken to ensure that everyone in the organization understands what the watchwords mean and why they are important to the long-run success of the organization. This process is straightforward in the firms that have had serious financial difficulty. Constant allusions are made to learning the

lessons from the past and how attention to the watchwords will help avoid similar crises in the future. In the organizations that have not experienced hardships, the tactic is different. Usually a reference is made to a successful, or dominant, competitor as a model of how things have to improve. This process seems necessary to provide a commonality of purpose and focus at all levels in the organization. This process is the key to developing a system that ties what matters in the long run to the factors that operations-level people focus on in the short run.

3. Choosing What to Measure to Accomplish What Matters
The idea that senior executives can specify, and use, aggregate financial measures to motivate and control short-run operational performance is not supported in the firms that we visited. We found that, once operations people accept the watchwords of the organization, they develop operations control systems that guide the firm toward the activities implied by the watchwords. The operations people take the watchwords and specify how their work will be undertaken and improved in order to pursue the corporate watchwords and how to best measure and assess their performance in achieving the watchwords' goals.

In other words, organization goals are communicated top down, but control in the organization is bottom up. Most of the systems to monitor, evaluate, and improve short-run performance are systems put in place by operations people. These systems track operations data such as quality measures; percentage on-time delivery; productivity rates; yield rates; and measures that assess the use of the key cost-causing resources of the firm. The force for change and improvement in operations has to come from the operations people assuming responsibility for the process. Management's challenge is to get operations personnel to buy into the cooperative style of management.

Data derived from the financial accounting process, such as costs, revenues, variances, and profits, are not used to control short-run performance. On the other hand, traditional cost accounting measures, such as unit costs and variances, are used to evaluate the efficacy of short-run control systems. In other words, unit costs and variances are used in the strategic sense of comparing the organization's performance to competitors' or in comparing plant performance in the organization. The day-to-day activities, however, are monitored by operational systems that also diagnose problems and suggest improvements.

The effective synthesis of corporate objectives (as embodied in the watchwords) with the activities of operational personnel (as embodied in the control and monitoring systems that they design) requires management skill, cooperation, and an atmosphere of trust and mutual respect. This reinforces our belief that behavioral considerations are the critical elements of the process.

We recently discovered the following comment by Schonberger (1986) that effectively captures what we saw in our study:

A factory is like Moby Dick, and the managers are like Captain Ahab. They sink a few harpoons and hang on for dear life. The only way to steer Moby Dick is to surround it with a thousand boats and have a thousand harpooners penetrate the whale's hide. Likewise, the only way a factory can be steered is for the factory people to sink a thousand probes. There are enough people there. The trick is to get them to sink the probes.

In effect, top-down control is doomed to failure. Effective control requires that everyone at every level of the organization pitch in and try to steer the organization. The first question is, How can the activities of the individual participants be coordinated? The answer?—through the effective meshing of the corporate watchwords with the productivity systems of the organization. On a second question, How can participation by all organization members be motivated? Schonberger comments:

Data recording comes first. The tools are cheap and simple: pencils and chalk. Give those simple tools for recording data to each operator. Then make it a natural part of the operator's job to record disturbances and measurements on charts and blackboards. The person who records data is inclined to analyze, and the analyzer is inclined to think of solutions. Success depends on recording the right kind of data at the right time.

This opinion, that the job environment itself can provide an intrinsic motivation, is not universally held in the firms that we visited. Some managers feel that in order to secure motivation, compensation must be tied to performance. This difference of opinion is arguable, and we have no further insights into its resolution.

We summarize our observations as follows:

Successful organizations are driven from the top down in terms of understanding what has to be done to improve the chances for long-run success. However, successful organizations are driven from the bottom up in terms of developing effective control systems to monitor short-run progress toward the long-run success indicators. The key is the mechanism that integrates the long-run success indicators with the short-run performance indicators. In particular, the key is to secure the acceptance of the long-run success indicators by operations personnel and to motivate operations personnel to develop the appropriate operations control systems to monitor and steer progress toward achieving these goals.

THE RELATIONSHIP OF OUR
RESULTS TO ANOTHER
PRODUCTIVITY STUDY

During the course of this study, we discovered a publication by the American Productivity Center (Belcher 1987). Based on his consulting experience, Belcher has proposed various principles that we were able to evaluate, indirectly, in our study.

These principles concern the following topics: management commitment to productivity improvement; organizational awareness of the focus and scope of the productivity program; the existence of specific productivity goals; a merit system that ties productivity improvements to financial and nonfinancial rewards; specific productivity measures that are widespread and visible throughout the organization; quality improvement as a specific performance variable; employee involvement in the productivity program; assessing the productivity of all resources; improvement techniques (such as quality circles and statistical quality control) used as tools rather than as ends in themselves; and productivity as an integral part of the budgeting, planning, and financial reporting systems.

A summary of Belcher's productivity success factors, and how our results confirm, or contradict, them, appears in Appendix 4.

OUR RESULTS AND HOW THEY
RELATE TO EXISTING MANAGEMENT
ACCOUNTING MATERIAL

Agreement between the perspectives of the people we met in our study and those of writers of conventional cost and management accounting texts is almost nonexistent. We observed instances of cost accounting practices, such as process costing, standard costing, variance analysis, joint costing, and cost allocation. However, the outputs from these cost accounting practices are not considered useful in measuring or directing productivity improvement efforts. Rather, their principal value appears to be in providing periodic, aggregate comparisons of the organization's performance with that of its competitors.

Second, our field work suggests that effective management accounting systems are not generic. They must relate to the particular strategic objectives and opportunities of each firm.

Third, the financial perspective of management accounting texts stands in stark contrast with the operational perspective of management accounting practice. Virtually all management accounting texts emphasize the manipulation of financial accounting numbers as the basis for effective organizational control and evaluation. This perspective reflects the general attitude that the firm can be managed through the judicious use of financial data without any real understanding of the physical processes that underlie these data. There is little mention in these texts of the need for operational data that relate to key organization success factors. Yet this appears to be the basis for effective organization control. To us, the contrast between texts and practice reflects the general lack of understanding on the part of academics of the environment in which management accounting is practiced.

Fourth, we found that operating managers had little use for, and paid little attention to, the elaborate variance reporting systems that exist in most organizations. These systems are, of course, the predominant topic in management accounting education.

If our observation of effective practice is confirmed in other studies of management accounting practice, a profound change must occur in the focus of management accounting education. The focus must move away from topics that are extensions of financial accounting conventions and move toward the design and use of operational systems that reflect the needs of management.

NOTES

1. The Silver, Craig and Harris, and Gold indices are perhaps the best-known approaches to defining aggregate productivity measures. These, and some other aggregate approaches, are described briefly in this paper.

2. The best-known individual productivity measures are materials yield and output per unit of labor.

APPENDIX 1

Sample Bibliography of Productivity Articles

Aggarwal, Summer C. "A Study of Productivity Measures for Improving Benefit-Cost Ratios of Operating Organizations." *International Journal of Productivity Research* 18, No. 1 (1980): 83–103.

Babson, Stanley M., Jr. "Profiling Your Productivity." *Management Accounting* (December 1981): 13–17.

Belcher, John G., Jr. *How Today's Best Run Companies Are Gaining the Competitive Edge.* Houston: Gulf Publishing Company, 1987.

Brittany, R. R., R. P. Kudar, J. Walsh, D. A. Johnston, and J. M. Legentil. "Planning for Productivity Improvement: A Management Perspective." *Business Quarterly* (Winter 1983): 38–42.

Coates, J. B. "Productivity: What is it?" *Long Range Planning* 13 (August 1980): 90–97.

Craig, C. E. and R. C. Harris. "Total Productivity Measurement at the Firm Level." *Sloan Management Review* 14, No. 3 (1973): 13–29.

Day, Charles R., Jr. "Solving the Mystery of Productivity Measurement." *Industry Week* 28 January 1981: 61–66.

Gass, Gerald L., Roger Benston, and Grover McMakin. "White Collar Productivity." *Management Accounting* (September 1987): 33–38.

Gold, Bela. "Practical Productivity Analysis for Management Accountants." *Management Accounting* (May 1980): 31–44.

Hayes, Robert H. and Kim B. Clark. "Why Some Factories Are More Productive Than Others." *Harvard Business Review* (September–October 1986): 66–73.

Hendrick, Gregory. "Organizational Structure: The Source of Low Productivity." *S. A. M. Advanced Management Journal* (Winter 1982): 20–30.

Mammone, James L. "Productivity Measurement: A Conceptual Overview." *Management Accounting* (June 1980): 36–42.

———. "A Practical Approach to Productivity Measurement." *Management Accounting* (July 1980): 40–44.

Meadows, Edward. "How Three Companies Increased Their Productivity." *Fortune* 10 March 1980: 92–101.

Mundel, Marvin E. "Measures of Productivity." *Industrial Engineering* (May 1976): 24–26.

Oishi, Osamu. "Productivity and Productivity Ideas." *Business Quarterly* (Summer 1982): 44–48.

Perry, Lawrence W. and Mary K. Sealey. "Measuring Productivity: Focusing on Key Resources and Added Value Management." *Cost and Management* (May–June 1981): 65–68.

Pigeon, P. J. "How to Measure Productivity." *Cost and Management* (May–June 1981): 14–21.

Roll, Y. and A. Sachish. "Productivity Measurement at the Plant Level." *Omega* 9 No. 1: 37–42.

Rowe, David L. "How Westinghouse Measures White Collar Productivity." *Management Review* (November 1981): 42–47.

Schonberger, R. J. *World Class Manufacturing: The Lessons of Simplicity Applied.* New York: Free Press, 1986.

Schroeder, Roger G., John C. Anderson, and Gary D. Scudder. "White Collar Productivity Measurement." *Management Decision* 24, No. 5 (1986): 3–7.

Shetty, Y. K. "Key Elements of Productivity Improvement Programs." *Business Horizons* (March–April 1982): 15–22.

Silver, M. S. "Appropriate Index Number Formulae for Productivity Measurement at the Plant/Organizational Level." *Managerial and Decision Economics* 3, No. 4 (1982): 244–250.

Taylor, Bernard W. and K. Roscoe Davis. "Corporate Productivity—Getting It All Together." *Industrial Engineering* 9, No. 3 (1977): 32–36.

Teague, J. and S. Eilon. "Productivity Measurement: A Brief Survey." *Applied Economics* 5 (1973): 133–145.

Tuttle, Thomas C. "Organizational Productivity: A Challenge for Psychologists." *American Psychologist* (April 1983): 479–486.

Wait, Donald J. "Productivity Measurement: A Management Accounting Challenge." *Management Accounting* (May 1980): 24–30.

APPENDIX 2

Summary of the Results of the Mail Questionnaire

A total of 164 responses was received to the 300 questionnaires that were mailed out. These responses were distributed as follows:

Productivity Questionnaire

Distribution of Responses

Item	Number
Questionnaires Returned Completed	103
Questionnaires Returned Blank	22
Envelopes Returned Unopened	39
Total	164

The questionnaires that were returned blank had the following explanations: not relevant for our firm (19) and refuse to answer these questions (3).

The envelopes that were returned unopened carried the following explanations: addressee has left the firm or has retired (9), the firm has been sold (11), and not at this address (19).

Of the 103 questionnaires that were returned completed, 81 stated that a productivity system was in place and 22 mentioned that there was no productivity system in place. Of the 22 indicating that there was no productivity system in place, 20 mentioned a reason why the firm did not use a productivity system. These explanations were as follows: now putting one in place (4); productivity measures not relevant in a services firm (4); productivity measures not relevant in a holding company (3); never bothered to develop a productivity system (4); productivity too difficult to measure (2); use a budget-based control system (1); company too diverse to develop a single productivity system (1); and productivity assessed informally (1).

In reviewing the 81 responses that stated a productivity system was in place, two striking features emerged. First, productivity is a very broadly perceived concept. Second, the most enthusiastic and thorough responses appeared to come from people in regulated utilities.

The questionnaire had five parts. The questions appeared on the questionnaire exactly as they are reproduced below and were provided with no accompanying interpretation or explanation. The following tables summarize the responses to each of the five questions on this questionnaire.

Question 1 Please indicate the major benefits that you feel are derived from measuring productivity.

Major Benefit	Number
To provide for improved motivation and accountability	30
To motivate better uses of resources and cost reduction	30
To assess trends in performance	24
To focus attention on the factors creating success	15
To provide a basis for comparison to competitors	13
To provide a basis to express and reward individual effectiveness	7
To allow prompt recognition of, and reaction to, changing conditions	7
To provide the means for evaluating capital expenditures	6
To provide a standard for performance	6
To improve quality	4
To identify opportunities for innovation or improvement	4
To provide a means to control inventory	1
To identify bottlenecks	6

Question 2 Please indicate the general principle(s) that you use to decide what activities ought to be subject to productivity measurements.

General Principle	Number
Pick the activity with highest potential for improvement	31
The activity must have a specific goal that is quantifiable	28
The activity must be controllable	18
The activity should be labor intensive	6
There must be an industry standard available for the activity chosen	5
The potential to measure all facets of the activity must exist	4
There must be a quality standard that can be defined and controlled	2
Activities must be related to volume of work	2
Choose an activity at the lowest level of output/ input control	1
Choose activities that have macro (financial) measurements	1
Choose activities that have micro (operating) measurements	1
Choose activities that evaluate investment decisions	1
Choose activities that are measurable over time	1

Question 3   Please indicate the general principle(s) that you use to decide how
               to measure the productivity of the activities that you have chosen
               to assess.

General Principle	Number
Must be chosen by person controlling activity and agreed by superior	10
Must be capable of incorporating material, labor, capital standards	10
Must be understandable by person controlling the activity	9
Must be meaningful and address all facets of the activity	9
Must relate some output measure to some input measure	9
Must be capable of objective measurement	8
Must be comparable to others in the industry	6
Must be simple	6
Must be consistent over time	5
Must be easy to calculate	4
Must measure performance relative to past, not absolute, performance	3
Must relate hours allowed to hours used	3
Must relate to cost effectiveness	3
Must use operating data in order to provide better control information	2
Must be related to factors creating success rather than costs or profits	2
Inputs must be expressed in dollars to provide comparability	1
Must focus attention on improvement areas	1
Must employ fundamental industrial engineering principles	1
Must measure a facet of the job controllable by the incumbent	1
Inputs must include all factors of production	1

Question 4   Please indicate what, in your opinion, are the two most important productivity measures used in your firm and why each is important.

Most Important Measure	Number
The consumption of the highest cost factor per unit	23
Shippable units of output per shift	16
People/equipment capacity usage ratios	11
Material yields	9
Sales or production per employee	8
Cost per unit of output	7
Ratio of largest component of cost to total cost	6
Ratio of sales to inventory or some other asset account	6
Ratio of allowed direct labor hours to total direct labor hours	6
Ratio of capital required to units of output	5
Return on sales or operating ratio	5
Ratio of flexible budget dollars to actual dollars	4
Rejects or sales credits issued per unit of time	4
Changes in the profile of activity costs in production process	3
Defect rates	3
Overhead cost per unit	2
Units of consumption of major resource per unit of output	2
Ratio of expense growth to margin growth	1
Payroll as a percentage of sales	1
Percent improvement in cost or performance measure	1
Units of productive activity by incumbent	1
Cost per unit of service by customer class	1
Payback period	1
Performance on agreed task by employee	1
Project completion relative to timetable	1
Total cost of moving goods through production/distribution system	1

Question 5   Please indicate the most difficult issue that remains to be resolved with respect to the use of productivity measurement in your firm.

Difficult Issue	Number
Securing trust in measurements so that they can serve as basis for action	14
Developing measures for non-repetitive skill oriented activities	10
Ensuring consistency of measurement over time	7
Developing measures for customer service	6
Controlling for the effect of production mix on the measure	4
Understanding the relationship between quality and productivity	3
Developing meaningful, comprehensive, and non-manipulable measures	3
Interpreting measures that do not relate directly to a GL account	3
Developing measures of corporate, rather than factor, productivity	2
Determining if measure is counterproductive or stifling	2
Adjusting measure when automation affects labor and overhead costs	2
Developing data to make comparisons to other firms	2
Developing comprehensive measures for an activity	2
Understanding the relationship between standards and expectations	2
Implementing just-in-time systems	1
Implementing statistical process control	1
Implementing vendor certification systems	1
Understanding the relationship between value-added and throughput	1
Evaluating cost-effectiveness of productivity systems	1
Dealing with discretionary cost items	1
Developing simple and objective numbers	1
Developing accountability with measurement	1

APPENDIX 3

Profiles of the Seven Field Study Firms

MANUFACTURING FIRMS

COLT STEEL

Major Business: Steel manufacturer
Size: > 10,000 employees
1987 sales—$2.8 billion

Brief Description

Colt Steel is one of the largest, fully integrated steel manufacturers in Canada, producing a variety of hot-rolled, cold-rolled, tin-plate, and galvanized steel.

Colt Steel experienced a traumatic period during the 1970s and early 1980s when a combination of overexpansion, economic recession, the rise of the mini steel mills, and high-quality, relatively cheap, Japanese steel caused the firm to close inefficient plants and lay off a significant portion of its work force.

During this period, action was taken to counteract these negative forces. It became clear that the critical success factors in maintaining a competitive position in the steel business are 1) output per employee and 2) yield. Steel is an intensely competitive industry: prices for raw materials and finished goods are virtually identical for all producers. Furthermore, industrywide collective wage agreements are common, and similar production technology is available to all competitors. Consequently, Colt Steel has little comparative advantage in terms of factor prices, quality, or the types of products that it produces.

The three variables that are controllable are 1) the quality of output (conformance to stated strength and metallurgical properties), 2) the rate of output (tons per shift or tons per worker-hour), and 3) the yield (ratio of weight of finished steel to weight of inputs) of the process. It is around these variables that the productivity program and the productivity measurement system has been organized.

Early each morning, a one-page report summarizing the results of the previous day's activities, organized along the dimensions of quality, rate of output, and yield, is prepared and forwarded to the vice president of manufacturing. By midmorning of each day, the plant superintendents call the vice president, discuss the report, and discuss what steps to take to correct any undesirable situations.

The labor productivity measure takes on added importance when comparisons with overseas competitors are made. Given that foreign competitors face similar prices for raw materials and finished goods and employ comparable technology capable of producing similar quality output, the critical relationship is that the sum of Colt Steel's labor cost per ton and freight cost per ton must be less than the comparable sum of the overseas competitor.

A capital-spending program had been undertaken to achieve yield improvements and cost reductions. During the ten-year period 1978–1987, capital expenditures averaged $165 million per year. The number of employees fell by 30%, and the number of tons shipped per employee rose by 32%. Many of the productivity improvement suggestions came from employees through a suggestion system that paid 20% of the first year's savings (up to a maximum of $100,000).

Although there are no rewards tied explicitly to the measurements provided by the productivity system, it is clear that the company's previous problems have fostered an awareness, throughout the company, that failure to achieve success on these productivity measures will result in the loss of jobs and the eventual demise of the organization.

MODERN MOTORS
Major Business: Manufacturer of cars and trucks
Size: > 45,000 employees
1987 revenue—> $15 billion

Brief Description

Modern Motors, a wholly owned subsidiary of a multinational corporation, operates multiple vehicle-assembly plants, including automobile-, truck-, and van-assembly plants. Its average annual output in recent years has exceeded 500,000 vehicles.

Faced with a deteriorating share of the total car and truck market, Modern Motors embarked on a major strategic initiative to regain markets. Central to its initiative is the establishment of a corporate-wide business plan that was adopted in 1987. The plan is hierarchical and establishes corporate values that are strongly customer-oriented. These values have led to specific strategies that, in turn, are implemented by specific techniques, including a productivity system. At the heart of the productivity system is a multifaceted definition of output. These facets consist of three variables that Modern Motors believes are critical to remaining competitive: quality, cost, and responsiveness.

Quality is the predominant concern, and reports of quality conformance receive high exposure. Each month, the measurement system reports on key quality indicators and ranks the relative performance of each assembly plant in Canada and the United States against these indicators, both in an absolute sense and relative to the competitor identified as the world-class producer in terms of quality.

Cost is reflected by a number of measures but the focus, despite the major move to automation, is the labor cost per vehicle since this is the cost factor that is the most controllable in the short run at the operating level. This cost measure is reported widely throughout the company and is a statistic used to compare the performance of different plants. The other major focus in monthly reports is the progress that the company is making toward reducing the cost for each vehicle relative to the cost of the world-class competitor for that vehicle.

Responsiveness is defined as the time needed to respond to internal and external customers, and reports summarizing responses to customer orders and production time in each department are widely distributed. Not only is the responsiveness factor related to customer service, but it also relates to the requirement to meet production schedules in order to support the on-going implementation of a just-in-time manufacturing operation. Responsiveness measures are communicated daily through the plants via overhead monitors and through the organization hierarchy via daily production reports that compare actual to planned production and note any overtime required to make up production deficiencies.

Although there are no explicit rewards tied to performance on the productivity measures of quality, cost, and responsiveness, there is a general feeling in the organization that failure to maintain performance on the three dimensions of productivity will lead to production losses, both to sister plants within the corporate system and to outside competitors.

ALLEN-BRADLEY CANADA
Major Business: Industrial controls
Size: 1,000 employees
Sales consolidated into parent

Brief Description

A subsidiary of a multinational conglomerate, Allen-Bradley Canada consists of three divisions that collectively produce eight types of products: industrial automation controls; sensing devices; programmable controllers; drives; voltage starters; color graphic systems; factory-floor computers; and software for industry.

In the mid-1980s, Allen-Bradley Canada was the market leader in several of its business lines. However, an economic recession, an explosion of global competitors, shrinking product life cycles, availability of automated machinery and advanced technology, and an inability to pass costs along to customers caused management to reevaluate its strategies and operating plans. Management believed that the only way to meet these challenges was to become a world-class manufacturer—a flexible, cost-efficient, highly automated producer of top-quality products.

To accomplish this, Allen-Bradley Canada has developed a formal productivity program that focuses on manufacturing resource planning, JIT manufacturing, computer-integrated manufacturing, and employee involvement and training. This strategy is supported by a sophisticated data base system and a belief in the concept of total quality control.

At Allen-Bradley Canada, the primary desire is to expend efforts to increase productivity, not to devise formulas to measure it. The company philosophy is that the overriding measure of success, and the one true measure of productivity, is profit. To convey the importance of this message, meetings are conducted to educate and inform supervisors, foremen, and line personnel on the financial aspects of the firm. In most cases, nonfinancial measures, such as yields and quality, are translated into dollar terms to add significance to their impact on the bottom line.

For purposes of the program, however, productivity is formally defined as the ratio of total outputs of goods and services to the number of employees. The strength of this measure is that it is simple, easily understood, and focuses on the company's critical input resource. Although labor is a small component of total manufacturing cost (4–15%), Allen-Bradley Canada views it as the component that makes the difference between earning and losing money.

During the period 1983–1987, Allen-Bradley spent about $30 million on productivity improvement programs and equipment. Between 1985 and 1988, productivity, as measured by the contributed value per employee, increased at an annual rate of about 10%.

Although rewards are not tied specifically to the productivity system, there is active employee participation in the productivity program. Participation is motivated by securing employee involvement in all aspects of the productivity plan and through the development of a sophisticated, real-time, statistical quality control system that focuses on providing employees with the opportunity for self-evaluation and improvement.

NATURAL RESOURCE/FOOD COMPANIES

J. M. SCHNEIDER INC.
Major Business: Manufacturer of processed meat products
Size: > 3,500 employees
     1987 revenue—about $700 million

Brief Description

J. M. Schneider Inc. is one of Canada's largest producers of premium-quality food products. In 1988, the company sold over 1,800 products in a wide variety of forms, including fresh, processed, fast-frozen, cured, cooked, custom-butchered, and cut meats to grocery and food services outlets.

Meat processing is a labor-intensive industry, and, in the early 1980s, wage settlements in Canadian meat-packing houses had reached levels that were uncompetitive in comparison with American meat packers. Responding to the competition, and as a reaction to inflating labor costs, J. M. Schneider embarked on a productivity program.

The productivity program focuses on the two factors that the firm believes are critical to staying in business: labor productivity and materials yields. Since labor costs amount to about 20% of each sales dollar, improvements in the output/labor input ratio have a major impact on corporate profitability. The productivity program was undertaken through continual upgrading of industrial engineering labor standards with the promise that no employee would lose his or her position due to productivity improvements. Once the labor-oriented program was underway, the yield improvement program was undertaken. Yield is considered a critical factor since materials costs amount to about 67% of the sales dollar.

Both the labor and yield productivity improvement programs are top-down initiatives undertaken by the industrial engineering department.

The labor and yield productivity programs are critical to the firm's survival. During the period 1984–1987, the labor and yield programs resulted in average yearly savings of $3.4 million and $3.2 million, respectively. To put these figures into perspective, the firm's annual average net income during this period was $2.6 million.

The program does more than contribute dollar savings, however. Executives in the company state that the industrial engineering-based program has improved scheduling, manpower usage, materials and equipment usage, problem solving and error correction, communication, and general knowledge of the business and has enhanced employee fulfillment. Due to these successes, the budget for labor and yield productivity programs was to be increased by 30% in 1988.

Although rewards are not tied to the productivity system, the system commands attention in the organization since it is generally believed, at all levels of the organization, that failure to continually improve the labor and yield performance will result in the demise of the organization.

FISHERY PRODUCTS INTERNATIONAL LTD.

Major Business: Fish processing
Size: 8,600 employees
1987 sales—$396 million

Brief Description

Fishery Products International Ltd. was created in the mid-1980s by amalgamating the operations of a number of financially troubled sea-products companies. With the financial backing of the federal government of Canada, Fishery Products International embarked on a major program to reduce its debt load and to modernize its fish plants. In four years, Fishery Products International Ltd. emerged from a position of heavy losses to a position of prominence in its industry. In 1988, it had the largest fish allocations off Canada's Atlantic coast and was the largest foreign supplier of seafood to the United States.

The productivity program at Fishery Products International Ltd. was developed during the restructuring that occurred in 1985 and is widely regarded within the firm as the centerpiece of the new management team's recovery strategy. Productivity at Fishery Products International is synonymous with cost containment and control. Productivity is defined and measured using 1) product yield—the ratio of finished product to raw materials input, 2) throughput—the amount of output per labor hour, and 3) quality.

The yield measure is the cornerstone of the productivity system and the focus of frequent, detailed reporting. The existence of stringent fishing quotas means that controlling yields is a critical factor in the firm's success.

Throughput and quality are the other key productivity measures. Throughput measures the efficiency of labor in producing good output; quality measures monitor both fishing and processing operations.

Management recognizes explicitly the contributions made by employees during the restructuring process and has adopted a system of both intrinsic and extrinsic rewards. Whereas the fishing industry generally is characterized by bitter strikes and militant unions, Fishery Products International uses its productivity system to develop a sense of common purpose within the organization and to convey to employees how the security of their jobs relates to the achievement of corporate goals. This has reduced friction and has helped to ensure goal congruence.

Fishery Products International employs three performance-related compensation schemes. First, there is a profit-sharing scheme that includes all employees. Second, there has been a generous distribution of stock to all employees. Third, in some of the plants, piece work incentives are tied into the corporate yield system. All of the piece rate plans are remnants of systems that existed in the individual firms that were amalgamated to form Fishery Products International. The vice president of Industrial Relations is considering the elimination of the piece work incentives on the grounds that they are inconsistent with the spirit of the productivity system, which holds that performance on yield and quality is a necessary, and not a meritorious, part of the company's continued success.

SERVICE COMPANIES

LONDON LIFE INSURANCE CO.
Major Business: Selling and servicing insurance policies
Size: > 5,000 persons
        Net assets of approximately $9 billion

Brief Description

London Life Insurance Co. is a full-service life insurance company. It employs approximately 5,400 people divided almost equally between administrative and sales positions. Operating from 165 regional offices, it has the largest sales force of any insurance company in Canada. The company does business with 1 of every 5 Canadian households and has over 2 million individual policies and 26,000 group policies in force.

The driving force behind the productivity program came from executives who had prior experience in retailing. Although they knew of no previous attempts to install formal productivity programs in the insurance industry, the president and vice president were convinced that, given the highly competitive life insurance market, the company that improved the productivity of its operating activities would enjoy a significant competitive advantage. Critical to future success, they believed, was using scarce resources in an effective and efficient manner. Since 70% of London Life Insurance's operating costs are personnel-related, the productivity program has concentrated on improving and measuring employee output.

A top-down approach was adopted, and a special unit that reported directly to the vice president, finance, created the program. In total, over 90 productivity measures were developed to measure the productivity improvement of office staff. Incumbents were asked to design appropriate productivity measures for their respective jobs (most jobs had multiple productivity measures). Most of the measures relate to units of work, or service, provided per employee-hour.

Output is measured by externally driven factors, that is, by factors not controllable by the employee. By insisting that input be measured in terms of equivalent employee-hours, individual productivity measures can be aggregated to compute a corporate productivity measure. Yearly improvements in corporate productivity form the basis of a corporate gainsharing system.

In an industry where productivity gains are low or negative, productivity improvement in London Life Insurance has averaged 8% per year. Despite a tripling of their business, the size of administrative staff support had remained constant. London Life Insurance has a policy of gainsharing with the employees. Each year, productivity gains in excess of 4%, up to a maximum of 10%, are shared equally between the employees and the firm.

BELL CANADA
Major Business: Supplier of telecommunications services
Size: > 50,000 employees
       1987 Net income—over $700 million

Brief Description

Bell Canada provides basic telephone service in an operating territory that covers several provinces. The organization serves a population of more than 16 million and handles more than one billion long-distance telephone calls a year.

Before the mid-1980s, Bell Canada was a highly regulated firm. In this monopoly situation, control focused primarily on employee costs and technical considerations, although there were some service quality criteria imposed on the firm by its regulator. By 1984, certain services had been deregulated, and Bell Canada faced a situation in which over 25% of its revenues were subject to direct competition—a trend that seemed certain to continue. This development caused the firm to shift its focus from efficiency considerations, a common perspective in a regulated utility, to one wherein quality of customer service took precedence.

To accomplish the reorientation from efficiency to service, a corporate productivity center was formed in 1985. Ensuring a high quality of customer service, both inside and outside the organization, became the focal point of the productivity effort. The center has three responsibilities: to heighten the company's awareness of productivity issues; to ensure consistent approaches to productivity; and to offer guidance on organizing for, implementing, and measuring productivity.

The company experimented with several commercially available productivity packages before adopting its own approach. Although initially designed to develop and monitor productivity for white-collar workers, Bell Canada's program is robust enough to capture blue-collar workers as well. Employees in each operating unit are charged with developing a mission statement, defining its customers (in most cases they are internal customers), and developing a series of non-manipulable measures that best track progress toward the mission statement.

Although still in its infancy, Bell Canada's aggregate productivity program registered a gain in 1986 of 6.7%, this compared with the less than a 1% gain in the general Canadian economy. Dramatic improvements in grievances, absenteeism, quality of work, timeliness, use of technology, teamwork, and cost have also been recorded. Beginning in 1987, nonunionized employees have been able to share in aggregate corporate gains based on a formula that measures achievements in financial returns and customer satisfaction indices.

APPENDIX 4

Productivity Project Summary

How Do the Results of This Study Compare with Those of Another Study?

Productivity Success Factor	London	Bell	Allen	Colt	MM	JMS	FPI
Management Commitment	yes	yes	yes	yes	yes	yes	yes
Organizational Awareness	yes	no	yes	yes	yes	yes	yes
Broad Targets for Productivity	yes	yes	yes	yes	yes	yes	yes
Reward System	yes	yes	no	no	no	no	yes
Productivity Measures	yes	yes	yes	yes	yes	yes	yes
Quality	yes	yes	yes	yes	yes	yes	yes
Employee Involvement	yes	yes	yes	yes	yes	yes	yes
All Resources	no	no	no	no	no	no	no
Improvement Techniques	yes	yes	yes	yes	yes	yes	yes
Productivity System Tied to Budgeting, Planning, and Financial Reporting Systems	no	no	yes	yes	no	yes	yes

Note: The productivity success factors appearing in this table were suggested by John G. Belcher, Jr., *Productivity: How Today's Best Run Companies Are Gaining the Competitive Edge* (Houston: Gulf Publishing Company, 1987).

PART II

Measures to Facilitate Organizational Learning

CHAPTER 5

Measurement, Coordination, and Learning in a Multiplant Network

W. Bruce Chew, Timothy F. Bresnahan, and Kim B. Clark

DURING the past several years, we and our colleagues have studied productivity of multiplant firms in over two dozen widely different industries, involving plants engaged in discrete part production and process flow and in high-tech and low-tech operations. In every environment, the research has identified large differences in plant-to-plant productivity within the same firm, even when the plants employed similar technologies and produced similar, occasionally identical, products. Performance differences between the best and the worst plants within a single company can be on the order of 3:1. After controlling for differences in the age and size of plants, their technology, and their location, differentials of 2:1 can still remain. Intrafirm productivity variations of this magnitude are both financially and competitively significant.

Understanding how performance differentials of this magnitude can arise and persist requires a broader view of decentralized production operations than has been typically taken in the economics, accounting, logistics and operations research literature. That literature views a multisite firm as an opportunity for optimizing material flows and minimizing costs in the network. This view, however, ignores the large opportunities for learning and sharing improvements across the many plants in the network. Innovative practices and policies can be developed at any location. Multiple production locations enable a firm

129

to leverage performance-enhancing ideas generated at one site to all the other sites in the network. The challenge for managers is to encourage the generation of performance-enhancing ideas at individual locations and then to ensure that the successful ideas become transferred to all locations in the network. With this view, the key tasks become not optimized production and materials flows but managerial decision making, knowledge creation, and the flow of knowledge and information. The critical actors become the people who discover, apply, and transfer the new ideas. General managers become concerned not only with the flow of materials but also with the flow of knowledge. Large, persistent variations in individual plant productivity among similar plants can only occur with a less-than-optimal management of network knowledge flows.

This paper examines the impact of management on network performance. We first develop a framework to identify the critical role for the general manager in the transfer of innovative practices within the network. We then examine the operation of a particular multiplant network to illustrate the extent of productivity variation and the role played by performance measurement, compensation, and personnel policies in the persistence of large productivity variation. The example studied—a commercial food operation—is a multisite operation in which all sites produce similar products, serve similar customers, and use similar technology. The example is particularly instructive since, under these conditions, plants should be able to learn extensively from one another and be able to transfer successful practices relatively easily. Yet, we found almost no transfer of knowledge within the network and persistent large differences in productivity among plants. The case study shows how a coherent, mutually reinforcing set of beliefs, policies, and practices prevent productivity-enhancing ideas from being transferred among plants. In the fourth section of the paper, we draw lessons about the choices firms face in designing and managing a network to stimulate the flow of know-how and reduce variation in productivity. We conclude with a brief summary and with implications for practice and further research.

NETWORK MANAGEMENT AND PERFORMANCE

In studying knowledge creation and information transfers among plants in a network, we must highlight the role played by the general manager. The general manager, with supporting staff, must perform two fundamental tasks. First, the manager must verify that the individual plants execute the tasks required for current operations; orders must be filled, bills paid, materials ordered, workers hired, trained, and paid, and so on. Second, to respond to competitive pressures and to increase profits, the performance of the network must improve over time.

Locally, plants improve by developing new procedures, new technologies, and new applications of existing technologies. Many local innovations may have applicability at other sites in the network. Transfer of these ideas to other plants will keep the network as a whole close to the highest performance possible. Thus, improvement of network performance requires both local innovation and interplant transfer of the local innovations.

Interplant transfer of knowledge is more important when the plants in a network are similar. If core technologies differ substantially (such as when a semiconductor wafer fabrication plant ships its output to an assembly plant), processes that improve performance in one plant may not apply to another. Similarly, if the plants operate in different environments—serving large versus small markets, serving a quality-conscious versus a cost-conscious market, or using high-skilled versus low-skilled labor—practices useful at one site may not easily transfer to another. Networks with similar products, processes, environments, and missions provide the best opportunity for sharing knowledge from plant to plant.

If plants are geographically dispersed and unlinked by physical flows, little opportunity may exist for communication about current practices. Information transfer is also inhibited when the plants are dominant in their local markets; without strong competitive pressures, plant managers may not feel continuous pressure for improvement. Unless the network general manager creates incentives for improvement, plant managers may become comfortable in their local niches, and information will not be transmitted or received around the network.

The information needed to improve network performance does not flow naturally among the plants in the network. The information is not standardized or routine. Thus, plant managers do not know when they have not received an important piece of information about a procedural innovation. Also, the information is not quantitative (unlike factors such as order size, price, or standard cost). Many process innovations, representing advances in know-how or new procedures or attitudes, are extremely difficult to communicate concisely and precisely.

Four critical phases are required for network information flow: creation, identification, transfer, and application. A failure in any one of these phases will prevent good ideas and management practices from disseminating across the network. In the *creation* phase, new management practices are developed at local plants. The *identification* phase requires that advances at local plants be recognized. This may not be easy. Good plant managers may be able to create a production revolution locally but be unable to recognize that the innovation may be useful elsewhere or be unable to distinguish between actions that were successful because of unique circumstances at their site and those that could be generally applied elsewhere. The *transfer* stage disseminates the created and identified practices to other sites in such a way that they can be usefully applied. And in *application*, managers at the other sites must be willing and able to apply the innovation to their local operations.

The general manager of the network can play an active role in the identification and transfer stages but must also strive to have local managers be receptive to new ideas for the application stage at each plant and encourage the creation of new ideas to begin with. Before commenting on the various ways in which the network manager can influence each stage, we will make these concepts more explicit by focusing on a case study that provides rich insights into the complex problems of network management.

NETWORK PERFORMANCE:
A CASE EXAMPLE

We studied a commercial food operation, a division of a large multibusiness firm, with over forty operating units that prepare, deliver, and set up food. The average kitchen at a plant is quite large, in excess of 45,000 square feet, and employs almost two hundred hourly employees. The kitchens serve an average of over two million meals annually. While customers vary considerably, each has a list of standard meals from which it orders. The variety of meals provided has precluded any significant automation to date. With the exception of dish washing, the work is done manually, using larger versions of equipment found in most well-equipped home kitchens.

The division experiences pronounced seasonal peaks in volume, but even more pronounced are the daily breakfast, lunch, and dinner peaks typical of restaurant kitchens. Unlike restaurants, however, the meals prepared by the division are delivered to customers and prepared for serving by the customers' employees. Thus, meals must be prepared well before the actual final number required is known with certainty. Plant managers' skills are tested by the constant need to scramble to accommodate last-minute changes in the number and type of meals desired by customers.

The division is an ideal research site for this study. The units are highly similar in both process and product; many plants produce identical products sold to the same customer in different regions of the United States. Its operations are entirely domestic, free of international influences. And no transshipping of either finished or unfinished product occurs, so that the division consists of a set of physically unlinked plants that produce similar products with similar processes. Thus, information sharing should be especially valuable.

The division is the clear leader in its industry, as indicated by the monopoly or highly dominant market share it holds in the majority of its local markets. The business is growing and has been profitable for years. Increased cost competition and the emergence of new markets and technologies, however, have recently been threatening the sustained success of the division and have increased managers' interest in improving local operations.

Measuring Performance

To identify plants where management practice is particularly good or bad, appropriate measurement tools are needed. We have chosen multifactor productivity as our measure. Profitability, perhaps the more obvious choice, will not serve as well for this purpose because profits are influenced by meal prices that are not determined at the local plant level. Meal prices are negotiated separately for each site by corporate marketing staff and vary widely from plant to plant, even for the same meal. The variation does not appear to reflect meal or service quality; it does reflect local differences in food prices, wage rates, efficiencies, and the competitiveness of the local commercial food business as well as the cost pressures of the local customers. Of these factors, only local efficiencies represent potentially transferable practices. Since our focus is on the role of network management in transferring information, we will set aside the other site-specific sources of variation and highlight the efficiency differences by measuring productivity, i.e., the ratio of unit outputs to unit inputs consumed in production.

To make a useful productivity index for comparing plants requires solving three distinct measurement problems.

First, measured output must be comparable across plants; few firms produce completely homogeneous output at all their sites. Since this is an important problem, we will discuss our index of plant output in detail. Second, all of the different inputs (capital, labor, energy, and materials) used at each plant must be aggregated into a single "unit input." Though this problem is important in many applications, our study concerned a very labor-intensive process, so there will be no important difference between labor productivity (output per labor-hour) and total factor productivity (output per unit input).

The third and most difficult measurement problem arises because not all plants operate in the same environment. Some may have higher productivity because they enjoy economies of scale in large markets or because local labor market conditions are favorable. Network management attempts to identify productivity advances that can be transferred to other sites. Differences in productivity arising from specific local factors are therefore of less interest to network management. Our productivity measurement framework will need to hold local environmental factors constant and to report variations in productivity above and beyond what would be expected because of environmental variation. We will use a regression analysis approach to control for local environmental conditions.

Output Indexes

The plants in our study operate high-volume commercial kitchens in many cities. They cook meals and then deliver and set up the meals at a customer's site. Meals can vary in type, and thus in the amount of labor input needed to prepare them. Setups can also vary in complexity and in the distance and time to the customer's site. Both of these effects are quantitatively important; thus, simply counting meals and setups will not give an accurate picture of real output.[1]

Our solution to the problem was to weight meals and setups using complexity indexes prepared by corporate staff. A simple meal produced by the majority of kitchens was selected as the standard and given a complexity value of one. All other meals were scaled against this standard based on their labor requirements at an average kitchen in the network. A meal requiring twice as many man-hours to prepare as the standard meal would have a complexity index of two, for example. Thus, for each meal, j, we have a meal complexity index value C_{mj}. Setups were treated similarly. We defined the setup complexity index for setup k to be C_{sk}.[2]

These complexity indexes make it possible for us to measure output in complexity-adjusted standard meal equivalents and standard setup equivalents.[3] To add them up into a single output measure, we weight them by the 1987 network average price for the standard meal and for the standard setup. Thus our index of output is

$$\text{Output}_i = p_m \sum_{j=1}^{n} C_{mj}(\text{meals})_{ij} + p_s \sum_{k=1}^{m} C_{sk}(\text{setups})_{ik}$$

where

p_m is the networkwide average price of meals excluding food costs

p_s is the networkwide average price of setups

$(\text{meals})_{ij}$ is the number of type j meals produced at site i (there are n varieties of meals)

C_{mj} is the networkwide complexity adjustment for meal type j

$(\text{setups})_{ik}$ is the number of type k setups performed at site i (there are m varieties of setups)

C_{sk} is the networkwide complexity adjustment for setup type k

Input Indexes

The inputs for our productivity measure present no unusual problems. Labor skill levels are basically the same at all sites. We measure labor input as total labor hours at each site, multiplied by the average 1987 hourly wage in the system as a whole. This prevents counting the more expensive but otherwise equivalent labor in higher-wage cities as more input. Were we to measure only labor productivity, we could simply use labor hours alone. We need to convert hours into dollars so that we may add it to other types of inputs.

A second important category of inputs is capital, in this case the plant's machinery and equipment.[4] Capital is not a particularly large component of cost in this production process, so its treatment has little impact on our findings. For simplicity, we assume that the annual cost of capital at each site is 15% of the gross book value of capital at the site.[5] This is a larger figure than depreciation since it assumes a longer asset life and includes a return-on-investment component.

Materials—food, beverages, ice, napkins—are billed through at cost directly to the customer. Therefore they do not create any real variation in performance. We do not include materials as an input, nor does the bill-through revenue affect our measure of output.

We therefore calculate our index of real input as

$$\text{Input} = W_A \text{ (labor hours)}_i + .15 \text{ (gross book value)}_i$$

where

$$W_A = \text{the networkwide average wage}$$
$$\text{labor hours}_i = \text{total labor hours at site } i$$
$$\text{gross book value}_i = \text{the gross book value of the equipment and vehicles at site } i$$

Productivity Index

Once real input and real output have been defined, productivity at a site i is simply their ratio:

$$\text{productivity}_i = \frac{\text{Output}_i}{\text{Inputs}_i}$$

$$= \frac{p_m \Sigma^n \text{(meals)}_{ij} \, C_{mj} + \Sigma^m \text{(setups)}_{ik} \, C_{sk}}{W_A \text{ (labor hours)}_i + .15 \text{ (gross book value)}_i}$$

Expressed in words, our productivity measure is standardized output divided by the sum of labor costs at a standard wage and an estimate of capital costs. In its simplest terms, the measure reflects how good a plant is at turning inputs, primarily labor hours, into output.

Variation in Network Performance: A First Look

Figure 5-1 presents the productivity index of each plant for the year 1987. We have rescaled the productivity levels so that the average plant has a productivity of one. The indexes in Figure 5-1 have been arranged in order of increasing productivity.

Figure 5-2 shows the profitability of each site. Again, the actual

Figure 5-1   Multifactor Productivity Index

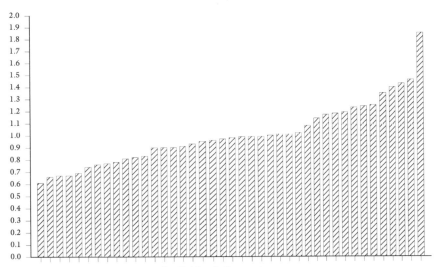

Individual Operations

values have been divided by the mean to give an index assigning a value of one to the average plant. The profitability indexes are arrayed in the same order as the productivity indexes in Figure 5-1. It is clear that while productivity and profitability are correlated (with a simple correlation of .677), the variations in price and wage do create a different picture of relative performance. The importance of this fact, as it relates to identifying the "best" plants, will be returned to below.

The most striking point about Figure 5-1 is the enormous variation in plant performance. Bear in mind that all sites are within the United States, all employ low-skilled labor, all utilize the same technology, and all serve similar if not identical customers and produce similar if not identical products. In short, this network should exhibit less variation than that found in most industries. Yet the most productive plant appear to be three times as productive as the least productive plant. The top-rated plant is over 80% above the mean; the bottom-rated plant is almost 40% below.

A variety of forces may account for the degree of variation exhibited among plants in this network, even with their considerable similarity of products and processes. One major consideration is the *size* of the operation. Some kitchens have up to eight times the square footage and produce up to nine times the meals of their smallest coun-

Figure 5-2 Profitability Index
(in order of increasing productivity)

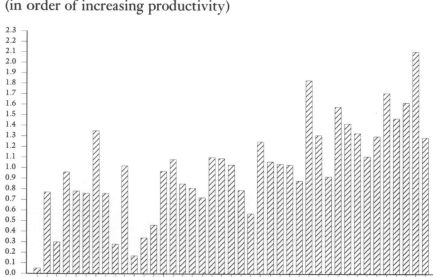

Individual Operations

terparts. This variation in size could create variation in performance. One must be careful in suggesting that size should affect performance, however, because causation could run in the other direction: performance could affect size. The better kitchens could be expected to grow more rapidly than their poorer counterparts. Perhaps we should say that the size of the local market affects performance and that the size of the local market, and performance, determine plant volume.

Although all the plants are in the United States and all employ low-skilled labor, there is a regional variation in *work force* characteristics. This variation may also be a source of differences in plant productivity. Similarly, although all the technology is fundamentally the same, differences in the *amount and age of equipment* may affect performance.

Even if all the sites were identical in terms of size, work force, and amount and age of equipment, variations in performance could still arise from certain environmental characteristics. If local markets value supplier attributes differently—if one market places a premium on quality and another on cost, for example—local managers might respond by trading off one attribute for another. In effect, the plants might have different *plant missions*.[6] If trade-offs differ as plants pursue different missions, then variation in our one-dimensional performance measure may simply reflect different choices among the different objectives. In other words, one plant may be less productive because it chose to be less productive while pursuing quality. Another important environmental characteristic is the presence of competitors. As noted earlier, if a plant has a local *monopoly*, management may slack off in terms of new-idea creation and adoption.

An additional, serendipitous component to performance exists, which cannot be captured by looking at size, work force, amount and age of equipment, plant mission, and monopoly. Ideas pop up more frequently or with greater impact at some sites than at others. Better management may have created an environment that promotes innovation, or perhaps one plant simply has more creative people. These localized *innovations* should affect plant performance. Some of these ideas are procedural; one plant developed a more efficient reference sheet distributed to workers at the beginning of a shift. Another plant instituted the use of colored dots to date meals. Some ideas involve technology; one plant developed a faster, safer loading dock ramp, another modified existing equipment to slice orange peels faster. Local innovations will affect plant performance, but they will increase variation only if they remain localized.

We now attempt to estimate variation due to implementation of local innovations by estimating (using regression analysis) the portion of the cross-plant productivity variation due to size, work force, amount and age of equipment, plant mission, and monopoly. A significant portion of the variation that remains after controlling for these factors should be due to local innovation in management practices, procedures, and equipment, much of which could potentially be transferred to other sites. After estimating the magnitude of the variation, we turn to the question of why such large interplant variation in performance still remains, implying that local innovations have not been successfully transferred from plant to plant.

Variation in Network Performance: Controlling
for Structural Variation

For our purposes, structural variables reflect site characteristics that are almost entirely beyond the plant manager's control. They are characteristics that are part and parcel of the decision to open a plant in a given area. Two of the factors discussed above fall into this category: the size of the local market and the characteristics of the local labor force.

Industry sources provide an accurate estimate of the institutional food market in each plant's region, supplying us with one key variable. It is likely that the size of the local market will affect productivity, but the direction of the effect is less clear. If economies of scale are important, then plants located in larger markets should be more efficient. However, increased volume can increase managerial problems. This may be especially true in an environment with pronounced peaks in demand and an inability to store the product for more than a few days without spoilage. If size-related managerial problems are significant, the plants located in larger markets may be less efficient.

The work force characteristics of greatest concern to managers are the plant's turnover rate and whether the work force is unionized. The managers are unequivocal in their expectations regarding the impact of these factors on performance. Turnover is a continual problem in the low-paying, low-skill jobs that characterize much of the work in these plants. In spite of the low skill required, there is still a learning curve associated with these jobs. Each customer account has different requirements. As workers gain experience, they are able to produce meals and set up customers with less referral to the often incomplete account descriptions.

Although labor's decision to unionize is clearly not independent of managerial actions, once a union is in place, it is likely to remain in place for a number of years. Unions, like turnover, are seen as negatively affecting plant performance. We are not referring to the increased wages unions may have negotiated. Because we have used the networkwide average wage, local wage rates, while affecting costs, do not affect our measure of productivity. The key union-related issue that the firm's managers focus on is strict interpretation of work rules, which can make it difficult to meet the last-minute changes in the number of meal orders that characterize this industry.

These managerial concerns reflect two work force variables, in addition to the size of the local market, that characterize the nontransferable structural factors faced by management. The first work force variable is the local unemployment rate to capture local labor conditions and to proxy for the exogenous turnover rate. The plant's actual turnover rate is to some extent endogenous, that is, it is affected by potentially transferable management actions making it unattractive as a structural variable. The second work force variable is a sim-

Table 5-1 Controlling for Structural Variation
(Dependent variable: log of multifactor productivity)

Independent Variables	Estimated Coefficient	Standard Error	Probability of Sign Error
Constant	.357	.330	.14
Log of city market size	−.063	.031	.03
Local unemployment rate	.060	.021	.00
Union dummy	−.147	.076	.03
$R^2 = .33$			

ple dummy variable to characterize whether or not a plant is unionized.

Using ordinary-least-squares regression, we can estimate the effect of these structural variables on multifactor productivity. Regression results are shown in Table 5-1. The model frequently uses the log value of some variables. The use of logs creates a diminishing effect as the variable's value increases.[7] In this way, effects are driven by percentage changes rather than absolute changes. The model is thus structured so that a 10% increase in a logged variable will have an X% impact on productivity.

The work force variables show the expected signs. High unemployment rates (associated with lower turnover rates) are associated with improved performance. This positive relationship is significant if above the 1% level, as suggested by a probability of sign error of .004.[8] The union dummy, significant at the 5% level, is negative.

The size variable, the log of the total meal and setup sales in city market in dollars, is negatively associated with productivity, suggesting that diseconomies dominate economies of scale in this environment.[9] This is not surprising. The technology of cooking a wide variety of meals does not lend itself to dramatic scale economies. Omelettes are made by an individual, one dozen at a time, each omelette in its own skillet. Increasing the number of omelettes produced simply means that each worker will work longer at omelette making. The task does not lend itself to further subdivision, nor is there a technology-based solution applied anywhere in the company.

While these coefficient estimates are interesting, the key result here is not in the coefficient estimates or even in their signs. The key fact in Table 5-1 is the R^2. The structural variables, while significant, account for only one-third of the variation in the log of productivity across the plants. The bulk of the variation is due to other factors.

Variation in Network Performance:
The Impact of Equipment

Plant managers are constrained by more than the local market and work force. They must also get network management's permission to invest in new equipment. If new equipment is not distributed uniformly, differences in the amount and vintage of equipment will arise among plants, and these differences may affect performance. It is important to understand the role equipment plays in determining performance variation. If superior performance comes from buying new equipment, then network management can eliminate interplant performance variation by manipulating financial flows (buying equipment) rather than by the more difficult task of controlling the flow of information.

As Table 5-2 shows, however, superior performance cannot simply be purchased from equipment suppliers. In Table 5-2, we add the log of gross book value divided by net book value of equipment as a proxy measure of asset age, not quantity. The positive coefficient, significant at the 5% level, implies that the plants with newer assets (having lower gross/net ratios) will have poorer productivity than those with older assets (higher gross/net ratios).[10]

The negative impact of new equipment on plant performance is not as surprising as it might seem. Similar relationships have been found in a variety of industry settings.[11] New equipment requires a lengthy period of debugging and adjustment. During this period, the new equipment may be an efficiency-impairing bottleneck requiring a disproportionate amount of management attention. Problems of adapting to newly installed equipment are especially difficult in this environment, where workers are low skilled, receive little training and, in many cases, do not speak English. Lessons learned in adjusting to new equipment are another example of information that should be shared across the network.

The impact of the local unemployment rate changes when the equipment age variable is added. The estimated coefficient changes from .060 (Table 5-1) to .033 (Table 5-2), suggesting that the division has been investing relatively more in low-unemployment-rate areas. At first glance, this policy makes perfect sense. Where labor is hard to get and hold (low unemployment), we are automating. The problem is that high-turnover plants are the plants most likely to have the greatest difficulty in learning to properly use new equipment; often, trained, knowledgeable people may leave, requiring additional train-

Table 5-2   The Impact of Equipment
(Dependent variable: log of multifactor productivity)

Independent Variables	Estimated Coefficient	Standard Error	Probability of Sign Error
Constant	.203	.315	.26
Log of city market size	− .059	.029	.03
Local unemployment rate	.033	.023	.08
Union dummy	− .111	.073	.07
Log gross/net book value	.255	.101	.01
R^2 = .43			

ing for new operators. Some of the equipment purchased may simply have been a bad investment. Concerns about new equipment reliability have led some kitchens to keep staffing levels high. (If new equipment breaks down at a critical time, this eliminates labor savings.) Some of the new equipment, in the field for over a year, has never even been unwrapped. These bad investments may reflect the lack of actual operating knowledge possessed by divisional staff members who evaluate and authorize equipment purchases.

Two immediate cautions arise regarding the interpretation of the estimated coefficient on the equipment age. The first is that age and level of assets may be intermingled here. This can be tested for in a straightforward manner, either by replacing the log of the gross/net ratio with the log of the gross stock or by adding the log of the gross stock to the estimating equation of Table 5-2. Neither of these approaches changes the interpretation that new assets reduce productivity. The gross (or net) stock in place of the gross/net ratio results in a negative coefficient estimated for the gross (or net) stock. Neither the gross nor the net stock are statistically significant if added to the Table 5-2 equation. It would seem, therefore, that it is the newness of the assets that creates the problems. The quantity of assets does not affect the basic "newer assets mean poorer performance" relationship.

A second concern is the direction of causality. Perhaps the phrase "newer assets mean poorer performance" should read "poorer performance means more new assets." The firm may buy new equipment for its bad plants in an effort to make them better performers. We explored this in discussions with managers and by replacing the gross/net ratio with equipment expenditures made in 1987. If managers were investing more heavily in the problem plants, then we should see a negative relationship between performance and the level of equipment expenditures. Both tests suggest that the relationship is, in fact, "newer assets mean poorer productivity." Management did not believe they were investing relatively more in problem plants, and 1987 equipment purchases did not show a statistically significant negative correlation when included as a replacement for the gross/net ratio in the equation of Table 5-2.

The plant's problems in adjusting to new equipment are consistent with problems seen in a number of industries (see Note 10). The implications for network management are clear. The firm cannot eliminate plant-to-plant productivity variation with a checkbook; the variation is not due to new, superior equipment at some sites. This leaves plant mission, monopoly, and innovation as primary sources to explain the 57% of the performance variation that remains.

Variation in Network Performance: Strategic Choices

As noted earlier, some plants may be less productive because of different missions. Some may have chosen to emphasize quality over productivity. Although the plants serve many of the same national customers, regional variation may still occur to meet a given customer's needs, and plant managers may have made decisions to reflect this variation. Our discussions with managers, however, suggest that this is not the case, but completeness requires that it be tested.

Table 5-3 shows the result of adding a dummy variable for superior quality to the equation of Table 5-2. This assessment is based on customer ratings. A dummy is used because no consistent, continuous variable was available. Contrary to the asserted quality-efficiency trade-off, the positive coefficient suggests that the highest-quality shops are 12% more productive than the average-quality shops. Far from making a strategic trade-off, plants that know how to produce more efficiently are also able to achieve better quality. Other coefficients remain effectively unchanged.[12]

Residual Variation

As discussed earlier, a plant manager enjoying a local monopoly may lack the incentives needed to improve on efficiency, especially if internal incentives also fail to reward efficiency. In Table 5-4, a dummy variable testing for the presence of a local monopoly appears to be

Table 5-3 Strategic Choices
(Dependent variable: log of multifactor productivity)

Independent Variables	Estimated Coefficient	Standard Error	Probability of Sign Error
Constant	.241	.305	.22
Log of city market size	− .065	.029	.01
Local unemployment rate	.036	.022	.06
Union dummy	− .113	.070	.06
Log gross/net book value	.232	.099	.01
Superior quality dummy	.121	.064	.03
$R^2 = .49$			

negatively related to performance, as predicted by our earlier discussion. The coefficient is only weakly significant (at the 10% level), but its magnitude is potentially quite large. Plants with local monopolies are, on average, 15% less productive than plants in competitive locations.

Again, even after adding additional explanatory variables, significant (51%) unexplained variation remains. We have introduced enough variables that we might be advised to look not at the simple R^2 but at the R^2 corrected for degrees of freedom.[13] Furthermore, the presence of the quality variable, a performance measure, may have inflated R^2. One could even begin to argue that the presence of three dummy variables in Table 5-4 may be overidentifying a handful of points, giving an inflated picture of the ability of the equation to explain the variation it accounts for. It is possible, then, that the R^2 overstates the amount of variation actually explained.

Yet, we have only accounted for roughly half the plant-to-plant variation. As shown in Figure 5-3, the absolute amount of variation has been significantly reduced by controlling for the effects of size, work force characteristics, age of equipment, plant mission, and monopoly's influence. But the remaining variation is still quite large. In dollar terms, it represents tens of millions of dollars in lost opportunity. If the below-average plants can be brought up to average performance (a conservative goal given that several plants are performing at 30–40% above average), total network profits will be increased by over 20%.

The high performance of some of the plants represents the development of innovative new practices that appear to have dramatically enhanced performance. In our field visits to top performers, we

Table 5-4   Local Monopolies
(Dependent variable: log of multifactor productivity)

Independent Variables	Estimated Coefficient	Standard Error	Probability of Sign Error
Constant	.649	.420	.07
Log of city market size	− .101	.038	.01
Local unemployment rate	.041	.022	.04
Union dummy	− .095	.071	.09
Log gross/net book value	.183	.104	.04
Superior quality dummy	.120	.063	.03
Local monopoly dummy	− .157	.113	.09
R^2 = .51			

saw unique work assignments, equipment modifications, site-specific documentation, and so on, which personnel from elsewhere in the firm believe contribute significantly to performance improvement. We cannot say why one plant came up with an idea that other plants missed. Perhaps they were simply lucky in the caliber of employees. We can, however, comment on why the know-how in this network tends to remain localized, and it is the localization of ideas that causes much of the variation we see here.

THE PERSISTENCE OF VARIATION

The evidence in the last section shows that multifactor productivity varies significantly within the network. Assuming our measures to be correct, the difference between the most- and least-productive unit is on the order of 3:1. Even after controlling for a variety of structural and other characteristics, we still find large differences in performance on the order of 2:1. Discussions with managers and our experience with plant networks studied over longer periods of time suggest that plant-to-plant variation is not a transient phenomenon and, in fact, has persisted for a number of years.[14]

The persistence of sizable differences in productivity suggests that opportunities exist for significant improvement in overall firm performance and reflects factors other than those included in the model. The persistence of large differences in productivity within the network is all the more intriguing once we recognize that the firm in question has been very successful, and, at least compared with other competitors in its industry, is regarded as exceptionally well managed.

Figure 5-3   Actual-to-Expected Productivity

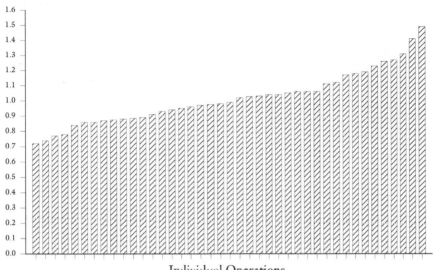

Individual Operations

The firm has been highly profitable, its sales and market share have been growing, and it is known in the industry for providing high quality at a competitive price. Why, then, has it missed the opportunity to improve performance by sharing productivity-enhancing knowledge among its many sites?

The reasons are complex and interrelated. We focus on four: the values and beliefs that guide management of the network, measurement systems, incentives, and staff functions. We shall examine each element individually, but what is most critical is the way in which they reinforce one another. Thus, throughout the discussion, we will identify important interactions among values and beliefs, measurements, incentives, and the role of the staff.

Culture of the Network

The management of the network is rooted in a set of beliefs and values about the nature of production, the character of customers, and the sources of high performance. Through interviews with managers within the network and through review of documented behavior, we have identified three basic beliefs that strongly influence the policies and practices managers use in directing the network.

1. *Plants are unique.* Since the founding of this firm in 1930, managers have believed that each plant faces unique circumstances and therefore poses unique managerial problems. In the early days, success depended on meeting the needs of the local customer regarding service and quality and not cost. For customers, meal costs were a small part of overall operating cost, and their own product markets allowed for significant pass-through of any costs incurred because of meals. The net effect was that priority in this firm was placed on meeting local demands for quality and service. Thus, the dominant focus of network management was the successful operation of a locally determined mission. With diverse customers and a focus on the local needs of those customers, it is but a small step to the belief that each plant is unique. That belief has persisted to this day, despite significant changes in the customer base and despite the innumerable common activities that now exist across today's sites. While all plants have unique features, their core business activities are strikingly similar.

2. *Managers are unique.* The belief that each plant is unique has been accompanied by the belief that each manager is unique. When the senior management of the firm speaks of the challenges posed by the various plants and the kinds of managers that are likely to meet them, it focuses not on aspects of the job that are common but on peculiarities of the local situation that call for unique characteristics. Thus, in reviewing managerial personnel with senior management, one executive remarked that while plant manager one was quite effective in Dallas, plant manager one was unlikely to be particularly effective in a much smaller operation such as that in Rochester, NY. While each manager is a unique individual, one would expect that certain managerial concepts and skills should be effective in more than one plant.

3. *The key to high performance is matching managers and plants.* With a belief that plants and managers are unique, the notion that performance comes from matching the right manager to the right plant is a natural and logical conclusion. This belief has a number of interesting implications. For example, if matching is the critical determinant of performance, there is little reason to engage in management development of a general sort. In fact, within this firm, managers rarely receive formal training or edu-

cation. The implicit assumption has been that managers, and potential managers, have inherent characteristics that need to be matched with environments in which those characteristics will be effective. The second implication has to do with personnel transfer. If managers and plants are unique, once one has found a good match—and a good match is recognized through the excellent performance of the plant—there is no incentive or reason to change or move the plant manager. In fact, with the exception of staffing new sites, plant managers move primarily because of a mismatch. Thus, personnel transfer, which might otherwise be a source of new ideas moving in the network, may have somewhat the opposite effect. The most mobile managers may be those who have not been effective.

The belief that plants and managers are unique reinforces a disregard for the problems of transferring know-how within a network. Clearly, if each plant is unique, variation is normal, and one plant cannot learn from another. The analysis in the previous section and evidence from our field work, however, show that many opportunities exist for transferring know-how within the firm. One incident illustrates this point well. A manager from a southeastern, one-customer, declining-volume plant visited the site of a rapidly growing, multi-customer plant in the northeast. According to the fundamental beliefs governing the network, the southeastern manager should not have been able to learn much from the northeastern operation. In spite of the significant differences between the two plants, however, in the space of one brief plant tour, the southeastern manager identified five different innovations to implement in his operation. Three had to do with equipment and two with managerial procedures. Our discussions with the manager suggested that he expected relatively significant improvements from these ideas, even though he spent no more than a couple of hours walking through the plant.

The southeastern manager's experience is but one example of many that came to light during this study. Simple, but effective, procedures such as checklists were being used at only some of the kitchens. Dozens of inexpensive adaptations of existing technologies had been developed at individual sites but had not been widely adapted in spite of their proven effectiveness. Many of these devices and practices had been previously identified as valuable by corporate staff. However, memoranda on them sent out by corporate staff to the plants had not been adopted. Plant managers must have assumed that innovations developed elsewhere were unlikely to be effective in their locations.

Thus, fundamental beliefs about uniqueness have driven the firm to meet the requirements of the local customer but have limited the flow of know-how within the network. These fundamental values permeate the organization and its management. They influence the way performance is measured, the incentives governing managerial action in the plants, and the role of the staff.

Performance Measurement

Given a culture that emphasizes the uniqueness of each operation, it is not surprising that few attempts have been made to develop uniform networkwide performance measures. The network managers focus on profitability as their measure of facility performance. But, given the use of unique local prices, the most profitable operations are not necessarily the plants where process knowledge resides. Focusing on profitability obscures the detection of those factors affecting productivity. Figure 5-4 makes this point clearly. The top graph shows the plants ranked by profitability. This is how network management ranks the plants. But the second diagram shows the multifactor productivity of the plants arrayed in the same sequence as the top figure, that is, in order of profitability. The difference between the profitability and productivity graphs reflects the impact of price variations across the network.

Even more striking is the actual-to-expected productivity data shown in the third diagram. This graph shows the performance of each plant after controlling for the structural and other variables of Table 5-4. (The plant sequence is, once again, identical to the order in the other two graphs.) A high, actual-to-expected productivity index suggests that the plant manager is able to achieve relatively more with the market, work force, and assets he or she has been given. A low index (below one) suggests that the plant manager is not achieving the level of performance one would expect based on that site's market, work force, and assets.

We believe that at least some portion of unusually high performance represents ideas that can be transferred to other sites. Some portion of the below-par plant's poor performance can be eliminated if the high performer's practices and ideas are adopted. Yet if network managers go only to the high-profitability plants for insight into good

Figure 5-4 Profitability Index

Profitability Index

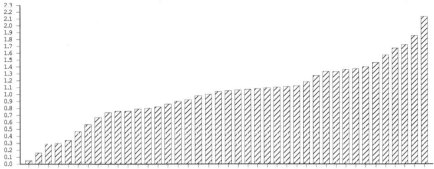

Individual Operations

Multifactor Productivity Index (in order of increasing profitability)

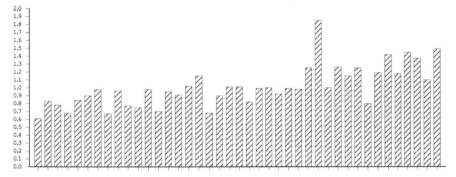

Individual Operations

Actual-to-Expected Productivity Controlling for Structural Factors
(in order of increasing profitability)

Individual Operations

management practices, they will miss a number of outstanding sites and may collect information from some below-average sites. Based on profitability alone, they may also miss some significant opportunities to improve the plants where productivity is low but profits are satisfactory.

Why is network management unable to see the lesson shown in Figure 5-4? First, it is not really looking for it. With plants that are unique, variation is natural and inherent, and network managers worry little about comparability. However, even when some of the staff have sought to create comparable measures, they ran into obstacles.

The firm has historically used man-minutes per meal and a separate man-hours per setup figure as a productivity measure. But, it was widely recognized in the firm that the site-to-site variation in meals and setups preclude using this figure for plant comparisons. Indeed, period-to-period changes in mix make it impossible for a plant to track meaningfully even its own performance over time. In order for a comparable performance measure in this firm to be credible, it has to be based on equivalent meals. Getting equivalent meals-data involves calculating the complexity of meals, customer by customer, at each local site (a time-consuming computation). Many managers know that the current productivity data are inherently incorrect and, being disinclined to compare facilities to begin with, choose to ignore any attempts to create comparable measures of performance. Thus, a variety of plants within the network simply does not collect the relevant data for computing equivalent meals. Some plant managers recognize the potential value of the data, but can not compute performance measures for other plants. Thus, the equivalent meals-data are fundamentally incomplete, and the firm is faced with a classic Catch-22: the financial staff does not attempt to get complete data because no one is using them; and no one uses them because they are incomplete.

Incentives for Plant Managers

Good organizational design requires that local managers have incentives to internalize the firms' goals.[15] Transfer of know-how in a network depends on the willingness of critical players in the network, like plant managers, to invest time in transferring know-how to other sites and to assist them in its application. In this company, the compensation system would appear, at least on the surface, to motivate plant managers to seek know-how transfer. Compensation includes a bonus calculated as a percentage of base pay; moreover, the bonus percentage awarded to plant managers is based on their performance against objectives and division profits.

While this arrangement could provide significant incentives for improvement, in practice, little incentive exists. First, senior management recognizes that current measures of performance do not identify plant managers performing above expectations. The performance measurement system provides little basis for determining which plant managers have done well relative to other managers. Furthermore, while each plant manager has a set of annual objectives to meet, those objectives are framed in the most general of terms. Because each plant manager's situation is assumed to be unique, the tendency has been for senior management to rate plant managers similarly. In fact, our review of performance ratings by plant shows that, in 1987, each plant manager received an identical rating. Each plant manager's bonus percentage was therefore the same—in spite of significant performance differences in profitability and productivity.

The compensation system reinforces the view that each plant is unique. The compensation system, as it is managed and practiced, dulls any incentive managers have for improving overall performance of the firm. One can still argue that, because the bonus is related to overall division profitability, actions that improve overall profitability will improve plant manager compensation, even if all plant managers receive the same share. Our discussions with senior managers and managers within plants, however, suggest that the relationship between know-how transfer and division profitability is perceived as indirect at best and not a driving force in their behavior. The overwhelming sentiment expressed by a number of plant managers and senior management personnel was that overall division profitability is dramatically affected by pricing and by customer relationships. While quality and service were perceived by management to be critical to division profitability, they saw much less connection between improving productivity performance and division profitability. Thus, any personal incentive to achieve excellence is undercut by the firm's focus on profitability, a measure dramatically affected by pricing decisions that are beyond the plant manager's control.

Staff Functions

It is possible for improvement to come even without incentives or a measure to identify the best-managed plants if the network staff has sufficient expertise to identify and communicate new management practices. Two groups in this firm could potentially fulfill this role: the central quality staff and the technology staff.

The quality staff plays an auditing and advisory role. It focuses, of course, on quality, and it has accomplished significant transfer of ideas about quality. However, our investigations into specific quality-related, know-how transfers revealed that the customer has been the most important source of quality insight and information. Although the quality staff travels regularly to review quality issues, information about which operations are performing at high levels and which operations need improvement comes from the customers rather than from the internal staff. Customers who have multiple operations served by the firm compile data on their perception of the firm's performance at different sites. That information is transferred to the firm for its use and review. The internal quality staff has developed no base of data on which to judge performance, nor do they have the internal skills necessary to identify high from low performance. Their primary role has been to represent the interests and concerns of the customer to the various sites and, to a lesser extent, to transfer know-how about quality performance from site to site.

In order for the quality staff to play an important role in transferring know-how about productivity, it must be able to recognize good practice. Unfortunately, there are no systems of measurement that allow it to identify good practice, nor is the quality staff particularly knowledgeable about plant operations. It is primarily trained for and knowledgeable about customer needs and has little experience in kitchen management—experience necessary to identify and transfer effective practices from plant to plant.

The technology group is the other staff group that could play a centralized information-transfer role. But the technology staff's role is to monitor the equipment technologies being developed outside the firm and to inform managers about what is available. Attempts by the technology staff to more actively transfer know-how in equipment operation—e.g., through a suggestion system—have run into the same problems encountered in attempts to create equivalent meals-data: indifference, lack of credible data, and a belief that only local ideas have local value.

Human resource staff could potentially transfer information through training or personnel assignments. As noted earlier, these opportunities are not exploited by this firm.

Future of the Network

We have painted a picture of a network fundamentally incapable of satisfying the basic conditions for reducing plant-to-plant variation in productivity. The most remarkable thing about this network is the self-reinforcing, self-sustaining nature of the managerial practices and procedures within it. Incentives to encourage creation or application of new ideas from outside the plant do not exist in this network. Meaningful incentives to motivate creation, transfer, and application of know-how are difficult to create without measures that identify good performance. Furthermore, the plant managers have little mutual contact to promote communication and would not know whom to call if they were looking for knowledgeable sites. The beliefs that govern the culture of the network reinforce the search for local solutions to local problems. Staff personnel are not familiar with plant practices and thus can neither create, identify, nor communicate innovations. Plant managers are compensated equally, with no incentives to transfer knowledge or know-how across the network. The system of performance measurement and compensation, the nature of the staff support groups, and personnel policies reinforce the view of the network as a collection of independent units with little to say to one another.

It would be wrong to assume that the network we have described is the result of perverse thinking on the part of senior management. In fact, this network has been extremely successful in accomplishing the basic mission laid out for it in the early days of the firm. That mission was to provide a very high level of quality and service to local customers in an environment where costs were insignificant. Over time, good ideas about improving local operations have essentially remained within the local units. In the current environment, however, cost has become a much more important part of competition. Moreover, competitors have begun to achieve comparable levels of service and quality. The net effect has been a fundamental rethinking of the operations side of the business, and a search for improvement in performance has begun.

Our analysis underscores the difficulty of changing the network. No single change will be sufficient. Appropriate systems for measurement and compensation, redefinition of the roles of the staff, new programs for training, and new organizational structure can influence the transfer of information. Before these changes are made, the firm should make some fundamental decisions about the architecture of the network. The challenge is not simply to effect a wholesale shift in emphasis away from quality to productivity, but rather to achieve improved quality while at the same time dramatically improving productivity. This requirement is similar to the situation facing a wide variety of firms and industries subjected to intense international competition. The issues surrounding the network we have described may therefore provide insights of more general value.

THE ARCHITECTURE OF
MANAGED NETWORKS

First and foremost, network managers need to recognize their obligation to manage information flows with at least as much attention as they manage physical flows. Some productivity variation among plants is inevitable, but innovative management practices that remain localized represent a major potential source of interplant variation and a major opportunity cost.

We see two core decisions in the design of an information network that will shape the plant manager's willingness to create and apply new innovations and the network's ability to identify and transfer these innovations. The first is the question of how *competitive or cooperative* the network will be. In a competitive network, plants and plant managers are rated against one another. Compensation and decisions regarding which units receive investment dollars, which are used as pilot sites, where customers are taken on tour, who gets promoted, whether plants are rank ordered, and so on can serve to create powerful managerial incentives if they present a common message about which managers are better than others. In a cooperative network, the well-being of the plant and its manager are not explicitly linked to comparative success. Instead, the corporation rewards managers for their contributions not only to their own plant's performance but to advances in the firm generally.

The competitive network gives plant managers incentives to excel. Those found to be below par will have a particular incentive to hustle. Thus the competitive design is particularly well adapted to environments where each plant is a local monopolist. It can replace the competitive incentives that are not coming from outside the firm.

An obvious implementation problem exists for a competitive system, however. Managers have to be rated and compared by some specific quantitative system. Otherwise, incomplete subjective data will be used; but such data cannot substitute for the clear incentives that come with outside competition. Managers will need to understand the system in some detail. For example, lagging managers will need to understand why they are lagging. If the quantitative measures of managerial performance are not true to the managers' performance, the system can go badly wrong. Managers will either ignore the system or strive to improve their performance along the direction in which they are measured, not in the direction that will improve overall corporate profitability. The successful implementation of a competitively based system demands a high-quality, quantitative plant performance measurement tool.

A more subtle point about the competitive system should not be missed. We argued above that a critical part of the problem of network management is obtaining the cooperation of managers in information transfer. What are the incentives for a successful manager in a competitive network? A purely competitive system gives no strong incentive to communicate ideas to others; in fact, it promotes the reverse. If some improvement in managerial practice places a plant out in front, the plant manager will be rewarded until the other plants achieve the same gains. Communicating the improvement to other plants simply shortens the period of time in which the manager is rewarded for being out in front. Thus, pure competitiveness can inhibit information flow.

Of course, the answer to this problem is to give the plant manager a positive incentive to cooperate, or at least to remove the negative one. But this implies modifying the competitive compensation scheme.

This trade-off makes the competition/cooperativeness choice a fundamental one. If senior management gives competitive incentives by measuring plants in a relative way, it will necessarily dampen the incentive to cooperate. Thus, an ideal network in most circumstances will not be fully competitive. On the other hand, if the network gives incentives only to cooperate, it will lose the opportunity to provide guidance to poor plants and may lessen the incentive for local managers to search out and implement productivity-improving actions. Thus, the ideal network in most circumstances will not be fully cooperative either.

Where along this continuum the firm chooses to position itself will shape the nature of network management's challenges. In the competitive network, network management must design accurate performance measures and identify and communicate outstanding management practices. In the cooperative network, network management must work to encourage the creation of innovative practices and promote their adoption. In effect, the firm must select a position on the competitive/cooperative continuum and then manage against its weaknesses by balancing the incentives created by compensation, promotion, investment, and the multitude of other factors influencing plant management's behavior.

The second core decision in designing the architecture of the network is to determine which functions will be *centralized or decentralized*. Just as physical flows can be determined at a centralized or decentralized level (through transfer prices and/or decision rules), so information flows can be managed in either fashion. Decentralization is not a laissez-faire approach. It means network management will manage the system, which promotes information flows, rather than manage the information itself. Again, a continuum of managerial choice exists, but, for explication, we will focus on the extreme points. Separate decisions must be made for each of the critical tasks of creation, identification, transfer, and application.

Creation of new management practices can be conducted in a decentralized or centralized fashion. If decentralized creation dominates, network management's key task is to create an environment that encourages innovation. Centralized innovation can be managed more directly as an independent activity. Having a central staff responsible for innovation may be a more efficient way to promote innovation, but efficiency may come at the cost of effectiveness. Innovators who are not involved in day-to-day management may be less likely to develop innovations that will address the plant managers' critical problems effectively.

Identification of good practices requires knowledge not only of the innovation but of existing practices as well. This means a huge amount of detailed information must be exchanged throughout the network. On a decentralized basis, this means plant manager meetings and on-site visits or transfers (an expensive proposal). On a centralized basis, this function can again be performed more efficiently, but the central staff must be able to detect outstanding performance at a distance, placing a premium on an accurate and timely measurement system.

Transfer on a decentralized basis is a by-product of the identification process. On a centralized basis, the staff must either travel extensively and learn to "speak the language" of local managers or learn to write unusually clear memoranda.

Application must be decentralized. While network management can mandate a given procedure, it cannot guarantee that it will be followed. Network management can purchase equipment, but it cannot ensure that plant managers will use it properly or at all. Because innovation so often requires a degree of local adaptation, successful application can only take place at the local level.

Fundamentally, network management faces a choice about which set of information flows it will manage. A decentralized approach means network management must develop incentives and systems to facilitate plant-to-plant information flows. Time spent on information transfer is expensive since a plant manager's time carries a high opportunity cost. Decentralized information transfer is also a process for which it is difficult to assign responsibility. When done well, however, the decentralized approach can effectively minimize plant-to-plant variation.

A centralized approach eliminates costly and difficult to manage plant-to-plant information flows; but in their place, plant-to-network management information flows must exist. Although cheaper, and easier to assign responsibility for, these flows must be carefully managed to ensure that the network staff has a clear picture of what's going on in the plants. Obtaining a clear picture is not an easy task since staff members are not involved in day-to-day operations, and plant managers may have incentives that make them unwilling to divulge everything going on at the plant level.

Neither fully centralized nor fully decentralized approaches are likely to be optimal. As with the choice of cooperation or competition, the best approach is somewhere in the middle, with built-in redundancies. Again, measurement will play an important role. If a central staff group seeks to identify innovations taking place at the local level, it must have information concerning where good ideas are likely to be. If plant managers are going to seek out good practices, they, too, must know where to look. The performance measurement system must fill that crucial need.

CONCLUSIONS

We have looked closely at the causes and consequences of interplant performance variation in a single firm. The variation is large in absolute dollar terms, even after controlling for a variety of differences between the firm's plants and markets. While some performance variation is inevitable, much of the remaining variation can be attributed to potentially transferable management practices.

These potentially transferable management practices remain localized, rather than being broadcasted to other plants where they could be useful. The existing culture of the firm, reflected in the firmly held beliefs of both plant and corporate managers, is an important reason why good ideas stay localized. People believe that sites cannot be compared well. The existing profitability indices are inadequate for spotting well-performing plants. Plant managers not only believe that other managers have nothing to tell them, they also believe that they have nothing to tell other managers. Thus, no well-functioning mechanism exists, either at the corporate level or in the plants, for communicating the good ideas underlying good performance.

The case study suggests that the extent and quality of innovation in the practice and transfer of know-how within a network depends on systems for performance measurement and compensation, on personnel policies, and on the activities of support staff. The policies and practices, in turn, are influenced by the values and beliefs that managers hold about the determinants of performance and the nature of the challenges they face. Moreover, these elements of network management reinforce one another, creating a self-sustaining system. Thus, improving the performance of a network in capturing and applying the know-how within it is likely to require coordinated changes in the elements of the system.

Our experience in a variety of industries suggests that opportunities to improve overall network performance through better management of the flow of information are widespread. Specific actions to improve performance will need to be tailored to the circumstances in specific networks, but important elements that are likely to be generally applicable can be identified. First, any attempt to improve know-how transfer must focus on the measurement system. Measurement is fundamental to the essential task of innovation identification.

Second, the ability of managers to influence information flow depends on the architectural choices about the nature of the network. We have tentatively identified two core decisions that network management faces in designing an effective network; they concern the degree of cooperation versus competition among plant managers and the centralization versus decentralization of information flows. The performance measurement system plays a critical role in both decisions, either facilitating or hindering efforts to promote information transfer.

Our study is merely a first step in exploring intrafirm, interplant performance variation. Researchers and managers must learn to look beyond local performance factors to the performance characteristics of the network as a whole. The tremendous variation that exists in most networks suggests that the importance of the transfer of information is equal to, and sometimes greater than, that of the far more visible flows of physical products.

NOTES

1. One possible solution, using prices to weight meals and setups, is inapplicable in this situation. The weights one would like to use are cost- or input-based weights. If markups differ across types of meals or across sites, then price weights will not closely track cost weights.

2. It should be noted that the company's complexity-index data were incomplete. Some sites had to be dropped as a result, leaving the forty-one plants discussed here. We have been forced to estimate the volume-weighted average complexity adjustment for some shops. This was never done without at least four months' data covering over two-thirds of factory volume. Discussions with managers as well as inspection of our data and results do not suggest any bias due to estimation.

3. Though these indexes do correct for variation in the type of meal and the difficulty of the setup, they do not explicitly account for variations in preparation quality or on-time setup performance. We return to these topics in the regression analysis later in the text.

4. Building and land were not included. They are typically not consumed in production.

5. This implies a fairly long asset life and reflects a roughly equal proportion of asset consumption and carrying costs. This number is, of course, only an estimate of the effective inflation-free capital costs.

6. The plant's mission is defined by the markets and priorities it will pursue. For more on this subject, see R. H. Hayes and S. C. Wheelwright, *Restoring Our Competitive Edge* (New York: John Wiley, 1984).

7. The use of logs in this context also implies that the underlying production function is multiplicative. This is consistent with the vast majority of economic models.

8. The probability of sign error denotes the likelihood that the sign shown on the estimated coefficient is incorrect. The figure .004, for example, means that the chances are 99.6% that high unemployment rates are truly associated with improved performance.

9. A variety of size measures were tested, including sales, employees, and square footage. When significant, the relationship between size and performance was consistently negative.

10. This result is not due to the presence of capital costs in the productivity index. More new assets are associated with less productivity even when only labor productivity is used as the dependent variable.

11. R. H. Hayes and Kim B. Clark, "Exploring the Sources of Productivity Differences at the Factory Level," in Kim B. Clark, Robert H. Hayes, and Christopher Lorenz, eds., *The Uneasy Alliance* (Boston: Harvard Business School Press, 1985): 151–188; W. B. Chew, "Productivity and Change: The Short-Term Effects of Investment on Factory Level Productivity" (Ph.D. diss., Harvard University, 1985).

12. Other strategic choice variables were explored. While they did not have any statistically significant correlation with multifactor productivity, their estimated signs suggest no trade-off between productivity and delivery (measured in terms of percentage on-time) nor between productivity and flexibility (measured in terms of the number of accounts).

13. A variety of other variables were explored, including plant square footage, recent volume trends, customer concentration, local market share, work force turnover, average years of service, management education levels, and number of competitors. These variables were either statistically insignificant, as in the case of square footage, volume, customer concentration, experiences, and education, or represented outcomes where value was determined by other variables in the model, making them poor choices as explanatory variables.

14. See Note 10.

15. See, for example, M. Jensen and W. Meckling, "Theory of the Firm," *Journal of Financial Economics* 3 (1976): 305–360.

CHAPTER 6

Managing for Cost Improvement in Automated Production

Anders Grönlund and Sten Jönsson

INTRODUCTION

W E report the results of the experiences of a three-year case study of local cost control by three production teams in the components company of the Volvo group. Three foremen and their teams were encouraged to manage their own costs with the help of a PC and some administrative support. Outcomes were very promising for one team and mixed in the other two. We pay the most attention to the successful team, trying to explain why it succeeded.

It seems essential to start with projects small enough to give participants a sense that they are in control. When a team has established itself as a respected actor in problem-solving projects, it can achieve great improvement in partnerships with neighboring teams. In this way, cost control efforts can spread throughout the organization, generating competitive advantages that can be exploited in a fine-tuned niche strategy.

The Location of Learning in Industrial Production

Industrial jobs have traditionally been designed to be simple and easy to learn. In our field work, we have frequently heard people reflect about the complete reversal in approach to job design that has recently occurred. Earlier, under the influence of scientific management, the idea was to minimize training costs due to high personnel turnover by making jobs simple; repetitive jobs should be designed so that the man off the street could be in full production in a matter of hours. Now, we have learned that the earlier approach alienates the people who hold those simple jobs and that the supposed solution aggravates the problem. Instead, jobs should be designed to provide variety and challenges. Workers should have opportunities for growth and development.

Still, personnel turnover always occurs; consequently, learning should be organizational as well as personal. Experience should be interpreted and encoded into routines, and this process should be built into the work organization. This integration cannot usefully be done by the accounting staff, since the routines that relate to outcomes are located in local production units. Learning cannot be done by top management since it does not receive the data to interpret. Under scientific management, top management, or rather its engineering staff, can do the encoding since it assigned the routines. (Formerly, management accounting systems provided relevant information [Johnson and Kaplan 1987] because organizational learning occurred centrally.) This study reports how organizational learning and design of routines must be located in the same unit if a steeply sloped learning curve is to be achieved.

Learning Is Not Automatic

In the 1970s (Delionback 1975), the learning curve referred to process improvement in a broad sense. The slope of the curve was generally specified in percentage resource use per unit with measures for every doubling of accumulated experience. The following factors were assumed to contribute to the continual cost reduction:

1. Operator learning
2. Improved methods, processes, tooling, and machines and improvements in design for manufacturability
3. Management learning
4. Debugging of engineering data
5. Rate of production

6. Design of assembly or part or modifications thereto

7. Specification or design of the process

8. Personnel factors such as fatigue, personal matters, or employee morale

9. Materials improvement or discount

Several different "theories" of learning evolved and had one feature in common: learning was assumed to be automatic. It occurred as a volume-dependent effect of production. The only problem with experience curves was how to estimate them. The underlying process was assumed to be mechanical, governed, as it were, by "laws of nature."

Earlier in the late 1960s, the Boston Consulting Group (BCG) considered the experience curve to reflect the combined effect of learning, specialization, investment, and scale. This combination of factors led BCG to postulate a considerably steeper experience curve than is actually observed. However, some additional overhead is introduced by the need to plan and coordinate changes to achieve a steeper experience curve. The curve was considered essentially to be a pattern of cash flow. Therefore, accounting cost data were misleading because of arbitrary classifications of expense versus capital.

Again, the analysis was based on the assumption that learning curves are the same for companies in a given industry if they use the same combination of the factors mentioned above. But, it is clearly wrong to assume that there is a mechanical learning function, derived from experience, that can be estimated once the appropriate amount of data is available. Learning is not a matter of "law" at all. It is a matter of focusing attention, wanting to take the risk of changing habitual behavior, and having access to the relevant information.

It may be customary to write learning requirements into contracts for large-batch deliveries, and this may be viewed as a forecasting problem by the buyer, but for the organization that has to supply it, learning is a long-term struggle.

Learning Is Organizational

It has been maintained that only individuals can learn. The behavioral theory of the firm (Cyert and March 1963), however, introduced the assumption that behavior in organizations is based on routine. Routines have a logic of appropriateness but are not a search for optimal consequences. Routines stabilize behavior. Furthermore, routines are largely developed and maintained through interpretation of the past more than through anticipation of the future. Still, organizations seek profitable outcomes. Judging whether a specific act contributes optimally to the joint outcome of organizational action can be so complex, however, that people resort to crude measures like success-failure or acceptable-unacceptable. Therefore, organizational learning requires that personnel engage in ongoing discussions on what constitutes good performance and how it should be measured.

Levitt and March (1988) argue that organizations learn by encoding inferences from history into routines that guide behavior. These routines include not only rules, roles, habits, and conventions, but also structures, strategies, and the technologies in which beliefs are embedded. In this way routines can be made sufficiently independent of the individual actors to survive personnel turnover.

An organization fortunate enough to have a steeper learning curve than that of competing organizations will have a competitive advantage in importing and implementing new technology. Better learning ability will enable it to solve startup problems and fine-tune equipment to achieve economic capacity quicker than competitors can. One precondition for successful local learning of new technology is that good vertical (central-local) communication occurs within the larger organization. Theories of new technology, as well as the design of production systems, are located with the central engineering staff, but actual observations of the process of production and of anomalies that cause or contribute to breakdowns are made by operators on the shop floor. These observations are particularly important in situations where new technology is introduced, because there is no reliable historic process data for interpreting chains of events. The organization must learn de novo.

If the engineering staff is competent and the competitive situation favors flexibility, the design of the production system will probably consist of a team-oriented organization, with groups managing sets of automated machines performing multiple operations in small batches. Production will be controlled by the inflow of orders from the market rather than by fixed plans. When local learning in an automated context is stressed, there is an increase in the horizontal flow of process information and a decrease in the vertical flow downward from the central management accounting system (MAS). Local learning is particularly useful in mature product areas, like the car industry, wherein competitive advantage (given the design of the product and the structure of the production system) is based on flexibility, productivity, and quality in small-batch production. Flexibility and quality are largely a function of automated production technology, while productivity improvement depends on attention, a will to improve, and relevant performance measurement.

We conducted a four-year experiment on the role of information support by studying three teams in different plants of the Volvo Components Corporation. Since the three teams work differently, it is not possible to give a complete account of all three processes. The experiences and results among the teams differ. At a two-day seminar marking the end of the field study, participants in the experiment unanimously declared that one could not write a manual on how to manage performance improvement of production teams. We, however, believe that some results are generalizable. We realize that on the shop floor, things are concrete, processual, and different; but although it is difficult to abstract from concrete events, and, for example, describe the consequences on accounts of the cost center report, it is not impossible.

UPSTREAMING THE CAR
PRODUCTION PROCESS:
THE FLOBY PLANT

Volvo Components was formed ten years ago as a subcorporation of the Volvo Corporation. It consists of eight production plants, formerly part of the parent company, delivering subassemblies and parts to Volvo's assembly sites. Its main products are engines and gear boxes. During the period of our study, Volvo Components invested heavily in new production technology and operations were at full capacity.

Although Volvo Components is a complete, limited company, it does not have all the normal functions possessed by many independent companies of its size. Product design, marketing, financial work, and some purchasing are performed outside of the subcorporation by the product companies. The Volvo Corporation is organized in a matrix fashion and the product companies (cars, trucks, and so forth) have worldwide responsibility for their output, from design to post-sale service, using a return-on-capital criterion.

A production plant in Volvo Components is subject to pressures from two directions: from the product companies to deliver high-quality parts—flexibly, promptly, and at a low price, without employing more capital than is absolutely necessary; and from Components headquarters to meet a strict cost budget, to be a reliable link in the materials flow, and to maintain a high-quality index.

Volvo Components' goal is to be a leader in the application of new technology to the production process. The threat that the product companies will buy subassemblies elsewhere is always present. Consequently, Components must carefully plan the installation of new technology to avoid production losses due to fine-tuning of new installations. In general, new technology means a higher and more homogeneous output and an opportunity to produce smaller batches economically; but the complexity and interdependence of installations makes downtime costly.

The Site

The main site of our study is the Floby plant, a rather small establishment built in 1957 since expanded, with 185 hourly and 24 salaried employees. The Floby plant produces brake discs for cars and hubs, and brake drums and drive shafts for heavy vehicles. As the figures that follow show, the plant has a fine productivity record. (Added value, or more simply, processing value is used in calculating the productivity index. Inputs as well as outputs are adjusted for price and volume differences and the resulting processing value is related to the standard value. Then the year's index is divided by the prior year's to determine improvement.)

1982	1983	1984	1985	1986	1987
7.4%	5.3%	2.1%	7.7%	8.8%	13.2%

The last three years are those of our experiment. About half the Floby plant is devoted to car brake discs. Our study deals with the responsibility center run by Borje A. His center produces hubs, brake drums, and drive shafts, which constitute the bulk of the rest of the plant's production. Hubs and brake drums are produced in similar lines (turning, drilling, grinding, cleaning, painting, control, and packing) with raw material coming from a foundry. The raw material for the drive shaft is not hardened at the forge. The shaft (with disc) is first turned, then spliced and hardened. After hardening, the shaft is cooled, the unit holes are drilled in the disc, and the unit is ground, balanced, and measured before being packed and sent to another plant for subassembly into back axles.

The production line is primarily numerically controlled (NC) machines coupled to a line with a controlling computer and one or more robots to handle materials. The machines on the shaft line and brake-drum line are about eight years old (a new hub line was installed in 1986). All three lines are run in two shifts, with 2–3 operators per line and shift. About 20 people were directly involved in our study. When we paid our first visit to the plant, we were struck by the low noise level. Most machines arc light green. The place looks tidy.

Borje supervises the three lines. He is a friendly person, keenly interested in improving things. In his younger days he was a mechanic for one of the national auto rally heroes, and this gives him prestige among auto operators. He has worked at the Floby plant since 1974 and had just completed a one-year, full-time production management course given by Volvo Components when we started the project in May 1984.

Magnus H. is Borje's co-partner. He came to the Floby plant in 1981 as a production planner. His duties were extended in a 1983 reorganization to include the management accounting and information systems functions of the plant. Magnus is an independent person with an analytic approach to and a thorough knowledge about operations.

Getting Started

The striking thing about the empirical evidence collected during the three years of the study is the individualistic nature of the observations. They are difficult to describe in abstract terms. We could, of course, give statistics on outputs, productivity, or cost curves, but since we are interested in organizational learning, we prefer to describe the dramatic events behind the improved performance figures. Again, we cannot really describe what actually occurred because we were not there to witness most of the events. We have accounts of what occurred, in the form of stories, and we have been able to observe the outcomes of learning (rather than learning itself). We have, therefore, chosen to use these stories to illustrate what goes on when local managers (operators) identify and do something about performance deficiencies. In this way, we believe we can contribute to a better understanding of what kind of information support best serves team self-management.

It is important to realize the significance of getting started in the right way with early victories. It is also important to realize that outcomes are often indirect and cumulative. What follows is how it went in Floby.

The main idea of the project was learning by doing, and we were anxious to get started without too much planning. Borje wanted to study the use of cutting tools in two lathes on the drive shaft line. Five different cutting tools can be attached to the rotating heads of the lathes. Each tool has a number of cutting edges, and when an edge is worn, quality declines, and they have to be shifted. Cutting tools are tracked by account 631 on the cost center report. Borje and Magnus felt that the standard was too high on tool costs. The team decided to do a manual follow-up on these tools by counting how many drive shafts had been processed for every cutting tool. Four weeks after the start of the project, the first follow-up report was ready. During the three days that the counting took place, the machine group produced 574 drive shafts with 52 cutting tools (the standard for cutting tool consumption was 74.3).

	Cutting Tool					
Tools used	Type 1	Type 2	Type 3	Type 4	Type 5	Total
Standard	22.9	17.2	11.4	11.4	11.4	74.3
Actual	19	14	9	6	4	52
Price/tool	20:00	28:00	15:00	21:00	18:00	
Cost savings compared to standard	78	90	36	113	133	450 skr

Better than standard! But was improvement because of operator awareness of the follow-up being done or because of a change in procedures? Even the question of whether the standard was too high could not be answered with certainty. But it was clear that the follow-up had generated an interest among operators. There was a motivating effect merely from finding out prices and volumes. There was also a welcome side effect: people cleaned out cupboards and reserves that had been stashed away as a buffer in case the materials department ran out of stock. An amazing number of half-empty packages of cutting tools had appeared. People seemed to realize that it was difficult to follow up tool consumption if unused tools were on reserve.

No one was really surprised by the findings of the first follow-up (30% lower cost than standard). People felt that the standard was on the high side. They decided to continue manual follow-ups as a warm-up before the PC, included in the project plan, was installed. "Keep it simple so that we know what we are doing," seemed to be the argument. A new routine had been designed, it worked well, so people started to think about what else could be improved.

Borje and Magnus pointed out to us that sometimes cutting tools were changed, either because there was a new supplier or a new version of the tool. The new procedure could be used to test new tools; when the production technology unit received a new tool, it tested it and took responsibility for its being phased in properly to the materials unit's supply.

The operators also decided to produce statistics on the consumption of all cutting tools during the fall of 1984. These data could be used to set a new standard, but of more importance, they would come in handy in budget discussions to back up claims that the group could meet, say, a 5% cost cutting requirement for the next year, by a specified amount on account 631 (tools). Collecting a larger amount of operating statistics also provided a good argument for the installation of the PC and for operators to attend a course on the PC software.

In 1983, the outcome on the 631 account was close to budget; and the cutting tool cost per shaft was 4.69 skr. During the whole of 1984, cutting tool per shaft costs continued to decline, ending at 3.67 skr per shaft in the last quarter. The budget on the account was 405,300 skr for 1984. Borje accepted a budget of 350,000 skr for 1985, with the same production volume, although the budget should have been revised upward because of an expected price increase of 5.7% on those tools.

This was the start-up phase in the Floby plant. Nothing spectacular was done. There were no lectures and no speeches; there was just a follow-up on cutting tools—a simple, manual counting exercise. The economic effects were astounding; the cutting tool cost had dropped from 4.69 skr to 3.67 skr. Was it that easy? What had really happened? Obviously, the outcome was a result of increased attention and motivation on the part of the operators. No routines had been changed, but a large number of half-empty tool packages had been cleared out of cupboards and shelves. No causal links between activity and costs had been clarified, but the operators' attention had been aroused by collecting information, doing something with that information, and getting quick results.

Sustained Improvement

Productivity has been the principal performance measure in Volvo for as long as most people can remember. It is based on value-added and adjusted for volume and price changes. The calculation of productivity improvement is rather complicated. When we confronted top management with the lack of understanding by operators (or anyone else) about the calculation, we were told that it is not really that important to understand them. The theory was that as long as you realize that you improve productivity by producing more with the same resources or by using less resources to produce the same output, you are on the right track.

If the cost center report says that the budgeted productivity improvement is 4.1% for the year, and the outcome to date is only 3.2%, what should be done? Top management would say, "Try harder!"

Toward the end of 1984, an educational program in cost management for operators was initiated by Borje and Magnus. It consisted simply in going through the cost center reports, explaining some cost concepts, and, where possible, breaking down the budget figures into concrete physical measures and discussing causes of changes. Training the shift teams in cost management was new in Floby. The operators learned two new things: first, Floby management was seriously interested in the follow-up of cutting tools; second, they were asked what they thought about operations. The troubles with the hub line were a case in point. During the latter part of 1984, many stoppages and malfunctions had occurred on the hub line. (It was replaced in 1986.) The maintenance account showed a large negative productivity: 110,400 skr for the last reporting period alone, although the budget for the entire year was set at 60,000 skr. In fact, the whole Floby plant was in the negative on maintenance productivity and the cause was almost exclusively traceable to the hub line. The cost figures and the productivity decline could be related to specific incidents. The incidents could be discussed, and thereby be viewed as controllable. The new approach meant asking operators, "What do *you* think?"

Episodes

Cutting tools continued. During much of 1985, statistics on cutting tool consumption were collected. Several episodes concentrated operators' attention on the turning operation on the shaft line. During the first tests in 1984, they found that they could do, on average, 33 shafts per cutting tool. The first reporting period of 1985 brought 46 shafts per tool, which was 13 better than standard. But, toward the end of period two (week 12), something went wrong. The number of shafts done before the operator had to shift tools went down to 11. A couple of cutting tools were performing well below standard. The operator sounded the alarm. In the following weeks they worked on the problem. Was the raw material too hard? Too soft? Was the machine set right? Was it human error? Production technology could not find an answer. Finally, the team approached the supplier forge and asked what was going on. The supplier said, "Didn't you know? The friction-welded joint between the shaft and the disc is a little harder because of higher quality standards!"

The problem with cutting tools consumption now turned into a question of whether a different tool could cut the joint better than the old tool could. Normally, the standard would have been adjusted to the new situation; now, a period of testing other cutting tools began. During this time, the division manager came to the Floby plant to see how things were going. The operators demonstrated how they had solved the problem. By the time summer vacation started, they had shifted to a somewhat more expensive tool, but it cut an average of 66 shafts before it had to be replaced (the earlier standard was 33!).

Production targets. In the third quarter of 1985, a new wage system was introduced in the Floby plant: operators decided themselves on the production rate they estimated they could maintain during the next six-month period. Under the new system, the rate was based on the piece rates used in production planning. The model was built on the precalculated production time (e.g., 0.166 hours per passed widget) according to the standard. Actual time was divided by the standard for a ratio. The base ratio was 117%, with 125% the highest possible ratio for the first six months. The outcome would set the base for discussions about the next six-month period. The operators received a fixed salary per month but would negotiate every six months to set a new target. Borje and the operators of the three lines he supervised agreed to go for 123% for hubs, 121% for shafts, and 123% for drums. (The outcomes six months later turned out to be 123%, 123%, and 126%, respectively.) On this occasion, Borje asked the operators what they intended to do to meet the production target they had set. This focused attention on how to avoid lost production. Two factors were taken up: rejects and downtime. The drum line initiated a follow-up on rejects, which are classified as M-faults (materials) or P-faults (caused during processing inside the cost center). They managed to reduce M-faults substantially by setting up communication with a supervisor at the supplying foundry and reporting immediately when, for example, sloppy sandblasting in the foundry caused processing problems in the drum line. P-faults remained largely the same (below budget) throughout the period.

It was believed that the other factor, downtime, could be reduced by rationalizing production methods and increasing flexibility. The latter was paid the most attention. It was recognized that the reduced number of operators in the teams created problems: with one person absent, the whole team produced at reduced speed. Furthermore, operators were specialists, which made the teams vulnerable if there were absences. A program was set up to teach every operator how to run the entire line. Breakdowns or setups were used to teach each operator how to operate the machines. The drum line increased its average output from 5.0 drums per time unit in 1984 to 5.6 in 1985, primarily because of reduced downtime and because absences did not cause the problems they had caused previously.

Consequences

The production target episode made operators more willing to take charge of production planning and to assume responsibility for meeting the target. Operators started to call in indirect personnel, such as maintenance people and forklift drivers, without clearing their decisions with the foreman. They also started to sign for indirect materials requested from the materials department. Toward the end of 1985, all three lines received an extra 1% in salary, justified by the increased responsibility of operators.

In preparing (in early fall 1985) the budget estimates for 1986, operators participated in setting estimates for the first time. Some operators were rather passive, others active, and the discussion concerned, account by account, how costs could be controlled and what was a reasonable target figure for next year. Because of the training program Borje and Magnus had initiated, a meaningful discussion could be held and causal chains explored. The amount to budget on account 606 (overtime and shift surcharges) was dependent on unplanned downtime, which sometimes has to be compensated for by extra shifts. By reviewing the outcomes from earlier years, operators could see that machine stoppages caused cost increases on many accounts. It was easy to identify downtime as an important cost driver, but relations were unclear. On the cutting tools account, budgeting was very easy because the team had reliable statistics on cutting tools.

After the budget work was finished, the team decided to stop collecting data on cutting tools consumption and to go into an ad hoc mode, i.e., start a follow-up only if output figures showed that something was wrong.

No End in Sight

We collected a great deal of empirical evidence in this three-year project. It is difficult to account for all the changes that occurred. The actions form causal chains, or rather spirals, whereby one achievement constitutes the basis for a subsequent step. When we stopped observing the process, all three of Borje's lines were better than budget on all indicators. Furthermore, he had been allowed two days a week to design a course in local cost management (at the request of the division head). Borje stated his philosophy in a closing interview: "I want the operators to be driving me instead of my driving them!" So, if any trouble on the hub, shaft, or drum lines arises that the operators cannot handle themselves, they call Borje at home. They can usually agree on what should be done over the phone. He has managed himself out of the supervisory job and is becoming a teacher. The Floby experience will be transmitted to other units through "contagion." If other units want to know what worked in Floby, Borje is ready to tell his story, with good slides and case descriptions, in the tradition of teaching by story-telling. His audiences are always interested because Borje knows his business and his story is about how to be a little smarter and not to work harder than necessary.

Costs and quality. In the meantime headquarters had initiated a "Quality 100" program. Quality 100 means that a product is within tolerance limits on all measurements. Special inspectors take five random pieces from every week's production and perform a number of measurements. On the hub line, there are ten different measures to meet. An "index 100" means all five products are within tolerance on all ten measures. (Measures essential for the functioning of the part are taken on every produced piece.)

Operators are skeptical about the wisdom of some of the quality requirements. Why the obsession with smoothness on the inside of the brake drum? After the brakes have been used ten times, the smoothness is gone anyway! One of the other teams in the study had many cog wheels for gear boxes rejected because normal air dust interfered with the measurements. Were parts for heavy gear boxes to be produced in "clean rooms" or even in a vacuum? The skepticism seems to increase with consciousness about the costs of rejects.

In one instance, the sample from the hub line did not meet measure eight on three of the pieces. That measure concerned the fixture of the piece in one of the machines. The sample measure deviated 62 thousandths of a millimeter from the stipulated measure and the tolerance was 50 thousandths. After some deliberation, the team decided that minuscule metal chips must have stuck on the hubs or the fixture. They decided to rinse all parts as well as the support plate of the fixture. A simple thing to do. They could now keep within tolerances on measure eight. But was it the best possible solution?

For drums there was never a problem in keeping close to the index 100, but for the shaft and hub lines an extra effort during 1988 was required to surpass the index value of 85 that had been reached in 1987. These higher quality requirements can seemingly be met without any significant effects on controllable costs in the teams Borje manages.

Summing Up

The three lines in the study have increased output while decreasing the number of man-hours used. (On the hub line, new machinery was introduced in 1986, but the technological level was not much different). The following figures (pieces per man-hour) have been achieved:

	1984	1985	1986	1987
Hubs	5.05	5.23	6.13	6.76
Shafts	3.66	4.03	4.30	4.71
Drums	5.02	5.60	5.92	5.82

(In 1987, the drum line required a permanent night shift, and some extra weekend shifts had to be used. This increased man-hours proportionally more than it increased production.)

Although crude, these figures indicate a successful cost improvement operation. It is difficult to pinpoint a specific cause or a single decision that brought about the improvement. This was a low-key, every day kind of project—one that will continue and become a way of life in the Floby plant.

THE LINDESBERG PLANT

The Lindesberg plant, employing about 650 people, specializes in producing rear axles for heavy vehicles. It was set up in 1972 and was soon very busy producing tandem axles with reduction gears for heavy trucks. These axles give trucks extra power and the ability to move off roads (e.g., in sand). Reduction gears need many cog wheels. In a few years, however, the demand for reduction gears declined rapidly, mainly because of the cancellation of a large order by the new regime in Iran. When our project started in the summer of 1984, there was overcapacity in cog wheel processing in Lindesberg. This was one of the reasons why the company wanted to include the cog wheel department in the study.

In Lindesberg, some traditional Tayloristic views lingered. These views tended to be strengthened by the overcapacity situation. Managers had mixed feelings about the wisdom of experimenting with self-management at a time when central coordination seemed required to solve problems. Also, a strong centralist was in charge of the computer department serving Lindesberg.

Getting Started

At the first meetings with our team in Lindesberg, the foreman and his second in command clearly identified their most pressing problem: the piece count system. The current system was an old-fashioned time clock one, wherein production orders were stamped in and out and the number of pieces produced registered on the order card.

The team produces straight and conical cog wheels. The wheels are processed in 12, cog-cutting machines (Coniflex machines) that are located in three groups of four machines. The operator is surrounded by four machines and performs the following operations:

- Loading the machine with a turned blank. The machine cuts 10–15 cogs an hour, depending on cog size. The cogs are cooled with oil, which makes the place a bit greasy.

- Stamping an identity number with a hammer and tool on each cog.
- Grinding the cog wheel.
- Packing the wheel in Volvo crates.

Cutting tools are changed by specialists called in by the operators as needed, a process that causes about 20 minutes of downtime. The main part of the operator's job is to load and unload machines, and since one operator serves four machines, there is plenty of loading. The technology of the machine groups is not very advanced, and operators are rated in the lowest wage class. The Coniflex department has been looked upon, and used, as an introductory station on the way to more-advanced jobs in other machine groups. The machines are run in three, six-hour shifts. The standard is 52 minutes an hour of processing time (allowing eight minutes for loading and setup). There are about 15 variants of cog wheels, and the average production order is for 2,000–3,000 pieces. With a machine processing about 12 wheels an hour, each operator produces 288 pieces per shift (six hours, four machines). To get a good balance among the four machines, an operator will normally run 2–3 different variants at the same time. That means there are up to 27 production order cards at the Coniflex department at any one time (three shifts, three operators, three machine groups). The order cards conform to production orders. Finished orders are reported in a special internal delivery routine. Only then does the wage manager have a definitive basis for wages, calculated from passed pieces and time used to produce them. A production order can take several weeks, and until it is accounted for, the operator receives an advance payment. There are several problems with this system:

- Operators have difficulty checking their wages.
- Operators have to stamp order cards several times during a shift.
- Supervisors have difficulty knowing the status of a specific production order.
- Cards disappear, time is spent chasing down errors and correcting them, and overproduction is common ("to be on the safe side").

Everyone agreed that significant improvements could be realized by replacing the production order card system with a local PC-based system. To start the project, a plant controller gave a short course (five sessions, two hours each) in costing and relevant concepts and routines to each of the three shifts. The second step was to set up a task force to specify what requirements a PC-based system should meet. A specialist from the computer department was a member of the group, which generated a long list of information that the new system should be able to provide.

So far so good; although some operators found some of the concepts difficult to grasp, expectations ran high as to how much easier everything would be when the new PC system was operational. Discussing the team, operators indicated repeatedly that they preferred to work as they always had: each operator in complete charge of his or her own machine group. They could not see any problems that concerned them as a group.

Sustained Improvement

The PC arrived and operators went through a seven-lesson computer course. They expected the new information system would be ready about a month later, but things started to go wrong. The computer expert who was going to do the programming recommended a new software package and in order to design the new system, he had to learn the new software. The programmer was not located in Lindesberg; there were communication problems; the system requirements were changed after the programming had started. The first version of the system did not work properly. Errors occurred that were difficult to trace. The programmer was tightly controlled by his boss. A wait-and-see attitude emerged from all parties. The system did erroneous summations and mixed up batches. Operators grew suspicious! This system generated more correcting work than the old card system! And in order to substitute the new system for the old one, the personnel department demanded that security measures be built into it; production planning had its demands and debates on the new system, which tended to involve more outside people. The programmer left and his replacement had to be trained. The project came to a virtual standstill.

By early 1988, the team was running the two systems in parallel. Because of personnel turnover, the team was completely new; no one knew how to use the new software, and any increase in productivity that may have been registered was due to other factors.

THE KÖPING PLANT

The Köping plant is large and produces manual gear boxes. Our study included three lines producing cog wheels and shafts for heavy boxes. The shaft line (A5) processes eight varieties of gear box shafts, each weighing 5–15 kilograms. It produces 15–30 shafts per shift, in two shifts, each shift having two operators. The line consists of 11 machines positioned along a transfer line; its technology is fairly recent, with computerized process control and automated transfers between machines. During the latter part of the study period, a new shaft line (A6) using FMS technology was installed. So the attention of the people involved was divided among

- producing shafts for the old gear box models
- installing new production technology
- starting to produce shafts for the new models of gear boxes using new technology

The three activities competed for attention and resources throughout the project. The average batch size on A5 was about 500 shafts, which took 25–50 hours to produce depending on the variety of shaft. The setup for the next batch took about 20 hours. Since the trend was toward increased flexibility and smaller batches, setup times were a significant problem.

Getting Started

In Köping the atmosphere of the starting phase was different from that in Floby. There was no open conflict, but there was an undercurrent of negotiation. It more or less boiled down to an employee demand: "If we are going to increase productivity, we want half of the gain." The issue obviously came up in the other plants, but it was stated most bluntly in Köping. (Union traditions explain the difference; Köping was used to solving problems by confrontations.) The will to improve was present, but there seemed to be less trust between parties.

In a sense it was a good start because the next issue automatically became "How can any improvement be attributed to operators, rather than to planners, maintenance, or other factors?" The answer was that the team needed a local system to keep track of operational factors that influence productivity. Even if the discussion on how the productivity gain would be split between the parties caused some turbulence, we do not believe that it had a significant effect on the course of events. Still, it was part of the context in which the experiment was conducted.

Rejects

The team decided to gather statistics on rejects (causes thereof) and real processing times (in relation to precalculated). Initially, they focused just on collecting the information. During the last six weeks of 1984, the number of rejects equalled about 2%, and the team noted where in the machine line errors had occurred and what were the causes. During that period, there had been 20 setups of the line, and, on average, 1.5 rejected shafts could be directly attributed to problems in setup. Setup problems will only increase, since the product companies are pressing for greater flexibility and smaller batches.

Processing Time

During the last reporting period of 1984, the team found that it had used 368 hours for the 20 setups (against a standard time of 291) in spite of a drive, initiated after a visit by a Japanese expert, to decrease setup times during the prior six months. The team first debated what could be done to reduce setup time; after the debate the setup time for the focused machine dropped from 195 to 66.4 minutes. The team then used video filming and further analysis (which peeled off another 32.4 minutes). Still, setting up the whole line in normal, operational conditions seemed to differ from the laboratorylike conditions of the focused study. But, at least the team had a record of the most important delays and their causes.

Processing time was also above the precalculated rate (498 hours against a standard 411). This meant that customers had paid for 702 hours during the period, while the team had worked 866, an efficiency of 81%.

Although the data showed that the team's actual processing times exceeded the budgeted times, the startup of the project seemed to have gone quite well. The team had set up routines to collect the operational data it wanted. Now it was time to install the PC and to have some training in management accounting. The team set up a computer group (which included the department manager), acquired help from the computer department, and even used a consultant. Maybe the fascination with the ongoing installation of the gigantic new FMS line in the same department influenced the group to go for too sophisticated a solution with high-level language software. As a consequence, it was a very long time before the PC was operational. Once the FMS line (and PC) was in operation, the team began to do follow-ups and to improve operations, but there was not enough time to achieve the same kind of success as the Floby plant had achieved.

One interesting episode that illustrates how learning can be interpreted differently from different perspectives involved an experiment with a designated maintenance man for the three lines involved in our project. It went on for a little more than a year. The maintenance man taught the operators how to tend to the machines to avoid breakdowns and explained what signals and noises indicated imminent problems. The outcome was encouraging. Maintenance costs decreased by 150,000 skr between 1985 and 1986. Furthermore, there was less downtime, because of faster service. However, this experiment had to be abandoned. The team's maintenance man worked only day shifts, while his colleagues in the maintenance department worked two shifts. His colleagues were jealous, especially of his socially satisfying work relations with the team. They complained, and, after union pressure, the team's maintenance man went back to the traditional form of maintenance. (It was also said that a maintenance man who works only with the trivialities of one machine group will lose competence, but we are not convinced that this is a valid argument, at least not if one man can help a department cut its maintenance cost so significantly.)

In Köping, the team's start was delayed by interference from the FMS installation and from the overambitious PC-installation process. But once it got started, it seemed to be moving in the right direction. The limits to team self-management are aptly illustrated by the maintenance incident.

ANALYSIS

The experiences from this field experiment illustrate the potential and the limitations of the team self-management approaches. The Floby (drums, hubs, and shafts) success shows how a step-by-step development, wherein the team has a firm grip on what it is doing and why, generates chains, or rather spirals, of motivation and action that spread outside the team. In Lindesberg (cog wheels), we see how an old technology, which ties operators to the manual handling of inputs and outputs from the process, preserves a Tayloristic view of work, and a consequent lack of perception of group problems. Instead of a team, there is a group of individual, piece rate workers who are dissatisfied with the production order system. The lack of automation seems to get in the way of team problem solving. It should be noted that the problem that was attacked by the Lindesberg team—allocating the right amount of production output to the right period (shift) and person in a situation with interaction between periods—is a classical accounting problem with no solution.

In Köping (gear box shafts), the experiment was distracted by the installation of a fascinating FMS complex and by the choice of an overly advanced software package for the PC. The team was doing the right thing in collecting data on its own operations, but because of these distractions, it really did not act on the results.

In analyzing the experiences of these three-year experiments, one should be aware that, even if special care has been taken to place the initiative firmly in the hands of the teams and their foremen, all kinds of interventions can occur. Even though Volvo gave special attention to these groups (the company has a long tradition of experiments with group-oriented production structures), Hawthorne effects cannot be excluded, limiting our ability to generalize. Still, some tentative conclusions worthy of further investigation can be drawn.

Controllability

The semi-fixed costs of the reject or cutting tool type are the keys to cost control in the kind of cost centers studied in this paper. The semi-fixed costs are more controllable than are costs of materials and labor. Labor is controllable in the sense that operators of automated machinery have time to conduct projects while they oversee the machines. To the extent that operators are bound to the production process, as in Lindesberg, by manual operations (like loading and unloading several machines), it is more difficult to conduct self-management. Projects are likely to be possible only with outside help; in such cases, however, the self-management properties of the project tend to become dominated by experts, which in turn diminishes responsibility and motivation.

A striking feature, throughout our observations, was the preeminence of action over analysis and planning. Although the teams in all three plants indicated that statistics on operations would be useful in coming budget negotiations, the driving factor behind the projects was the will to know more about the effects of action. Knowing is owning; and owning is, by definition, having control.

The crucial importance of ownership of the data and of the projects was obvious in the successful Floby team, which initiated and largely carried out all projects by itself (or on its terms). The Floby team chose to work with problems it thought it could handle. When it asked for outside help, it was able to specify what the problem was and thus establish criteria for an acceptable solution.

In Köping and Lindesberg, the teams were not given a proper chance to take ownership of their projects, maybe because support from higher levels in the organization was too intrusive. In setting up their first projects, both teams involved other departments, conspicuously the computer department, which blocked the formation of a team identity that could serve as the platform for action. In Floby, actions also involved other departments, but only after the team had established itself and learned how to cooperate to solve common problems. In Köping and Lindesberg, the teams became dependent on other departments for the success of their main project, demonstrating to team members the need for outside assistance. When a project drags on, it is easy for team members to attribute lack of success to the environment and to shun responsibility. Furthermore, it is obviously demoralizing if the team believes it has improved operations, but cost center reports show no improvement or, worse, show deterioration.

Doing something, having success, and realizing that you have control are, as we all know, potent motivating forces. Our foremen agreed that team spirit is central to success. Team spirit takes a long time to build but can be destroyed almost instantaneously. We believe that it relates to the feeling of being in control, but this factor is something that could not be observed properly in this kind of study.

Attention

Academics tend to see the world through models, whereby processes are treated as black boxes and described with the help of relations between inputs and outputs. The teams are inside the boxes. The closer one gets to the process, the less one can get an overview. To compensate for the lack of distance from the ongoing process, one has to focus attention on a few things at a time and work with standard procedures in areas to which attention is momentarily drawn. Attention is a limited commodity to be applied with wisdom. Learning is a useful tool in establishing standard procedures that do not require much attention once they are established. But learning requires attention. Teams have a strategic choice: What factor is judged to be critical for success at a given instance? Part of the process deserves an interactive approach; other parts must be delegated to programmed control (Simons 1987).

Interactive control of operations and changes in those operations within the limits set by the context, require information not normally accessible to operators. A lot of data is displayed on screens in the machine group (data about the depth of holes being drilled and so forth), but those measures are physical and directly coupled to the machines. To understand data relating to the performance of the group in economic and strategic terms requires an interpretational leap to meaningful issues worthy of attention. Interpretation means a translation between operational activities and financial measures in both directions so that a reversible figure-based situation (one set of measures providing the explanatory background for the other set, and vice versa) is established. To interactively construct interpretational schema, the team must build these translations into its work routines. Once a new routine has been confirmed as reasonable, it may be delegated to programmed control as part of a normal procedure, until it comes to the fore again on another interpretative occasion. We maintain that the relevance of data emerges in such interactive episodes that temporarily focus attention. Consequently, the local need for data on operations is also temporary. Few local performance data are needed or wanted all the time. Physical measures like temperatures and so forth are another matter, but performance in terms of costs or quality is learned by organizations by being built into routine behavior.

If this claim is valid, it follows that data for organizational learning are needed only temporarily, i.e., when searches and problem solving are occurring. When things are normal, the relevant information exists in standards, such as how many rejects per shift correspond to those in the cost center budget, or how many shafts should normally be turned before a tool needs to be changed. Deviation from normalcy may arouse attention and lead to problem solving, if the deviation is put on the agenda. One interviewee said that a foreman receives a large number of signals every shift. Operators tend to report observations and complaints to the foreman as he passes by. A good foreman has the ability to register those signals that form patterns. When a pattern is interpreted to be a problem, the foreman should publicize the problem to the group: "We have this and that problem." Once the problem is put on the agenda, operators will start to think about it, and if the foreman communicates continuously with the group, this will generate most of the pieces of the puzzle that constitute the solution. Attention generates group problem solving, and the will to know—to be in control of your own operation—drives the members of the group to provide tentative solutions to parts of the problem. The foreman's task is to integrate information and to gather the holders of pieces of a solution together in a joint session at the right time. The resulting solution will be the property and responsibility of the group.

The Will to Know

To assume responsibility for performance and to take action for improvement are acts of will. The mobilization of that will in the team is largely the task of the foreman. In our study we saw different types of foremen. One was primarily interested in technology and tended to search for solutions by adjusting machines. Another believes that if operators are happy with their work conditions and the social environment, they will keep machines going even if technical readings indicate a probable need for a stoppage. Finally, there was the problem-oriented foreman who worked in the following sequence:

- find out what is wrong (follow-ups)
- analyze what can be done (problem solving)
- act and see whether there is improvement
- end the sequence

In the latter approach, Borje, the foreman in the Floby plant, seems to have gone to extremes of leadership. His statement, "I want the operators to drive me, instead of me driving them," suggests a role in which he mainly represents the team in its dealings with the outside world. He does play an active role in initiating follow-ups but delegates most of the decision making under normal conditions to his operators.

To a large extent, we believe that the leader of the team establishes the identity of the team. Having an identity as a responsible unit that can act as a partner in cooperative problem solving with other units is quite important for the motivation of the team. When the team interacts with expert staff units (like the computer department), unless it has a strong identity, the relationship between the two very easily turns into a subservient relationship wherein the team has difficulties in articulating its problem and the expert imposes his favorite models on the team, taking away any sense of responsibility it might have had. Partnership in cooperative problem solving presumes an identity as a responsible, knowledgeable unit. The team thus needs a track record of successes, a leader to represent them in negotiations, and some attention from top management.

The importance of identity was highlighted by the responses of participants from the teams during a final seminar on how a written manual on team work (as the teams experienced it) should read. The answer was, unanimously, that such a manual cannot be written. Circumstances are so different, the tasks so complicated, and the teams so unique that one cannot pronounce any general rules on how to go about working as a team. The proof of uniqueness was that no other team would (could?) have done it the way each of the participants did it! As researchers, we do not agree with that statement, but find it challenging.

CONCLUSIONS—ANY GOOD ADVICE

The study, as conducted, does not allow for any safe scientific conclusions, since we did not have all the independent variables under control (and since we did not really know what our dependent variable was). We have studied a three-year process of organizational learning in three locations with similar, but differently aged technology, and we are trying to make sense of what we observed. Further research will provide a sounder basis for conclusions.

We list a number of observations we think relevant in applying a local cost management approach in industrial settings.

1. In the beginning of the paper, we referred to nine factors assumed to contribute to cost improvement. We saw improvements on all factors and we believe that these factors interact in a complex way. This complexity has to be dealt with, and there is not time enough to map out all interactive links before com-

mencing action. Instead, the approach should be to try to initiate "good circles" through action. The knowledge gained in this way is provisional and may be challenged in the next project, but organizational learning occurs, and *opportunities for learning are quite rare* in most environments.

2. *The information needed in local teams is different in kind from the information needed by a central manager.*
The information support needed for management of local cost control is dependent upon but different from that of the management accounting system. The objective of a local information system is to assist in detecting causes of unacceptable performance measures registered in the central system. Thus, the local system is always complementary to the central one.

3. *Organizational learning occurs in small steps—solving one problem at a time.*
Our observation is that the necessary conditions for organizational learning are attention and a will to change (create improvement). This means that organizational learning occurs in episodes of increased attention and motivation. The will to change means a will to break away from customary behavior and to risk failure. In order for teams and their members to take calculated risks, it is imperative to have projects that are manageable and comprehensible. Operators should not be required to undertake changes greater than those undertaken by other people. After all, top managers do not switch from the car industry to publishing in one day. Changing the procedures in a machine group may constitute a revolutionary change for the operator.
Operators, like top managers, have limited allotments of attention to pay to different aspects of their work. Since attention is a scarce resource, it should be focused on one problem that can perhaps be solved in a reasonable length of time. Problems that require lengthy investigations and complex design cannot be dealt with successfully on a part-time basis (the only basis an operator usually can afford). Large projects should be delegated to project groups that do not have the same organization as production teams have.

4. *What is normal should be described in several dimensions.*
The trick in managing the local economy is to link the output measures of the responsibility center with a variety of measures

on operational activities. Managing is maintaining a dialogue between activities and outcomes in goal dimensions. Therefore, the cost budget must be translated into physical measures such as the budgeted number of rejects per shift or shafts per cutting tool. Knowing what is expected or viewed as normal helps one see deviations.

5. *Thinking of cost improvement as a series of projects.*
   In our study, the most successful team developed a pattern in its improvement activities by taking the following steps: problem discovery, follow up, analysis/decision, action, and confirmation.

   Recognition of a problem establishes the parameters of a project and of the information needed. The follow-up phase collects the data needed. The data are interpreted by team members who are directly involved in the project. (It is not necessary to involve every member in all projects, nor is it useful to have a lot of meetings unless something important needs to be discussed.) Those involved in the problem must commit themselves to carrying out their part of the decision. The cost center report for the next period confirms that the project solved the problem satisfactorily or that another effort has to be made.

   The important thing is to design projects that end before everyone's attention is exhausted.

6. *Information technology cannot substitute for a thorough knowledge of the production process.*
   We had mixed experiences with local PCs in this study. In two of the teams the chosen software was too complicated to be used by the team, and the computer experts were not able to communicate well enough for the PCs to become a useful instrument during the three-year period. In Floby, simpler software was used and some of the programming was done by students from the local schools as field work. In this way the team was in command of the information technology at all times. Information technology did not get in the way of dealing with the problems.

   Local information needs seem to be transient, being relevant to the immediate problem on the agenda. This poses some problems for structuring the information flows in the organization and for providing systematic reports in relation to ad hoc information needs. It is, of course, tempting for the computer department to take over, professionalize, and integrate local information systems into the central one. We believe that it may be a misconception to view local data banks as "systems." It would be better to see them as investigative capacities supporting operational knowledge.

7. *The important effects will probably come through the horizontal communication between teams solving joint problems.*
   When a team has established a platform of responsibility for its own development, it can enter into cooperative problem solving with other teams. One can argue that central coordination and planning are impossible if local units change the coefficients as they learn. To a certain extent this is true. Like most other planned economies, a corporation of any size will have a planning system that is persistently out of step with the real process. And the effects may be more severe in a highly automated production system.

Instead of striving to create a perfect, integrated planning system with no deviations, corporate managers are well advised to go for the more effective solution of having central coordination rely on more robust and simple plans while allowing local units to learn and to innovate.

The main benefit of cost improvement activities is shorter throughput times in local units. Since there is no benefit in having processed products ready ahead of schedule wait for shipping (time won in processing being lost in stock), the local unit should initiate communication with units responsible for subsequent production stages to adapt schedules. A cost saving can not be realized until the product has reached the customer.

Coordination without complete control from the center is possible provided that local (and central) units have communicative competence and responsibility (van Gunsteren 1976). This requires developing the managerial role of foremen by sequences of projects such as those described above.

This report may seem to contain no spectacular conclusions or few new ideas. But this is precisely the point. Cost improvement is much easier to talk about than to accomplish.

Having followed the successes and failures of three production teams for three years, we are convinced that the Tayloristic approach to work design will be replaced by an approach designed for learning in the way we have tried to describe. It is a slow and vulnerable process that requires good local leadership. If successful, people grow, efficiency increases, and personnel turnover decreases. That is the impressive side of this low-key approach!

REFERENCES

Cyert, R. M. and J. G. March. *Behavioral Theory of the Firm*. New York: Prentice-Hall, 1963.

Delionback, L. M. *Guidelines for Application of Learning/Cost Improvement Curves*. NASA Technical Memorandum X-64968. Marshall Space Flight Center, Alabama 1975.

Gunsteren, H. van. *The Quest for Control*. New York: Wiley, 1976.

Johnson, H. Thomas and R. S. Kaplan. *Relevance Lost: The Rise and Fall of Management Accounting*. Boston: Harvard Business School Press, 1987.

Levitt, B. and J. G. March. "Organizational Learning." *Annual Review of Sociology* (1988): 319–340.

Simons, R. "Planning, Control, and Uncertainty: A Process View." In *Accounting and Management: Field Study Perspectives*, edited by W. J. Bruns, Jr., and R. S. Kaplan. Boston: Harvard Business School Press, 1987: 339–362.

CHAPTER 7

An Architecture for a
Process Control Costing System

Ramchandran Jaikumar

INTRODUCTION

ALL manufacturing processes evolve over time. Technical know-how related to any particular process at any given time is at best imperfect. Even when a process is well understood, the need for new products that entail the development of new processes will move process capability once again to the level of imperfect understanding. To date, process improvement has occurred without systematic economic valuation of alternative process capabilities. Costing, which is supposed to provide such economic valuation, is primarily motivated by the need to provide information on product costs. It is our premise that rapid advances in information-intensive processing capability have made it possible to provide an economic basis for systematically choosing among the many different options available for controlling processes.[1]

Material transformation processes and how they are achieved must be understood to effectively value the choices that are available. To identify the demands on a process control costing system, this paper links costing to the historical evolution of process control. Section 2 shows that the information required for process control costing is part of the world of computer-integrated manufacturing (CIM). Section 3 develops a framework for combining the information that is required with that which is available as a basis for developing an architecture for a process control costing system. The final section describes a process to which this architecture is currently being applied.

THE EVOLUTION OF
PROCESS CONTROL

The purpose of any manufacturing process is to effect a transformation, according to closely prescribed specifications, in the form, physical characteristics, or finish of a component. A measure of the effectiveness of a process is the degree to which products produced by it conform to specifications. Some degree of variation is implicit, inasmuch as the performance of a process is never perfect. People, machines, and procedures, as well as the object being fabricated, can all constitute sources of variation. Control of variation—which entails studying the kinds of variances that can occur, the sources of these variances, and the means by which they can be managed—is termed *process control*. The effectiveness of process control can be measured by the degree to which variances are minimized.

In measuring the characteristic being transformed for a specific lot of components produced by a particular process, the frequency of occurrence for a given measure will follow the distribution in Figure 7-1. The difference between the actual and desired values of a measure tells us how close we have come to satisfying our requirements; it is a measure of the *accuracy* of the process. The standard deviation tells us to what degree a process is capable of repeating a specified performance; it is a measure of *precision*, and is attributable to limits in the ability both of a machine to execute identical performances and of the persons and procedures that direct the machine. Variance due to machines is defined as *repeatability*, variance due to people and procedures, as *reproducibility*.

The mean of the process for sequential lots of the same component changes over time. The standard deviation of the mean of the process, defined as the *stability* of the process, is a measure of how well it performs over time. System variance is the net variance due to accuracy, precision, reproducibility, and stability.

All of the measures of variance assume that we have not made any adjustments to the process. In practice, we always make adjustments to a process when something goes wrong, and a process that accommodates adjustments is obviously desirable. Accuracy, as noted earlier, is the systematic bias in a process; stability, the manner in which that bias shifts over time. To the extent that we can adjust a

Figure 7-1   Frequency of Occurence for a Given Measure

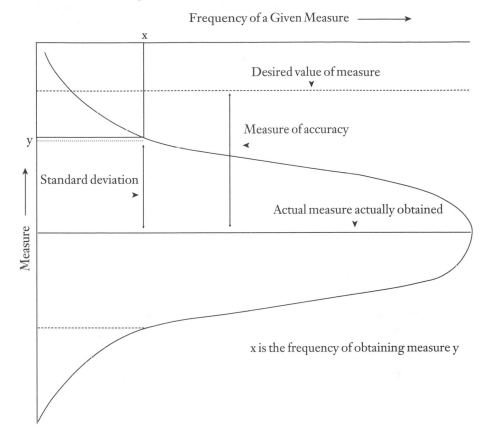

process, we can correct the bias and bring it closer to the desired standard. The capability of a process to support dynamic adjustments that correct for bias is termed *adaptability* and is measured as the variance between system variance and variance in repeatability.

The requirement for adaptability is quite different depending on whether we want to make one component or a large number of identical components. To be adaptable with a sample of a single component, a process must have a high degree of accuracy. More important in a process for producing large numbers of identical components are precision and stability, which allow us to compensate for accuracy by making adjustments. The greater the stability of a process, the less frequently it will have to be adjusted.

Versatility, inasmuch as it has nothing to do with variances in product characteristics, is quite different from the notions discussed above, yet it has important implications for process control. Versatility is the ability of a process to accommodate variety in process specifications. Greater versatility usually reflects greater complexity in a task, and hence, more sources of variance.

The nature of process control has changed dramatically over time. We have documented the evolution of process control through six epochs, each characterized by a fundamental shift, or "revolution," in the organization of work and the nature of the firm. We studied this evolution and documented the epochs in Beretta, a firearms firm that dates from the 1400s. The analysis of Beretta revealed, among other changes, those shown in Table 7-1.[2]

The six epochs of process control occurred in the following sequence:

1. The invention of machine tools and the English system of manufacture (1800);

2. Special-purpose tools and interchangeability of components in the American system of manufacture (1850);

3. Scientific management and the engineering of work in the Taylor system (1900);

4. Statistical process control (SPC) and the dynamic world;

5. Information processing and the numerical control (NC) era;

6. Intelligent systems and computer-integrated manufacturing (CIM).

Each epoch focused on a particular process attribute—accuracy, precision, reproducibility, stability, adaptability, and versatility. In the early epochs, we developed measures, then gained control of the process. Next, we mastered variability, first in the machine, then in the human. Finally, we studied, and then controlled, contingencies in the process until we were able to extract general principles and technologies that we could apply in a variety of domains. (See Table 7-1; note that the dates refer to the epochs not in an absolute sense but as they occurred at Beretta.)

The First Three Epochs—the Mechanistic View

The first three epochs—the English, American, and Taylor systems—were characterized by an emphasis on mechanization. Each

Table 7-1 The Six Epochs of Process Control Reflected in Changes in One Firm

	English System 1790–1850	American System 1850–1910	Taylor Scientific Management 1910–1950	Dynamic World 1950–1975	NC Era 1975–1985	Computer-Integrated Manufacturing 1985–?
Number of Machines	3	50	150	150	50	30
Minimum Efficient Scale (Number of People)	40	150	300	300	100	30
Staff/Line Ratio	0:40	20:130	60:240	100:200	50:50	20:10
Productivity Increase over Previous Epoch	4:1	3:1	3:1	3:2	3:1	3:1
Cumulative	4	12	36	54	162	486
Number of Products	Infinite	3	10	15	100	Infinite
Engineering Ethos	Mechanical	Manufacturing	Industrial	Quality	Systems	Knowledge
Process Focus	Accuracy	Repeatability	Reproducibility	Stability	Adaptability	Versatility
Focus of Control	Product Functionality	Product Conformance	Process Conformance	Process Capability	Product Process/Integration	Process Intelligence

epoch saw the manufacturing world as a place of increasing efficiency and control, witnessed the substitution of capital for labor, and gained progress through economies of scale. These objectives were obtained through an engineering focus on machines and what could be done with them. Labor was increasingly expected to adapt to the machines and the contingencies of the environment, and, ultimately, to become yet another machine. Concurrently, the machines themselves became more elaborate, capable of ever greater precision and control. The single principle that seemed to underlie these developments was increasing mechanical constraint, which fostered a reductionist orientation emphasizing smaller and smaller tasks with a high volume of production. Increasing mechanization reduced the scope of work, while the specialization of machines reduced discretion as to what could be made.

By 1950, the world of mechanization had reached its zenith, and the power of information processing was beginning to be recognized. People, processing information, became the means to transform a collection of individual machines into a manufacturing system. The integration and intelligence needed to make these collections of machines function have been the focus of the subsequent three epochs. In the dynamic world, the NC era, and the present computer-integrated manufacturing era, the trends of mechanization are reversed: we see increased versatility and intelligence; substitution of intelligence for capital; and economies of scope. Machines, designed to enhance the cognitive capabilities of the human being, have become extensions of the mind. The versatility of information technology and freedom from mechanical constraint suggest a new managerial imperative.

Figure 7-2 traces the progress from high to low discretion and back again, and from increasing mechanization in an essentially static world to increasing intelligence in a more volatile, dynamic world.

. . . as conversion processes that formerly were supplied at a price through market exchanges became performed within organizations, a demand arose for measures to determine the "price" of output from internal operations. Lacking price information on the conversion processes occurring within their organizations, owners devised measures to summarize the efficiency by which labor and material were converted to finished products, measures that also served to motivate managers who supervised the conversion process.

The early accounting management measures . . . focused on conversion costs and produced summary measures such as cost per hour or cost per pound produced for each process and for each worker . . . and involved some

Figure 7-2 Work, Mechanization, and Intelligence in the Evolution of Process Control

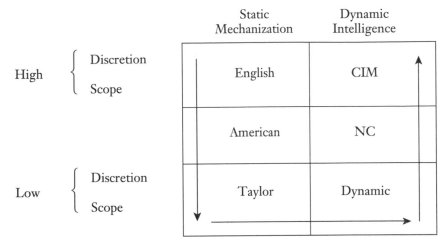

attribution of overhead. The goal of the systems was to identify the different costs for the intermediate and final products of the firm and to provide a benchmark to measure the efficiency of the conversion process . . . [and] to provide incentives for workers to achieve productivity goals.[3]

Frederick Taylor's realization that the speed and efficiency of the machines available at the end of the nineteenth century were constrained by worker-related activities precipitated the third epoch. The idea that these human activities could be measured, analyzed, and controlled by techniques analogous to those applied to physical objects was the central theme in what Taylor put forth as the theory of "scientific management." During this epoch, the average number of machines per shop, and the staff function, tripled over what they had been in the previous epoch, while line workers only doubled.

Taylor's scientific management practice evolved as a means to gather detailed information about the efficiency of complex processes and the people who carried them out. It aimed at finding the "one best way" to do any task. By reducing a task to a series of very small inputs, it became possible to establish "standard" rates at which material and labor should be consumed in manufacturing tasks. Standard rates provided a basis for assessing variances between actual and standard costs and for differentiating variances due to controllable conditions from those beyond management's control. This information was used to compare actual performance against prescribed performance, rather than for making judgments relative to process improvement.

The cost of observing and documenting the actual consumption of material, labor, machine time, and indirect resources for every physical transformation of a material was, at that time, prohibitive. Therefore, in practice, variances were calculated at very high levels of aggregation. A common approach was to aggregate all of the operations that were the responsibility of a single manager and use the resulting variances to evaluate that manager. The effect was to treat information as a scarce resource and the manager as an *intermittent* observer concerned with making sense of what happened between observations from aggregate data.

The Latter Epochs—Time, Information, and the World of CIM

Time and information enter for the first time in the fourth epoch, with the development of statistical process control (SPC) in the 1930s. While the average number of machines per shop did not change significantly during this epoch, the ratio of staff to line workers grew to 1:2 (see Table 7-1).

SPC assumes that all machines are intrinsically imprecise, that an identical procedure will produce different results on the same machine at different times. The degree to which results vary depends on a machine's ability to maintain precision. SPC enhances the process capability of machines by recording on charts the process behavior of a sample of parts at specified intervals of time. With SPC, it becomes important to distinguish between *random* and *systematic contingencies*. SPC can be effectively employed to manage systematic contingencies in the short run, and to manage process capability over the longer term by controlling sources of random variability.

For the first time, we see a divergence between process control and costing systems. The statistical notion of process control, the ability to distinguish between random and systematic contingencies, was not reflected in costing systems. Still locked into the rigid logic of the scientific management epoch, costing systems did not provide managers with information about the costs of different control strategies that would help them manage contingencies. The costing system did not distinguish between random and systematic contingencies, nor did it identify the short- and long-term value to be derived from operating in control, or the costs to be incurred from operating with a lack of control.

To understand the two most recent epochs, we need to understand how the microprocessor fundamentally altered the nature of automation. The new automation, called flexible automation, differs in several important ways from the automation of the Industrial Revolution. First, it integrates information and materials processing, which were very much separate in traditional technologies. Second, it relies on greater machine intelligence (unlike traditional automation, which relies on the intelligence of machine operators). Third, it affords flexibility, precision, productivity, and versatility simultaneously. Traditional technologies typically provide one of these at the expense of the others.

These differences give rise to the most important characteristics of microprocessor-based automation: *flexibility* and *reproducibility*. The machines of the microprocessor-based automation can produce different components in varying amounts, and they operate most efficiently in small groups, thus minimizing economies of scale. In contrast, the machines of traditional automation were designed to churn out one thing in enormous quantities. Reproducibility is achieved through the tight integration of information and materials processing. In a flexible manufacturing system (FMS), the process is under the "complete" control of computer programs. Product and process specifications exist as computational *procedures* that are fed into these programs. The specifications must anticipate every possible contingency, that is, every potential problem with the product and process must be anticipated and solved. A process done right need never be modified again.

When every part made using a particular set of specifications is exactly the same as every other part, the highly skilled people who write the procedures have achieved *precise reproducibility*. In this context, firms are distinguished primarily by the software and programs available to them, as these determine the range and type of products they are capable of manufacturing. Consequently, a firm's *intellectual assets*, that is, the people who write the procedures and resolve the contingencies of production, become more valuable than the firm's hardware.

The existence of procedures also contributes to the *transportability* of product and process information, as software can be moved both physically and via telecommunications. Stored specifications enable one to produce an identical part on any one of many different machines in many different places. With computer communication, such procedures can be used to control production at locations remote from the place where the procedures are run.

The fifth epoch, characterized by this new form of automation, followed the development of SPC by a mere forty years. With the fundamental change in the nature of automation, the average number of machines per shop required to maintain an efficient scale of operations dropped to the levels of the midnineteenth century (at the beginning of the American system), while the ratio of staff to line workers climbed to 1:1. Microprocessor-based NC machines, which use electronic gauges to replace the control chart, require operators to work with information in the form of procedures rather than with physical objects. Measurement in a metal-turning operation, for example, now consists of introducing machined parts into an electronic gauge, and automatically feeding measurements along four different dimensions into a controller, which integrates them with data on parts previously produced.

As the NC machine has some built-in variability and its sensors some measurement error, we would not expect parts to be identical, but rather to range randomly within certain bounds of precision. We need a procedure that, taking account of this random variability and the historical data, can detect a systematic change (e.g., jaws misaligned) or a trend (e.g., tool wear). Having detected a change, we need to make an adjustment to the cutting program. The machine can then automatically adjust the tool movement as appropriate. With such *adaptive control*, it becomes possible to expend all the effort required to effect systematic changes (e.g., creating a program) prior to production.

With microprocessor control, the procedure becomes the object of analysis. Managers exert control by modifying procedures to effect change, hence controllable costs are directly related to contingencies in procedures. With many products, and a wide variety of manufacturing procedures, each subject to a variety of contingencies, we need a process control costing system that provides the ability to evaluate different procedures.

The CIM era, which arrived a mere two decades after the NC era, brought the potential to automate the manufacturing process from beginning to end—from loading machines, through changing, setting, and operating tools, to unloading processed products. The average number of machines per shop dropped further, and for the first time the number of staff exceeded the number of line workers.

A CIM system is a computer-controlled configuration of semi-independent work stations, connected by automated materials handling systems, designed to efficiently manufacture more than one kind of part at low to medium volumes. The system shown in Figure 7-3 consists of three CNC machining centers connected by a materials handling system that incorporates a conveyor arranged in a loop. The loop constitutes a buffer area where pallets on which the workpieces are mounted keep moving until the machine required for the next operation becomes available. As all system operations (with the exception of inspection) are under precise computer control, effects of part-program changes, decision rules for priority assignment, contingent control, and part-portfolio mix can be captured.

The far-reaching effects of this technology are control over the process, repeatability, and reprogrammability. Dynamic contingencies remain a part of the environment, and skill is still required to identify and eliminate errors. Neither the computer control systems, nor the persons employed to operate them, are capable of recognizing systematic errors in these machines. The "feel" for the machine is absent. New skills, those of manipulating abstract procedures and entities and of recognizing, and learning from, the relationships between procedures and tolerances, are required.

FMS technology and "unmanned" machining compounds the accuracy problem. As an FMS is merely a number of standard NC machines connected by an automated materials handling system, it has all the problems common to NC machines. But it lacks the standalone NC machine's constant attention from an operator who can compensate for small machine and operational errors. Determining the source of an "out-of-tolerance" problem in an integrated FMS can be difficult. The error might be caused by one or a combination of factors, such as tool wear or interface alignments (e.g., tool/spindle, part/fixture, fixture/pallet, pallet/machine). Proper diagnosis entails knowing which tools were used on which workpieces on which machines, and, if more than one part program was used, which was in use when the problem occurred.

In contrast to NC, which allowed us to detect and correct for specific contingencies in a procedure, CIM allows us, through systems integration, to observe procedures in relation to one another, and through intelligence, to recognize patterns in contingencies over time. It effectively renders the manager an *omniscient* observer. (With NC, the manager is still limited to *intermittent* observation.)

With CIM, the process control cost system must help us determine the actual system cost of errors and contingencies. We need to be able to measure the effect of (and assign a value to) reducing specific errors. More value will accrue to eliminating some errors than to

Figure 7-3   A Computer-Integrated Manufacturing System

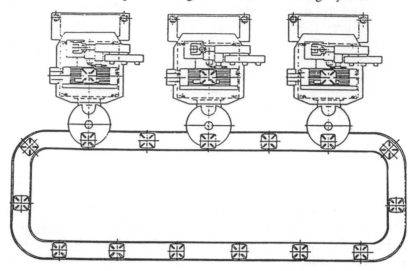

eliminating others, and we need to know which are more costly. A costing system should also help us understand the value of information gained from experiments conducted to improve a process.

THE COMPUTER COMPONENT OF CIM

In the early evolution of mechanization and automation, attention was focused on the transformations done to a product. The effect of this orientation was to reduce the variable cost of manufacture. But many auxiliary activities are not transformational in nature. Some, such as burr removal and machine qualifying, are machine related; others, such as materials handling, information processing, tool management, and fault diagnosis, are factory system related. Cost accounting has always had problems reporting and assigning the costs of these activities to products or to cost centers.

In conventional factories, virtually no information is collected on auxiliary activities, except the occasional recording of the time required to set up machines. In flexible manufacturing factories, the situation is quite different: 1) the computers that coordinate and control the flow of products, tools, process information, and other resources in these factories automatically also capture information on auxiliary activities; and 2) many formerly manual auxiliary activities have been automated.

The Hierarchical Structure of Process Control

The architecture of factory work that integrates information and materials processing, automated auxiliary functions, and high flexibility and versatility would probably be hierarchical. The system would use specialized, dedicated computers to operate machines, materials handling facilities, and inspection processes, and to manage the cells and the factory. Such a hierarchical orchestration is used in almost all existing FMSs.

The five levels in the hierarchically structured flexible manufacturing facility (FMF) shown in Figure 7-4—the facility, shop, cell, work station, and equipment—correspond to the vertical organizational structure of most present-day factories. The type of decision making usually associated with these factories is also present in the hierarchical computer system. At the lowest level of the hierarchy, where decision making must be adaptive to the environment, is the process control information. At the second level, where the different manufacturing operations are managed and contingencies and conflicts are resolved, there are machine controllers. The principal decision-making function at the cell level is coordination and management of resources, and at the facility level, the management of experimental procedures, capacity, and knowledge bases.

The lowest level of the hierarchy, the process control level, performs problem solving. The complexity of problem solving in an FMS is an order of magnitude greater than in a manually tended machining center. Thus, if the operator of an NC machine is once-removed from the "feel" of machining, the supervisor of an FMS is twice-removed. An analogy is useful to understand the difficulty associated with diagnosing problems in an FMS. Consider a person of limited vocabulary, using only the English language, attempting to write instructions for drawing a picture of a donkey. If this exercise proves easy enough, then consider the following: each of three people are given instructions for drawing a different part of a donkey (using different vocabulary and syntax); and their drawings are brought to a central location where a fourth person assembles them. Now, if a fifth person says that the donkey looks like a horse, how will you go about correcting the problem and issuing new instructions?

Recognizing, diagnosing, and learning from contingencies re-

Figure 7-4   A Control Hierarchy for an Automated Manufacturing Facility

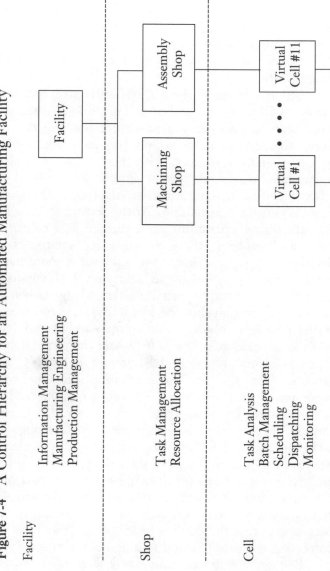

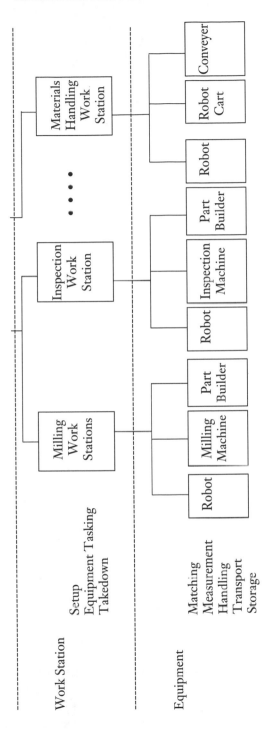

quires a high plane of technical intelligence. Operators must be trained in the scientific method in order to understand how various machine tool errors can cause parts to be out of tolerance, how to measure and correct such errors, and how to make accurate parts. Operators are typically alerted to contingencies by a product's lack of conformance to specifications. Discrepancies, whether of size, shape, location, or surface finish, can result from one or a combination of errors in the three broad categories—mechanical, thermal, and operational—elaborated in Figure 7-5. Mechanical and thermal errors can be further classified as attributable to either a machine or a part.

The frequency of errors is also of concern. Errors can be systematic (static), whereby they occur with approximately the same magnitude each time a manufacturing task is performed, or random (dynamic/fluctuating), occurring each time with different magnitudes and without apparent pattern. (See Table 7-2.)

The Temporal Structure of Process Control

Another view of the computer, quite different from the hierarchical one just described, derives from what transpires in the temporal domain. In a computer-integrated manufacturing situation, the controlling computer operates much as a motion picture does, recording every event in every location (that is, every *finite state*) as a series of frames, allowing us to produce a "freeze frame" for the state of the entire factory at any given moment. Computers can record hundreds of thousands of these states every second. The computer can examine the nature of one state and control its activity by some defined procedure in the form of "if state AXYZ then do . . ." and then move on to the next state. The ability of a computer to observe a phenomenon in one state and control an activity in the next state is called *contingent control*. In a manufacturing operation, adaptive control allows us to continually manage uncertainties in the environment.

These computer-stored "snapshots" are significant for process control. They allow a manager to compare the current state of a system to the expected state and to relate an event to corrective action. For example, if a cutting tool begins to overheat, the contingent controller can increase the flow of lubricant to the tool and/or slow the machine down.

Though these snapshots occur with such frequency that a number of them must be aggregated to provide a single picture that encompasses a sufficiently long time frame to interest managers, the

Figure 7-5 Sources of Error in an FMS

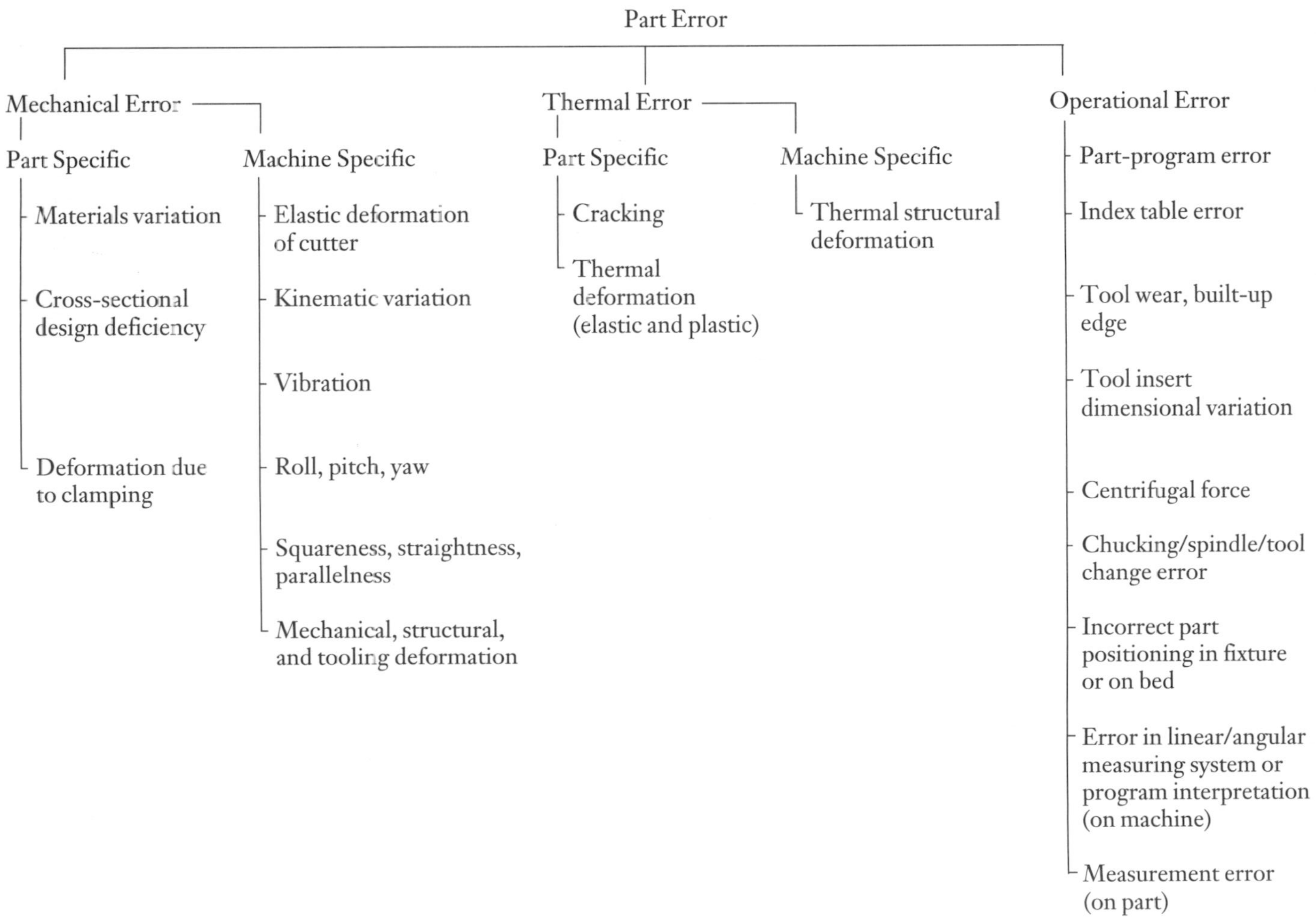

Part Error

Mechanical Error

Part Specific
- Materials variation
- Cross-sectional design deficiency
- Deformation due to clamping

Machine Specific
- Elastic deformation of cutter
- Kinematic variation
- Vibration
- Roll, pitch, yaw
- Squareness, straightness, parallelness
- Mechanical, structural, and tooling deformation

Thermal Error

Part Specific
- Cracking
- Thermal deformation (elastic and plastic)

Machine Specific
- Thermal structural deformation

Operational Error
- Part-program error
- Index table error
- Tool wear, built-up edge
- Tool insert dimensional variation
- Centrifugal force
- Chucking/spindle/tool change error
- Incorrect part positioning in fixture or on bed
- Error in linear/angular measuring system or program interpretation (on machine)
- Measurement error (on part)

Table 7-2   Classification of FMS Errors

Errors	Systematic/Static	Random/Dynamic
Part-Specific Mechanical	Materials variation Cross-sectional design deficiency Deformation due to clamping	Materials variation Deformation due to clamping
Machine-Specific Mechanical	Elastic deformation of cutter Kinematic variations: roll, pitch, yaw Squareness, straightness, parallelness Mechanical, structural, and tooling deformation	Elastic deformation of cutter vibrations
Part-Specific Thermal	Thermal deformation	Cracking Thermal deformation
Machine-Specific Thermal	Thermal, structural deformation	Thermal, structural deformation
Operational	Part: program error Index table error Centrifugal force Error in linear/angular measuring system or program interpretation (on machine)	Index table error Tool wear, built-up edge Tool insert dimensional variations Chucking/spindle/tool change error Part incorrectly positioned in fixture on bed Error in linear/angular measuring system or program interpretation (on machine) Measurement error (on part)

manager in such an environment is effectively omniscient. The difference between omniscient and intermittent observation can be likened to the difference between identifying diseased trees in a forest (intermittent) and making sense of the nature of the forest from the trees and trying to understand the impact of an observed disease in a tree on the growth of the forest (omniscient).

The omniscient observer can undertake process control costing in a fundamentally different way. Because variances can be reported as the outcomes of events that disrupt the production process, the omniscient observer can identify events as they occur, and trace the economic consequences of those events as they unfold. In contrast, the intermittent observer, constrained to view the production process as a black box, can only report on the relationship between factor inputs and outputs.

As the quantity of data available to a process control costing program vastly exceeds its requirements, excess information must be discarded on a continuous basis. This requires that the process control costing program be constructed around a *features of interest processor*, designed to identify and store only information of interest. Such a processor is event-oriented and attempts to examine the consequences of any event and the conditions that might have caused it. For example, a manager might be interested in how a new procedure is functioning and any problems it is causing. These *interesting events*, as we call them, are dynamic and, typically, part of an investigative or problem-solving activity. The processor interprets an event using all the relevant states that need to be observed and then behaves as an omniscient observer of those states. It also interprets the language used by the manager in conceptualizing interesting events in terms of the logical states and corresponding locations in common memory. Having obtained the information, the processor runs the analysis programs to examine the significance of the events.

A more fundamental change in the process control costing approach can be made by focusing on the cause of the variance and attempting to capture all the associated economic consequences. The new costing system views the production process as running exactly as expected unless disrupted by an event. The cost system recognizes such events, identifies all the effects of each event on the entire production process, and reports this information to management by event. The power of this approach lies in the ability to simultaneously identify events and their economic consequences.

We can examine the impact of computer systems on observation, classification, and correction of contingencies by placing the feedback times for these activities along the temporal line shown in Figure 7-6. This line, drawn on a logarithmic scale, assigns to ten different levels feedback times ranging from 1/100th of a second to three months. A feedback time of one second, for example, is a level 0 feedback time. Similarly, a level 2 response is a feedback time of 1.5 minutes.

Figure 7-6 Time Scales of Feedback Control Mechanisms

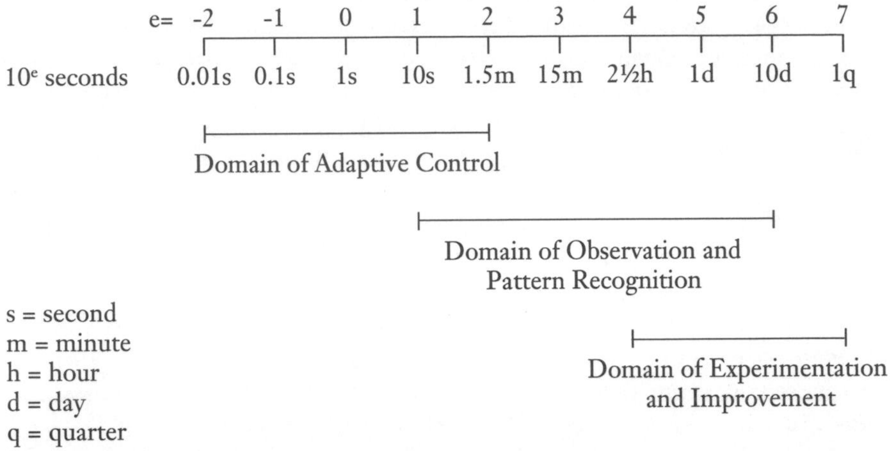

e=	-2	-1	0	1	2	3	4	5	6	7
10^e seconds	0.01s	0.1s	1s	10s	1.5m	15m	2½h	1d	10d	1q

Domain of Adaptive Control

Domain of Observation and
Pattern Recognition

s = second
m = minute
h = hour
d = day
q = quarter

Domain of Experimentation
and Improvement

Feedback time starts when a particular contingency is first observed, includes the time it takes to recognize a pattern of similar contingencies, and concludes when an appropriate procedure to control the contingency has been performed. Feedback time might be a second, an hour, or a day. Through the six epochs of process control, feedback time has been progressively reduced; in some cases, computers respond to contingencies at microsecond intervals.

Having briefly described the evolution of, and role of computers in, process control, we can now begin to develop a framework around which a process control costing system can be built.

A NEW FRAMEWORK FOR MANUFACTURING SYSTEMS

Figure 7-7 presents a manufacturing model for the CIM environment. In this model, the programs, procedures, and mechanical fixtures used in production are created by a firm's intellectual assets (the upper block in Figure 7-7). In an ideal world, once we have created a factory's physical assets, we can run it entirely without people. We can dispense completely with intellectual assets, and the fully automated factory can produce any feasible mix of products within the capacity constraints imposed by 1) its physical assets and the intelligence programmed into them, 2) the availability of raw materials and other inputs that can be purchased on a competitive market, and 3) the demand for its output in the consumer market. This is the world

Figure 7-7   A Framework for Manufacturing Systems

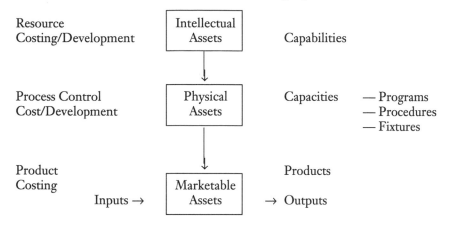

described earlier, in the discussion of CIM, as the "unmanned" factory.

To compete effectively in the ever-changing, real-world environment, however, we need to make process improvements constantly, which entails developing our intellectual assets in order to be able to create new procedures and adapt old ones. Projects, which grow out of decisions about which procedures to improve, what fixtures to build, and what resources to develop, are undertaken on the basis of some uncertain notion of the value that will accrue from the projects' output. Because all costs are sunk once a project is completed, and controllable costs are thus negligible, a process control costing system is needed to identify which of a variety of procedures need to be improved, and to provide an economic basis for making a choice among the possible controls that can be developed.

Improving processes for existing products not only enhances the efficacy and efficiency for these products but also augments the knowledge base available for the development of new product designs requiring even greater process capability. Thus, the benefits of such improvements are twofold and must be seen as such.

Managing Assets

Compare, in Table 7-3, the ratio of manufacturing to engineering overhead in a conventional U.S. factory (2:1) and in an FMS (1:3). The sixfold change in this ratio indicates just how much the emphasis

Table 7-3 Manpower Requirements for Cutting the Same Number of Identical Metal Parts

	United States	Japan	FMSs Japan
Engineering	34	18	16
Manufacturing overhead	64	22	5
Fabrication	52	28	6
Assembly	44	32	16
Total number of workers	194	100	43

Note: There is no column for FMSs in the United States because, at the time of this study, no domestic machine-tool producer had an FMS "on line."

has shifted from "minding the store" to creating new products and processes.[4]

The firm's *physical assets* (the middle block in Figure 7-7) are its production machinery. These assets determine the kinds of products that can be made and the total capacity of production across the entire portfolio of products for any given period of time. Management of physical assets is management of capacities. Management's task is to manage the portfolio of products that can be produced so as to maximize the firm's net revenues (i.e., revenues less materials costs). Management must also determine how well the firm's physical assets are performing with respect to the existing portfolio of products and how well they might perform with a potentially more desirable portfolio of products.

The performance levels of the physical assets are related to the two types of contingencies discussed earlier: 1) those related to the efficacy of the process being used, and 2) uncertainties about capabilities required by new products and processes. If neither type is present, no new development is required. It is the presence of contingencies that leads to further development. A process control costing system is needed to value contingencies to guide the development activities of the firm's intellectual assets for the next period. Thus, the need for a process control costing system rests on the following premises:

- the principal goal in production is process improvement;
- for any manufacturing system comprising one or more process steps, our technical know-how consists of a model for the control of each step;
- imperfections in such a model give rise to contingencies in production and incur costs to the firm;

- to the extent that we can improve the model, we can enhance control of the process steps; and
- we can build a costing system that focuses attention on, and assesses the relative importance of, contingencies in production, thereby facilitating refinement of the model. We can do this because the costing model will be identical to the underlying model for production control.

As we can see in Table 7-4, the domain of observation is concerned with scientific models of production and how procedures can effectively utilize technical know-how for adaptive control. Such models, which might include fishbone diagrams or causal trees that link events with their potential causes, are derived from an imperfect understanding of the physical world of production. Other models, relying on pattern recognition, might involve making inferences statistically or by analogy. Models such as these, which are not models of the production process but are related to them, form the basis of a process control costing system.

Event Analysis

The basic unit of analysis in process control is a contingent event—an unexpected disruption in the flow of the process or a discrepancy between specified product parameters and the actual product. An organization's response to a contingent event can range over a broad spectrum, from altogether ignoring the event to directing a massive allocation of attention and effort to its complete elimination. Choice enters into the organizational response due to the large numbers of possible events and the variety of possible responses to each. A process control costing system can impart an *economic* value to these choices. It can assign an economic value to reducing the occurrence of different kinds of contingencies, to increasing process capability, to securing additional information needed to resolve uncertainty, and to understanding the history of, and responses to, events.

Returning to Figure 7-6, we see the three domains within which events can be analyzed. Process control costing systems deal with the domain of observation and pattern recognition (levels 1 to 6). Here we observe procedures and the contingencies they create in the domain of adaptive control (levels -2 to 2) to derive information that has economic consequences when applied in the domain of experimentation and improvement (levels 4 to 7). To relate an event to perfor-

Table 7-4 Domains of Feedback Control

Domain	Models	Economics
Adaptive Control	Scientific model of production process	Economics of process control mechanism
Observation and Pattern Recognition	Deviations in the environment Deviations in the control parameters Deviations from process model	Economics of adjustment and learning
Experimentation and Improvement	Design of experiments Refinement of scientific models of production Systems effects of local changes	Economics of resource allocation and knowledge development

mance measures, and then subsequently to control a process, we need the following:

- the ability to translate the event and the performance measure into money;
- a scientific model that relates production parameters to process parameters;
- an economic model that relates resource utilization to process capacity;
- all the controllable parameters and constraints on production;
- a time scale for every controllable feed-back and feed-forward loop; and
- the relationship between a set of controllables and a set of resources.

An Example of Process Control Costing

How are events, contingencies, and process improvements costed out? Consider, as an example, machine downtime. We first determine the value per unit of time for the machine. This is the "shadow cost" of capacity and can be obtained through a variety of methods related to capacity utilization. A production monitoring system provides information about all occurrences of machine shutdown (e.g., causes, duration, and so forth). We classify the events by category and aggregate the events within each category. Given the opportunity cost of downtime, we can now calculate the benefit of reducing or eliminating each category of downtime.

Continuing with the example of machine failure, we now require a logical model of machine failure that relates different kinds of failure, mean times between failure, and causes of failure. Such models are, by their very nature, imprecise. As we gather more information about production processes, we can begin to assess the impact of different causes on machine failure. The model needed for process control costing is precisely the model we need to control a process. A process control costing system adds to this model the economic value and economic cost of reducing or eliminating the different causes of failure. The benefit realized is given by the time saved multiplied by the opportunity cost of that time. The cost is the cost of the resources—in terms of new procedures, maintenance, new sensors or tools, personnel, and so forth—required to make the change.

In a factory, managers must choose from among a great many opportunities for making process improvements. These opportunities could be ranked by calculating for each the ratio of the benefit divided by the cost in order to determine which process improvement activities will yield the "most bang for the buck." More sophisticated models could be developed to relate the variety of cause and effect relationships in a large system to benefit measurement.

AN APPLICATION OF THE NEW ARCHITECTURE FOR PROCESS CONTROL COSTING

We illustrate our process control costing system with an example drawn from the manufacture of wire. Process control in the wire-drawing industry has evolved through the first four epochs depicted in Table 7-1. The industry is just beginning to use information-intensive processing, giving rise to an interesting case study—normatively building a process control costing system in this evolving environment.

Much of the wire-drawing industry works in the world of Taylor, with isolated pockets of statistical control. Know-how is an art, and involves the use of mechanical equipment. The typical plant houses more than a thousand wire-drawing machines, laid out functionally. Even though, as we shall see, process competence is the key to competitive advantage in wire-drawing, the industry's cost systems are tailored to product costing, and not to systematically evaluating process choices. The recent introduction of microprocessor control, circa 1985, and the rapid adoption of CIM have afforded us the luxury of being able to build a new architecture for costing.

The Wire-Drawing Process Today

A typical wire-drawing plant receives wire rod in spools, tests the rod for properties related to the raw material, and then stores it in a warehouse. The spools are subsequently sent to a pickling operation, in which the wire is cleaned in acid in preparation for dry wire-drawing. In the drawing operation, the spools are loaded into an unwinding spool bin and the wire is pulled through a series of dies of progressively smaller diameter. This reduces the diameter of the wire and lengthens it, adding stress and changing its crystalline structure.

The wire is then heat-treated to relieve the stress and coated with different substances to change the surface structure. The thinner-gauge wire is wound onto other spools and transported to a wet wire-drawing operation, similar to the dry wire-drawing operation. The spools are then sent to finishing operations, where the wire can be cut, galvanized, and coated with adhesives or processed in whatever way is desired to customize the final product. Finished spools are packaged, palletized, and returned to the warehouse.

A typical factory will have two large pickling machines, 200 dry wire-drawing machines, 20 heat-treating installations, 1,000 wet wire-drawing machines, and 100 finishing lines. The plant will make 100–1,000 different products. The value-added in such a plant has the components shown in Table 7-5. As we can see, fully half of direct labor is related to disruptions in the process. Most of the indirect labor and maintenance is also related to disruptions in the process.

Figure 7-8 provides a simple illustration of the wet wire-drawing operation. The wire is pulled through a series of dies, like the one depicted in the illustration, by an unwinding spool. On the average, the wire fractures about every 200 kilometers.

Finding the reasons for wire fractures is similar to finding the reasons for a break in a chain—one locates the weakest link and identifies the characteristics responsible for its weakness. In a statistical distribution of the different treatments on a wire, the worst sequence of treatments will lead to poor product properties, which will be reflected in the extreme tails of the treatment distribution. Thus, it is not the mean process parameters that dictate product/process failure,

Table 7-5   Percentage Breakdown of Value-Added in a Wire-Drawing Plant

Direct Labor		33%
Loading and Unloading	30%	
Machine Breakdown and Wire Fractures	50	
"Other"	20	
Indirect Labor		15
Maintenance		25
Overhead		27
Total Value-Added		100%

but the tails of the distribution, which reflect poor product properties. Hence, we need to manage the wire-drawing process so as to reduce process variance. Process variables number in the hundreds, as do possible responses to a wire fracture. Thus, the degrees of freedom one has, not only to respond to a given fracture but also to reduce its incidence, are many. Table 7-6 provides an example of the kinds of process parameters involved in various steps in the process. In a plant with more than 1,000 machines, the choices available at any given time are many: one needs a system that will help operators focus attention on the right problems and use the appropriate control mechanisms.

Today, an economic valuation of process alternatives is not done—costs are maintained by production order and information on fractures and machine reliability is based on monthly production reports. The different steps in the process are located in different parts of the plant, each of which has its own supervisory structure. Information about the impact of heat-treating, which is done in one part of the plant, or on wire-drawing, which is done in another part, is not captured. In fact, no systematic analysis of process variance is performed—a process that is out of control is resolved by ad hoc engineering analysis. Consequently, little or no learning occurs and history repeats itself, over and over again.

The Automated Wire-Drawing Process

An automated, continuous flow wire-drawing process is being developed in which the process flow described previously is under the control of one system for similar products. The new process eliminates

Figure 7-8   Typical Operation in a Wet Wire-Drawing Process

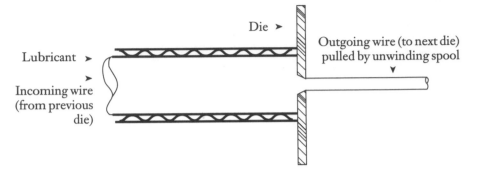

many machines—an automated plant would probably still have two pickling machines, but only ten dry wire-drawing machines, one heat-treating installation, 500 wet wire-drawing machines, and 50 finishing lines.

As spools are handled by automated materials-handling equipment between operations, loading and unloading of machines is no longer in the province of direct labor. Returning to Table 7-5, we find that *all* the work of direct labor now relates to machine breakdowns and fractures in the wire. Hence, the source of competitive advantage is now *entirely* process control.

In an automated facility, all of the microprocessor-controlled machines, and the processes that run on them, are integrated and use the hierarchical structure already described (see Figure 7-4). We now have systems integration, so let us see what an omniscient observer might do in the wire-drawing process.

For one thing, the omniscient observer can track all the process parameters that operate on every meter of wire that goes through the line. During heat-treating, for instance, the omniscient observer can know the location of a given meter of wire as different furnace burners are opened and closed. Thus, at any given time, the omniscient observer is aware not only of the ambient temperature in the furnace but also of the finite states of a number of operating parameters. When a fracture occurs, the omniscient observer has data on the sequence of events concerning the particular meter of wire that suffered the fracture; such data were never before available.

Let us consider just the wet wire-drawing process. Certain parameters related to the incoming product, certain parameters to the outgoing product, and certain fixed parameters are the same for the

Table 7-6 Some of the Process Parameters Observed in an
Automated Wire-Drawing System

Pickling	Dry Wire-Drawing	Heat-Treating	Wet Wire-Drawing
Furnace Temperature	Drawing Wire Temperature	Furnace Temperature	Total Reduction
Furnace Burner Temperature	Cooling Water	CO Percentage in Furnace	Lubricant Temperature
CO Percentage in Furnace	Atmosphere at Payoff	Wire Temperature at Furnace Exit	Tension
Volume of Furnace Burner Gas	Drawing Speed	Speed	Residual Lubricant
Speed		Furnace Burner Temperature	Head Die Reduction
Atmosphere at Take-Up		Volume of Furnace Burner Gas	
		Wire Temperature at Furnace Burner Exit	
		Thermo Diffusion	
		Take-up Tension	
		Payoff Tension	
		Outside Atmosphere	

entire spool. Control parameters change with every meter of wire (see
Table 7-6). One can use the information gathered on fractures to make
changes in the microprocessor controller during the process and affect
key process variables in the outcome. The algorithm used for control
can be changed, the results of the experiments observed, and new
changes introduced.

In a normal production operation, with more than 1,000 machines running, an operator has a number of options available—at the
first intimation of a problem, he has to ask, How long can I keep
running? Which machines should I speed up or slow down? and

Given a number of problems to solve, which should I solve first? There are also more routine questions, such as When should I change dies? and What products should I run on which machines? One would like to be able to make an economic choice among these process alternatives. An omniscient observer could use the kinds of information described earlier in both day-to-day production decisions and in the development of algorithms to create new process capability over the long term.

The process control costing system just described is event-based, statistical in nature, attention-focusing, and allows us to build, and subsequently refine, models of production processes. These characteristics enable us to distinguish between systematic and random events, detect novel events and patterns of events, and evaluate features of interest. It enables us to capture a complete picture of events, compare those events with expectations and alternative procedures, assign an economic value to the procedures, and suggest variations and experimentation.

CONCLUSION

Eight months ago, we started construction of a CIM system for wire-drawing on one line. To date, we have realized a fourfold reduction in fractures on the line and expect a tenfold increase in productivity. The architecture described in this paper is general—many different implementations are possible. The company is currently working on a number of specific implementations whose outcomes will be reported in a subsequent paper.

NOTES

1. See Robert S. Kaplan, "One Cost System Isn't Enough," *Harvard Business Review* (January–February 1988): 61–66.

2. Ramchandran Jaikumar, "From Filing and Fitting to Flexible Manufacturing" (Harvard Business School Working Paper, 1988).

3. Thomas H. Johnson and Robert S. Kaplan, *Relevance Lost: The Rise and Fall of Management Accounting* (Boston: Harvard Business School Press, 1987): 7–8.

4. Ramchandran Jaikumar, "Postindustrial Manufacturing," *Harvard Business Review* (November–December 1986): 69–76.

PART III

Measures for Product Design Improvements

CHAPTER 8

Activity Accounting: An Electronics Industry Implementation

George Foster and Mahendra Gupta

INTRODUCTION

ACTIVITY accounting systems (AASs) are attracting considerable interest.[1] Advocates of activity accounting claim a long and diverse list of possible benefits.[2] The growing number of organization units adopting variants of AAS will enable us to probe the descriptive validity of these claims. These adoptions also provide insight into implementation issues associated with the changeover to an AAS.

This paper discusses the implementation of an AAS by an electronics instruments manufacturing facility (disguised as Instruments Inc.) that assembles and tests over 800 products (including options and accessories). These products include electronic measurement instruments. Manufacturing personnel number approximately 300. Instruments Inc. first adopted activity accounting in May 1988. This was the culmination of over four years of experimentation, led initially by a materials engineering manager. The accounting group did not become involved in the project until late 1985. In November 1988, a substantial revision in the AAS was made; the revision

This paper would not have been possible without the cooperation and enthusiasm of the personnel of Instruments Inc. Detailed comments by A. Atkinson, C. Horngren, and R. Kaplan helped tighten the analysis and exposition.

changed the recording of indirect activity costs. This paper examines product cost figures reported in both the May 1988 and November 1988 versions of activity accounting as well as those reported by the pre–May 1988 system. We will cover the following topics:

- The firm's prior internal accounting system
- Criticism of the prior system
- Iteration to activity accounting
- Implementation of activity accounting system(s)
- Comparison of reported product costs
- Explanation of changes in reported product costs
- Implementation suggestions: a retrospective viewpoint
- Behavior changes associated with implementation of AAS

THE FIRM'S PRIOR INTERNAL ACCOUNTING SYSTEM

Instruments Inc.'s internal accounting system prior to May 1988 had a heavy focus on product costing. The two direct product cost categories were direct materials and direct labor. Indirect costs allocated to products comprised manufacturing overhead (MOH). Two MOH cost pools were used in this allocation:

- MOH cost pool 1—allocated to products based on their direct materials dollar component
- MOH cost pool 2—allocated to products based on their direct labor dollar component

(See Appendix A, Section 1, for a numerical example of this system.)

Exhibit 8-1 (Panel A) presents distribution data on the ratio of each cost category in the pre–May 1988 system to the total manufacturing product cost for each of the 298 products with budgeted production volume in 1988.[3] Each of the three cost categories is independently ranked and the associated ratios for the other two cost categories calculated. Columns 2, 5, and 8 present the independently ranked cost categories. The median ratios for these columns are

- Direct materials cost/total product cost   .64
- Manufacturing overhead/total product cost   .33
- Direct labor/total product cost   .02

Instruments Inc. sells its products in a highly competitive market. Price, product quality, and service are each perceived as important

Exhibit 8-1 Distribution Statistics on Manufacturing Product Cost Structure at Instruments Inc.

Deciles of Distribution (1)	Direct Materials (Ranked*) (2)	Manufacturing Overhead (3)	Direct Labor (4)	Manufacturing Overhead (Ranked*) (5)	Direct Materials (6)	Direct Labor (7)	Direct Labor (Ranked*) (8)	Direct Materials (9)	Manufacturing Overhead (10)
Panel A: Old System (pre–May 1988)									
.1	.49	.45	.06	.24	.76	.00	.00	.75	.25
.3	.61	.36	.03	.29	.70	.01	.01	.72	.27
.5	.64	.34	.02	.33	.65	.02	.02	.61	.37
.7	.69	.30	.01	.36	.61	.03	.03	.62	.35
.9	.75	.25	.00	.42	.54	.04	.05	.54	.41
Panel B: AAS I (May 1988)									
.1	.42	.58	—	.17	.83	—	—	—	—
.3	.54	.46	—	.28	.72	—	—	—	—
.5	.62	.38	—	.38	.62	—	—	—	—
.7	.72	.28	—	.46	.54	—	—	—	—
.9	.83	.17	—	.58	.42	—	—	—	—
Panel C: AAS II (November 1983)									
.1	.44	.56	—	.14	.86	—	—	—	—
.3	.56	.44	—	.27	.73	—	—	—	—
.5	.62	.38	—	.38	.62	—	—	—	—
.7	.73	.27	—	.44	.56	—	—	—	—
.9	.87	.13	—	.56	.44	—	—	—	—

*Cost category used to rank the 235 products from lowest to highest. Distribution points for other cost categories (category) pertain to products at deciles for the ranked variable.

factors in customer decisions. Product profit margins have been under considerable pressure in the 1980s. Listed prices of the products examined range from $12–$9,700, with a median of $417.

CRITICISM OF THE PRIOR SYSTEM

Criticism of the prior accounting system came from at least three areas: product design, manufacturing, and marketing.

Product Design. Product designers believed that the cost buildup of products based only on direct materials cost and direct labor cost and their associated burden rates lacked credibility. A typical concern was

Why is it when I use a $0.20 part (X), the materials overhead charge is $0.02, whereas when I use a $100 part (Y), the materials charge is $10? Part Y does not consume 500 times the resources used to procure and move part X.

Product designers started to develop their own "closet" sets of cost guidelines. However, the guidelines developed by individual designers were inconsistent. Moreover, the resulting product cost estimates failed to link up with the product costs subsequently reported by the internal reporting system. These closet costing systems did not promote the learning that arises when individual designers frequently discuss and refine a cost system widely used at a facility.

Product designers reported that the prior system provided "few believable guidelines on how to reduce product costs." The myopic focus on designing-out direct labor was mentioned in many interviews. Under the pre–1988 system, every $1 of direct labor designed into a product "attracted" almost $6 of manufacturing overhead. The system communicated a clear cost guideline: design products with minimal direct labor content. Many designers argued that this was "simplistic" at best. Some argued that it was "straight wrong." The following comment by a designer captures the latter viewpoint:

The implication of the design-out labor guideline, given that we are not highly automated, is that we should become a final-parts assembler. I simply do not buy that. We are adding value to products that would be lost if we simply subcontracted out every activity that required a sizable direct labor component.

One product designer noted that while the direct labor content of products had been reduced in recent years, there was little evidence that manufacturing overhead had declined.

Manufacturing. The pre–1988 system was perceived by manufacturing personnel to assume more homogeneity than they believed existed in their operations. Exhibit 8-2 presents a classification scheme that captures their concerns.

- **Activity Cost Pool Diversity.** At one end of the spectrum is homogeneity: all activities have the same cost driver and each cost driver has the same overhead rate. At the other end of the spectrum is heterogeneity: each individual activity has a different cost driver (or those with the same cost drivers have different overhead rates).
- **Product Usage of Individual Activities Diversity.** At one end of the spectrum is homogeneity: all products pass through the same activities and make equivalent use of the facilities in each activity. At the other end of the spectrum is heterogeneity: each product makes unique use of the facilities at each activity.

Manufacturing believed its operations were in the northeast corner of Exhibit 8-2, i.e., heterogeneity existed in both activity cost pools and in product usage of individual activities. The previous costing system implicitly assumed Instruments Inc. was in the southwest corner of Exhibit 8-2. The alleged consequence of this mismatch was product costs for individual products that manufacturing personnel argued were "not credible." For example, some products that made extensive use of high-cost activity areas were reported to have lower indirect costs than several other products that made extensive use of low-cost activity areas.

Manufacturing personnel interviewed had three specific criticisms of the prior system.

- Failure to reinforce design-for-manufacturability (DFM) considerations. Manufacturing in the 1980s had been paying increasing attention to DFM, e.g., reducing the part count in products and increasing the number of parts used in more than one product. The pre–May 1988 accounting system did not explicitly capture DFM considerations.
- Failure to signal the cost of manufacturing products with low volume. One supervisor in the printed circuit area noted: "It encouraged a proliferation of low-volume products, many of which were subsidized by the high-volume products." Another supervisor noted that "direct labor was a poor representation of manufacturing overhead cost behavior, especially for manufacturing low-volume products."

Exhibit 8-2   Homogeneity/Heterogeneity Classifications Related to Activity Accounting

	Homogeneity	Heterogeneity
Heterogeneity		Manufacturing Personnel's Perception of Product/Activity Area Environment ↗
Activity Cost Pool Diversity	Product/Activity Area Environment Implicit in Pre–May 1988 Accounting System ↙	
Homogeneity		

Product Usage of Individual Activities

- Low visibility of individual activity area cost drivers. Manufacturing personnel perceived individual activities differed in the variable(s) that drove cost levels, but the differences were not reflected in the prior accounting system. The phrase "increase the visibility of cost drivers" was used by many of those interviewed when discussing the perceived benefits of AAS over the prior accounting system. The pre–May 1988 system emphasized the development of product costs. Starting in the 1983–1984 period, manufacturing at Instruments Inc. increased the focus of its activities on processes rather than on products (especially in the printed circuit board part of the facility). However, the internal accounting system was not designed to support analysis of costs of **individual activities.** In the words of one manufacturing manager, "The prior accounting system simply was irrelevant to our cost control decision making."

Marketing. There is considerable diversity in the volumes Instruments Inc. sells of individual products. Selected points on the distribution of estimated six-month unit production volume for the 298 products examined here are

Percentiles of the Distribution						
.01	.10	.30	.50	.70	.90	.99
1	5	18	45	122	485	1811

The range is from a minimum of 1 unit to a maximum of 4,826 units. Several marketing personnel reported they were having problems being cost competitive on their high-volume products when they felt that they should be most competitive with these products. They believed one possible explanation for this could be found in systematic biases in the product cost figures reported by the existing accounting system.

ITERATION TO ACTIVITY ACCOUNTING

In May 1988, Instruments Inc. replaced its existing accounting system with an activity accounting system. The phrase "process cost accounting" (PCA) is used internally to describe this system. Over the 1983 to 1988 period, Instruments Inc. iterated toward the AAS adopted in May 1988. The early efforts were led by a materials engineering manager. It was not until late 1985 that accounting personnel became involved in the AAS developments.

In late 1983, a materials engineering manager experimented with ways to reduce the materials-related costs in the products assembled. Out of these efforts, a manufacturing cost model (MCM) evolved. The model had 45 separate cost drivers and reflected how individual products used activity areas at the facility. Running parallel to these efforts was a task force (led by the R&D/product design manager and the manufacturing manager) to promote design-for-manufacturability (DFM). The task force was expanded in late 1985 to include the materials engineering manager and representatives from accounting and manufacturing engineering. One issue discussed was whether to give specific guidelines to designers (e.g., reduce part count or eliminate hand load) or to use an accounting system to signal the relative costs of design choices. The DFM task force opted for the latter, in part because it delegated more decision making to the designers. Its choice led to increased interest in the MCM.

There were two concerns with the MCM as it existed in early 1986. First, it was perceived to be overly complex. One product designer commented: "You had to be a rocket scientist to comprehend it." Second, it was not integrated into the internal accounting system. One designer pejoratively referred to it as a "a back of the envelope cost model." The DFM task force then decided to set up a cost driver task force to explore the adoption of a version of AAS as the internal accounting system.

The cost driver task force had three members: the materials engineering manager who developed the MCM as well as one representative each from accounting and information systems. The materials engineering manager reported to the manufacturing manager and was viewed as the spokesman for manufacturing. The R&D/product design group was not represented on this task force. At no stage did marketing have a representative on either the DFM task force or the cost driver task force.

The initial plan was to have an AAS operational in November 1987 and to run both the prior system and the AAS in parallel for the six months from November 1987 to April 1988. During this six-month period, there would be debugging of the AAS, e.g., adjustments to standards to take account of any large variances in the AAS. This plan was not fulfilled, in part because of the limited resources available for AAS development at the facility. The project team included enthusiasts, but it had not yet developed broad-based support for activity accounting. One member of the team noted that even in October 1987 it was still a "skunkworks project." The date to start on-line with the AAS was pushed back to May 1988. Rather than run two systems in parallel, starting in May 1988, only AAS-based numbers were reported. Given the delays that had already occurred, it was believed that an exclusive and immediate focus on AAS numbers would speed the development of the system.

Objectives of AAS at Instruments Inc.

Internal presentations, made in the initial months of the implementation of AAS, listed the following five objectives:

1. Provide manufacturing managers with a tool to monitor costs by production process in order to
   • Drive each operation's cost down
   • Build each product in the most economical fashion
   • Improve "ownership" and responsibility for cost cutting of processes

- Identify cost-saving opportunities with regard to adding processes, eliminating processes, purchasing equipment, and so
forth
- Improve decision making
2. Provide R&D with product costs that accurately reflect actual
cost to manufacture in order to
  - Allow costs to reflect design decisions
  - Provide a meaningful "report card" of designer performance
  - Improve new product evaluations
3. Provide R&D with a "what if . . ." capability to easily test
the impact of design alternatives on total manufacturing cost
4. Provide marketing with product costs that accurately reflect ac-
tual cost to manufacture in order to
  - Improve pricing of products
  - Improve discount policy by product
  - Improve new product evaluations
5. Provide finance with the tools to
  - Cost all products by process
  - Report variances by process
  - Report actual process rates by process

All of the above was to be achieved with minimum changes to
existing systems and to existing staffing levels. The focus of the behavior changes sought in the initial phases of the AAS implementation was on manufacturing and its upstream activities (e.g., product
design and process design). The following phrases, also used in many
internal presentations, reinforced this focus: "allow design trade-offs,"
"quantify and make manufacturing costs visible," and "provide a common reference point for design/manufacturing decisions."

Instruments Inc. implemented AAS to change the behavior of
line personnel. At least two approaches to changing behavior were
debated by members of the task force:

1. develop "accurate" activity cost data and let them guide behavior, or

2. "adjust" the cost data to increase their signaling component over
and above (1).

An example of (2) was a proposal to "artificially double" the standard
cost of using the masking activity area. The purpose was to encourage
product designers to reduce the masking component on boards being

designed. The task force rejected the proposal and opted for approach (1); this was perceived to increase the credibility of the AAS numbers. One member of the task force expressed strong opposition to (2): "We shouldn't mess with the cost data to manipulate behavior. Estimate the activity costs as accurately as possible and then let the chips fall whichever way they do."[4]

Activity Area and Cost Driver Choices

The AAS implemented in May 1988 is based on a breakdown of 14 activity areas (see the section on implementation and Appendix A). This number of activity areas was a compromise between a) the product design and accounting groups, which wanted a system with fewer than 14 activity areas and, b) the manufacturing group, which wanted a system with more than 14 activity areas.

Internal presentations noted four requirements of a cost driver at each activity area:

- it must be "systematically accumulable"
- it must "control a large number of dollars"
- it must have a "diagnostic capability"
- it must have the capability to "impact design decisions" or to be a "vehicle for process cost management"

The last factor is consistent with the targeted behavior changes of the AAS aimed at manufacturing and its upstream activities.

Manufacturing personnel had the largest voice in the choice of the individual activity areas and the cost driver at each area. The choices were based on their knowledge of the operations. Data analysis (e.g., correlation studies) played a minimal role in their choices. Manufacturing initially proposed having several cost drivers at each activity area. However, accounting was "very negative" to this proposal. One member of the accounting group noted: "We responded, 'Time out! Let us get the system up and running first and then at a later stage add the refinement of multiple cost drivers.'" Both Phase I and Phase II of the AAS restricted each activity area to only one cost driver. Several manufacturing personnel interviewed still believe further refinement of the AAS is possible, by assigning multiple drivers at each activity area or by increasing the number of activity areas.

IMPLEMENTATION OF ACTIVITY ACCOUNTING SYSTEM(S)

Phase I Implementation (May 1988–October 1988)

Fourteen activity areas were distinguished in the Phase I implementation (see Exhibit 8-3). Activity areas 1 to 12 cover printed circuit board assembly while areas 13 and 14 cover the instrument buildup and testing activities. Total product cost in phase 1 consisted of 4 components.

1. **Direct product costs:** These comprised only direct materials costs. Simultaneous with the adoption of AAS, Instruments Inc. started classifying all labor costs as indirect costs. By May 1988, direct labor costs were less than 5% of total product cost for over 90% of the products (see Exhibit 8-1).

2. **Activity area-based indirect product costs:** These costs were built up from the use individual products made of the 14 activity areas in Exhibit 8-3. Up to three cost functions at each area were recognized:[5]

   a. **Driver quantity-based.** A cost driver was chosen for each activity area and a cost per unit of driver estimated. For example, the driver in the axial insertion area was the number of axial insertions. The quantity-based indirect cost was based on the total number of axial insertions in the PC boards incorporated into a product times the activity cost per axial insertion.

   b. **Assembly unit-based.** In three activity areas (hand load, hand add, and board test) an additional indirect cost was attributed to each product that utilized the resources of that activity. This cost was a function of the number of assembly units. A single PC board was the assembly unit in each of the first 12 activity areas.

   c. **Batch size-based.** In six activity areas (axial insertion, dip insertion, robotic insertion, hand load, hand add, and board test), a third indirect cost was attributed to products that utilized the resources of that activity. An indirect cost charge was made for each production batch; this charge was assigned to individual assemblies based on the number of assemblies in the production batch. This batch-size cost function means that each product can have N different actual costs if it is assembled in N different batch sizes in a given period. (The product costs analyzed here are based on standard batch sizes.)

3. **Period-Based Indirect Product Costs:** These costs are a function of the direct materials dollar component of each product.

4. **Other Indirect Product Costs:** This cost category comprises those indirect costs not in (2) or (3). In Phase I, the magnitude of the costs included in (4) was relatively small. These costs were attributed to each product on a percentage of the activity area-based indirect product costs.

Appendix A, Section 2, presents a numerical example to illustrate product costing in the Phase I implementation of AAS

Phase II Implementation (starting November 1988)

In November 1988, a major change was made in the cost buildup of individual activity areas. A sizable component of the total costs of each activity in Phase I comprised indirect activity costs. These costs related to support and other functions that provided resources to each of the 14 activity areas in the AAS, e.g., EDP, manufacturing engineering, and production planning.

Manufacturing personnel at Instruments Inc. raised strong objections to the magnitude of the indirect activity costs included in the activity cost buildups in AAS Phase I. The following comments are typical of their objections:

- Allocating the costs of other activity areas into my activity area seems like a make-work task for accountants. I can only manage those costs for which I have ownership. I have no ownership of the costs incurred in other areas.
- The fundamental goal should be to make the accounting system track true process (direct activity) costs and to give supervisors the skills and tools to manage process costs. This implies a low nonprocess (indirect activity) component of the cost bucket.
- You want the costs at the activity areas to be controllable. The indirect costs were a "pure tax" on the activity and we felt we had no representation on how the tax was set.

Exhibit 8-3 Activity Areas/Cost Drivers at Instruments Inc.

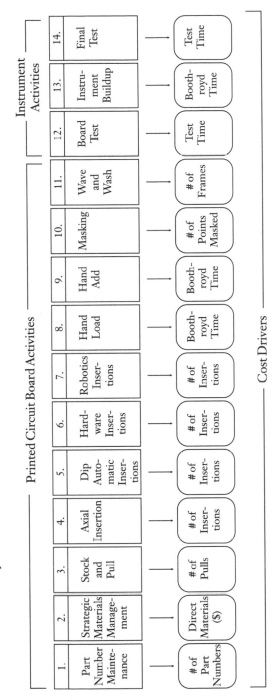

The phrase "I have no ownership of those [indirect activity] costs" was heard many times during interviews with manufacturing personnel.

The Phase II version of AAS retains the same activity areas and the same cost drivers as Phase I. The key change in Phase II is a reduction in the indirect activity costs included in the 14 activity areas.[6] These costs are now classified as "Other Indirect Product Costs," i.e., component (4) of product costs in Phase I. Exhibit 8-4 compares the percentage of total indirect activity costs at each activity area in Phases I and II. Activity areas 1 (Part Number Maintenance) and 2 (Strategic Materials Management) have the largest reductions in indirect activity costs in Phase II vis-à-vis Phase I. Appendix A, Section 3, illustrates the Phase II implementation of AAS.

The percentage of total indirect costs in the Other Indirect Product Costs category increased from 6% in Phase I to 33% in Phase II. This change is viewed as an interim step. The hope is that subsequent analysis of these costs will either facilitate more activity areas (each with its own cost driver) or lead to the elimination of the activity. Phase II is viewed as a transition step that recognized the concerns of manufacturing and increased the visibility of the magnitude of indirect activity costs. It is well recognized at Instruments Inc. that the existing cost driver (activity area-based indirect product costs) has little cause-and-effect relationship with costs included in the Other Indirect Product Costs category.[7]

Panels B (AAS Phase I) and C (AAS Phase II) of Exhibit 8-1 present distribution data on the ratio of the two cost categories in AAS to the total product cost for the 298 products examined here. The median ratio of direct materials to total product cost is .62 and the median ratio of manufacturing overhead to total product cost is .38 in both AAS versions.

Heterogeneity Recognized in AAS

One complaint against the prior accounting system was that it assumed more homogeneity than existed at Instruments Inc. The AAS system developed can be used to gain insight into the heterogeneity with which individual products use each activity area. The cost driver units used at each activity area by each product are added (assuming one unit of each is assembled). Products at each activity area are then ranked in terms of the number of cost driver units used (from highest

Exhibit 8-4   Comparison of Total Indirect Activity Costs at Each Activity Area in Phase I and Phase II

Percentages of Total Indirect Activity Center Costs

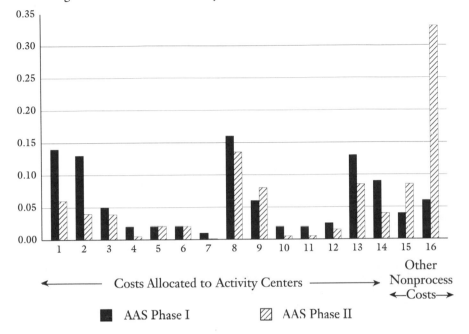

Costs Allocated to Activity Centers ⟶

Other Nonprocess ←Costs→

■ AAS Phase I   ▨ AAS Phase II

Notes: Activity Centers 1–14 as per Exhibit 8-3.
Activity Center 15: Period-Based Indirect Product Costs.
Activity Center 16: Other Indirect Product Costs.

to lowest). The percentage of the total drivers used by the first 5%, 10%, 15%, 20%, and 40% of products (assuming one unit of each is assembled) is then calculated. Panel A of Exhibit 8-5 presents the actual distribution of the percentage of total drivers used by selected percentages of the 298 products assembled. The expected distribution of the percentage of total drivers used by selected percentages of products, assuming all products are homogeneous in terms of use of cost drivers, is presented in Panel B of Exhibit 8-5. The actual distribution in Panel A differs markedly from the expected distribution in Panel B. A small subset of products at each individual activity area uses a disproportionately large number of the cost drivers at that activity. For example, selected observations underlying Exhibit 8-5 are as follows:

Activity Area	Cumulative Percentage of Cost Drivers Used by		
	5% of Products	10% of Products	20% of Products
Part Number Maintenance	40.0%	54.0%	61.9%
Axial Insertions	31.3	49.2	59.1
Robotic Insertions	86.1	100.0	100.0
Hand Add	42.2	57.1	64.2
Masking	79.8	91.6	93.6
Final Test	64.6	81.4	86.7

The patterns in Exhibit 8-5 are consistent with the considerable heterogeneity existing at Instruments Inc. in the way individual products use the resources at each activity area.

COMPARISON OF REPORTED PRODUCT COSTS

Instruments Inc. uses a standard product costing system. Actual product costs have not been computed in either Phase 1 or Phase 2 of their AAS. All comparisons of product costs in this section are based on standard costs. To facilitate comparisons with the prior costing system, Instruments Inc. retained data on the standard costs previously classified as direct labor in the pre–May 1988 system. Data on individual product costs for three accounting systems were made available:

$$X = \text{Pre–May 1988 system}$$
$$Y = \text{AAS Phase I Implementation (AAS-I)}$$
$$Z = \text{AAS Phase II Implementation (AAS-II)}$$

Two cost numbers will be analyzed for each product i:

$\text{IMPC}_i = $ indirect manufacturing costs of product i, and
$\text{TMPC}_i = $ total (direct and indirect) manufacturing costs of product i

Three product cost comparisons will be made:

$$\frac{Y}{X} = \frac{\text{AAS-I}}{\text{Pre–May 1988 System}}$$

Exhibit 8-5   Usage of Total Drivers at Activity Centers

Panel A: Distribution of Actual Usage of Drivers by Products
Usage of Driver (%)

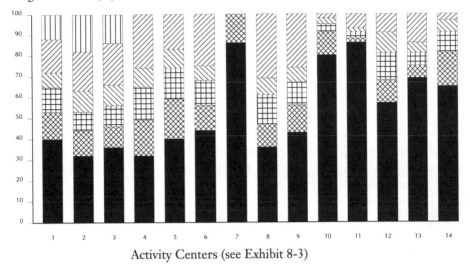

Activity Centers (see Exhibit 8-3)

Panel B: Distribution Assuming Homogeneous Use of Drivers by Products
Usage of Driver (%)

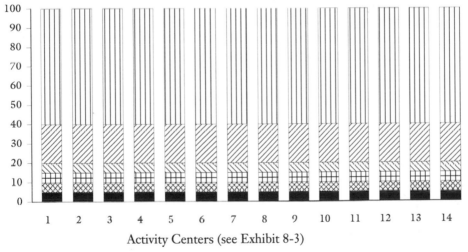

Activity Centers (see Exhibit 8-3)

Key: ■ 0–5   ⊠ 6–10   ⊞ 10–15   ◩ 16–20   ▨ 21–40   ⊡ 41–100
Percentages of Products

$$\frac{Z}{X} = \frac{\text{AAS-II}}{\text{Pre–May 1988 System}}$$

$$\frac{Z}{Y} = \frac{\text{AAS-II}}{\text{AAS-I}}$$

Exhibit 8-6 presents distribution statistics for the three product cost comparisons for both the $IMPC_i$ and $TMPC_i$ variables. Plots of the distribution of AAS-I/Pre–May 1988 and AAS-II/AAS-I for $IMPC_i$ are in Exhibits 8-7 and 8-8.[8] The distribution of reported costs under AAS-I and AAS–II vis-à-vis the pre–May 1988 system is positively skewed. Over 10% of products have increases in reported indirect costs under AAS-I of more than 100% vis-à-vis the pre–May 1988 system; 5% have increases of 300% or more.

The distribution of product cost differences in Exhibit 8-6 is most dispersed when either AAS-I or AAS-II is compared with the pre–May 1988 system. However, there are still some marked differences when the AAS-II product costs and the AAS-I product costs are compared. For example, the .1 and .9 deciles of the distribution for indirect costs of AAS-II vis-à-vis AAS-I are .74 and 1.31, respectively.[9] These differences between AAS-I and AAS-II highlight the fact that simply describing a cost system as an "activity accounting system" in no way implies that the resultant product cost numbers represent "truth" or "reality."

EXPLANATION OF CHANGES IN REPORTED PRODUCT COSTS

An analysis of variables associated with the reported product cost changes documented in Exhibits 8-6 to 8-8 was made. A summary of the results is now presented. Further details appear in Appendix B. Four categories of variables were examined:

- *Volume*-based variables, which relate to the level of output of each product, e.g., budgeted production volume.
- *Complexity*-based variables, which relate to the characteristics of products that potentially are "drivers" of manufacturing overhead costs, e.g., number of part numbers in a product.
- *Efficiency*-based variables, which relate to activities that increase the throughput time for assembling products, or do not add value

Exhibit 8-6 Comparison of Indirect Manufacturing Product Costs and Total Manufacturing Product Costs under Alternative Systems for 298 Products

Percentiles of Distribution (1)	Indirect Manufacturing Product Cost			Total Manufacturing Product Cost		
	AAS-I Pre–May 1988 (2)	AAS-II Pre–May 1988 (3)	AAS-II AAS-I (4)	AAS-I Pre–May 1988 (5)	AAS-II Pre–May 1988 (6)	AAS-II AAS-I (7)
.01	.16	.23	.29	.37	.54	.53
.05	.29	.39	.64	.63	.74	.83
.10	.52	.48	.74	.80	.86	.90
.20	.71	.66	.84	.91	.92	.96
.30	.88	.89	.90	.96	.99	.98
.40	1.00	1.00	.95	1.00	1.02	1.00
.50	1.11	1.17	.99	1.04	1.08	1.02
.60	1.22	1.25	1.04	1.08	1.12	1.05
.70	1.33	1.33	1.10	1.13	1.15	1.07
.80	1.60	1.55	1.16	1.22	1.22	1.10
.90	2.05	1.89	1.31	1.39	1.37	1.18
.95	3.01	2.91	1.52	1.74	1.75	1.41
.99	20.76	14.34	3.36	5.01	4.87	3.92

Key: Pre–May 1988 = Pre-Activity Accounting System (See the section on the Firm's Prior Internal Accounting System)
AAS-I = Phase I Implementation of AAS (See Appendix A, Section 1)
AAS-II = Phase II Implementation of AAS (See Appendix A, Section 2)

Exhibit 8-7   Distribution of Total Indirect Manufacturing Product Costs (Manufacturing Overhead and Direct Labor) AAS-I/Pre–May 1988

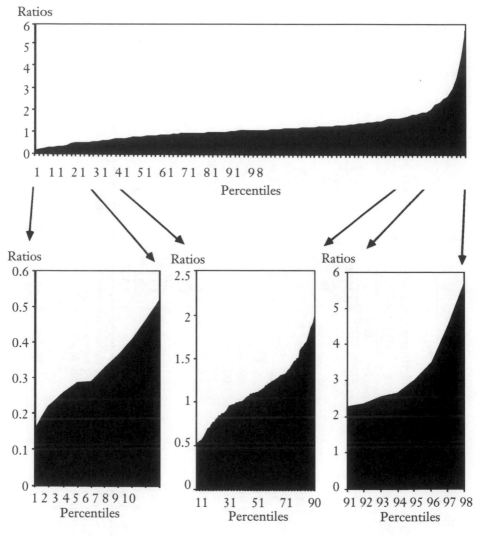

Note: Vertical scale is ratio of AAS-I/pre–May 1988 for indirect manufacturing product cost.

Exhibit 8-8 Distribution of Total Indirect Manufacturing Product
Costs (Manufacturing Overhead and Direct Labor) AAS-II/AAS-I

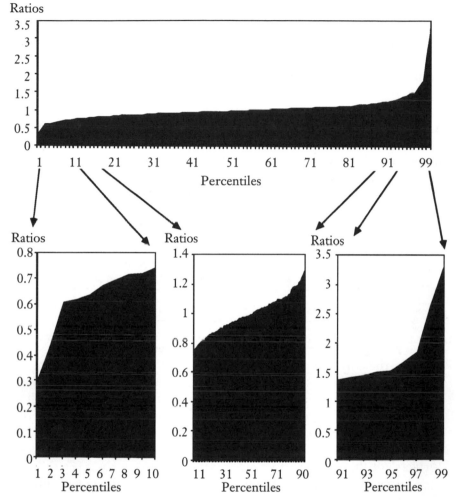

Note: Vertical scale is ratio of AAS-II/AAS-I for indirect
manufacturing product cost.

to the product as perceived by customers, e.g., setup time in component insertion areas.
* *Market*-based variables, which comprise the listed product price and the contribution margin percentage.

The volume, complexity, and efficiency variables capture variables explicitly incorporated into the AAS. The market variables were included to address comments made during interviews at Instruments Inc.

Significant univariate correlations exist between changes in the AAS-I or AAS-II product costs vis-à-vis the pre–May 1988 system, and variables in each of the volume, complexity, and efficiency categories. The five variables statistically significant across several multivariate regressions are

Category	Variable
Volume-Based	• Direct materials dollars
Complexity-Based	• # of part numbers • # of pulls in stock and pull • Boothroyd time in hand add
Efficiency-Based	• Test time for boards

These results are consistent with the considerable heterogeneity existing in the way individual products use the 14 activity areas in the AAS and with the cost driver choices in the AAS capturing this heterogeneity. All the data analysis is based on standard costs rather than on actual costs. The result is that much of our analysis examines the validity of the heterogeneity assumption implicit in the AAS. Our data analysis does not examine the validity of the chosen variables as "drivers" of the actual cost at each activity area.

Three findings in Appendix B support the following intuitions of many of those interviewed at Instruments Inc.

* Products with low (high) production volumes have increases (decreases) in reported product costs.
* Products with low (high) consumer listed prices have increases (decreases) in reported product costs.
* Products with low (high) contribution margin percentages have decreases (increases) in reported product costs under AAS vis-à-vis the pre–May 1988 system. None of these three results is an

artifact of the construction of the AAS numbers at Instruments Inc.

IMPLEMENTATION SUGGESTIONS: A RETROSPECTIVE VIEWPOINT

A "rich learning experience" (or variants thereof) is the phrase most often used at Instruments Inc. to describe the implementation phase of their AAS. Looking back, there is general agreement about some key aspects of an "implementation blueprint."[10]

Steering Task Force with Full-Time Leader and Representatives from All Key Areas.

A task force can provide several benefits. These include

- providing a visible (and ongoing) signal to all personnel that the AAS project is a priority one,
- promoting a group learning experience, and
- providing a set of individuals who can respond to enquiries, concerns, and so forth arising with the implementation.

Instruments Inc. operated with an AAS task force from the outset. This task force, which included several enthusiasts and "true believers," played a central role in maintaining momentum on the project. There is general agreement on two areas where the task force could have been further strengthened:

Having a full-time leader. AAS was implemented at a time when many other changes were occurring at Instruments Inc. The result was that efforts to solve implementation problems with AAS had to fight for priority with efforts to solve problems in other areas. The AAS task force leader had other responsibilities, several of which consumed large blocks of time (at not always predictable points). Having a full-time task force leader means that AAS implementation issues are given top priority on a continual basis by at least one person in the organization.

Having representatives from all key areas. Activity accounting systems are implemented to affect change in the decisions made in one or more functional areas. Involving members from all functional areas whose behavior is targeted for change gives them an opportunity to influence the AAS developments. It also may increase the "buy in" that each functional area has toward AAS. The product design group at Instruments Inc. has played a limited role in the cost driver task force discussions and in the implementation of AAS. One subset of product designers fully endorsed the concepts underlying AAS and reported that the system(s) implemented has been a very useful tool in their design decisions. Another subset of designers has yet to "buy into" the AAS, claiming it conveys no additional insights beyond those already available from existing design guidelines. One member of this second group views AAS, along with the design-for-manufacturability (DFM) program, as an inappropriate attempt by manufacturing to affect the behavior of designers.

Project Plan That Includes Objectives and Time-Lines

A project plan facilitates AAS having a profile of its own with communicable objectives. Setting time-lines has several advantages: the preparation of the time-lines itself can provide much-needed discipline on those planning the project, and progress on the project can be measured on an ongoing basis.

The objectives of AAS were outlined in every internal presentation. A general time-line was informally used; however, this was not developed from a detailed "bottom-up" analysis of the specific steps necessary in the implementation. All key players involved in AAS activities at Instruments Inc. reported that they considerably underestimated the time commitment and other resources required in the first year. For example, integrating data from files that had been kept separate and had been the responsibility of different groups (e.g., purchasing files, bill of materials files, manufacturing routing files, and quality testing files) was far more time-consuming than initially thought. The additional time demands required to implement AAS weighed very heavily on the accounting function at Instruments Inc. This function was being downsized in the 1987–1988 period due to an overall corporate goal of reducing the ratio of staff to line personnel.

Systematic Education Effort

The prior accounting system was familiar to many and relatively simple to outline. The AAS implemented by Instruments Inc. requires considerable effort to understand, even to those with a good knowledge of the operating activities. The education effort adopted in the first six months consisted primarily of presentations and one-on-one assistance. Many of those interviewed stressed the importance of having a larger budget (especially in manpower) devoted to AAS education efforts. This was pinpointed as one area where sizable underinvestment occurred in the initial stages of the implementation. Suggestions made in interviews included advice on

- A detailed user manual for consultation on an ongoing basis. This manual should include the objectives of the AAS, examples of how activity cost pools and activity cost driver rates are developed, and examples of how product costs are built up. The manual should also list the personnel responsible for the development and integrity of the data bases accessed in the AAS. (Two booklets on AAS were produced at Instruments Inc., but not all of those interviewed were aware of their existence.)
- Training sessions in which preparers and users developed hands-on experience relating to the AAS being implemented. One user of AAS information noted that the most effective training sessions were interactive ones that involved the development or use of the AAS numbers. He expressed his feelings with the oftheard expression, "Tell me and I will forget. Involve me and I may remember."
- Exposure sessions in which examples of other companies' implementation of activity accounting are discussed.
- Regular forums in which implementation issues are discussed and suggestions gathered on how to approach the issues raised.
- A "question and answer" on-line file that includes the most frequently raised questions and responses to them. This file should be updated on a regular basis.

Phase-In Period

The first time-line drawn up by the AAS task force included a six-month period in which both the prior system and the AAS would be operating in parallel (November 1987–April 1988). When the adoption of AAS was delayed six months, it was decided to move straight to the AAS and not have a phase-in period. Activities associated with the prior accounting system were stopped in May 1988. Many personnel at the facility emphasized the pressure and strain that the nonphase-in period caused. One member of the accounting group noted that, in the initial months after adoption of the AAS in May 1988, "Everyone went into overload." There is now heightened appreciation at Instruments Inc. of the learning that can be achieved by having a period in which the AAS is run off-line alongside the system it will replace.

Personnel interviewed at Instruments Inc. consistently stressed two notions as pivotal to a successful implementation:

- the credibility of AAS
- the believability of the AAS numbers

One person interviewed was emphatic that every aspect of the implementation activities should have to pass a two-question checklist on a frequent basis: "Does it promote the credibility of the AAS?" and "Does it increase the believability of the AAS numbers?"[11]

These implementation suggestions are a composite of individual comments made in numerous interviews. They are reinforced by written responses to an internal survey conducted in October 1988. Appendix C provides a summary of the responses to this survey.

BEHAVIOR CHANGES ASSOCIATED WITH IMPLEMENTATION OF AAS

Several problems exist in assessing behavior changes resulting from the implementation of AAS at Instruments Inc. First, a controlled experiment is not possible. More than just the adoption of AAS has occurred in the post–May 1988 period, e.g., increased emphasis on design for manufacturability (DFM) and increased adoption of just-in-time by manufacturing. Any observed behavior changes could be the result of these factors rather than the adoption of AAS. Second, the time period since the switchover to AAS has been short, especially relative to the time at which behavior changes in some areas were projected to have occurred. Consider product design. The designs of most of the existing products being assembled were developed prior to implementation of AAS. Any changes in product design associated with the implementation of AAS will be reflected in the next generation of products to be assembled.

Internal presentations at Instruments Inc. included the following list of "Tangible Changes Expected" from implementation of AAS:

1. Designers will actively seek process [activity cost driver] rates to better understand the cost of their design. CAD will include process rates and provide quick and accurate costing.

2. Designs will be driven by the selection of process cost drivers.

3. There will be better understanding of manufacturing costs in R&D.

4. Process owners will have visibility of their process costs on a monthly basis. Change in production throughput will cause changes in plans.

5. The mix of processes in products will change to lower costs (i.e., fewer low-volume parts, fewer hand-loaded parts, lower parts count, more externally sourced assemblies, etc.).

6. Process owners will make do with less services to lower their rates. Service organizations will be under pressure to reduce costs. Process owners will want to do their own service.

7. Process owners will tend to become more interested in the "numbers." The expense report will be less important than the process rate. Throughput will be as important as spending.

8. Some processes will be driven to obsolescence. New ones will take their place. Redesign will be required to accomplish this.

9. The cry for a separate low-cost overhead accounting system will disappear.

10. Focus will shift from product (vertical) to process (horizontal). Organization changes will take place to better align responsibility.

11. There will be an increase in comparisons between divisions. The potential exists for different divisions to bid on making the same product.

Product designers interviewed at Instruments Inc. gave mixed responses to the question, "Has it affected your behavior?" A subset responded, "Only at the margin." Another subset responded "Yes" and were fully supportive of AAS. One designer, while enthusiastic about AAS, cautioned about being "too mechanical" in assessing how AAS affects his behavior:

I understand and support AAS and its design signals. I can easily design instruments that have low reported costs under AAS. For example, use fewer parts, higher-volume parts, less hand add, etc. However, in some cases, you want to experiment with higher part products, lower-volume parts, and more hand add. We don't want to squash these experiments. I can envision instruments with low-budgeted volume in their first year that still may be worth doing. Today's low-volume products may well be tomorrow's high-volume products.

This designer emphasized his support of AAS, but was concerned lest it "discourage the innovation essential to stay ahead of the competition."

The manufacturing group at Instruments Inc. continues to be the most enthusiastic about AAS. It is the line group making the most suggestions and the one most willing to commit efforts to further refining it. One manager interviewed noted that activity-area cost driver rates were becoming informal targets and that several personnel were now examining shop-floor practices that would help reduce these rates. Another manufacturing person interviewed noted: "AAS is a very physical system. It is based on variables that I can influence. It is a big improvement over the prior system."

Most marketing personnel interviewed noted that they had had limited involvement in the AAS project and that their job had been little affected by its implementation. The marketing subgroup most receptive (in our interviews) to AAS were those who sold Instruments Inc. products internally to other divisions. One person noted that he now shares the AAS costing model with other divisions when explaining how a quoted price was arrived at. He cited several instances of using the model to illustrate to another division how a change in product specifications could sizably reduce the quoted cost. He termed AAS a "very useful costing model to take on the road" when dealing with customers who are very price sensitive.

One behavior change that has been occurring at Instruments Inc. in the last year is increased communication across functional areas. There is general agreement that this change is a very positive one. AAS is one of several programs that has helped create interfunctional communication in a constructive way.

CONCLUSION

AAS developments at Instruments Inc. are ongoing. This paper has focused on only the first 10 months of the implementation. Personnel associated with the implementation have been under considerable pressure in those 10 months because of several factors:

- ambitious targets were set—the AAS implemented was relatively more complex than many systems implemented by other organizations;
- the educational and coordination efforts necessary for implementation were underestimated;
- downsizing was occurring in the accounting function; and
- significant changes were occurring in manufacturing organization and products.

Notwithstanding the pressure, the commitment to AAS is now considerably more broad-based at Instruments Inc. than when AAS was initially implemented.

One consistent viewpoint expressed by many people interviewed is that the system implemented is *not* "overly complex." This may be surprising to many outside the facility, especially to those familiar with product costing systems with one or two allocation bases. Manufacturing personnel at Instruments Inc. manage activities first (and products second) and view the AAS as "more physical." Product designers stress that the design function itself is complex; they note it should not be surprising that a credible costing system encompasses a sizable number of activity areas and cost drivers. Those in marketing now using the AAS find its level of detail a plus when discussing ways Instruments Inc. can assemble lower-cost products. It is likely that subsequent AAS developments at Instruments Inc. will add to the existing level of detail by recognizing more complex cost functions at each activity area.

NOTES

1. The distinguishing feature of an activity accounting system is the pivotal focus on activity areas of the organization. Activities are identifiable areas or operations in which resources are consumed or received. Product costing in an AAS includes analysis of the use each product makes of the individual activity areas. Alternative terms used to refer to AAS include "activity-based costing (ABC)," "cost driver accounting," and "transaction-based accounting."

The literature on activity accounting is rapidly expanding. Examples include
1. General writings: e.g., Berliner and Brimson (1988); Cooper and Kaplan (1988); and Johnson (1988).
2. Individual facility focused papers: e.g., Berlant, Browning, and Foster (1988).
3. Teaching cases based on individual facilities: e.g., Kaplan (1986) and Cooper and Turney (1988).
4. Minutes of CAM-I (Computer Aided Manufacturing—International) "Activity Accounting Work Group" meetings: February 22–23, 1988; May 4–5, 1988; November 3, 1988; and November 9–10, 1988.

2. Romano (1988, 74), outlines a list of 11 claimed benefits. He comments: "Does this sound like a list of positive benefits that only a Sunday preacher would dare to promote from the pulpit? While it might be premature to suggest that all of the above benefits can be derived through activity-based accounting systems, they are surely possible."

3. The data provided by Instruments Inc. covered 882 products; 298 had budgeted production volume in the May–October 1988 period. The data analysis here is restricted to the 298-product sample. Three of the 298 products use only support facilities. Appendix B presents analysis for the 283 products that have the full set of data available for the analysis in that Appendix.

4. Further discussion of this issue is in Cooper and Turney (1990).

5. See Cooper (1989) for further discussion of different cost functions in activity accounting systems.

6. One other change also occurred between Phase I and Phase II. The cost driver for the "wave and wash" activity area was changed from number of boards (Phase I) to number of frames (Phase II).

7. Several nonmanufacturing personnel are less enthusiastic about the change in indirect costs in Phase II. A product coordinator for R&D noted: "Lumping [indirect activity] costs in a general bucket causes them to lose their definition. It is a general blob." A finance supervisor commented: "Pulling costs out of the activity areas and lumping them in a single bucket is a step backward."

8. Only the .01 to .98 percentiles are plotted in Exhibit 8-7 and the .01 to .99 percentiles are plotted in Exhibit 8-8 to avoid extreme observations dominating the vertical scale.

9. Some of the differences between Phase I and Phase II were due to data errors during the switchover from one phase to another.

10. The accounting literature contains little analysis of issues arising in the implementation of new accounting systems. Useful insights from implementing manufacturing system changes are in Blache (1988).

11. The importance of having visible top-management support is frequently emphasized in discussions on successful implementations—see, for example, the papers in Blache (1988). People interviewed at Instruments Inc. did not stress this factor, noting that it was not "part of their culture to have top management leading the change on each new program." They noted that for them the norm was to have individuals or groups compete with each other to sell projects. Over time, top-management "buy in" was developed.

REFERENCES

Banker R. D., S. M. Datar, S. Kekre, and T. Mukhopadhyay. "Costs of Product and Process Complexity." Chapter 9 of this volume.

Banker, R. D. and H. H. Johnston. "Cost Driver Analysis in the Service Sector: An Empirical Study of U.S. Airlines." Working paper, Carnegie-Mellon University, 1988.

Berlant, D., R. Browning, and G. Foster. "Tomorrow's Accounting Today: An Activity Accounting System for PC Board Assembly." Working paper, Stanford University, 1988.

Berliner, C., and J. A. Brimson, eds. *Cost Management for Today's Advanced Manufacturing: The CAM-I Conceptual Design*. Boston: Harvard Business School Press, 1988.

Blache, K. M., ed. *Success Factors for Implementing Change: A Manufacturing Viewpoint*. Dearborn, MI: Society of Manufacturing Engineers, 1988.

Cooper, R. "Cost Classification in Unit-Based and Activity-Based Manufacturing Cost Systems." Working paper, Harvard University, 1989.

Cooper, R., and R. S. Kaplan. "Measure Costs Right: Make the Right Decisions." *Harvard Business Review* (September–October 1988): 96–103.

Cooper, R., and P. B. B. Turney. "Tektronix: Portable Instruments Division" (A), (B) and (C). HBS case series #9-188-142, #9-188-143, #9-188-144. Boston: Harvard Business School, 1988.

———. "Internally Focused Activity-Based Cost Systems." Chapter 10 of this volume.

Foster, G., and M. Gupta. "Manufacturing Overhead Cost Driver Analysis." *Journal of Accounting and Economics* (1989).

Johnson, H. T. "Activity-Based Information: A Blueprint for World-Class Management Accounting." *Management Accounting* (June 1988): 23–30.

Kaplan, R. S. "John Deere Component Works." HBS case series #9-187-107 and #9-187-108. Boston: Harvard Business School, 1986.

Romano, P. L. "Activity Accounting." *Management Accounting* (May 1988): 73–74.

APPENDIX A

Product Costing at Instruments Inc.

The product costing example (XYZ) in this Appendix relates to a measurement instrument. Assumptions made in the computations include

- Estimated production volume for the current year is 1,000 units.
- Standard production batch size is 10.

- There are 22 material parts in XYZ. These include one printed circuit (PC) board and nine other different part types; several part types are used more than once.

Section 1 illustrates the pre–May 1988 accounting system. Phase I of the AAS at Instruments Inc., in operation from May 1988 to October 1988, is illustrated in Section 2. Phase II of the AAS (started in November 1988) is illustrated in Section 3.

Section 1: Pre–May 1988 Accounting System

The pre–May 1988 system comprised two direct cost categories and two indirect cost categories. The total manufacturing product cost of $165.60 is computed as follows:

1. Direct Product Costs			
• Direct Materials	$90.00		
• Direct Labor	8.40	$98.40	59.4%
2. Indirect Product Costs			
• MOH Cost Pool 1 (0.42 × $90.00)	$37.80		
• MOH Cost Pool 2 (3.50 × $8.40)	29.40	67.20	40.6
		$165.60	100.0%

Section 2: AAS Phase I

Exhibit 8-9 presents a detailed buildup of the "Activity Area-Based Indirect Product Costs." The total manufacturing product cost of $149.46 is computed as follows:

1. Direct Product Costs (comprising direct materials)		$90.00	60.2%
2. Activity Area-Based Indirect Product Costs (see Exhibit 8-9)	$41.55		
• Driver Quantity-Based			
• Assembly Unit-Based	6.00		
• Batch Size-Based	5.30	52.85	35.4

3. Period-Based Indirect Product Costs
   (5% of Direct Materials Dol-   4.50   3.0
   lars)
4. Other Indirect Product Costs
   (4% of Activity Area-Based   2.11   1.4
   Indirect Product Costs)
                                                    $149.46   100.0%

Section 3: AAS Phase II

In Phase II, Instruments Inc. reduced the amount of the indirect activity costs included in the cost pools of the fourteen activity areas
outlined in Exhibit 8-3. These indirect activity costs were reclassified
as "Other Indirect Product Costs." This change resulted in a reduction in the cost per unit in the driver quantity-based indirect cost
computations and an increase in the rate that "Other Indirect Product
Costs" are attributed to products. Exhibit 8-10 presents the revised
buildup of the "Activity Area-Based Indirect Product Costs." The
revised total manufacturing product cost of $147.37 is computed as
follows:

1. Direct Product Costs (com- $90.00   61.1%
   prising direct materials)
2. Activity Area-Based Indirect
   Product Costs
   (see Exhibit 8-10) $22.81
   • Driver Quantity-Based
   • Assembly Unit-Based   6.00
   • Batch Size-Based   5.30   34.11   23.1
3. Period-Based Indirect Prod-
   uct Costs
   (5% of Direct Materials Dol-   4.50   3.1
   lars)
4. Other Indirect Product Costs
   (55% of Activity Area-Based   18.76   12.7
   Indirect Product Costs)
                                                    $147.37   100.0%

Exhibit 8-9 AAS-I: Activity Area-Based Indirect Cost Buildup for Product XYZ

| | | Production Planning Costs | | | | Production Scheduling Cost | | | | | |
| | | Driver Quantity-Based | | | | Assembly Unit-Based | | | Batch Size-Based | | |
Activity Area	Cost Driver	Units of Parts (Part #)	# of Driver Units	Cost per Unit $	Total Cost for Assembly $	Indicator Variable	Cost per Setup $	Total Cost for Assembly $	Indicator Variable	Cost per Batch Setup $	Total Cost for Assembly $
PC Board Assembly											
1. Part Number Maintenance	Part #	22(10)	10(a)	0.30	3.00	—	—	—	—	—	—
2. Strategic Materials Management	D.M$	—	$90	0.10	9.00	—	—	—	—	—	—
3. Stock and Pull	# of Pulls	22(10)	10(b)	0.10	1.00	—	—	—	—	—	—
4. Axial Insertion	# of Ins.	7(2)	7	0.05	0.35	—	—	—	1	4.00	0.40
5. Dip Insertion	# of Ins.	4(2)	4	0.10	0.40	—	—	—	1	15.00	1.50
6. Hardware Insertion	# of Ins.	2(1)	2	0.20	0.40	—	—	—	—	—	—
7. Robotic Insertion	# of Ins.	0	0	0.30	0.00	—	—	—	0	2.00	0.00
8. Hand Load	B-Sec.	3(1)	60	0.06	3.60	1	3.00	3.00	1	14.00	1.40
9. Hand Add	B-Sec.	2(1)	10	0.08	0.80	1	2.50	2.50	1	15.00	1.50
10. Masking	Points	—	10	0.10	1.00	—	—	—	—	—	—
11. Wave and Wash	Frame	—	.25(c)	4.00	1.00	—	—	—	—	—	—
12. Board Test	Test Hr.	—	.05	80.00	4.00	1	0.50	0.50	1	5.00	0.50

Final Instrument

13. Instrument Buildup	Hour	3(2)	.15	60.00	9.00	(d)	–	–	–
14. Final Test	Test Hr.	–	.08	100.00	8.00	(d)	–	–	–
					$41.55		$6.00		$5.30

Notes: a. Part Number Maintenance rate is $300 / Part Number / year under AAS-I and is $200 / Part Number / year under AAS-II.
  Let n be the estimated usage of Part number among all products in the current year, then
  Part Number Maintenance / Part number = $(300/n) / Part number.
  For our example, n = 1,000, therefore,
  PN Maintenance / PN = $.30 under AAS-I
  PN Maintenance / PN = $.20 under AAS-II.

b. Stock and Pull rate is $2.00 / Pull under AAS-I and is $1.50 / Pull under AAS-II
  Let m be the standard production volume per week for the assembly, then
  # of pulls/PN = 1/# of assemblies per week = 1/m.
  For our example, m = 20, therefore, # of pulls/PN = .05
  Stock and Pull/ PN under AAS-I = .05 × $2.00 = $0.10
  Stock and Pull/ PN under AAS-II = .05 × $1.50 = $0.075

c. Wave and Wash rate is $4.00 per frame
  Let b be the number of boards per frame, then
  # of driver units used per board (assembly) = 1/b
  For our example, assume 4 boards per frame, therefore,
  # of driver units = .25 frame.

d. For final instrument buildup and final test, setup costs are included in standard cost driver hours.

Exhibit 8-10 AAS-II: Activity Area-Based Indirect Cost Buildup for Product XYZ

| | | Production Planning Costs | | | | Production Scheduling Cost | | | | | |
| | | Driver Quantity-Based | | | | Assembly Unit-Based | | | Batch Size-Based | | |
Activity Area	Cost Driver	Units of Parts (Part #)	# of Driver Units	Cost per Unit $	Total Cost for Assembly $	Indicator Variable	Cost per Setup $	Total Cost for Assembly $	Indicator Variable	Cost per Batch Setup $	Total Cost for Assembly $
PC Board Assembly											
1. Part Number Maintenance	Part #	22(10)	10(a)	0.20	2.00	–	–	–	–	–	–
2. Strategic Materials Management	D.M$	–	$90	0.15	4.50	–	–	–	–	–	–
3. Stock and Pull	# of Pulls	22(10)	10(b)	0.075	0.75	–	–	–	–	–	–
4. Axial Insertion	# of Ins.	7(2)	7	0.02	0.14	–	–	–	1	4.00	0.40
5. Dip Insertion	# of Ins.	4(2)	4	0.08	0.32	–	–	–	1	15.00	1.50
6. Hardware Insertion	# of Ins.	2(1)	2	0.15	0.30	–	–	–	–	–	–
7. Robotic Insertion	# of Ins.	0	0	0.12	0.00	–	–	–	0	2.00	0.00
8. Hand Load	B-Sec.	3(1)	60	0.04	2.40	1	3.00	3.00	1	14.00	1.40
9. Hand Add	B-Sec.	2(1)	10	0.02	0.20	1	2.50	2.50	1	15.00	1.50
10. Masking	Points	–	10	0.05	0.50	–	–	–	–	–	–
11. Wave and Wash	Frame	–	.25(c)	1.60	0.40	–	–	–	–	–	–
12. Board Test	Test Hr.	–	.05	50.00	2.50	1	0.50	0.50	1	5.00	0.50
Final Instrument											
13. Instrument Buildup	Hour	3(2)	.15	32.00	4.80	(d)	–	–	–	–	–
14. Final Test	Test Hr.	–	.08	50.00	4.00	(d)	–	–	–	–	–
					$22.81			$6.00			$5.30

See Notes in Exhibit 8-9.

APPENDIX B

Explanation of Changes in Reported Product Costs

This Appendix examines relationships between product cost changes documented in Exhibit 8-5 and variables in the following four categories: volume, complexity, efficiency, and market. The volume, complexity, and efficiency categories capture variables that have been examined in prior research on manufacturing overhead cost drivers (see Banker et al. 1990; Banker and Johnston 1988; and Foster and Gupta 1989). The market-based variables are included, in part because of comments made by marketing personnel about the products whose costs were most affected by the AAS.

Volume-Based Variables. These relate to the level of output of each product:

- Budgeted production volume in next six months (VOL)
- Direct labor dollars per product, as reported in pre–May 1988 system (DL$)
- Direct materials dollars per product (DM$)

Complexity-Based Variables. These relate to characteristics of products that potentially are drivers of manufacturing overhead costs. The AAS includes four subcategories of such variables:

- # of part numbers in the product (PART #s)
- # of pulls in stock and pull (# PULLS)
- # of insertions in   -axial activity area (INS-AXIAL)
                        -dip activity area (INS-DIP)
                        -hardware activity area (INS-HW)
                        -robotic activity area (INS-ROB)
- Boothroyd time for -hand load (BT-HL)
                      -hand add (BT-HA)
                      -instrument buildup (BT-INST)
- # of points masked (# PT. MASK)
- # of frames washed (# FRAME W.)

Efficiency-Based Variables. These relate to activities that increase the throughput time for assembling products, or do not add to the value of the product as perceived by the customers. There are two subcategories of these variables:

- Setup activities -in axial insertion (SET-AXIAL)
                    -in dip auto insertion (SET-DIP)
                    -in robotic insertion (SET-ROB)
                    -in hand load (SET-HL)
                    -in hand add (SET-HA)
                    -in board test (SET-BT)
                    -in final test (SET-FT)
- Test time for boards and final products (TEST)

Market-Based Variables. These relate to the market in which the products of Instruments Inc. are sold:

- Catalogue listed product price (PRICE)
- Contribution margin percentage, as reported in the pre–May 1988 system (CM%)

Several of the individual variables represent more than one category. In part, this is because the four categories are not mutually exclusive. Also, individual variables are measured in a particular way. Consider the number of part numbers in a product, which we classify as a complexity variable. In the AAS, the part number maintenance cost of a part is affected not only by its uniqueness but also by its overall usage (a volume-driven factor).

All the correlation and regression results reported in this Appendix are based on the ranks of each variable. Restriction to ranks is appropriate given the widespread evidence of nonnormality in the distributions of the variables examined. Using a Kolmogorov-Smirov goodness of fit test, the distribution of every one of the variables in the volume-, complexity-, efficiency-, and market-based categories exhibits statistically significant (at the .01 level) evidence of departure from normality. Similarly, none of the cost change variables in Exhibit 8-5 has a normal distribution.

Correlation Evidence

Exhibit 8-11 presents Spearman rank correlations between pairs of the three cost change variables (AAS-I/Pre–May 1988; AAS-II/Pre–May 1988; AAS-II/AAS-I) and 24 variables in the volume-, complexity-, efficiency-, and market-based categories. The percentage of correlations in each category that are significant (at the .05 level) are

Cost Measure/Variable Category	AAS-I pre–May 1988	AAS-II pre–May 1988	AAS-II AAS-I
Indirect Manufacturing Product Cost			
Volume-Based Variables (3)	66.7%	66.7%	33.3%
Complexity-Based Variables (11)	100.0	90.9	63.6
Efficiency-Based Variables (8)	100.0	87.5	0.0
Market-Based Variables (2)	50.0	100.0	50.0
Total Manufacturing Product Cost			
Volume-Based Variables (3)	66.7%	33.3%	33.3%
Complexity-Based Variables (11)	90.0	81.8	9.1
Efficiency-Based Variables (8)	100.0	87.5	0.0
Market-Based Variables (2)	50.0	100.0	100.0

The significant correlations for the volume-, complexity-, and efficiency-based variables (capturing the cost drivers in the AAS), support the heterogeneity assumption underlying the implementation of AAS at Instruments Inc. If homogeneity existed in the way each product utilized each activity area, cross-sectional differences in the effect that the AAS has on individual products would be minimal.

Regression Analysis

Regression analysis was undertaken to gain extra insight into the relative importance of the variables examined in Exhibit 8-11. Rank regression methods are used because of the marked evidence of nonnormality in both the dependent and independent variables.

Exhibit 8-12 reports regression results for indirect manufacturing product costs. Similar results were also observed when total manufacturing product costs were used in computing the dependent variable. Two regressions—(i) and (ii)—are reported for each cost change variable examined.

Regression (i). All activity areas in the AAS are ranked in the order of total cost incurred at the activity level. The activity level with the

Exhibit 8-11 Spearman Rank Correlations between Change in Product Costs and Volume-, Complexity-, Efficiency-, and Market-Based Variables

Code	Variable	Predicted Sign	Change in Indirect Manufacturing Product Cost			Change in Total Manufacturing Product Cost		
			AAS-I Pre–May 88	AAS-II Pre–May 88	AAS-II AAS-I	AAS-I Pre–May 88	AAS-II Pre–May 88	AAS-II AAS-I
	A. Volume-Based							
VOL	Budgeted production volume	–	-.14**	-.11**	.02	-.12**	-.07	.06
DL$	Direct labor dollars pre–May 88	–	.05	.07	.24**	.06	.05	.12**
DM$	Direct materials dollars	–	-.16**	-.20**	.01	-.14**	-.18	-.04
	B. Complexity-Based							
PART #s	# of part numbers	+	.10**	.11**	.23**	.09*	.08*	.07
# PULLS	# of pulls in stock and pull	+	.29**	.30**	.11**	.28**	.28**	-.02
INS-AXIAL	# of axial insertions	+	.29**	.34**	.14**	.30**	.34**	.04
INS-DIP	# of dip insertions	+	.22**	.25**	.10**	.23**	.24**	.02
INS-HW	# of hardware insertions	+	.34**	.36**	.08*	.35**	.35**	-.03
INS-ROB	# of robotic insertions	+	.11**	.07	-.06	.11**	.07*	-.06
BT-HL	Boothroyd time in hand load	+	.33**	.36**	.11**	.34**	.35**	-.01
BT-HA	Boothroyd time in hand add	+	.37**	.41**	.13**	.39**	.39**	-.00
# PT. MASK	# of points masked	+	.25**	.28**	.12**	.28**	.30**	.07
# FRAME. W	# of frames in wave and wash	+	.31**	.32**	.09*	.32**	.32**	-.01
BT-INST	Boothroyd time in instrument buildup	+	.29**	.30**	.02	.29**	.25**	-.10**

C. Efficiency-Based

SET-AXIAL	# of setups for axial insertion	+	.36**	.40**	.08*	.38**	.41**	-.02
SET-DIP	# of setups for dip insertion	+	.27**	.27**	.04	.27**	.26**	-.05
SET-ROB	# of setups for robotics insertion	+	.14**	.09*	-.04	.14**	.09*	-.09*
SET-HL	# of setups for hand load	+	.38**	.44**	.15*	.40**	.42**	.00
SET-HA	# of setups for hand add	+	.39**	.44**	.13*	.41**	.42**	-.01
TEST	Test time in board area	+	.32**	.37**	.11*	.34**	.37**	.04
SET-BT	# of setups for board test	+	.32**	.37**	.11*	.34**	.36**	.05
SET-FT	# of setups for final test	+	.17**	.15**	.01	.18**	.17**	-.04

D. Market-Based

PRICE	Catalogue listed price	–	-.23**	-.23**	.19*	-.22**	-.21**	.18**
CM%	Contribution margin %	+	.08*	.15**	.12**	.11*	.13**	.11**

Key: ** Significant at the 5% level (one tailed-test)
  * Significant at the 10% level (one tailed-test)

highest accumulated cost is ranked first and the one with the lowest accumulated cost is ranked last. The variables are entered in the analysis in their rank order (first to last). All variables that are significant at the .10 level or less are retained in the regression model. This regression model provides insight into the subset of the activity areas that contribute most to explaining differences across products.

Five variables appear in more than one of the regressions reported in Exhibit 8-12.

Category	Variable
Volume-Based	• Direct materials dollars (DM$)
Complexity-Based	• # of part numbers (PART #s) • # of pulls in stock and pull (# PULLS) • Boothroyd time in hand add (BT-HA)
Efficiency-Based	• Test time for boards (TEST)

The regression results are consistent with products differing significantly in the use of these variables and with these differences being translated into sizable cost revisions by the AAS.

Regression (ii). The analysis in (i) is repeated, except that the budgeted production volume (VOL) variable is entered first. The rationale for this analysis is to examine the relative significance of the VOL variable. In all four regressions for (ii) in Exhibit 8-12, the VOL variable is consistently significant. The negative coefficient on VOL is consistent with lower- (higher-) volume products having reported product cost increases (decreases) under AAS vis-à-vis the pre–May 1988 system.

APPENDIX C

Feedback from Instruments Inc. Personnel: An Internal Survey

In October 1988, an internal survey was made of internal customers, e.g., a manufacturing analyst, a materials supervisor, and a production scheduler. Ten responses were received. Respondents were asked to answer the following three questions, on a scale from 1 ("no understanding") to 7 ("complete understanding"):

Exhibit 8-12 **Rank Regression Results for Variables Explaining Differences in Indirect Manufacturing Product Costs under Alternative Costing System**

(i)(a)   AAS-I/pre–May 1988 = 51.13 + 0.20 PART #s − 0.75 DM$ + 0.35 # PULLS + 0.25 SET-ROB + 0.40 BT-HA + 0.15 TEST

    (2.94)   (3.17)   (−12.14)   (4.34)   (2.32)   (5.26)   (2.15)

Adj. R^2 = 0.441   N = 283

(i)(b)   AAS-II/pre–May 1988 = 71.03 + 0.26 PART #s − 0.87 DM$ + 0.30 # PULLS + 0.37 BT-HA + 0.23 TEST − 0.17 H FRAME

    (7.69)   (4.81)   (−16.23)   (4.36)   (4.02)   (4.01)   (2.40)

Adj. R^2 = 0.58   N = 283

(ii)(a)   AAS-I/pre–May 1988 = 98.77 − 0.72 DM$ + 0.33 # PULLS + 0.29 INS-DIP + 0.23 INS-ROB + 0.33 BT-HA + 0.23 BT-INST − 0.40 VOL

    (6.32)   (−13.24)   (4.94)   (3.55)   (2.39)   (4.51)   (4.02)   (−8.38)

Adj. R^2 = 0.534   N = 283

(ii)(b)   AAS-II/pre–May 1988 = 116.0 − 0.81 DM$ + 0.34 # PULLS + 0.30 INS-DIP + 0.36 BT-HA + 0.15 TEST + 0.19 BT-INST − 0.36 VOL

    (13.05)(−17.03)   (5.90)   (4.16)   (5.32)   (2.70)   (3.94)   (−8.69)

Adj. R^2 = 0.642   N = 283

	Mean Response	*Range*
• How well do you understand the reasons for implementing AAS?	5.5	4–7
• How well do you understand the differences between AAS and the costing system we used before AAS?	6.0	4–7
• How well do you understand your responsibilities relative to AAS?	5.2	3–7

Internal customers were asked to name "three actions that you think would most significantly increase your understanding of AAS." A sample of responses follows:

- A conceptual overview of objectives and operations
- Explanation of the reasons for implementing AAS
- A concise overview of
  - Reasons for AAS
  - Philosophy behind AAS
  - Expectations for its use
  - Operating tenants
- An understanding of how AAS is supposed to be used and how it should not be used
- Training
- Explanation of how can it make my job easier
- Explanation of how this helps contribute to our bottom line
- Series of brainstorms with supervisors on the use of AAS

Internal suppliers (those with the responsibility for developing the AAS data, e.g., the manager of data for the board test area) provided written responses to the following question: "What could be done to resolve your concerns with your current AAS data maintenance process?" A sample of the responses suggested

- Written documentation
- A knowledgeable user reference point
- More organization
- More understanding of the system
- More training and initiation on AAS
- Training sessions for persons responsible for data integrity, input, and updates
- Frequent training

CHAPTER 9

Costs of Product and Process Complexity

Rajiv D. Banker, Srikant M. Datar, Sunder Kekre, and
Tridas Mukhopadhyay

INTRODUCTION

PRODUCT designers play an important role in influencing the total life cycle costs of a product. Accounting systems have traditionally focused on monitoring and controlling costs incurred subsequent to the design process. In manufacturing environments where product complexity significantly influences costs, a large proportion of the costs is determined at the design stage, although the cash flows that the accounting systems monitor take place later. It is therefore essential that systems be developed to inform the designer of the cost implications of alternative design choices. Such systems should isolate the various factors that are under the control of design engineers and that can be used to influence manufacturing costs. Lacking such systems and tools, corporations tend to add more features and design more complex products because the price and market share advantages are perceived to outweigh the additional costs of designing,

Support by the National Science Foundation—Engineering Design Research Center, Grant No. CDR8522616 at Carnegie-Mellon University, is gratefully acknowledged. The research assistance of Jeffrey Duffy, Holly Johnston, Jay Michael, Neeraj Nityanand, William Orr, Tanzel Ozyar, and Peter Steiner is gratefully acknowledged.

manufacturing, and supporting complex products. Manufacturing intricate products, however, results in high manufacturing overhead costs incurred for such activities as supervision, quality control, inspection, machine and tool maintenance, and production control. In a typical cost accounting system, manufacturing overhead costs are grouped together and allocated to products on the basis of direct labor or machine-hours. Unfortunately, direct labor and machine-hour allocation bases do not reflect the demands placed on resources by products that are more difficult to manufacture. Product costs thus become distorted, leading to a biased analysis of design-for-manufacturability, product profitability, outsourcing, and make or buy decisions.

In plants that manufacture a wide range of products, the more complex products tend to be undercosted. Undercosting of complexity biases the decisions of design engineers and marketing managers in favor of designing and manufacturing more complex products than may be warranted. Conversely, simple products tend to get overcosted. Their reported low profitability causes them to be purchased rather than made in-house. In the case of a decentralized corporation where one division makes components to be used by another, and where transfer prices are based on costs, overcosting of simpler components results in the user-division seeking outside vendors rather than purchasing the component parts internally. A more accurate cost accounting system that better identifies the costs arising from product complexity can influence design and operating decisions by providing information necessary for evaluating alternative product designs and outsourcing strategies.

Activity-based costing (ABC) has been proposed as a method that captures variations in demand placed on shared resources by individual products (Cooper and Kaplan 1987, 1988). The ABC method identifies a cost driver that measures the particular activity that causes the cost to arise. A frequently cited example of a cost driver is the number of setups incurred. Setup costs entail both the direct labor incurred in setting up the machine and the indirect costs of supervision, production control, and inspection. If a low-volume product requires a proportionately larger number of setups, then a greater amount of setup-related costs are attributed to that product in the ABC framework. Differing degrees of product complexity, however, create a new problem. A homogeneous measure of the activity or cost driver may be difficult to obtain. For example, the volume and number of setups may be identical for two products of different complexity levels. The more intricate product, however, requires additional care and attention on the part of supervisors and inspectors. As a result, the appropriate cost driver used to assign setup costs should address the varying degrees of complexity associated with individual setups.

We will describe how costs such as those of supervision and quality control, typically treated as overhead costs, can be directly traced to individual products. Our methodology allows us to evaluate the impact of design-engineering factors on product costs. We analyze the time that the indirect personnel spend on different products to distinguish the products that demand a disproportionate amount of time and costs. We compare the original overhead costs assigned to various products by a conventional cost accounting system to the revised, directly traced costs. The differences in these costs are explained in terms of the complexity of the product and process.

We develop and illustrate these ideas in the context of a division of a leading automobile manufacturer. The automaker is constantly innovating product designs to meet market pressures. At the same time, overseas competition has led to an increased emphasis on lower production costs. User-divisions continuously evaluate which products to outsource based on internal price (and cost) quotes. Over time, the focus on outsourcing has increased. Evaluating the impact on cost of product and process complexity and identifying product costs have thus become critical in this environment.

Our field site is a plant that manufactures a variety of rear, park, signal, and other lamps for a wide variety of automobiles and trucks. Some of the lamps, such as park and signal lamps and license plate lamps, are relatively simple products to manufacture, compared with some of the complex rear lamps. To distinguish various models of automobiles and to make the overall appearance of the car attractive to customers, several of the lamps (particularly rear lamps) have special features such as multicolor molding, horizontal and vertical stripes (called "flutes"), curvatures, and special contours (called "wrap around"). Injection molding of lamps with special features requires molds with complex, high-precision moving parts.

The existing cost system allocates supervision costs to products on the basis of direct labor hours, allocates quality control and inspection costs on the basis of direct inspection hours, and allocates tooling costs on the basis of machine-hours. Although the multiple-allocation base system may seem sophisticated, it does not adequately reflect the additional demands placed on support resources by the more complex products. The product costs, therefore, do not reflect the costs of complexity. We identify several product design features that explain the difference between the costs directly traced by us to products and the costs originally allocated to products by the existing cost system.

The corporation had recently commissioned a leading consulting firm to evaluate which products could be best outsourced. Our analysis shows that those products classified as outsourcing candidates (based on a comparison of internal manufacturing costs and external prices) were precisely the simpler products that were being overcosted by the existing cost system.

THE RESEARCH SITE

A wide variety of lamps is manufactured at the research site, ranging from simple lamps such as license plate lamps to expensive rear lamps that fit across the width of the car. Each lamp has at least one lens, which is assembled onto a housing with fixtures for mounting the lamp to the vehicle. In a finished vehicle, the lens of a lamp is visible while the housing is not. The lens and housing are designed to meet optical specifications depending on the functions performed by the lamp.

The primary manufacturing operation is molding. The lens and housing are molded separately in machines ranging in capacity from 50–2,000 tons, depending on the size and production volume of the lamp components. The molding operation consists of injecting molten plastic into a mold that gives the product the desired shape and form. The mold is cooled, allowing the part to solidify, and the part is then ejected.

The primary molding operations are followed by one or more secondary operations such as painting, aluminizing, and hot-stamping to provide finish and appearance to the part. The painting and aluminizing operations on the housing give the lamp a reflective surface. The hot-stamping and ornamentation are finishing operations that provide styling to the lens and lamp.

The lens can be attached to the housing in various ways—ranging from a simple method such as a snap fit with gaskets to sonic-vibration welding. In the final assembly stage, ornaments such as bezels are attached. The lamps are tested and inspected before being packaged and shipped.

The cost structure of the plant is described in terms of the various cost categories listed below.

Direct materials cost	41%
Direct labor cost	17
Fabricating burden	28
General burden	7
Commercial burden	7
Total	100%

Overhead costs have been steadily increasing as a percentage of total costs. These costs are the focus of our study. Fabricating burden refers to the factory-related overhead costs associated with the manufacture of the product. This burden is more susceptible to change as product complexity and mix of products increase. We report on the results of an analysis of three major categories (supervision, quality control and inspection, and tool maintenance) that comprise 33% of the fabricating burden. In future work, we will analyze machine maintenance, depreciation, utilities, production control and materials handling, and scrap. The above-mentioned cost categories constitute 80% of fabricating burden. The remainder consists of sundry items such as laboratory work, storage rack repair, and process-related support services.

General burden consists of the costs of administration, accounting, personnel salaries, and related administrative expenses, including depreciation and maintenance of office buildings. Commercial burden largely relates to the costs of planning and coordinating with user-divisions.

Molding is the most important activity in the manufacturing process. Over 75% of the total cost of supervision, quality control and inspection, and tool maintenance is incurred in molding departments. Molding is far more complex for some products than for others. Lamps that are curved so that they can "wrap around" the car, and lamps with multiple functions such as a combination rear, backup, and license plate lamp or with multicolor molded parts, require many moving parts in the mold. The moving parts must align and fit with accuracy and precision. Each stage of the setup operation must be carefully supervised. Supervisors and inspectors first ensure that all moving parts in the mold function smoothly, since each moving part (such as roller, lift, or sliding core) plays a crucial role in determining the quality of the component. Often, further adjustments need to be made, supervised, and inspected in order to ensure that the mold reaches the required thermal/mechanical equilibrium. Only then are the first test runs made. Since each stage of the setup is critical to the subsequent production of the part, inspectors and supervisors give considerable attention to the setup activity in the case of a complex mold with several moving parts. "Fixing" a mold after production commences is a costly and difficult task. Breakage and wear and tear on the tool (mold) is considerably greater when the tool has a number of moving parts. Tool maintenance costs increase with tool complexity.

The size of the part and its length also affect the care and attention required of supervisors and inspectors. Larger parts require that machine pressure and the heating and cooling cycle be carefully balanced. The basic requirement is for the molten plastic to flow evenly over a large area and to cool uniformly. The increased probability of violating dimensional tolerances and aesthetic, optical, and mechanical performance specifications means that supervisors and inspectors spend more time monitoring the production of these products.

Cost Allocation

In the existing cost accounting system, a traditional two-stage procedure allocates indirect factory overhead costs to products. Indirect costs are allocated to production departments in the first stage and allocated from departments to products in the second stage.

Supervision costs. Supervision costs are allocated to productive departments on the basis of direct labor dollars incurred in each department. Departmental supervision costs are then absorbed in components manufactured in the department based on the direct labor dollar content of the component. The present allocation reflects the premise that supervisory costs are incurred to supervise direct labor in a department. With this procedure, a simple part, with proportionately higher direct labor content but requiring little supervision because of its simple mold, could absorb a proportionately higher amount of supervisory burden than a more complex part.

Indirect quality control and inspection costs. Inspection is carried out in two ways. Some of the inspection is direct inspection performed by operators on the line. This inspection, called direct inspection labor, is included as part of the direct labor incurred to produce a part. Many quality technicians and inspectors also perform quality assurance and maintain production processes. These indirect quality control and inspection costs are allocated to departments and then to products based on the direct inspection labor dollars. The current allocation presumes that indirect inspection costs are incurred to supervise and monitor the direct labor inspectors who perform a largely appraisal function. More complex parts, however, require additional attention from these highly skilled technicians both during the setup stage and during production. The inspection and quality control indirect labor also devote considerable time to preventive activities, which vary with the complexity of the manufacturing activity.

Tool maintenance overhead costs. Tool maintenance costs are the costs incurred to repair and maintain the molds used in the manufacture of lamps. Tool maintenance costs have two components: 1) the direct labor incurred on each tool and 2) indirect labor, including tool room supervision, stocking and tracking of tools, and maintenance of tool room equipment. The direct labor incurred is identified to a particular molding department but not to the individual product or component for which the tool is used. Indirect tool maintenance costs are allocated to departments based on direct labor maintenance dollars incurred in various departments. The total direct and indirect tool maintenance costs allocated to each department are allocated to components and products based on machine-hours. The allocation is based on the assumption that the tool maintenance dollars incurred on individual tools are on average a function of the number of hours that the tool has been used. As indicated earlier, however, tools with more complicated components and moving parts have very tight tolerances and demand greater precision. These tools require repair and maintenance work at more frequent intervals for a given number of machine-hours relative to simpler tools.

Design Engineering Factors

Our earlier discussion suggests that many overhead costs are not caused by the direct labor dollars or direct machine-hours currently used to allocate overhead costs to products. One approach to identifying the overhead costs associated with individual products is to determine the costs incurred on various activities such as setups, part administration, and production orders and to compute an activity rate for each activity. The volume of activity associated with each product can then be used to distribute the total cost pool for that activity to individual products. In our case, it was difficult to use this method since the overhead resources demanded by simple products for one activity, say setup, varied greatly from the resources demanded for one setup by complex products. Thus it was difficult to compute a single homogeneous rate for the activity (setup) across products.

An alternative method is to directly identify the overhead costs such as supervision, inspection, and tool maintenance, to individual products. In general, this approach may be difficult (e.g., in the case of supervision costs, if the supervisor manages a large number of products). However, because of the specific nature of production flows and assignment of work responsibilities at the plant in our study, it was possible to obtain a relatively reliable number. Molding operations, the focus of this paper, are departmentalized such that each component is produced in no more than one or two molding departments. Supervisors are assigned to specific departments so that they become familiar with particular products. The supervisor generally oversees the production of only ten to fifteen components.

The time spent by supervisors on individual components was determined through detailed interviews by a member of the research team. This figure was corroborated by informal logs maintained by supervisors and through sampling and observation by team members. The information collected from the supervisor was carefully reviewed and rechecked based on our field operations. In the few departments where the number of components was large, supervisors first grouped components into product families and estimated the time spent on each family. The supervision cost to components of similar complexity within a family was then assigned on the basis of the direct labor content of the components.

The data collection methods for identifying quality control and inspection overheads in the molding departments to components paralleled the method employed for supervision.

We employed a different method for assigning tool maintenance costs to individual components. Plant records are available for the labor dollars (the major portion of tool maintenance costs) spent on the repair and maintenance of the individual tools. Since each tool (mold) is unique to a specific component, we were able to identify precisely the direct labor costs of repairing each tool. Recall that the existing method identifies direct labor costs of tool maintenance to the production departments rather than to the component, and then allocates departmental tool maintenance costs to components using machine-hours.

Analyzing tool maintenance costs raises different problems. Tool maintenance is a discretionary expense that may relate to production activity during past years as well as during the current year. Therefore, data were also collected for the tool maintenance costs and the production runs during the previous year with the objective of examining tool maintenance expenditures over a longer time period.

Although this approach is adequate to identify overhead costs to individual products, it provides no information to product designers or to manufacturing managers as to what product and process features create the demand for the various support activities. It is essential to identify these factors if the cost analysis is to be useful in influencing design choices and manufacturing practices. We had extensive discussions with managers to identify several product and process complexity factors that determine supervision, quality control, and tool maintenance support. These factors included number of moving parts in the mold, number of functions, multicolor molding, rejects, and length of part. Managers were unable to identify one factor as the sole determinant that would predict the amount of time supervisors would spend on production runs. Moreover, the identified factors related to product and process characteristics and not to the specific activities of supervisors. The various product and process complexity factors were identified by managers and were collected at the component, as well as subassembly, level. Managers did not cite number of setups as a statistic that would identify the overhead resources demanded by various components. The number of setups per unit of production was regarded as largely uniform across products.

Our research team included six students who worked at the site over the course of a year. The bulk of the data was collected over the summer months of 1988 by three students. Each student was responsible for collecting data on one of three overhead cost categories: supervision, quality control and inspection, and tool maintenance. The team also identified the complexity factors associated with these costs.

Number of moving parts. This is a measure of the complexity of the mold. Data on moving parts in a mold were obtained via a tool specification report and cross-checked with the tool audit report.

Multicolor molding. This is a complex operation in which molten plastics of two different colors are injected into the mold during the molding process. Multicolor molding eliminates the need for the secondary operation of painting. It also gives the product an excellent finish. Multicolor molding, however, is complex because the plastic that is first injected must completely dry out and solidify before the second color is injected. Otherwise the two colors will mix. Rejects from the operation cannot be reused. Multicolor molding requires that the temperature and pressure systems be carefully monitored throughout the process. Data on multicolor molded parts were obtained from the product design records and cross-checked with the tool specification report.

Number of functions. This refers to the number of distinct functions performed by a single lamp. Multifunction (or combination) lamps have lenses that must be molded together in order to meet the functional requirements of each lamp. Combination lamps require simultaneous satisfaction of tolerances and complex interactions among tolerances. Data on the number of functions were obtained from detailed part drawings.

Length of component. This is a measure of complexity attributable to the size of the component (in contrast to the shape of the part, which partly governs the moving parts in the mold). Greater length means greater care must be taken to avoid spots, cracks, and short shots (which occur when the entire mold is not filled with molten plastic). Data on component length were obtained from design records and detailed part drawings.

Number of rejects. This refers to the rejection percentage during molding operations. This variable measures the inherent complexity of manufacturing a component as well as the tightness of tolerances. Data on rejections were gathered from the molding load report.

Moving parts influence supervisory costs mainly during setup operations; they increase the complexity of the setup. The remaining variables were believed by managers to affect the production runs.

Cost Distortions and Outsourcing

Data collected on indirect labor hours spent on individual components directly provide revised measures of unit costs by overhead category and component. A natural question to ask is how well the unit costs allocated by the existing cost system match revised costs. A widely used method to measure the degree of this match is to examine the correlation between the two sets of costs. A correlation of one indicates perfect agreement between the existing and revised methods; a correlation of zero implies no agreement. The correlations between the original unit costs of components and the revised unit costs for the different categories of overhead costs are described below.

Overhead Cost Category	Correlation Coefficient
Lens supervision	0.51
Housing supervision	0.63
Lens quality control	0.78
Housing quality control	0.66
Lens tool maintenance	0.52
Housing tool maintenance	0.46

These correlations indicate that the existing cost system, which allocates overhead based on direct costs (direct labor dollars in the case of supervision, direct labor inspection dollars in the case of quality control, and machine-hours in the case of tool maintenance), does not match well with the overhead resources actually demanded.

The next question of interest is whether cost distortions are systematically related to the characteristics of the product. We examine this issue by referring to a study conducted by a leading consulting firm on the competitiveness of this division relative to its competitors. The study was based in part on the existing cost accounting system. The consulting firm obtained educated estimates of prices of outside suppliers and compared these with the unit manufacturing costs within the division. Of the three primary product groups manufactured at the plant, Group A (complex rear lamps) was viewed as competitive; Group B (noncomplex rear lamps) and Group C (park and signal lamps) were considered to be at a disadvantage relative to external competition.

Table 9-1 provides the relative ratios of revised to original costs for the three groups. For Group A, the ratio for each of the three cost categories is greater than one, indicating that this group of products is systematically undercosted by the existing cost system. An allocation of a higher cost to Group A is not likely to change the decision to produce the products in-house. Although the division has a cost advantage over competitors for the complex products, it is not the

Table 9-1   Ratio of Revised Costs to Original Costs by Product Category

	Supervision	Quality Control	Tool Maintenance
Group A—Complex Rear Lamp	1.04	1.04	1.27
Group B—Noncomplex Rear Lamp	0.97	0.96	0.68
Group C—Park and Signal Lamp	0.88	0.78	0.73

most critical factor in the decision to source in-house. The complex lamps require complicated machinery, special tooling, and labor skills that are only available within the division. The corporation also has a conscious strategy to maintain technological superiority in the area of injection molding. Producing complex parts in-house rather than having them outsourced is one way for the corporation to achieve its goal.

Products in Groups B and C can be outsourced because these products, unlike those in Group A, do not contribute to maintaining a technological edge. Table 9-1 indicates that the products in Groups B and C are systematically overcosted by the existing cost system. A cost comparison with competitors' products, based on the existing cost accounting system, would unduly penalize in-house production. This suggests that the cost accounting system may be at least part of the reason why products in Groups B and C appear to be cost-disadvantaged relative to outside suppliers.

Whereas Table 9-1 describes the average of revised costs to original costs for each group of products, Figures 9-1 through 9-4 provide more detailed information on how the revised costs compare with original costs for lenses and housings. In each figure, the horizontal axis reflects the ratio of revised costs to original costs. Using the graph, we can read off, on the vertical axis, the percentage of products (lenses or housings weighted by their respective revised costs) that have a ratio of revised costs to original costs less than the corresponding number on the horizontal axis.

Figure 9-1 presents the data for lenses in Group A (more complex lenses), and Figure 9-2 presents the data for lenses in Groups B and C together (less complex lenses). Figure 9-1 indicates that only 29% of Group A lenses are overcosted and 71% are undercosted; Figure 9-2 suggests that the split between undercosted and overcosted lenses is 50–50 for Groups B and C together. In fact, only 12% of the lenses in Group A are overcosted by more than 100%, whereas 22% of lenses

Figure 9-1 Cumulative Distribution Function: Lenses—Group A

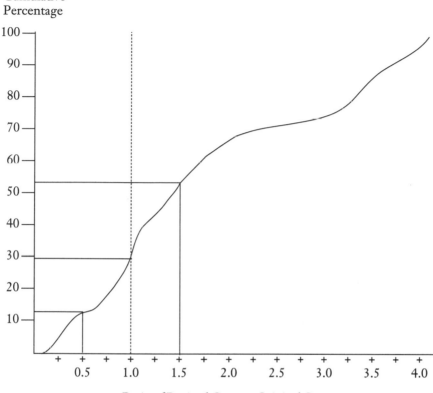

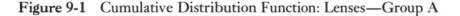

Ratio of Revised Costs to Original Costs

in Groups B and C show such overcosting. On the other hand, 48% of Group A lenses are undercosted by more than 100%, but only 15% of lenses in Groups B and C are 50% undercosted. Similar contrasts between Group A housings and housings in Groups B and C are reflected by Figures 9-3 and 9-4. Figures 9-1 through 9-4 thus support our conclusions that the existing cost system undercosts complex products and overcosts simple ones. The recommendation of the consulting firm to outsource some of the less complex products in Groups B and C (the ones more apt to be overcosted by the existing cost accounting system) can now be seen to be based on distorted data.

Figure 9-2   Cumulative Distribution Function: Lenses—Groups B and C

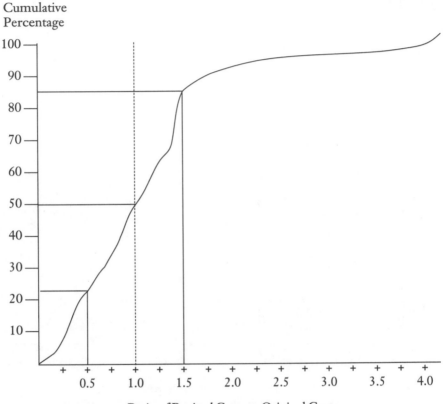

Cumulative
Percentage

Ratio of Revised Costs to Original Costs

Impact of Complexity Factors

The objective in this section is to examine whether the distortions in product costs documented in the previous section can be traced to product complexity factors. Identifying the impact of particular complexity factors on costs is essential for understanding how cost reduction can be achieved by redesigning and re-engineering products to facilitate manufacturability. Determining complexity factors that most influence cost is important so that these factors can be pointed out to the product designers and marketing personnel.

Our discussions with managers led us to identify five complexity factors. These factors were used to develop the following regression

Figure 9-3   Cumulative Distribution Function: Housing—Group A

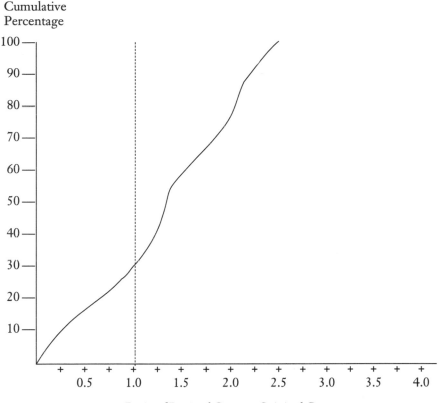

Ratio of Revised Costs to Original Costs

models for the various overhead costs incurred in the molding departments.

Revised Unit Cost = β_0 + β_1 DIRLABHRS/UNITS + β_2 MVGPTS/UNITS
of Supervision   + β_3 MULTCLR + β_4 NUMFUNC + β_5 LENGTH
                 + β_6 REJECTS + ε

Lens supervision costs. In the regression model that appears below, the independent variable DIRLABHRS/UNITS measures the direct labor hours per unit and is used by the existing cost accounting system to allocate supervisory costs to products. MVGPTS/UNITS measures the number of moving parts in the mold. Since we are estimating a unit cost model, we divide the number of moving parts by vol-

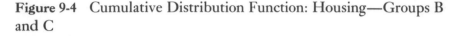

Figure 9-4 Cumulative Distribution Function: Housing—Groups B and C

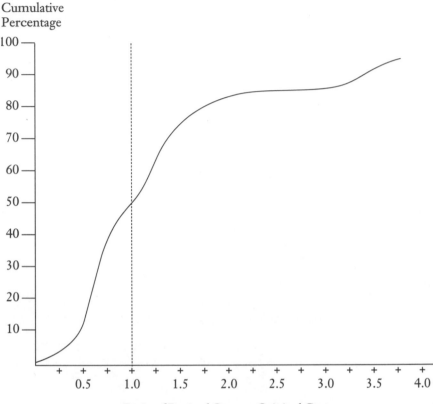

ume. It is assumed that the complexity of a setup (and hence the supervisory effort) is proportional to the number of moving parts. The cost impact of the remaining variables is believed to vary with the number of units produced. MULTCLR is a dummy variable that takes on the value 1 when the molding operation is multicolor and 0 otherwise. NUMFUNC measures the number of functions in the lens, and LENGTH, the length of the lens in inches. REJECTS measures the defect rate per hundred.

Lens quality control and inspection costs. The regression model for lens quality control is identical to the model described for lens supervision except that the dependent variable measures revised per unit cost of quality control and inspection. The independent variable DIR-LABHRS/UNITS is replaced by the direct labor inspection hours per unit, which is the basis used by the existing cost accounting system to allocate quality control and inspection costs to products.

Lens tool maintenance costs. In the case of the lens tool maintenance model, the dependent variable is the revised per unit cost of tool maintenance. The independent variable used by the existing cost accounting system to allocate tool maintenance costs is machine-hours. Consequently, the independent variable DIRLABHRS/UNITS is replaced by MACHOURS/UNITS.

The regression models for supervision, quality control, and tool maintenance costs for housing operations are identical to the corresponding models for lenses except that the independent variables MULTCLR and NUMFUNC are dropped since these variables only apply to lenses.[1] Housings are never multicolored and do not perform multiple functions.

The measures for complexity and labor hours, which constitute the independent variables in the regression equations, can be obtained relatively accurately, based on the detailed plant and accounting records mentioned previously. The dependent variable is an estimate of the actual amount of time spent on each product and is likely to be measured with error. As a result, it is more difficult to reject a hypothesis that a particular complexity variable has no effect. Consequently, although we can be reasonably certain that complexity factors that are significant in the regressions do indeed influence costs, some of the variables that appear not to have strong effects may affect costs more strongly than the reported regression results suggest.

The empirical results reported here are based on the actual data multiplied by a constant in order to protect the confidentiality of the data. The regression results for each cost category—supervision, quality control, and tool maintenance—for both lens and housing are presented in Tables 9-2 through 9-7.[2] In each case, the variable currently used by the firm to allocate overhead costs to products is very significant except in the case of tooling (lens and housing). This result supports the fact that supervision and quality control efforts are to some extent determined by direct labor involved in production. The use of machine-hours to explain tooling maintenance cost, however, cannot be validated from the regression results (see Tables 9-4 and 9-7).

Table 9-2 Regression Results
Revised Cost per Unit: Lens Molding Supervision

Independent Variable	Coefficient	Standard Error	T-ratio
Intercept	$-.01$	.03	$-.25$ (0.80)*
Direct Labor Hours/Volume	15.67	9.27	1.69 (0.09)
Moving Parts/Volume	698.90	30.62	22.83 (0.00)
Multicolor	.08	.05	1.56 (0.12)
Number of Functions	.01	.03	.57 (0.51)
Length of Component	.00	.00	-1.31 (0.19)
Percentage Rejects	.00	.00	$-.64$ (0.52)

R-squared = .75, F-statistic (6,113) = 56.40, pr < .00
F-statistic for Additional Cost Drivers: 221.38, pr < .00
*Data in parentheses are the significance levels.

Table 9-3 Regression Results
Revised Cost per Unit: Lens Quality Control

Independent Variable	Coefficient	Standard Error	T-ratio
Intercept	$-.01$	.00	-2.59 (0.01)*
Direct Labor Hours/Volume	1.44	.32	4.52 (0.00)
Moving Parts/Volume	145.26	3.42	42.48 (0.00)
Multicolor	.00	.00	1.23 (0.22)
Number of Functions	.00	.00	1.38 (0.17)
Length of Component	.00	.00	$-.82$ (0.41)
Percentage Rejects	.00	.00	1.64 (0.10)

R-squared = .97, F-statistic (6,113) = 615.91, pr < .00
F-statistic for Additional Cost Drivers: 2894.74, pr < .00
*Data in parentheses are significance levels.

Table 9-4 Regression Results
Revised Cost per Unit: Lens Tooling Maintenance

Independent Variable	Coefficient	Standard Error	T-ratio
Intercept	$-.02$	.01	$-.30$ (0.76)*
Machine-Hours/Volume	-6.98	21.21	$-.33$ (0.74)
Moving Parts/Volume	947.61	179.20	5.29 (0.00)
Multicolor	.69	.34	2.00 (0.05)
Number of Functions	.09	.04	2.26 (0.02)
Length of Component	.00	.01	.46 (0.64)
Percentage Rejects	.00	.00	.30 (0.76)

R-squared = .97, F-statistic (6,75) = 8.79 pr < .00
F-statistic for Additional Cost Drivers: 30.50, pr < .00
*Data in parentheses are significance levels.

Table 9-5   Regression Results
Revised Cost per Unit: Housing Molding Supervision

Independent Variable	Coefficient	Standard Error	T-ratio
Intercept	− .01	.01	− .81 (0.42)*
Direct Labor Hours/Volume	1.73	1.21	1.43 (0.15)
Moving Parts/Volume	132.86	106.40	1.25 (0.21)
Length of Component	.00	.00	1.45 (0.15)
Percentage Rejects	.00	.00	2.40 (0.02)

R-squared = .46, F-statistic (4,99) = 21.24, pr < .00
F-statistic for Additional Cost Drivers: 13.66, pr < .00
*Data in parentheses are significance levels.

Table 9-6   Regression Results
Revised Cost per Unit: Housing Quality Control

Independent Variable	Coefficient	Standard Error	T-ratio
Intercept	.00	.01	.44 (0.66)*
Direct Labor Hours/Volume	3.39	1.08	3.13 (0.00)
Moving Parts/Volume	276.55	178.50	1.55 (0.12)
Length of Component	.00	.00	.27 (0.79)
Percentage Rejects	− .00	.00	− 1.31 (0.19)

R-squared = .60, F-statistic (4,99) = 36.61, pr < .00
F-statistic for Additional Cost Drivers: 30.50, pr < .00
*Data in parentheses are significance levels.

Table 9-7   Regression Results
Revised Cost per Unit: Housing Tooling Maintenance

Independent Variable	Coefficient	Standard Error	T-ratio
Intercept	− .13	.07	− 1.76 (0.08)*
Machine Hours/Volume	9.95	9.77	1.02 (0.31)
Moving Parts/Volume	2481.51	879.70	2.82 (0.00)
Length of Component	.00	.00	.44 (0.66)
Percentage Rejects	.02	.01	1.55 (0.12)

R-squared = .34, F-statistic (4,46) = 5.85, pr < .00
F-statistic for Additional Cost Drivers: 10.69, pr < .00
*Data in parentheses are significance levels.

From the standpoint of this study, an important question is whether the complexity factors have any impact on the costs of supervision, quality control, and tool maintenance both for lens and housing molding operations. Indeed, our results show that taken together the complexity factors are significant in each of the six cases. The statistical evidence clearly shows that the allocation basis employed by the existing cost accounting system, while generally relevant, is not adequate by itself to identify the overhead resources demanded by the different products. The use of complexity variables is required in explaining and understanding the reasons for the changes in the cost per unit of the overhead costs incurred.

Of the complexity variables used in this study, moving parts in the mold has a significant positive effect on various categories of costs in all six cost equations. The importance of moving parts across all cost categories examined did not come as a surprise. In our discussion with managers and shop-floor personnel, the difficulty of aligning and matching many moving parts and the susceptibility of such parts to wear and tear were repeatedly mentioned. The results of our analysis, however, lend strong support to conjectures made by managers and can help to focus the attention of product designers to this factor.

In the case of lenses, the product and process complexity factors of number of functions and multicolor molding are also important and increase overhead costs.[3] Increasing the number of functions requires meeting many types of tolerances simultaneously; using multicolor molding necessitates close monitoring of temperature and pressure during the molding process to ensure that one color solidifies before another is injected. As a result, both factors tend to make additional demands on support services such as supervision, quality control, and tool maintenance. The plant needs to focus on both of these complexity factors in the design of a more detailed cost accounting system. On the other hand, we had no statistical evidence that length of component and percentage of rejects drive overhead costs in molding operations.

A significant implication of our analysis is that the existing cost system presents an incomplete picture to management by focusing solely on the current allocation basis (e.g., direct labor hours for supervision cost) to control overhead resources. Our results indicate that efforts to reduce the costs of support services should start at the product design phase. The demand on support services can be contained and manufacturing burden reduced by closely monitoring product and process characteristics such as moving parts, number of functions, and multicolor molding, all of which increase the complexity of the manufacturing process.

CONCLUSION

We have documented the distortions in product costs that occur even in a fairly elaborate cost accounting system characterized by multiple second-stage cost drivers. The cost driver for each overhead cost category in the existing system was chosen to best correspond to the consumption of the respective resources. We adopted an approach that allowed us to determine product costs in the presence of product and process complexity.

While recent developments such as ABC methodology yield product costs accurately, they do not provide the cost information to the designers in terms of the design factors that can be used to influence costs at the design stage. Our methodology extends the ABC methodology by analyzing the determinants of activities in terms of product and process design features. By relating complexity factors to costs, we identify important factors that act as explanatory variables for the consumption of overhead resources. This information can thus be used in the design of a cost accounting system for evaluating alternative product designs.

It is important to note that our analysis focuses on the complexity factors that drive costs in the current manufacturing environment. As processes and product mixes change, these factors may change. A particular characteristic that could have a significant effect on overhead costs in the future may not show up as a cost driver in our analysis because too few components in our data possess that characteristic.

We have examined and reported on our analysis of three overhead cost categories within molding operations. More information and insight may be provided as we expand our analysis to other overhead cost categories and to secondary and assembly operations. The study should result in a system that will provide valuable information to the designers by providing cost implications of alternative design choices.

NOTES

1. We estimate a unit-cost model to alleviate heteroscedasticity problems. The Goldfeld-Quandt (1972) and White (1980) tests indicate residual heteroscedasticity even after this correction. We adjusted for this and obtained consistent estimates of

the coefficient and the variance covariance matrix using White's procedure. Multi-collinearity diagnostics including Belsey, Kuh, and Welsch (1980) condition indices and eigen vector-based diagnostics did not reveal any problems.

     2. The results for tooling are based on 1988 model-year data. The results are robust when cumulative production data are used instead.

     3. Recall that multicolor molding and number of functions are not relevant for lamp housing.

References

Belsey, D. A., E. Kuh, and R. S. Welsch. *Regression Diagnostics*. New York: Wiley, 1980.

Cooper, R., and R. S. Kaplan. "How Cost Accounting Systematically Distorts Product Costs." In *Accounting and Management: Field Study Perspectives*, edited by W. J. Bruns, Jr., and R. S. Kaplan. Boston: Harvard Business School Press, 1987: 204–228.

————. "Measure Costs Right: Make the Right Decisions." *Harvard Business Review* (September–October 1988): 96–103.

Goldfeld, S. M., and R. E. Quandt. "Some Tests for Homoscedasticity." *Journal of the American Statistical Association*. (June 1965): 539–547.

————. *Nonlinear Methods in Econometrics*. Amsterdam: North Holland, 1972.

White, H. "A Heteroscedastic-consistent Covariance Matrix Estimator and a Direct Test for Heteroscedasticity." *Econometrica* (May 1980): 817–838.

CHAPTER 10

Internally Focused Activity-Based Cost Systems

Robin Cooper and Peter B. B. Turney

Several recent papers have emphasized the more accurate product costs reported by activity-based cost systems (for example, see Cooper and Kaplan 1988a, 1988b).[1] Activity-based systems have emerged in firms facing increased competition, where management decided that the fastest way to become more profitable was to gain a better understanding of what it cost to make their products. The more accurate product costs enabled management to take actions on pricing and product mix to increase overall profitability. Thus, the systems were designed to lead to modifications in the *external* marketing strategy of the firm.

Recently, another way to take advantage of activity-based systems has emerged. In some firms, management has decided that the fastest way to improve profitability is to reduce product costs through improved design and more efficient processes. These firms are characterized by products with relatively short life cycles; thus, the firms quickly reap benefits if new products can be manufactured more efficiently. They use activity-based systems to send specific messages to product designers and process engineers about how to improve the manufacturing capability of the firm. Their systems are designed to lead to modification in the *internal* strategy of the firm.

We identified and visited three companies, all in the electronics industry, that use internally focused activity-based systems. The three firms produce a diverse mix of products, have high fixed over-head, and have recently implemented continuous improvement programs in response to increased competitive pressures.

We first describe the activity-based cost systems developed in each company. We then analyze our findings—particularly, the conditions that favor internally as opposed to externally focused systems.[2] These conditions include 1) established competitive strategies and 2) products with short life cycles. The structural differences between the two types of systems are explored, especially the number and nature of their cost drivers.

The analysis of the difference between the systems relies upon relatively few examples. We know of fewer than ten documented activity-based cost systems. Our analysis is a preliminary one.

THE EVIDENCE

The three companies illustrate how activity-based cost systems can be designed to motivate improvements in the manufacturing capability of a firm. The primary objective of the system at the Portable Instruments Division of Tektronix was to reduce the number of unique components in their products. Hewlett-Packard's Roseville Network Division's objective was to improve the design of its products via better cost/performance trade-offs. At Zytec, the objective was to reduce the elapsed time from the ordering of components to the shipment of the finished product.

Tektronix: Portable Instruments Division*

Portable Instruments Division (PID) produces portable electronic os-cilloscopes. It recently implemented a continuous improvement program to help make it competitive with Japanese products. The program consisted of just-in-time production, total quality control, and shop-level personnel involvement. The changes in the production process resulting from this improvement program, coupled with a sig-

---

*The material for this section is taken from Robin Cooper and Peter B. B. Turney, "Tektronix: Portable Instruments Division," 9-188-142/3/4. Boston: Harvard Business School, 1988.

nificant decrease in the direct labor content of its products over the last few years, helped make PID's direct labor-based cost accounting system obsolete.

Therefore, management initiated a special study to identify the factors responsible for overhead. The study determined that half of all overhead costs related in some way to the number of different part numbers handled. To trace this overhead to products, management selected the cost driver called "number of part numbers." This driver divided overhead costs by the number of different part numbers used in the facility. Dividing the cost per unique part number by the volume of each part number used created a charge that was assigned to each product, depending on the overall usage of that part.

Management believed that using the number of part numbers as a cost driver would increase the product designers' awareness of the high costs associated with using low-volume parts. This awareness was important because the designers had used many special components to achieve product functionality; thus, the total number of different part numbers used by the division was very high. Management believed it could reduce overhead costs by achieving a reduction of both the number of part numbers in future products and the range of part number-related activities, such as maintaining bills of materials and expediting parts.

Management considered the "material burdening" approach a success, and the product designers acknowledged the beneficial effect of the system on their decisions. (PID uses the term "material burdening" for the assignment of parts-related overhead costs.) For example, according to the engineering manager:

> The way we allocate manufacturing overhead costs affects the way we design products. We design products differently under material burdening from the way we did under the old system, where all overhead was charged to labor. With material burdening, we now recognize the acquisition cost plus the carrying costs of components. This knowledge affects us during the design process, automatically guiding the process to the minimum true cost of doing business, not just to the lowest parts-cost.
>
> Today, we take a hard look at what parts we really need and deliberately minimize the proliferation of equivalent parts. Three major factors force us to limit part numbers: automatic assembly equipment can only handle a limited number of parts; each additional type of part complicates the task of establishing and maintaining high-quality sources of supply; and each part type complicates the logistics and cost of operating the production process.

Hewlett-Packard: Roseville Network Division*

The Roseville Network Division (RND) of Hewlett-Packard produces networking devices that allow computers to communicate with other computers and peripheral devices. The rapid introduction of new computers in the last few years has dramatically reduced the life expectancies of RND's products, while increasing the number of different products it has to sell to remain competitive.

RND's strategy is to keep the products up-to-date and to design them in a cost-effective manner. The shorter lives and increasing number of its products require a continuous flow of new products from design to production. Careful attention to the design of the products to reduce their overall cost of manufacturing is also needed.

The goal of the new cost system is to encourage the product designers to choose the least expensive alternative among designs with equivalent functionality. The cost system provides cost information on each production process so that the costs of different designs can be compared. A manager deeply involved in the implementation of the new system stated:

> The purpose of cost driver accounting was not to prevent the engineers from introducing new technology. [RND uses the term "cost driver accounting" to refer to its activity-based cost system.] Rather, it was to get the engineers to think about cost and not to go for elegance every time. Cost driver accounting put product costs on the backs of the engineers. It encouraged them to design for manufacturability.

The initial system design was quite simple. It had only two cost drivers: direct labor hours and number of insertions. However, over several years, a team from accounting and engineering sequentially added new cost drivers to the system as its understanding of the economics of design improved. For example, early in the development of the system, an engineer believed that the reported cost of a product was too high. A special study confirmed his belief and showed that axial insertions were about one-third the cost of dual in-line processor (DIP) insertions. The cost system was modified to differentiate between the two types of insertion.

During a four-year period the cost system went from two drivers to nine. The first six of the drivers are surrogates for direct labor or

---

*The material for this section is taken from Robin Cooper and Peter B. B. Turney, "Hewlett-Packard: Roseville Network Division," 9-189-177. Boston: Harvard Business School, 1989.

machine-hours. These unit-based drivers, however, are much more meaningful to product designers. Designers find it easier to think about the number and type of insertions their designs require than to think about how long they take to manufacture. The nine drivers were

1. Number of axial insertions
2. Number of radial insertions
3. Number of dip insertions
4. Number of manual insertions
5. Number of test hours
6. Number of solder joints
7. Number of boards
8. Number of parts
9. Number of slots

The designers did not, however, use the cost data blindly. As one designer commented:

I do not design to minimize the reported cost of the product as this will change across time with the introduction of new cost drivers. Instead, I design what I think is the lowest-cost product for a given level of reliability and functionality. It is important not to design to minimize cost because the model does not capture all of the relevant costs.

The cost system affected the decisions made by the product designers by allowing them to develop a series of design heuristics that helped guide the design process. For example:

1. Manual insertion was three times as expensive as automatic insertion.
2. Connectors that could not go through the wave solder machine and were manually inserted, or needed special presolder treatment, added approximately $2–3 to the overhead cost of the board.
3. Ease of availability was similarly critical. Selecting a component that had excess production capacity in the industry and could be supplied by multiple vendors reduced the risk of component shortages. A rule of thumb was used to adjust for availability: a low-availability component had an additional cost of ten times its materials cost.

Once the designers had developed these heuristics, they did not go back to the cost system for cost information. However, each time a new cost driver was implemented, the designers studied its effect on the economics of production and adjusted their design rules accordingly.

The new cost system thus played an important role in the design of new products. Even though it was based upon historical data, management believed it was successful in changing product design to improve the performance of the firm. The engineering manager at RND described how the design process changed:

> We created a lot of tighter relationships among accounting, research and development, manufacturing, and marketing. We were all learning about the business. We have broken the back of the cost system design problem and are now refining it and our intuitions about the economics of product design. Overall, the whole experience forced us to understand our design process.

Zytec Corporation*

Zytec Corporation is an independent producer of custom power supplies for computer peripherals and other electronic products. It was formed in a leveraged buyout in 1984. Zytec management embarked upon a continuous improvement program in late 1984. It has implemented just-in-time production techniques, total quality commitment, and people involvement programs. The continuous improvement program was extremely successful; for example, over a three-year period, the reported cost of one product fell from $530 to $325, and the cycle time was significantly reduced.

One of the major elements of this continuous improvement program was a "management by planning" system implemented in late 1988. This system identified six objectives that management believed to be critical to the success of the firm during 1989. All departments were expected to identify improvement targets for the six objectives. The objectives were to

1. Improve total quality commitment implementation
2. Reduce total cycle time

---

*The material for this section is taken from Robin Cooper and Peter B. B. Turney, "Zytec Corporation (B)," 9-190-005. Boston: Harvard Business School, 1989.

3. Improve service to customers
4. Improve profitability and financial stability
5. Improve housekeeping and safety
6. Increase employee involvement

The changes in the production process brought about by the continuous improvement program coupled with a general decrease in the labor content of the products rendered the existing cost system obsolete. The team assigned to redesign the system was told to design one that reinforced the just-in-time philosophy. Zytec's controller explained why:

We wanted to pick a set of drivers that was meaningful to the people on the floor. We wanted these drivers to capture the essence of our drive for continuous improvement. In particular, we were convinced that the cost system could become a potent tool for behavior modification. The only real limitation we placed upon ourselves was that the cost system not require any special measurements.

The design team identified four potential cost drivers:

Yield: a test of the quality of production that measured the average number of pieces that did not have to be reworked. Yield was considered a cost driver because of the high cost and shop-floor disturbance associated with rework.

Cycle Time: A measure of the average time taken by a product to go from raw material to finished goods. Cycle time reductions could be achieved only by improving the yield to reduce rework.

Supplier Lead Time: A measure of the average time taken by a supplier to deliver an order to Zytec. Supplier lead time was considered a cost driver because long supplier lead time was a significant roadblock to the flexibility Zytec sought to provide its customers.

Linearity: A measure of the average absolute deviation of actual production to the daily production plan. For example, if the planned output is 10 units and the actual output is either 12 or 8, then the daily linearity is said to be 80%.[3] Management believed that higher average linearity lowered overall costs.

After a series of discussions with management, the team simplified the cost system design and retained only two of the four drivers: cycle time and supplier lead time. All manufacturing overhead, previously allocated using direct labor hours, was allocated according to cycle time, and all materials overhead, previously allocated using materials dollars, was allocated proportionately to supplier lead time.

The team did not use linearity and yields as cost drivers because it had little confidence that the formulas it had developed for them would correlate with cost. The controller commented:

We wanted to build a system that fit manufacturing's need. They [manufacturing people] felt that cycle time and supplier lead time were most important, so we constructed a system based on these factors.

Despite limiting the design of the system to the two cost drivers that management felt were most important, the team found that reaction to the system was predominantly negative. One designer commented:

The initial reaction to the cycle time portion of the new system was dominated by confusion. Everybody wanted to compare the old and new numbers and have us explain the differences. Unfortunately, we could not satisfy them about the causes of the differences.

Reaction to the supplier lead time system was even more negative. In particular, the purchasing manager argued that supplier lead time was not under his control. He could not see any way to change his behavior to reduce supplier lead time. He felt unable to react to the new system.

Given the negative reaction, the new cost system was modified. Material burdening was treated as a period cost and only manufacturing burden was allocated to the products using cycle time.

ANALYSIS

Activity-based systems, both internally and externally focused, typically appear in firms experiencing intense competitive pressure and in firms where the benefits from the more flexible but more costly and complex activity-based system exceed the costs of designing, implementing, and operating such a system (Cooper 1988b, 1988c). The three companies studied face intense competitive pressure—PID from the Japanese, RND from changes in the product life cycle, and Zytec from a number of competitors. Similarly, they demonstrate the conditions that cause the benefits of an activity-based system to exceed the costs: a diverse product mix and high fixed overhead (Cooper and Kaplan 1988a).

Firms that have introduced internally focused systems differ from those that have introduced externally focused systems. A key difference is the extent to which the competitive strategy of the firm has been clearly established. A second difference is the length of the time from introduction to withdrawal of the product. The length of the life cycle affects the orientation of internally focused systems.

The Role of an Established Strategy

Internally focused systems are used to make internal improvements in order to better implement a chosen strategy. They are used to facilitate improvements in product or process design. This was the case in all three of the internally focused systems. At PID, for example, the system was purposely designed to support the firm's strategy. As one cost system designer commented, "We recognized that we had already chosen our strategic direction. What we needed was a cost system that would drive behavior in that direction."

At RND, the strategy was to keep the product lines as up-to-date as possible. The short product life cycles reflected this approach. Management implemented a cost system that motivated the design of products that could be manufactured more efficiently. At Zytec, the strategy was to improve manufacturing capability, with particular emphasis on improving cost, quality, and flexibility. The focal point for implementing this strategy was the reduction of total customer lead time, the primary motivation behind the design of the new cost system.

In contrast, most firms that implement externally focused systems use the new product costs to help establish a new strategy. The benefits of the cost system to these firms comes from the improved profitability resulting from changing the product mix, product prices, and other factors relating to the firm's approach to its external customers.

The need to establish a strategy before introducing an internally focused system is understandable. First, the cost system can be designed to support and enhance the strategy; e.g., it can be focused on motivating specific improvements in the firm's manufacturing capability. Second, an established strategy creates a receptive environment for the new system. A system that brings the message "reducing the number of unique components will make it easier to introduce new products" will be better received in a company whose strategy focuses on continual introduction of new products than in a company that has yet to decide if new products are beneficial.

Not all companies with a well-established strategy have internally focused systems. At least one firm, the Electric Motor Works at Siemens, has implemented an externally focused system to sustain its new strategy.[4] They chose this route because the new strategy rendered the existing system obsolete. Without a new system they would have been unable to tell which orders were profitable, and their new strategy would have failed.

The Role of Products with a Short Life Cycle

All three firms implementing internally focused cost systems had products with a short life cycle.[5] The product life cycle at PID was about 18 months, at RND about 24 months, and at Zytec about 36 months. In contrast, the product life cycles at firms that install externally focused cost systems are typically much longer. The role of product life cycle in determining the type of cost system to install can be understood by considering how the length of the life cycle affects the speed at which different benefits can be achieved. If a firm's existing product mix is insufficiently profitable, and the products have long life cycles, the fastest way to improve performance is often to change the mix of products or prices charged. To make these changes requires understanding relative product profitability.

In contrast, if the product life cycle is relatively short, the fastest way to improve performance is often to design new products that can be manufactured efficiently. Hence, designers need to be motivated to design products for manufacturability.

At PID and RND, the primary focus of the cost system was to improve the design of the product. The firms had already made their production processes highly efficient. Management believed that larger cost reductions could be achieved by better design of the next generation of products than by improved efficiency of the existing products or production process. The manufacturing manager at PID described this perspective:

Part number burdening is of little immediate use to the manufacturing manager. Its real value is to drive the next generation of products to have fewer parts. Manufacturing cannot do much, in the short run, about the number of parts. The reduction in the number of parts can only be significantly reduced through product redesign.

The focus of the system at Zytec was slightly different. The longer product life cycle increased the benefits from improving the production process for current products. Consequently, the system focused on improving both the current production process and the design of new products.

Simplicity

Internally focused systems tend to be simpler than externally focused ones. Simplicity helps ensure that the system is understood by management and product designers and is therefore more likely to produce the performance improvements desired. For example, at PID, management purposely kept the system simple so that the users understood the "message":

> Our objective with the cost system was to change the behavior of the division management. We did not go to a more complex system, say an eight-driver system, immediately, because we wanted to take incremental steps and change behavior permanently. If we had tried to introduce a massive change, we might have created such confusion that the benefits would have been lost. The beautiful thing about taking this incremental step was that the behavior change we wanted was almost instantaneous. On day one we thought the old way, and on day two we were thinking the new way.

However, this approach will only be effective if management can react to the message. At Zytec, for example, the "supplier lead time" cost driver was poorly accepted because the purchasing manager did not control supplier lead time and therefore could do nothing about it.

The danger of simplicity is that the reported product costs may be somewhat inaccurate and lead to poor decisions. The message is strong: if the reported cost per unit of a cost driver is higher than it should be, this approach risks improvements being made that are not cost justified. The firms' original direct labor-based allocation systems suffered from this problem. As one PID manager commented:

> Engineering could justify a $10,000 project to remove five minutes (of direct labor) from an instrument because that five minutes was leveraged by the labor burdening system. In reality, they were adding to the size of burden and doing little to reduce costs.

The designers at all three companies were aware of the risks of reporting inaccurate product costs. One designer at PID commented:

The product costs reported by our system are accurate enough to guide behavior in the direction we want to go. They are not 100% correct, nor are they as accurate as we want them. I did not attempt to calculate the economic or financial impact of the designers' individual decisions. This was not necessary because collectively their decisions would take us where we wanted to go—common parts, standard parts throughout the product line, and modifications to existing products using existing components. I was more interested in forcing a move toward standardization than in being able to say that replacing two unique parts with one common part would save exactly $4.93.

The designers at PID and RND had strategies for dealing with the lack of accuracy of their systems. PID had identified two possible approaches. One was to change the drivers once the message had been accepted. As a manager at PID commented:

The number of parts will cease to be a useful behavioral cost driver when the design engineers see the value of common parts. When they come to believe that it hurts our competitive position to proliferate parts, they will naturally design the products with common parts, and we won't have to continually remind them to do so.

The cost system will be used to cause behavioral change in a series of steps. I can see that in a few years the system will use different cost drivers, for example, cycle time burdening.

An alternative approach was to add more drivers to the system sequentially. This approach was used by RND. Over time, in response to engineers' expressed concerns, the system was modified to make it more accurate. An engineer commented on the process of continuously changing the cost system:

I would have preferred one transition, but I do not believe it could have been done that way. Accounting simply did not understand enough about the production and design process. If we had attempted one transition, we would have risked freezing the firm on the first system we designed, and we would not have been able to change it to reflect new insights we gained from it.

However, this additional accuracy was achieved at the expense of the simplicity of the system. Personnel at RND were concerned that its system was becoming too complex. According to one engineer on the design team:

We could improve it [the cost system] to capture more costs, but we would risk it becoming too complex to understand and hence use. This is especially true for new college hires. They have never been taught to design with cost in mind.

The designers at Zytec were less successful in resolving the accuracy issue. Their system was so focused on motivation that management and engineers did not believe in the accuracy of the costs reported. For example, supplier lead time is not a good driver for product costing because it does not capture enough of the complexity of materials acquisition costs: one vendor may have a long lead time but deliver high-quality products, while another may deliver low-quality products with a short lead time. Failure occurred when management tried to interpret the new cost numbers in light of the old ones.

When the driver that sends the strongest message is not the one that most accurately reports product costs, designers will have to choose between the strength of the message and the accuracy of the reported product costs. Clearly, choosing a driver that does not send the desired message risks not achieving the desired improvements. Choosing a driver that does not report very accurate product costs risks management making poor decisions based on the costs reported. We know very little about how to decide which type of driver to choose. More research is required before we understand the nature of this trade-off.

CONCLUSIONS

This paper introduced the concept of internally focused activity-based cost systems. These are activity-based systems designed to influence internal decisions such as product or process design. They can be contrasted with externally focused systems designed to report accurate product costs and to allow the firm to modify its strategy.

The firms implementing internally focused systems made products with short product life cycles and had well-established strategies. Those implementing externally focused systems made products with longer life cycles and usually were searching for a new strategy. Between the two types of systems, two structural differences were identified: the number and the type of cost drivers selected. On average, internally focused systems are simpler than externally focused ones, and they use cost drivers that send a clear message, in contrast to systems that report accurate product costs.

An important question emerging from our study is whether cost systems should be designed to influence internal decisions. We believe the answer is yes. First, at both RND and PID, managers strongly believe that the cost system is a potent method to improve the firm's manufacturing capability. There is also strong evidence at RND that designer behavior was modified by the cost system. Second, ignoring the motivational effects of cost systems can lead to decisions that negatively affect performance. There is evidence at PID and Zytec that the driver "direct labor hours" resulted in incorrect product and process design decisions.

A second important question is the extent to which cost system designers should allow motivational effects to dominate the need for accurate product costs. First, the cost system is frequently the only source of information on product costs. Second, designing a cost system solely to motivate behavior can lead, as it did at Zytec, to acceptance problems (because reported product costs lack credibility). Finally, internal decisions can be influenced by other means such as performance measurement systems or by legislating policy. At Zytec, for example, a performance measurement system was used to reduce cycle time. At PID, designer behavior was modified by setting policies for new designs, such as restricting the sets of parts, limiting the number of subassemblies, and eliminating the need for repositioning the product on the bench during assembly.

We recommend that a firm, prior to designing an activity-based cost system, examine the main source of potential benefits from installing the system. If the main benefit is external, the system should be designed with sufficient cost drivers to provide reasonably accurate product costs. If the main benefit is improved internal decisions, the system should be designed to clearly communicate the link, via the cost drivers, between these internal decisions and cost. The designers of internally focused systems must be careful, however, not to sacrifice too much accuracy. This is particularly true in firms where cost information is used for external as well as internal purposes. Accuracy should only be decreased when the benefits of sending a clear message outweigh the costs of reporting less accurate cost information.

NOTES

1. Activity-based cost systems are distinguished from their conventional counterparts by the cost drivers, or allocation bases, they use to relate the consumption of inputs to products. Conventional systems rely solely on unit-level cost drivers, such as direct labor hours or dollars, machine-hours, and materials dollars. A unit-level cost driver assumes that inputs are consumed in direct proportion to the number of units produced. Activity-based systems, while retaining unit-level drivers, also use nonunit-level ones. Nonunit-level drivers assume that costs are not consumed in

direct proportion to the number of units produced. These drivers include number of part numbers, number of vendors, and number of setups (see Cooper 1989d).

2. Our analysis is based in part upon findings from earlier studies on externally focused systems. See, for example, the following Harvard Business School case studies: R. Cooper, "Schrader Bellows," #9-186-272 (1988): R. S. Kaplan, "John Deere Component Works," #9-187-107,108 (1987) and "Kanthal," 9-189-129 (1989).

3. The absolute value of (10–12) and (10–8) is 2. The linearity is therefore 80% [(10–2)/10 stated as a percentage].

4. R. Cooper and K. Wruck, "Siemens Electric Motor Works (A): Process Oriented Costing," #9-189-089. Boston: Harvard Business School, 1988.

5. For more information on the linking of manufacturing and product life cycles, see Hayes and Wheelwright (1979).

REFERENCES

Cooper, R., 1988a. "The Rise of Activity-Based Costing—Part Two: When Do I Need an Activity-Based Cost System?" *Journal of Cost Management for the Manufacturing Industry* (Fall 1988): 41–48.

———, 1989b. "The Rise of Activity-Based Costing—Part Three: How Many Cost Drivers Do You Need, and How Do You Select Them?" *Journal of Cost Management for the Manufacturing Industry* (Winter 1989): 34–46.

———, 1989c. "The Rise of Activity-Based Costing—Part Four: What Do Activity-Based Cost Systems Look Like?" *Journal of Cost Management for the Manufacturing Industry* (Spring 1989): 38–49.

———, 1989d. "Cost Classification in Unit-Based and Activity-Based Manufacturing Cost Systems." Working Paper, Harvard University, 1989.

Cooper, R., and R. S. Kaplan, 1988a. "How Cost Accounting Distorts Product Cost." *Management Accounting* (April 1988): 20–27.

———, 1988b. "Measure Costs Right: Make the Right Decisions." *Harvard Business Review* (September–October 1988): 96–103.

Hayes, R. H., and S. C. Wheelwright. "Linking Manufacturing Process and Product Life Cycles." *Harvard Business Review* (January–February 1979): 133–140.

PART IV

Measures for Production Planning
and Evaluation

CHAPTER 11

Measuring Delivery Performance: A Case Study from the Semiconductor Industry

J. Michael Harrison, Charles A. Holloway, and
James M. Patell

INTRODUCTION

This paper describes a set of interrelated programs undertaken by a commercial producer of semiconductor products in order to improve customer service. The emphasis is on operational decision making, booking customer orders, releasing production lots to factories, assigning priorities to production lots queued at factory work centers and on the information systems and performance measurement systems that support and influence those decisions. Our report is based on a detailed field study of a single company, National Semiconductor Corporation (NSC).

The two most frequently cited dimensions of manufacturing performance are cost and quality, but in many industries the timeliness

We are indebted to Gary Dean and Edward Pausa of National Semiconductor Corporation (NSC) for their sponsorship of our field study, to Court Skinner for his help in establishing the research relationship, and to John Groves, Butch Holmberg, Robert Kocher, Philip Lorson, Ted Malanczuk, Manfred Nieder, Charles Riley, Darius Rohan, and the other NSC managers who cooperated in the undertaking. Financial support was provided by the Stanford Graduate School of Business and by the Semiconductor Research Corporation through a grant to Stanford's Center for Integrated Systems. Finally, we are indebted to Robert Kaplan for his help in setting the scope and focus of this paper and to other participants in the "Measuring Manufacturing Performance" colloquium for helpful comments on a previous draft.

of production is equally important for competitive success. Good delivery performance consists of order lead times that are both short and reliable; it can be achieved either through short manufacturing cycle time and good production scheduling or by using inventory to buffer customers against lengthy manufacturing delays. For a variety of reasons, the latter option is becoming less attractive to semiconductor manufacturers, so there is pressure throughout the industry for better cycle time control and improved scheduling systems.

Semiconductor manufacturing involves a great deal of uncertainty and private information, a combination that virtually forces a decentralized system of operational control. There is general agreement that current scheduling practice in the semiconductor industry leaves much to be desired, but there also is a serious discrepancy between the issues of primary concern in real semiconductor companies and the issues that dominate the academic literature on production management. To comprehend the full scope of the subject, it is necessary to expand the traditional view of "production scheduling" to include information processing and performance measurement as well as scheduling logic.

The NSC system for high-level production scheduling is based on what we call a "clockwork" model of manufacturing flows in which factory capacities and production lead times are treated as known, fixed parameters; the model suppresses recognition of any statistical variability in actual processing times. Moreover, the parameter values that the schedulers use are essentially performance commitments made by operating managers, and NSC's "on-schedule delivery" performance evaluation system may induce managers to provide ultra-conservative lead time estimates. Thus, we suspect that there is a trade-off between order-by-order accountability and aggregate efficiency, as execution of the production schedule turns conservative planning lead times into self-fulfilling prophecies.

We start with a quick overview of the process by which integrated circuits are made. Then, we describe the essential elements of the production scheduling problem at NSC in relatively abstract terms. The next section is more reportorial in nature, describing in broad outline how NSC approaches production scheduling, performance measurement, and related information processing. This section contains the data from our field study. Finally, we return to a more analytical mode, describing some trade-offs that NSC confronts in designing its operating systems and discussing alternative approaches that might be adopted.

SEMICONDUCTOR MANUFACTURING PROCESSES

Throughout this paper, a generic semiconductor product will be referred to as an integrated circuit (IC) or semiconductor chip. This section contains a brief and highly simplified description of the IC manufacturing process.

Wafer Fabrication and Wafer Sort

An integrated circuit, consisting of miniaturized electronic components and their interconnections, is produced in a four-stage process portrayed schematically in Figure 11-1. The process begins with raw wafers of silicon or (less commonly) gallium arsenide; these polished discs are three to eight inches in diameter and a few millimeters thick. In the first stage of IC production, called *wafer fabrication*, wafers are grouped in lots (a typical lot size is 20–100 wafers) that travel together in a standard container and are subjected to identical processing operations. The integrity of the lot usually is maintained through the second stage of production, called *wafer probe* or *wafer sort*.

The term *wafer fab*, or just *fab*, commonly is used to mean a clean room in which wafer fabrication is conducted. During this initial stage of production, the intricate miniature circuitry for a number of identical chips is created on each wafer. An individual chip-to-be is called a *die*, and the number of die per wafer may vary from just a few to many hundreds. The processing sequence required to create the circuitry involves many steps and many pieces of equipment, through which lots are routed in traditional job shop fashion. A distinctive feature of wafer fabrication is that routes consist of repetitive loops, so a production lot may visit a given work center within the clean room a dozen or more times; the term *re-entrant flow* has been coined to describe this process characteristic. Most fabs support between 10 and 100 distinct *process flows*, each of which is used to produce a large family of related products. Two process flows may differ in the number of operations to be performed, the order of operations, or the precise physical parameters associated with particular operations.

Most wafer fabrication facilities operate on a three-shift basis, five to seven days per week. However, scheduled maintenance, equipment failures, and other sorts of unscheduled downtime reduce the

Figure 11-1   IC Manufacturing Process

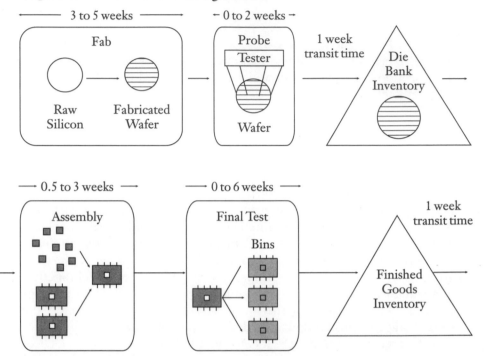

number of hours actually available for processing wafers. If one were to add up the processing times for the hundreds of individual operations required to fabricate a complicated integrated circuit, taking realistic account of such overhead factors as loading and unloading time, the total might come to something like 120 hours (one five-day working week with three shifts per day). But the industry-average fab cycle time (the number of working hours that elapse between a wafer's entry into the clean room and its exit) for such a product is, in fact, typically three to five weeks; even ten weeks is not unimaginable.

For the most part, this difference is due to queueing time—the time that lots spend at work stations waiting for other lots to complete processing there—which arise because of statistical variability in the operating environment. The ambient level of statistical variability in wafer fabrication is at the high end of the scale for industrial operations; most of it is associated with unscheduled equipment downtime (i.e., equipment failure, recalibration, or readjustment), but in many fabs a good deal of variation also occurs in both the input rate of new lots and the input mix by process flow.

In the wafer probe or wafer sort stage of IC production, each die on each wafer is tested for functionality; die that fail the functional test are marked with an ink dot and eventually discarded. The total time to probe a lot of wafers is seldom more than a few hours, but the total elapsed time between completing fabrication and completing probe usually is measured in days, and it may go as high as two weeks. As with wafer fabrication, the cause of congestion and delay in the probe area is statistical variability, primarily associated with tester failures but also with variability in the mix of products emerging from fab.

Wafer probe usually is done at the same physical location as wafer fabrication, with little or no intermediate logistical delay, and therefore we use the term "fab facility" to mean a physical installation at which both fabrication and probe operations are conducted.

Assembly and Test

After they have been probed, wafers are placed in protective containers and (usually) shipped to another location where they are put into *die bank* inventory. They are withdrawn from die bank when a production lot requiring die of that type is scheduled for release in an assembly plant. That release initiates the third stage of production shown in Figure 11-1, called device *assembly* or *packaging*. In this stage wafers are scored or sawed to physically separate individual die. Then each die is placed on a *lead frame*, electrical leads are attached to the die at appropriate contact points, and finally the whole assembly is sealed in a package made of molded plastic, ceramic, or (less commonly) metal. The result is called a *packaged device*. Manufacturing cycle times for device assembly may range from a few days to several weeks. Usually there are a number of distinct "process flows" through an IC assembly plant, but unlike wafer fabrication, the routing is a linear flow through the major work centers with no loops or cycles.

The fourth and last stage of IC manufacturing, called "final test," usually is done at the same physical location as assembly, and we will use the term "assembly plant" to mean a physical installation at which both device assembly and final testing are performed. The final test process may involve several stages of functional testing, and it also may include a burn-in operation whereby devices are operated for a specified interval in a high-temperature environment. As a result of this testing, packaged devices may be categorized into a number of different *bins* depending on the measured values of one or more attributes such as device speed, power consumption, tolerance of voltage fluctuations, and so forth. The overall throughput time or cycle time for final test and burn-in usually falls between one day and one week, but the figure can go as high as six weeks when a lengthy burn-in procedure is required.

BASIC ELEMENTS OF THE
SCHEDULING PROBLEM

To introduce the scheduling problem at NSC, we will first describe its basic elements in relatively abstract terms. In this discussion, IC manufacturing will be viewed simply as a two-stage process, with the fabrication stage (actually, fab and sort) and the assembly stage (assemble and test) done at different physical locations.

Customer Orders versus Production Lots

The word "order" carries a heavy burden in the literature of production planning and control, because we must deal with both customer orders and manufacturing orders. Manufacturing orders are generated internally, and they initiate either the production of intermediate products like die or the production of finished products. To avoid confusion, we will use the term "production lot" in place of "manufacturing order."

Production lots may not correspond to customer orders in a one-to-one fashion, for two reasons. First, management may choose to produce finished products in anticipation of future demand, or at least to produce die in anticipation of demand. Second, management may choose to employ a standard production lot size, in which case a large order must be broken into multiple production lots and a small order may trigger a production lot containing more than the requested number of items.

Scheduling in a Clockwork Environment

To facilitate a step-by-step explanation of production scheduling complexities, let us first imagine an idealized factory environment where equipment downtime is completely predictable and can be managed so as not to interfere with the processing of production lots. Let us also assume that processing times are completely deterministic and that new production lots are launched into each factory at uniform rates in accordance with a fixed set of *capacity allocations* for process flows. The capacity allocations dictate the overall start rate, in lots per day, for each process flow supported by each factory; because many different products can be made with one process flow, the capacity allocations constrain but do not determine the array of products ultimately manufactured. Assuming that the capacity allocations are consistent with equipment availability, work will flow through factories smoothly with little or no queueing. That is, the only queueing delays that occur in our hypothetical *clockwork environment* are the minor interference effects associated with re-entrant flows in fabrication; the total factory cycle time for each process flow is very nearly equal to the naive sum of its associated processing times, and there is essentially no shop-floor control problem.

The major operational scheduling problem that *does* exist in this hypothesized scenario is that of booking customer orders that are consistent with the capacity allocations. The sales force must generate both a volume and a mix of business that are consistent with the allocations, dynamically adjusting promotional effort or rationing demand to assure a smooth flow of work through the factory network.

In addition, managers must quote delivery dates for individual customer orders and must time the release of individual production lots in a fashion that is consistent with those quotations. One can envision this in terms of paper tapes on which the production schedules for individual factories are written (see Figure 11-2). Imagine that each vertical segment of the tape corresponds to one working day and that the production lots to be released on a given day are written on the corresponding portion of the tape. The total number of lots started each day and their mix by process flow must be consistent with capacity allocations, which are represented in Figure 11-2 by the numbers on the order tapes. The darkly shaded portions of the tapes in Figure 11-2 correspond to lots currently in process, and the lightly shaded portions correspond to future lot releases that are already firmly scheduled. In this particular example, the manufacturing cycle time for both "fab flow a" and "fab flow b" is five days, the manufacturing cycle time for both "assembly flow s" and "assembly flow t" is two days; flow a is firmly scheduled three days into the future, flow b one day into the future, flow s three days into the future, and flow t five days into the future.

Suppose that a customer asks for a delivery quotation on a prod-

Figure 11-2   Schematic Representation of Order Backlogs

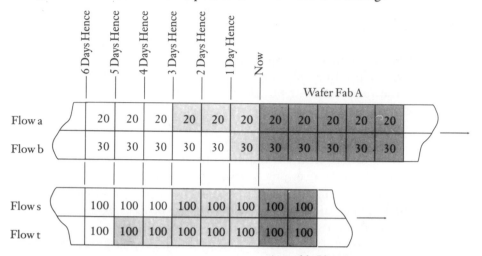

Wafer Fab A

Assembly Plant L

uct whose die use fab flow a and whose assembly requires flow t. If the product is available in finished goods inventory (FGI), then immediate delivery can be promised. If there is sufficient die bank inventory, but no FGI, the earliest feasible delivery date is eight days hence, and, if that is acceptable to the customer, an assembly production lot must be scheduled for release six days hence (that is, at the first available opportunity) once the order is booked. Finally, if neither die bank nor FGI is available, readers may verify that the earliest feasible delivery date is eleven days hence, and, in that case, booking of the order will trigger the release of both a fab production lot and an assembly production lot at appropriate points in the future. In general, all of the following questions are potentially relevant when generating delivery quotations: 1) Is the product in question currently available in FGI? 2) Are there assembly lots for the product currently in process or scheduled for release that will yield more units than required for currently booked orders? 3) Are die for the product currently available in die bank inventory? 4) Are there fab lots currently in process or scheduled for future release that will yield more of the die in question than required for current orders? 5) What are the current production release backlogs for the relevant fab flow and assembly flow?

Given the answers to these questions, and assuming that currently scheduled production lots cannot be leapfrogged or appropriated, the logic required to calculate the delivery date for a new customer order, and for scheduling of new production starts if the quotation is accepted, is straightforward. Because we have assumed away all variability in factory operations, these calculations are exact, and they will be referred to as *clockwork* planning calculations in the remainder of the paper.

Scheduling in a Statistical Environment

Holding everything else fixed, let us now suppose that equipment downtime is at least partially random in character. To be more specific, suppose that the mean time between failures and the mean time to repair for each equipment type yield exactly the same *average* availability as that assumed in the clockwork scenario above, but also suppose that there is a substantial variance in the distributions. Even if factory input rates remain perfectly constant and there are no other sources of processing variability (in real factory operations there definitely *are* other sources of variability), the operating environment and associated scheduling problems are changed drastically.

When statistical variability is introduced in the processing environment, both queueing theory and actual experience in factory operations predict the following effects. First, the manufacturing cycle time for each process flow will be a statistical distribution rather than a single number. Second, the mean of that distribution will be larger than the total processing time for the flow in question, because of queueing time, and the average queueing time actually may be much longer than the processing time. Finally, both the mean and the variance of the cycle time distribution increase as the overall factory production rate increases (given constant capacity), and the relationship between mean cycle time and total production rate has the characteristic convex shape portrayed in Figure 11-3, with catastrophic degradation of cycle time performance as throughput is increased to approach the effective system capacity.

How is the operational scheduling problem changed by statistical variability? First, a real shop-floor control problem now exists within the factory. Machine operators typically will have a queue of production lots from which to choose when they are ready to begin work on

Figure 11-3   Illustrative Relationship between Production Rate and Mean Cycle Time

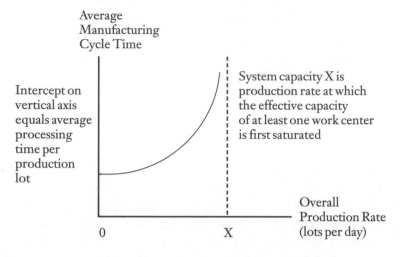

a new lot, and real efficiency gains may be realized by conditioning that choice on the current factory status. For example, by routinely giving low priority to lots that are headed next to heavily congested work centers, or by giving high priority to lots that are near completion, it may be possible to shift the cycle time distribution to the left for all process flows simultaneously. In factories where individual jobs have associated "due dates," shop-floor control systems typically award increasing priority according to the proximity of the due date. But such a system tends to degrade aggregate cycle time performance, while increasing the reliability of delivery for individual orders.

Now consider the impact of statistical variability on the process of generating delivery quotations. A production planner asks, "If appropriate production lots are added to the lot release backlogs today, how long will it take to fill this order?" Obviously, in this setting, the question does not have a deterministic answer. The answer must be statistical; or, expressed differently, the only meaningful question is whether a given delivery date can be met with sufficiently high probability.

Suppose, then, that the question is rephrased: "Can this order be delivered within x days with 95% probability?" To reply, we would like to have historical data on cycle time distributions, but even more information is needed. In particular, the current status of the lots in production, the shop-floor control system being used, and the system being used to release new lots will influence the cycle time distribution for a given lot.

In a statistical environment, physical efficiency considerations also create a motivation to vary input according to factory status. For example, a manager may wish to decrease the overall lot release rate when equipment failures are frequent and congestion mounts and to increase the release rate when good uptime performance is achieved. Such dynamic adjustments of mix and volume should, in principle, allow a factory manager to improve overall throughput and aggregate cycle time performance relative to a rigid, prespecified lot release schedule.

Information Flows and Organizational Relationships

In most large, complex manufacturing environments, production scheduling requires both communication among multiple decision makers and a performance evaluation system that aligns the various decision makers' individual incentives toward a common goal. We will consider three basic organizational functions—Sales, Manufacturing, and Production Control—that typically exist as separate divisions of a functionally organized firm.

1. Sales	The sales organization is the firm's interface with its customers. Sales is responsible for forecasting and communicating customer needs and for negotiating specific customer orders, including dynamic renegotiation if necessary.
2. Manufacturing	Manufacturing physically produces the product. Manufacturing managers are responsible for shop-floor control decisions, including the precise timing of individual production lot releases.
3. Production Control	The production control (PC) organization mediates between sales and manufacturing. It monitors order status, inventory status, and

the production backlog. PC devises the high-
level production schedule that "loads the factories" with production lots, and provides delivery quotations to Sales for potential new orders.

Figure 11-4 portrays these three organizational units, the data
bases they maintain, and the messages that pass among them. Each
organizational unit possesses a huge store of detailed information that
is too large, too diverse, and too complex to transmit completely to
the other units. Sales, for example, maintains knowledge of each customer's current and future needs. While some of this information may
reside in a computerized order entry system, the best salespeople have
developed personal relationships with customers that transcend records of quantities and prices. They understand the customer's business, the competitive environment, and the personalities involved.

Similarly, Manufacturing may maintain a computerized lot-
tracking system, a spreadsheet containing the detailed production
schedule, and perhaps even a computerized equipment status display
and maintenance plan. However, particularly with high-tech production processes involving state-of-the-art equipment and a highly
skilled labor force, much of Manufacturing's "specialized expertise"
remains undocumented. In addition, Manufacturing has specialized
knowledge about (and some control over) the actual cycle times for
jobs that are released for production.

Production Control (PC) acquires a large, private data base in its
role as coordinator. While PC admittedly receives only condensed
versions of the data residing in Sales and Manufacturing, it organizes
that data in ways that are not visible outside of PC. For example,
Manufacturing may not know what part of the production schedule
that it receives from PC arises from specific orders and what fraction
is "produce to forecast" inventory replenishment. Similarly, Sales
may not know whether a delivery quotation from PC involves inventoried items, new production orders, or reassignment of items originally slotted for another customer.

Since each organizational unit has private access to a large array
of information, communication protocols that specify the coordinating messages to be passed between units are needed. Communication
protocols determine how each unit distills the essence of its relevant
knowledge for other managers' use. That is, the communication protocols specify what type of information is to be passed (e.g., factory

Figure 11-4 Organizational Relationships and Information Flows

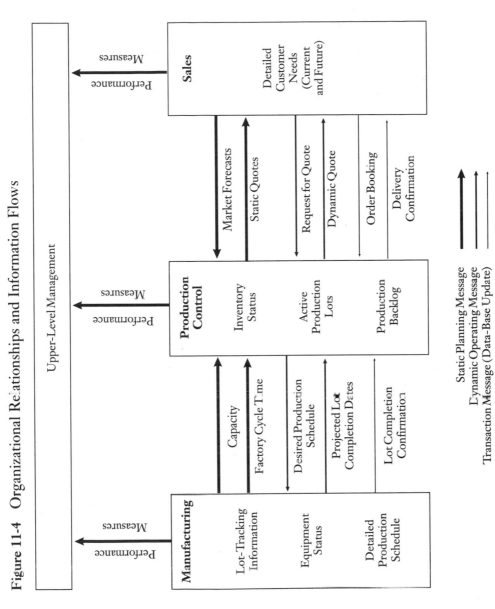

cycle time), the form in which the information is to be passed (e.g., a single number versus a probability distribution), and the rules for computing the message from the data at hand. Communication protocols reflect both how a firm "models" its own operations and what goals it seeks to attain. If, for example, a firm thinks that its manufacturing processes are well represented by the deterministic "clockwork" model of production, we would not expect to see probability distributions communicated. Similarly, one expects that the types of information passed in a firm that is concentrating on cost control or quality will differ from these in one emphasizing timeliness.

In Figure 11-4, we distinguish among three generic types of messages sent among units: static planning messages, dynamic operating messages, and transaction messages.

Static planning messages. Static planning messages are extremely condensed summaries of complex underlying situations. They are updated relatively infrequently and often are treated as fixed parameters in the scheduling process. We identify four static planning messages:

- Capacity. Although the concept of capacity is complex and imprecise, Manufacturing provides PC with an estimate of the amount of product that can be produced per unit time, subject to product mix constraints.
- Factory cycle time. Manufacturing provides PC with an estimate of the time interval required for a unit to pass through all stages of production.
- Market forecasts. Sales provides PC with aggregate, long-range forecasts of demand for each product.
- Static quotes. PC provides Sales with a set of standard responses regarding quantities and lead times that can be promised to customers without directly consulting PC about an order.

Dynamic operating messages. Dynamic operating messages contain operational information about the current state of the system. They occur frequently, and they can involve interactive communication between the concerned parties. The interactive nature is apparent in the two sets of back-and-forth messages we identify:

- Desired production schedule. PC "loads" Manufacturing at regular (monthly or weekly) intervals with a time pattern of production lot releases (i.e., the schedule of "starts").

- Projected lot completion dates. Manufacturing responds to PC at regular intervals with an estimate of the time pattern of emerging finished or intermediate goods (i.e., the schedule of expected "outs").
- Requests for quotes. Sales will inquire of PC whether a particular order can be supplied on better terms (e.g., more quickly) than the standing offer listed in the standard quotes.
- Dynamic quotes. PC responds to Sales with a specific delivery promise that can be offered to a particular customer request.

Transaction messages. Transaction messages correspond to the data-processing entries in a computer file that are necessary both to record contractual agreements with outside parties and to allow the organizational units to update their own internal data bases. These messages occur frequently and are part of the standard lot-tracking and accounting systems.

- Order bookings. Sales accepts customer orders and passes them through to PC.
- Lot completion confirmation. Manufacturing informs PC when finished or intermediate goods are available for inventory or shipment.
- Delivery confirmation. PC informs Sales when finished goods have been shipped to fulfill a customer order.

Performance Measurement

In addition to the coordinating information sent among Manufacturing, PC, and Sales, performance information is passed from each of these organizational units to the upper levels of the corporate hierarchy (see Figure 11-4). As in the case of the messages among the functions, communication protocols (content and form of message) must be established for these performance measures. The managers of the organizational units are rational individuals who understand the criteria by which they are judged and take actions to score well on those criteria. Thus, it becomes crucially important that the performance measures and incentives are consistent across units and that they resonate with the firm's overall goals.

Managers face two sorts of decisions: what actions to take within their own organizational units and what messages to communicate to other units. It is clear, for example, that the Manufacturing managers' performance goals should motivate them to be clever and diligent in orchestrating production lots on the shop floor. At the same time, the Manufacturing managers understand that the capacity and factory cycle time estimates that they provide to PC ultimately influence the production schedule; overly optimistic estimates may come back to haunt them as unreasonably tight deadlines.

In establishing the protocols for messages sent among functional units (and from these units to upper-level management), two criteria must be considered. First, the information transmitted should lead each unit manager to make decisions that are optimal for the overall company. That is, to the extent possible, the decisions made by the unit managers should coincide with the decisions that would be made by a completely informed top executive acting in the company's best interests. Both interunit communications and performance measurements can affect the ability and motivation of a unit manager to make these optimal decisions. The second criterion dictates that the protocols should provide incentives for each manager to send the necessary coordinating messages in a timely and unbiased manner. Again, both interunit communications and performance measurements can affect the managers' incentives to provide unbiased information.

The Expanded Scheduling Problem

With this background, we see that the "scheduling" problem may take on several forms. If no statistical variability arises in the production process, then there is no shop-floor control problem; once capacity and factory cycle times are fixed, PC can transmit a production schedule that can be executed exactly. Moreover, PC can provide reliable (exact) quotes on delivery dates to Sales for any system status. To provide these schedules and quotes, the firm needs a detailed information system that can track orders, production lots, inventories, cycle times, and capacities and that can make straightforward calculations from these data. There is no problem designing performance measures that induce the right information flows and the right operating decisions, at least in Manufacturing, because there is no private information that is critical to other functions. Fixed cycle times and capacities provide an adequate model of the manufacturing function, and no real scheduling decisions remain.

The problem changes drastically when the manufacturing process exhibits statistical variability. Shop-floor control decisions may advance some production lots at the expense of others, and delivery quotations must consider both the priority status of various lots and the statistical variability of factory cycle times. In addition, the design choices for the communication protocols and for the performance measurement system become substantive issues.

For example, a performance evaluation system that measures a Manufacturing manager on aggregate efficiency should motivate that manager to maximize productivity. However, if the PC manager is measured on the basis of meeting delivery commitments, he or she will be motivated to increase the reliability (i.e., reduce the variance) of the factory cycle times. And if Sales is evaluated on sales volume, Sales managers will seek shorter lead times (by shortening factory cycle times) and reduced prices (by reducing costs). This scenario results in conflicting incentives for the three functional units. And, from the perspective of scheduling, quite different shop-floor and production lot-release systems will respond best to each of these performance measures.

Moreover, the operation of the overall system will depend on the combination of performance measures and communication systems chosen. Continuing the example, when the Manufacturing manager (who is evaluated solely on aggregate efficiency) is asked to provide a cycle time planning number to PC, he or she may report a single representative number, such as the mean of the distribution. Manufacturing has little incentive to invest great care in the estimate. The manager also has little motivation to ensure that a particular production lot meets that cycle time. However, if a Manufacturing manager's performance evaluation criteria are augmented to include meeting cycle time commitments on specific lots, one would expect changes in both operating and communicating decisions. The cycle time estimate transmitted to PC, on which the commitments will be judged, likely will be longer than the mean of the cycle time distribution, to reduce the risk of late delivery. For the same reason, individual lots' due-date proximity probably will affect scheduling decisions, perhaps at the expense of aggregate efficiency.

The issues here are complicated and it is very difficult to find general rules. Extensive theoretical analyses of this type of multiperson problem indicate that uniformly best policies seldom exist, and, typically, one must sacrifice some production efficiencies within units to encourage beneficial communication among them.

AN OVERVIEW OF NSC OPERATIONS

NSC is one of the world's largest commercial suppliers of semiconductor devices, and its product line is among the broadest in the industry. The company markets six major product lines that encompass many tens of thousands of distinct NSC products, ranging from simple linear and logic devices that sell for as little as ten cents (such low-priced commodity products are commonly called "jelly-beans" in the industry) to sophisticated microprocessors that sell for hundreds of dollars.

One of the six NSC product lines is application-specific integrated circuits, or ASICs, which accounted for about 10% of FY87 sales. As the name suggests, ASIC products are customized to user specifications, which means that neither finished goods nor die bank inventory for the products can be manufactured in anticipation of future demand. Conventional wisdom holds that the future for merchant semiconductor producers lies in ASIC products, but this market segment has been slow to develop, and is fiercely competitive, so ASIC sales for both NSC and its major competitors have been somewhat disappointing thus far.

NSC has wafer fabrication facilities at five different locations in the United States and Europe and has assembly plants at four locations in Southeast Asia. The company's customer base is concentrated in the United States, and sales are divided almost equally among three customer categories: major OEM customers, a set of about 20 original equipment manufacturers who have been designated for special treatment; other OEM customers; and distributors, who resell NSC products to other companies.

The Role of Die Bank Inventory

The great bulk of NSC wafer fabrication is done to forecast; the company maintains a strategic die bank inventory rather than fabricating die for specific customer orders. On the other hand, except for a few high-volume commodity products produced on a "run rate" basis, finished goods are assembled and tested only when firm orders are in hand. The policy of fabricating to forecast and assembling to order arises for several reasons. First, as in many industries, there is a major "product fan-out" after fabrication, with an average of 10–20 final products per die type, so it is much more efficient to carry an inventory of semifinished goods (die) than final products. Second, wafer fabrication is much more time-consuming than assembly, so the strategic die bank greatly reduces delivery lead times to customers. Finally, fabrication is capital intensive and subject to hard capacity constraints, whereas assembly capacity is more easily adjusted in the short term. Thus, there is a higher premium on stability of the production plan in fabrication; a decoupling intermediate inventory facilitates such stability. As a consequence of the NSC inventory policy, fabrication managers have been largely insulated from short-term market urgencies, whereas assembly managers are accustomed to think in terms of specific orders and identifiable customers.

Top managers at NSC believe that the company must learn to operate with greatly diminished die bank inventory, and perhaps must learn to do it quickly, for three reasons. First, it is physically impossible to maintain die bank for ASIC and other custom products. Second, the die bank is too costly, especially in light of the obsolescence costs arising from rapid product turnover and increasing fragmentation of the product line. Finally, a manufacturing productivity issue often is raised in support of the just-in-time manufacturing philosophy: final testing and burn-in of packaged devices provide information about wafer fab operations that cannot be obtained in any other way, and this informational feedback is retarded by the time wafers spend in die bank inventory.

The Drive for Service Leadership

Some NSC history is required to understand our emphasis on timeliness, communication, and performance measurement. Until at least the late 1970s, virtually all semiconductor companies were technology driven; managers focused their attention primarily on the development of faster, smaller, more sophisticated devices and on the development of manufacturing processes to produce them commercially. (In the semiconductor industry, product technology and process technology are so inextricably intertwined that the distinction between the two is almost meaningless.) The emphasis on technology development arose from the desire for increased functionality and higher performance. For example, denser packing of elements on a chip leads to faster circuits, and increased speed opens up new domains of application. But denser packing (smaller features) also allows a more commercial product to be derived from each wafer, and thus technology development is also a key to cost reduction.

The rate of innovation in basic semiconductor technology has slowed somewhat in the last decade, and Japanese companies have established a dominant position as low-cost, high-quality producers of commodity products (in some cases very sophisticated commodity products), such as basic computer memory chips. Thus, many industry observers feel that U.S. semiconductor manufacturers, especially the commercial suppliers, can succeed in the future only if they become service oriented, or customer driven, rather than technology driven.

In 1986, NSC launched a campaign with the expressed goal of achieving industry leadership in customer service by 1989; the word service now figures prominently in the NSC company culture. The service orientation is exemplified by the following precept: "The role of NSC operations (manufacturing, materials management, physical distribution, customer service, and production control) is to provide the products that customers require, in the amounts required, on the date required."

The service campaign emphasizes delivery performance, and by the end of FY87 the following goals had been formally established with respect to on-schedule delivery (OSD):

Major OEM customers	98% OSD
Other OEM customers	93% OSD
Distributors	no established goal

No numerical goals were established for the length of delivery lead times imposed on customers, the stated objective being to retain parity with major competitors on this dimension. On the other hand, the numerical goals cited above for reliability of delivery commitments are intended to achieve a true leadership position. The disparate treatment of lead time performance and OSD performance seems to arise, at least in part, from a time-phased strategy for development of a service-oriented company culture. Once systems are in place for disseminating and reinforcing commitments to customers, the reasoning goes, then more formal steps can be taken to reduce delivery lead times. That is, it does no good to reduce the delivery lead times promised to customers until attitudes and systems are in place to assure the reliability of those commitments.

Nonetheless, NSC is concerned that competitive pressure may

necessitate drastically reduced delivery lead times in the not-too-distant future. At the end of FY87, delivery lead time quotations were often in the 8–12 week range, even when die bank inventory for the product was available; the manager of Customer Service felt that this was causing NSC to lose potential business. In his words, "We need four to six weeks to be competitive on major accounts. We're not getting that now because we don't have the necessary systems in place. Also, we need die bank to hit that kind of lead time." That same manager, while emphasizing the absolute necessity of reliable delivery promises, conceded that some incentive problems are created by a formalized system of OSD performance reporting: "We're holding everyone's feet to the fire on OSD, and that's leading to some conflicting goals. Production managers get very conservative on the lead times they'll commit to, like 12 weeks, and the customer just goes elsewhere. Some customers are really pressing us for short delivery lead times, saying they absolutely need it, but buyers lie to me a lot."

A senior marketing manager, taking a longer-term view, said that NSC must start thinking in terms of two- to four-week lead times: "With efficient wafer fabrication and geographically concentrated operations, we should be able to achieve four-week delivery lead times without die bank inventory." A senior member of the corporate MIS staff said, "If we carry strategic die bank inventory, we can probably give one-week delivery. Our assembly operations and physical distribution are as fast as anyone's."

Computerized Information Systems

Figure 11-5 is a schematic diagram of the relationships among three major computer systems at NSC. Together they are called the "service systems architecture," and the development of this integrated management information system is a keystone in the company's campaign for service leadership. The left side of Figure 11-5 represents a work-in-process (WIP) tracking system that we call WIPSYS. (In reality, NSC has two interlocking systems that have different names.) It performs a number of functions beyond simple WIP tracking, such as test data management and shop-floor scheduling, but for our purposes WIPSYS is viewed simply as a data base that contains up-to-date information on 1) production lots currently active in both wafer fabrication and final assembly plants, 2) production lots firmly scheduled for future release, and 3) die bank and finished goods inventory currently on hand. The right side of Figure 11-5 represents an order entry system known within the company as SWISS, the heart of which is a data base on customer orders firmly booked but not yet delivered. SWISS also contains other data needed by Customer Service and Sales representatives in the order entry process, such as the quote guide referred to below. All SWISS data are available to NSC sales representatives around the world, and much of the data must be entered from remote locations. To maintain and disseminate timely information, the system contains telecommunication links that are comparable to its computing and data storage components in importance and expense.

The middle block in Figure 11-5 represents a production control module, called Advanced Semiconductor Planning and Control (ASPC), that is still under development. The intended functions of this module are 1) to execute the logic required to derive delivery quotations, using real-time system status information from SWISS and WIPSYS, and 2) to use that same logic to generate appropriate time-phased production lot releases once the quotation is accepted and the customer order is booked. Thus, ASPC is designed to automate most of the PC planning function, but ASPC is not viewed as a decision-making system by its developers in NSC's corporate MIS group. Rather, in their words, it is "an execution system that automates the mechanics of doing business," routinely generating delivery quotations and production lot releases based on "real product availability" and "real capacity commitments."

NSC has invested heavily in development of its information systems, and top management, through the ASPC project, now is striving to leverage that investment and make gains in the customer service domain. With millions of units in inventory, thousands of orders outstanding, and facilities spread all over the world, the information-processing requirements to support NSC operations are prodigious, and the company's managers tend to equate good production control with high-quality information systems.

The Quotation Process

Figure 11-6 is a schematic representation of the information flows involved in responding to a customer's request for quotation. The customer specifies a particular product and the quantity desired, and NSC must respond with a quotation that specifies both the price and

Figure 11-5 Computerized Information Systems

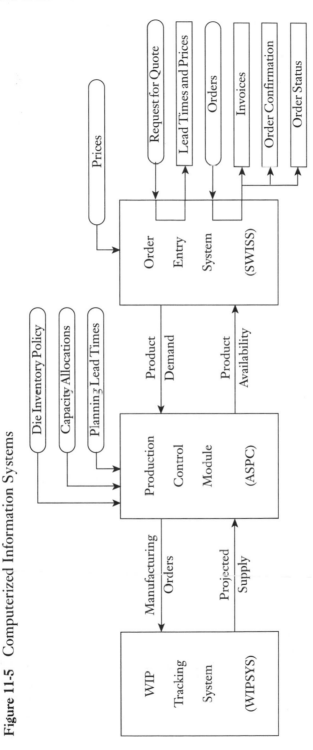

the delivery lead time for the order. If the order involves no special conditions, then a sales representative can obtain both price and delivery quotation from a "quote guide" that is part of the SWISS data base. We classify the delivery lead time specified in the quote guide as a "static quotation" because it is not necessarily based on up-to-date system status information. Rather, it is a figure that has been provided by a PC planner responsible for the product in question, a figure that he or she has implicitly certified as "safe to promise." As inventory levels and order backlogs change, quote guides obviously must be revised, and weekly updating is frequently cited as "ideal practice." However, in dealing with tens of thousands of products, PC planners often are unable to achieve the ideal, and because they ultimately are measured on the reliability of promised delivery dates (see below), the tendency toward conservatism in setting static delivery quotations is overwhelming.

As Figure 11-6 shows, a customer's request for quotation may receive individualized attention if special conditions prevail. One such condition occurs if the SWISS quote guide simply contains no information on the requested product. Another arises when the customer has a long-term agreement that guarantees either a price or a delivery lead time more favorable than that cited in the quote guide. Most important for our purposes, however, is the special condition in which a customer is simply not satisfied with the static delivery quotation, and either the customer or the order is important enough to merit personalized attention. In that case, as shown in Figure 11-6, an NSC sales representative will seek a price quotation from the appropriate product line marketing organization and request a delivery quotation from the cognizant Customer Service Account Manager (CSAM).

The NSC Customer Service organization is composed of about 30 CSAMs, plus supervisors, clerical support staff, and a Customer Service manager who heads the organization. The Customer Service manager plays a leadership role in the company's service improvement campaign, promoting service awareness among factory managers, bringing customer representatives into factories to explain their needs, and so forth. Members of the Customer Service staff also are involved in planning computerized information systems that support their needs, but the staff functions primarily as an internal advocate or representative for customers. In generating a delivery quotation for a customer when special conditions prevail, a CSAM either works from information that has been supplied by PC, or else directs an inquiry to a PC planner, explaining the customer's needs and asking

Figure 11-6   Quotation Process

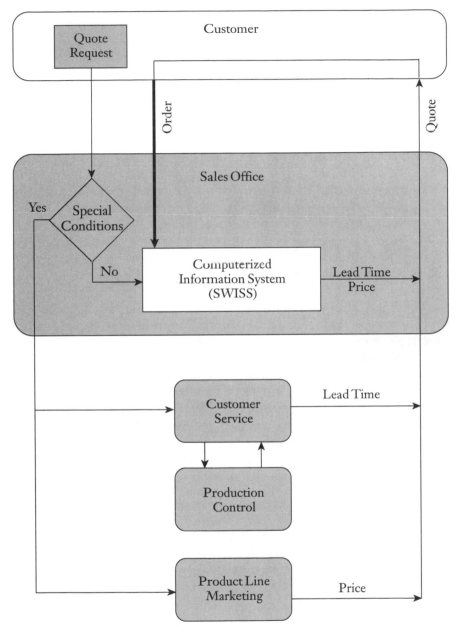

for the best possible terms of delivery in light of current inventory levels, order backlogs, and capacity commitments.

The logic that a PC planner uses to determine a "dynamic" delivery quotation is explained below. The delivery lead time ultimately quoted still may be quite conservative, with various safety factors built in to hedge against uncertainty, but it almost always will be shorter, often much shorter, than the worse case figure in the quote guide. Ultimately, NSC management would like all quotations to be dynamic in nature, based on up-to-date information on product availability and existing commitments. With current manual procedures, that practice would impose an unbearable burden on Customer Service and PC, but the ASPC module of NSC's "service systems architecture" is intended to automate dynamic lead time calculations and thus obviate the static quote guide.

Once a lead time quotation is accepted by a customer, the names of both the CSAM and the PC planner who collaborated in that quotation are included in the order entry data, and if the NSC manufacturing organization fails to achieve the promised delivery date, a key performance measure for those two individuals is affected adversely. The CSAM continues to track the customer order through the manufacturing system, alerting production control and manufacturing managers to actions that may be required to assure on-time delivery.

Incidentally, the price quoted to a customer may depend on many different factors, but delivery lead time generally is not one of them. To charge a premium price for fast delivery or to give a discount when imposing a long delivery lead time is considered by marketing people to be unsavory behavior; a product line marketing manager described it as "a distributor's game" and said that such practices would create a bad market image for a major supplier like NSC.

Calculating Delivery Lead Times

We will describe, in general terms, the logic being built into the ASPC system for automated delivery quotation. This is roughly the same procedure currently used by PC planners to determine delivery lead times manually, but many nuances and complexities are suppressed in our description.

One important input to ASPC is a set of capacity allocations for fabrication and assembly plants. These allocations dictate the overall start rate or production rate for each process flow supported by each

NSC factory, and they are revised on a quarterly basis. A second critical input is a set of planning lead times, one for each process flow within each factory. Roughly speaking, a planning lead time represents a total factory cycle time (measured from the moment of order release) that the plant manager feels can be achieved with high probability, assuming that order releases respect the agreed-upon capacity allocations. As we will see shortly, capacity allocations and planning lead times play a central role in high-level production scheduling as well as in quote generation, and they are established by negotiation among representatives of the Manufacturing, PC, Customer Service, and Marketing organizations.

In addition to capacity allocations and planning lead times, ASPC uses information from WIPSYS on current finished goods inventory, current die bank inventory, currently active production lots, and production lots firmly scheduled for release, as well as information from SWISS on the current backlog of customer orders to which those inventories and work-in-process may be committed. Given all of this information, ASPC will execute the algorithm we defined earlier as "clockwork planning logic" to determine an earliest feasible delivery date for a new order, treating the planning lead times as if they were deterministic factory cycle times. That is, the program first checks to see whether a new order can be filled from finished goods inventory, then whether it can be filled from an assembly production lot already released or scheduled for release, then whether it can be filled from existing die bank inventory, and so forth, using capacity allocations, planning lead times, and the current production backlog to determine release dates and completion dates for new production lots when they are required.

Timing the Release of Production Lots

Once a quotation has been accepted and the customer order has been entered in SWISS, the delivery lead time calculation obviously suggests release dates for whatever new production lots may be required to fill the order, and when it is fully operational, ASPC will automatically generate time-phased lot release authorizations in precisely this fashion. For each die type that continues to be produced on a make-to-stock basis, the computer system also will release production lot authorizations when the die bank inventory falls below a designated reorder point.

The ASPC system is designed to provide a tight linkage between fab operations and market conditions, but large amounts of die bank inventory make such linkage unnecessary, and PC planners currently do not dictate the precise timing of fab releases. Rather, at the beginning of each month, planners simply specify the set of production lots that they wish to have released during that month. The fab manager and staff then are free to determine the day-to-day schedule of releases as they see fit (equipment failures are a major consideration in this process), but they often are strongly influenced by shortage-related pressure from PC planners.

The clockwork planning model used by ASPC to calculate delivery lead times and lot release dates does not quantify or even acknowledge the existence of statistical variability. Of course, everyone involved with production at NSC recognizes the high levels of statistical variation in real operations, and they know that the capacity and lead time figures used for delivery quotation and production scheduling are set conservatively as a hedge against uncertainty. But there is equally broad acceptance of the notion that one should or must base quotations and high-level production schedules on a fixed set of capacities and lead times that have been negotiated and agreed upon throughout the organization.

This is entirely consistent with practice in other manufacturing industries, where materials requirements planning (MRP) is used widely for the coordination of purchasing and work order releases, given a desired schedule of outputs. In the clockwork factory model that underlies MRP calculations, each work center or process stage is represented simply by a planning lead time, perhaps differentiated by order type. In the real factory, manufacturing cycle times typically form a widely dispersed statistical distribution, and the planning lead time chosen for schedule coordination is usually far out in the right tail of the distribution. Such a choice provides an appropriate hedge against uncertainty (the usual reasoning goes), and there is little dispute over the notion that one should plan as if each stage of production had a well-defined manufacturing cycle time.

Measuring Delivery Performance

We now describe NSC's procedures for measuring on-schedule delivery (OSD) performance, and then we will explain the role these measurements play in the company's compensation plan. The formal OSD accounting process focuses exclusively on performance against commitments to customers, but there is a strong sentiment within the company for measuring individual OSD performance at each manufacturing stage.

When a customer order is entered in SWISS, two delivery dates actually are recorded in the data base, each of which is visible to NSC sales representatives, Customer Service Account Managers, and PC planners anywhere in the world. The first is a customer requested date (CRD), which is supposed to represent the delivery date originally requested by the customer at the time of the quotation request, although as we explain below, this is not always the case. The second is the schedule due date (SDD), which was quoted to the customer, perhaps after some iteration and haggling, when the order was accepted. The SDD is never earlier than the CRD, and in many cases the two are identical, meaning that the offered terms of delivery were acceptable to the customer. The SDD will be later than the CRD if the customer was willing to book the order despite a later delivery date, perhaps because no alternative vendor could offer earlier delivery.

The CRD and SDD remain in SWISS until the order is delivered, but under some circumstances the dates may be updated as time passes. Specifically, if a customer revises his CRD to a time later than the SDD, then the SDD is revised to agree with the new CRD, and no record of the original values is retained. Alternatively, an order's SDD may be set later if the order is placed on hold for some period. A hold may occur, for example, if the customer is delinquent in paying a bill, or if the product is put on product specification hold because of a design flaw revealed by field failures. Such occurrences are relatively rare.

In OSD accounting procedures at NSC, a customer order is considered to be a "hit" (that is, to be delivered on schedule) if its invoice date (triggered by a freight forwarder executing a SWISS "ship confirmation") is no later than the SDD. Separate percentage figures for OSD are compiled for many different subsets of the order population, such as orders shipped from a particular assembly plant, orders quoted by a particular PC planner, orders for devices in a particular product line, and so forth. When a customer places an order for several different device types, each line item is considered as a separate order in the OSD accounting process; if an order includes four different device types, and three are delivered on time in the desired quantities and one is shipped late, the OSD accounting process will record three hits and one miss. We should note that the overall hit rate computed in the OSD accounting process does not give greater reward for on-time delivery of a large order than for on-time delivery of a small one, and it assesses the same penalties for missing a delivery date by one day or by one month.

The manager of NSC Customer Service noted that when PC planners confront a request for quotation with a tight CRD, knowing that ultimately they will be measured against the percentage of OSD, they often will propose an SDD substantially later than the CRD, but they also informally communicate a willingness to strive for a delivery date closer to the customer's stated desire. Thus, the SDD recorded in SWISS does not fully reflect the understanding reached with the customer, but the PC planner has gained some insurance in terms of the formal performance evaluation system.

In addition to the CRD and SDD figures recorded in the SWISS data base, each order also carries a current schedule date (CSD) in SWISS. The PC planner who originally quoted the order can update the CSD by executing a SWISS transaction to reflect a change (usually an unfavorable one) in anticipated delivery due to unforeseen circumstances. This revision will be seen by the relevant Customer Service Account Manager (CSAM), who typically calls the PC planner for an explanation and then passes the information along to the customer. Depending on the customer's reaction, the CSAM and PC planner may begin to look for ways to expedite the order: appropriating work-in-process nominally committed to other purposes, jumping to the head of an assembly plant's order release queue, and so forth.

Even if no remedial action is feasible, the NSC Customer Service manager believes it imperative that customers be warned of impending delays and told of the causes, and therefore the updating of current schedule dates by PC planners is an important element of good service. Asked what direct motivation the PC planner has to provide schedule updates (the immediate effect is an angry phone call and cross-examination), the Customer Service manager noted that customers sometimes will agree to move back their customer request date when unforeseen problems arise, which causes the SDD to move back accordingly and thus protects the PC planner (and others) against unfavorable performance measures.

Personal Goals and Performance Reviews

OSD performance is a significant factor in NSC's well-established process for individual performance reviews. Twice each year supervisors send a written set of specific, personal performance goals to each exempt employee and assign weights to each goal. At the same time, the supervisor assigns weights to a set of standard performance characteristics, such as analytical ability, initiative, and interpersonal skills, for the employee's particular job.

At the end of each semiannual evaluation period, the supervisor assigns a numerical score for each objective or goal, using a ten-point scale. The relative weights are used to compute separate indices for goal attainment and performance characteristics. Finally, the supervisor establishes relative weightings for goal attainment versus performance characteristics (the weighting between the two indices varies, but it is usually about 50–50, although goal attainment may carry as much as 60%) and computes an overall performance index. These overall performance indices are used as a basis for salary and promotion decisions. In addition, about 230 top NSC managers participate in a bonus plan that is directly tied to the goal attainment index.

Figure 11-7 shows the weights attached to various goal categories for a sampling of managers, and their direct reports, in different parts of NSC. For example, OSD carries a 25% weight in the statement of goals for a product line production control manager, and the corresponding weight is 30% for a PC planner reporting to him.

Delivery performance goals for all levels of NSC operating managers actually may be even more influential than the percentage figures in Figure 11-7 suggest, for several reasons. First, although a numerical score ultimately is assigned to each of an employee's personal goals and performance characteristics, most of those numbers are assigned subjectively by the employee's supervisor. As in most organizations, such subjective numerical ratings tend to cluster around an established norm reflecting good performance, and even large perceived differences in individual performance tend to result in small numerical deviations from that norm. For many employees the only goal rating based on objective measurement is the OSD percentage figure.

Second, OSD goals are considered to be met only if all categories of OSD meet their goals. For example, the manager of the Customer Service department is given the goal of 98% OSD for major OEM customers and 93% OSD for other OEM customers in the United States. If the operating organization as a whole fails to achieve *either* of these objectives, the Customer Service manager receives a *zero* as his score for the OSD goal category. Even when there are other measurement-related goals (for example, cost performance or manufac-

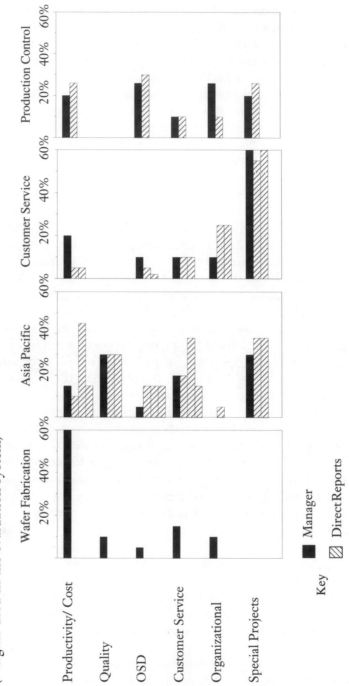

Figure 11-7 Performance Goals
(Weights used in the evaluation system)

turing yield), the corresponding numerical rating normally is not awarded on an all-or-nothing basis. Thus, the OSD goal category often accounts for a large portion of the variation in overall individual performance indices.

Measuring Performance for Wafer Fabs

OSD receives a relatively small weight in the goals of high-level wafer fabrication managers (typically 3–5%), and no weight at all at lower levels of the wafer fab organization. The reasoning behind this practice, of course, is that wafer fab operations are far removed from final delivery of goods to customers, and the heavy reliance on die bank inventory decouples individual production lots in a wafer fab from individual customer orders. Thus, wafer fab managers have little or no control over bottom-line delivery performance measures.

However, one measure of internal OSD has been tracked for three years. At the beginning of each month, the PC planners "load the fab" by specifying the quantities of each die type to be produced both for major OEM customers and for other OEM customers. Fab managers commit to these specified quantities of wafer-outs by die type. A fab OSD number is calculated as the percentage of all die types for which the out-quantity commitment is met during the period. Success is measured in the same 0–1 manner for each die type, and no credit is awarded for exceeding the commitment.

The critical performance measures for the fab organizations, as seen by top management, concentrate on physical and financial measures of efficiency. Three physical measures are calculated regularly:

- Cumulative fab yield: The percentage of wafers that physically survive the process.
- Die yield: The percentage of die that are found to be good in the sort operation.
- Productivity: Labor hours per 1,000 wafer "moves." A move is defined as the completion of a major processing step, and moves are set to be roughly comparable in financial cost. Two measures are calculated: one for direct and one for indirect labor hours.

Two financial measures are monitored by top management. One is prime wafer cost, consisting of the actual direct cost, plus a partial corporate cost allocation, per good wafer-out. (The corporate cost allocation does not include overhead, R&D, or sales and marketing expenses.) This measure is computed for each site at the level of individual fabs, but not for the fab organization as a whole because wafer types differ so much between sites. Prime wafer costs are watched closely, and cost decreases are considered critical indicators of productivity improvement.

A second key financial measure for wafer fab operations is the profit and loss impact, which corresponds to a variance summary. This number is considered the most important measure of fab efficiency. A positive P&L impact number is the amount by which standard costs of production exceed actual cost, and it is composed of the labor variance, materials variance, yield variance, overhead variance, and inventory (obsolescence) adjustment.

The wide variety of fab performance measures makes an assessment of their overall impact a complex task. The issue of OSD performance is especially sensitive at NSC, and a significant proportion of NSC managers favor the adoption of an OSD performance evaluation system for fabs that has the following characteristics.

- Capacity allocations and planning lead times, for fab facilities and assembly plants alike, are set and agreed upon by production control and manufacturing personnel.
- Manufacturing order releases for both fabs and assembly plants are scheduled by PCs on a day-to-day basis, consistent with the capacity allocations.
- Internal due dates, or scheduled out dates, are associated with individual production lots, consistent with the planning lead times.
- Manufacturing managers are measured (but not exclusively) on internal OSD percentage, computed on a lot-by-lot basis.

Many high-level managers at NSC, especially those who anticipate a competitive environment in which die bank inventory is no longer feasible, feel that such a system of overall manufacturing control is absolutely essential for service leadership. Many also endorse the concept of planning lead times differentiated by order priority, i.e., establishing shorter planning lead times for production lots associated with major OEM customers and other urgent orders to ensure that such work falls into the left tail of the factory's overall cycle time distribution.

This overall OSD philosophy, emphasizing a factory's service mission through lot-by-lot or order-by-order schedule accountability, is not always consistent with fab efficiency performance measures.

When cost and efficiency factors are emphasized, fab managers understandably seek wide latitude in controlling the timing and mix of wafer starts. By accepting only broad aggregate constraints on factory input, a fab manager can tailor new starts to current factory conditions (most importantly, the unpredictable and often lengthy downtime characteristic of fab-processing equipment). This makes for a smoother flow of work and hence for better overall throughput, better process control and higher yield, and better control of average cycle time. Having been raised in this environment, many fab managers resist the notion of tightly specified input or output schedules, and lot-by-lot schedule accountability in general. Addressing this traditional manufacturing culture, a senior NSC marketing manager stated flatly, "The problem with fab people is attitude. They just don't know what a customer is—they've never talked to one."

COMMENTARY

As stated earlier, the two essential elements of delivery performance are the lengths of the delivery lead times quoted to customers (shorter lead times represent better performance) and the reliability of those quotations. We have identified three dimensions of system capability that affect delivery performance: 1) management information systems, including all aspects of data management; 2) production scheduling logic, usually referred to as "software" in the industry; and 3) systems for measuring the performance of individuals or organizational units and for evaluating, compensating, or reinforcing individuals on the basis of those measurements. Managers at NSC have very definite views on these aspects of overall systems design. Below, we highlight several perspectives that seem particularly significant to us.

Commitment, Control, and Accountability

The establishment of OSD performance measures for the manufacturing organization, including both wafer fab and assembly plants, is considered by most NSC managers to be an essential part of designing a system for production planning and scheduling. Why does one encounter such widespread emphasis on deterministic internal due dates and lot-by-lot accountability with respect to delivery schedules? First and foremost, the marketing organization wants to know that commitments made to customers by NSC sales representatives will be taken as sacrosanct by the entire operating organization. Sales reps work with PC planners in determining feasible commitments, and those planners shepherd orders through the manufacturing network. Thus, from a marketing perspective, it is critical that PC planners be measured on both their willingness to make commitments that are responsive to customer needs and on their ability to make good on those commitments. PC planners, of course, are constrained by the capacity allocations and planning lead times established by the manufacturing organization.

Because they are held responsible for meeting commitments to customers, PC planners want control over factory loading, and they want the performance measurement system to reward manufacturing managers for making good on their lead time commitments. Moreover, because they wish to give superior service to important customers and important orders, the various PC organizations want to be assured that lead time commitments are differentiated by priority classification and that success in meeting these commitments is reflected in manufacturing performance measures.

The Role of Management Information Systems

Scheduling logic and production control are subjects of concern and discussion at NSC, but NSC managers seem to agree that their needs can be met by very simple systems models and correspondingly simple scheduling logic. While effective dynamic scheduling of manufacturing and distribution will require massive amounts of computation, the actual computer programs will execute a fundamental logic accessible to anyone who understands the rudiments of semiconductor manufacturing. The ASPC approach views production scheduling as a problem of reliable routine execution rather than as an exercise in dynamic systems optimization. In day-to-day scheduling, the task is not to maximize profits or minimize costs but rather to make commitments consistent with capabilities and then to execute those commitments. Thus, the NSC managers see scheduling as primarily a management information systems problem.

Information and Incentives

Recognizing that all of the players in the production scheduling game have information inaccessible to others and that they also have their own private goals and ambitions, we see that the production coordination problem includes performance measurement and the design of incentives. An overly simplistic information economics approach to the problem might presume that if the employees of a firm are given the relevant information and the right incentives (bonus plans, promotion criteria, and so forth), everything will somehow come out right.

In a complex technological setting, such an assumption becomes unrealistic; employees also must be given systems, tools, and training, and even then we may achieve only second-best solutions. Nonetheless, this paradigm captures the essential thrust of the ASPC project, which views effective scheduling and production control as matters of getting the right information to the right people in a timely fashion—i.e., designing the right MIS system—and then making sure that the performance of each organizational unit is measured correctly—i.e., designing the right set of incentives.

Planning Lead Times—A Major Incentive Issue

In the system under development at NSC, as in most systems for coordination of discrete parts manufacturing, planning lead times play a key role in the interface between PC and Manufacturing. The details of the new NSC system have not been fully refined, but for the sake of discussion let us assume the following structure: 1) PC planners lay out a detailed schedule of lot releases for each factory, although actual release dates may differ somewhat from scheduled release dates; 2) factories establish planning lead times for each of the process flows that they support; 3) the scheduled completion date for each lot is defined as its scheduled release date plus the planning lead time for the relevant lot category; and 4) Manufacturing is held accountable for achievement of scheduled completion dates. Thus, if manufacturing managers are measured on lot-by-lot due date achievement (that is, on internal OSD percentage), planning lead times for different process flows become lead time commitments for specific lots. We discuss some implications of this use of planning lead times below.

Conservative Lead Times
and Self-Fulfilling Prophecies

When one recognizes the discrepancy between fixed planning lead times (a clockwork planning model) and the statistical nature of manufacturing reality, the following question naturally arises. Is there any harm in fixing a set of lead time figures for planning purposes and then making delivery quotations and timing the release of manufacturing lots as if those figures were precise characteristics of the operating system? Practical experience with MRP suggests the answer is yes. If performance against lead time commitments is a keystone of manufacturing performance evaluation, the motivation for understatement of true capabilities is very strong, and the technical complexity and high statistical variability characteristic of semiconductor manufacturing make the monitoring of factory commitments difficult. In order to achieve a reasonable level of schedule reliability, the planning parameters must be set conservatively, which means that actual manufacturing capabilities are systematically understated in the formal planning system. The parameters of the planning system tend to become self-fulfilling prophecies, because delivery quotations and production schedules are set in accordance with them, and the primary concern of operating managers is to meet their schedule commitments. This sort of "satisficing" ultimately means that one never finds out just how short cycle times could be or how much capacity really exists. An emphasis on reliability and service may result in planned mediocrity, especially when manufacturing is viewed as a neutral competitive factor rather than as an area in which the firm seeks true competitive advantage.

Ultraconservative Delivery Quotations

In a multistage manufacturing system, a tendency toward conservatism can be compounded. The use of conservative planning lead times *at each stage* will tend to cause even more conservative *overall* lead times. The result can be delivery lead times that are ultraconservative and uncompetitive. Consider, for example, a two-stage process in which cycle times for the individual stages may be viewed as independent random variables, and suppose that management wishes to achieve 95% reliability of its delivery promises. If that schedule reliability goal is enforced at the plant level, then each plant manager will set planning lead time at the 95th percentile of the cycle time distribution. But if T_1 is the 95th percentile of the first distribution and T_2 is the 95th percentile of the second, it is likely that $T_1 + T_2$ will be at the 99th percentile of the composite cycle time distribution for stages one and two together. Thus, a delivery lead time quotation equal to the sum of the planning lead times for the two manufacturing stages (this is the obvious clockwork planning calculation) is excessively conservative. A shorter delivery lead time can be promised, because of the opportunity for statistical averaging; but, to take advantage of that opportunity, two things must happen. First, the two distributions must be available. Second, goods must always be moved through the manufacturing process at the earliest opportunity and not be held up because they are ahead of some nominal schedule that is "good enough."

Potential Effects on Manufacturing Productivity

The satisficing scenario sketched in the preceding paragraph is not entirely true to life, because all parties concerned with the planning and scheduling process know that slack has been built into the parameters of a clockwork planning model, and this slack may be exploited in urgent situations. Specifically, if an urgent order is received from an important customer, high-level managers may feel justified in adding manufacturing tasks to the existing factory backlog, without rescheduling existing work, and may also attach due dates to new manufacturing orders that are directly determined by customer desires, without regard to the planning lead times that have been agreed upon and incorporated in the formal system. Given the understatement of real capabilities in the formal system, this may seem to be a reasonable practice, and many marketing managers equate service orientation with the willingness to accept such orders on an ad hoc basis. However, this results in a chaotic or (at best) poorly structured manufacturing environment, and the operating organization is constantly called upon to accommodate requests or demands made outside the constraints implicit in the formal planning system. A way often can be found, but the resulting disorder may seriously impede manufacturing productivity improvement.

Such a system produces a job shop environment wherein production lots are differentiated *on the factory floor* according to their relative urgency (as reflected in the relative proximity of lot due dates). It introduces an additional dimension of complexity in the manufacturing task, complexity unrelated to the actual physical tasks of processing and testing wafers or assembling and testing devices. A growing body of armchair speculation and empirical study, stimulated largely by the very simple manufacturing control systems employed by successful Japanese companies, suggests that this complexity retards improvement in manufacturing productivity. When shop-floor supervisors feel that they must schedule jobs to ensure that internal due dates are met, they cannot focus on the basic tasks of releasing jobs and specifying sequences at work stations so that utilization is maximized and overall average flow times are minimized.

Of course, the management of a manufacturing network requires differentiation among jobs according to their relative priority, especially in a make-to-order business, but such priorities need not affect factory floor operations. In highly structured, flow-oriented manufacturing operations, marketing commitments and local market conditions may strongly influence the sequencing of production lot releases, but these scheduling considerations can be made invisible to personnel on the factory floor. That is, the complexities associated with market interactions drive production controllers in their loading of factories, but the internal management of manufacturing activity is driven by process control and physical efficiency considerations. If manufacturing cycle times can be kept short enough (a situation that is greatly facilitated by regularized factory input and a simplified manufacturing environment), then management of the lot release queue by production controllers often can provide an adequate response to marketing priorities. Such insulation of the factory floor from market complexities is seen by many as a key ingredient of high-performance manufacturing.

Scheduling without Lead Time Commitments

We have discussed high-level production scheduling systems that ask manufacturing managers for deterministic lead time commitments and then hold them accountable for schedule reliability on a lot-by-lot basis. At the other extreme, one may consider a system in which 1) manufacturing retains control over the exact timing of lot releases within relatively long time intervals, and 2) the time dimension of manufacturing performance is measured simply by overall average cycle time, defined as average elapsed time between *actual* lot release and lot completion. Such a scheme leaves manufacturing with maximal latitude to pursue efficiency goals, but it also produces a great deal of uncertainty regarding the timing of flows between factories and ultimately to customers.

The communication interface between PC and Manufacturing at NSC and the firm's manufacturing performance goals could be designed in such a way that completion date uncertainty is reduced (relative to the extreme scenario just described) without using internal, lot-by-lot due dates based on lead time commitments. Consider, for example, the following system design: 1) PC planners generate a detailed lot release schedule, based on transmitted capacities, maintaining discretion to alter that schedule right up to the day of release (but always working within the constraints of the capacity allocations); 2) Manufacturing retains control over actual physical release decisions; 3) cycle time distributions are compiled for each process flow, with the cycle time of a lot measured from its *scheduled* release date; and 4) the performance measures for Manufacturing include summary statistics for the cycle time distributions, without regard to the identities of individual lots. These summary statistics need not be simply the distribution means. One could, for example, compute the square root of the second moment for each cycle time distribution (this is what electrical engineers call a root mean square or RMS performance measure) in order to penalize long individual cycle times in a nonlinear fashion.

Whatever summary statistics are used to determine a factory's aggregate cycle time performance, if lead time commitments and internal due dates are eliminated, then PC planners confront a statistical problem as they coordinate the flow of material through successive manufacturing stages. Although that may be uncomfortable, production scheduling is intrinsically statistical in character, and a system based on lead time commitments and clockwork planning calculations simply pushes all statistical analysis down to the factory level. Each plant manager is asked to determine planning lead times so reliable that production controllers can essentially count on them and thus can revert to clockwork planning calculations when determining delivery quotations and time-phased lot releases.

At least in principle, having production controllers study the statistical character of individual factories and of the transport operations that connect them, and having them base quotations and schedules on observed or synthesized flow time distributions through the entire manufacturing network, has some advantages. Such a system does not eliminate all of the incentive problems discussed above, but it can modify some of them and it should increase the efficiency of the manufacturing organization (e.g., by reducing the tendency for ultraconservatism in delivery quotations for multistage processes). Obviously, statistical analysis of past cycle time performance will be of little value if the production plan is highly unstable, and one must be wary of any operational scheduling system based on very subtle or complex computational procedures. Nevertheless, an explicitly statistical approach may permit significant improvements in manufacturing cycle time commitments and lot release scheduling.

ADDITIONAL QUESTIONS
FOR INVESTIGATION

Our commentary has addressed several performance measurement issues that we found to be important in the production scheduling system at NSC. Managers in Manufacturing, Production Control, and Sales have decisions to make that will be influenced by the information they receive and by the performance measures used to evaluate them. Manufacturing managers must decide upon the lots to release, the sequence in which lots flow through work centers, and the capacities, factory cycle times, and projected completion dates to send to PC. PC managers must set production schedules for Manufacturing and provide lead time quotations to Sales. Managers in Sales must decide on forecast information and determine orders to be booked. In designing the information systems and performance measures to support these decisions, researchers and practitioners alike must confront a range of questions:

- How can procedures and incentives be established to induce reliable market forecasts from Sales personnel?
- In what form should delivery date quotations for potential new orders be communicated?
- To what extent can delivery quotations be automated in a dynamic environment? This involves questions about the design of the company's management information system as well as the form of the delivery quotation.
- What specific customer orders are to be booked? In particular, how is demand to be metered or managed so that established capacities are respected?
- In what form should information on basic factory capacities and cycle times be passed to Production Control? And, where in the system should the impact of the statistical nature of the manufacturing process be recognized?
- Where in the organization should decisions on releasing lots to the factory and sequencing lots through work centers be made?

- Will lot-by-lot cycle time accountability improve or degrade over-all delivery performance, taking into account both the length and reliability of delivery lead times?

When "the production scheduling problem" is viewed broadly enough to include questions like these, managers are unlikely to achieve the uniquely optimal solution or optimal system design. However, we do believe that an expanded view is necessary if one wishes to capture the real problem. We hope that we have encouraged other academic researchers to adopt a broader view of production scheduling and that our research will improve the appreciation among managers and practitioners for the trade-offs encountered in systems design.

CHAPTER 12

Choosing Manufacturing Production Control and Cost Accounting Systems

Uday S. Karmarkar, Phillip J. Lederer, and Jerold L. Zimmerman

INTRODUCTION

Little is known about the determinants of cost accounting systems and production control systems.[1] For example, we do not understand why some firms use plantwide overhead rates and others use department or work station rates. We do not know what determines the frequency of accounting and production reports. The accounting literature has not moved beyond generic tautologies such as, "The primary criterion for judging System A versus System B is cost-benefit. . . . To apply that criterion, the motivational effects of System A versus System B deserve center attention" (Horngren and Foster 1987, 374–375). There is some recognition that accounting system choices depend on physical production characteristics. "The physical processes of production are the keys to the design of cost accounting systems. If the processes change, the cost accounting systems should also change" (Horngren and Foster 1987, 595). But, the key physical characteristics are not specified.

The literature in operations management has similarly been reticent on the choice of production control systems. By the term "production control system," we mean all nonaccounting systems used by managers to control production processes. These systems track materials flows and stocks and physical transactions rather than accounting data. They include capacity planning systems, materials requirements planning (MRP) and its variants, order release methods such as (Q,R) and Kanban, production scheduling systems, and production tracking and reporting systems. Apart from the paucity of specific rules on the choice of production systems, there are differences of opinion about the "right" approach. Possibly due to the complexity of the problem, the technical and research literature has few if any results on this subject. Nor have the discussions in the industrial literature about the merits of alternative production control systems converged on a common viewpoint.

In general, several levels of production control must be instituted, and, typically, these are organized hierarchically.[2] A representative scheme uses the control layers of

Capacity planning
Materials planning
Order release
Detailed scheduling
Task execution

An alternative scheme might require the scheduling layer to have multiple levels of execution at plant, area, and cell levels. Furthermore, even if the structure of the scheme is agreed upon, there still remains the choice of mechanism at each level, the model, the algorithmic approach, and the information and computational procedures to be used. For example, order release schemes are broadly categorized into "push" and "pull," with many distinct approaches in each category. In materials planning, MRP systems are generally taken to be the standard approach, but these systems vary widely and include approaches like rate-based MRP and just-in-time (JIT) MRP. Some levels, such as detailed scheduling, may be eliminated entirely in certain process environments.

An examination of standard introductory textbooks on operations management (e.g., McClain and Thomas 1985, and Schmenner 1987) reveals a general agreement that production control systems can be classified on the basis of process characteristics and demand characteristics. For example, McClain and Thomas (1985) classify production systems into independent and dependent demand, job shops (batch flow processes), and multistage manufacturing. Schmenner (1987) provides an extensive classification of processes into categories such as job shop, batch flow, paced assembly, and continuous flow.

These categories tend to be correlated with many aspects of information handling, materials handling, and labor management as well as with product characteristics. In these and other texts, however, no empirical evidence or formal argument link these categories with process characteristics and control systems.

Karmarkar and Shivdasani (1986) attempt to associate process characteristics with production control. They describe various classes of manufacturing process and suggest using the variability or predictability of manufacturing lead time as one way to characterize processes. However, their discussion is prescriptive and unsupported by evidence on the actual use of production control systems in different environments.

Our central hypothesis is that the choices of cost accounting and production control systems are affected by characteristics of the firm's output market and the production technology used. We hypothesize that choice of these systems is sensitive to the requirements the market places on the firm. For example, unpredictable product volumes should cause the firm to select production control and cost accounting systems different from systems for environments with predictable volumes. The relative competitiveness of product markets also should affect the choice of systems. And, the production process used by the firm will likely affect the choice of cost accounting systems as well as production control systems (since the nature of the process will affect the relative costs and benefits of different systems). A dedicated continuous flow, constant volume process like a chemical process has little or no variability in its materials flow patterns. This stability makes it unnecessary to track physical flows or stocks on an ongoing basis for materials management or production planning. The same stability makes it unnecessary to track costs and variances at each stage of the process or to use a job order system. As a consequence, the choices of cost accounting and production control systems are likely interrelated.[3]

Cooper (1988) offers some conjectures regarding the design of cost systems to be used for cost prediction. He first contrasts a traditional unit-based costing system to an activity-based cost system. A unit-based system tracks all costs directly consumed at the unit level and then allocates some or all remaining indirect costs, using direct traced measures (e.g., direct labor or machine-hours) as the allocation bases. An activity-based cost system, in addition to tracking direct costs at the unit level, also tracks costs at the "batch," "product," and "process-sustaining" levels. The latter three categories are joint and common costs that cannot be traced to the unit level but can be traced to some level above the unit level. For example, setup costs can be traced to the batch level and then allocated to the units in the batch. Under an activity-based cost system, units in larger batch sizes will have lower per unit setup costs assigned to them than will units in smaller batches (see Johnson and Kaplan 1987, 237–244).

Cooper hypothesizes that firms with diverse product lines, producing products with heterogeneous batch sizes and relatively large "indirect" (i.e., nonunit-level) costs facing competitive product markets are more likely to adopt activity-based cost systems. He argues that in these situations the benefits of having more accurate or precise estimates of product costs are likely to exceed the higher costs of designing and operating the activity-based cost systems.[4]

One of the few empirical studies on the design of cost accounting and control systems is by Howell et al. (1987); it used a questionnaire to survey cost accounting and production control practice for 350 firms. The survey reports data on the mix of production methods, manufacturing technologies, and various performance and financial measures used by firms but was of limited usefulness, from our perspective, because it did not report associations among the manufacturing process variables and the use of various cost systems.

To reiterate, we know little about the interrelation among the demand characteristics of a firm's products, the production technology used by the firm, and its production control and cost accounting systems. The lack of knowledge of these interrelations hampers the development of a theory that predicts and explains the choice of production control and costing systems. We lack basic definitions that allow us to characterize production technology concepts beyond rudimentary notions of "batch manufacturing" and "process manufacturing." We also lack good descriptors of the complexity of cost accounting and production control systems and lack data on the interrelations between actual manufacturing processes and production control and costing systems.

In this paper, we first hypothesize that physical characteristics of the production technology (e.g., complexity and product mix), the relative amount of indirect costs, and competition in the product market are key variables affecting the design of production control and costing systems. Second, we develop an operational method of measuring manufacturing complexity. Third, we construct and field test a survey instrument to gather raw data on independent variables, production control, and accounting system choices. During field testing of the survey, five manufacturing plants were visited. Brief case studies describing the plants' actual manufacturing sites and their control and costing systems are included in the Appendix. Finally, the questionnaire was used to gather data from thirty-nine other, randomly chosen, plants.[5] Small-sample issues and other problems limit the strength of our preliminary findings. But some insights emerge as do confirmations of some conjectures. Costing systems are more useful in satisfying external reporting requirements than they are for internal managerial purposes. MRP systems are more likely to be used in batch production environments than in continuous production environments. Setup to run time ratios are high and queueing times are a substantial portion of lead time for most plants. Some associations do exist between production characteristics and costing practice. For example, the relative frequency of cost reporting is higher for custom shops than for batch flow or continuous environments.

VARIABLES AND HYPOTHESES

We seek to establish empirically whether cross-sectional variability in costing systems depends on 1) the physical characteristics of the manufacturing process, 2) instability of the production process, 3) the relative importance of overheads, and 4) the extent of product competition faced by the firm.

The dependent variables in this study are

- production control system
  1. use of materials resource/requirements planning (MRP) systems
  2. lot tracking
- cost accounting system
  1. number of overhead cost pools
  2. number of standard cost variances reported[6]
  3. frequency and reporting lag of accounting reports
  4. degree of reporting performance evaluation data

The independent variables in this study are

- physical characteristics of the manufacturing process
  1. type of production process (continuous, batch, or custom)
  2. production complexity
  3. number of products
- instability of the production process

- relative importance of overhead
- extent of competition in the product markets

Dependent Variables

The study focuses on two sets of dependent variables—one for the production control system and one for the costing system. For the production control system, we examine the extent to which the plant uses an MRP system and the extent to which individual lots are tracked.[7] For the cost accounting system we examine the number of overhead cost pools, the number of standard cost variances reported, and the reporting frequency and lag.[8] Finally, we count the number of performance measures reported at the work station level.

We assume that decisions on production control and costing systems are independent. Clearly, this is a gross simplification. In reality, both systems are chosen simultaneously, and the correct way to model choices on the two systems is to use a simultaneous equations model. Given the early nature of our research and the small sample-sizes, simultaneous equations models are not feasible.

We infer that costing systems that report more frequently are "more elaborate." Also, if MRP systems, individual lot tracking, and multiple cost pools are used to assign overheads, they too are said to be more elaborate. The cost of operating more elaborate systems, as we define the term, is higher than that for less elaborate systems. Hence, more elaborate systems should be providing more gross benefits than less elaborate systems.

Independent Variables

Six independent variables are used: three physical characteristics of the manufacturing process (production process type, complexity, and number of products), instability of the production process, the relative importance of overheads, and the extent of competition in the product markets.

1. Physical Characteristics of the Manufacturing Process
    a. Production process. The operations management literature emphasizes that continuous process plants should have different control and coordination problems than custom job shop plants have. Continuous process flow plants are expected to

have simpler materials management problems because materials flow is predictable and regular. In contrast, custom or small-batch processes have complex product flows, varying rates of resource usage, and many inventory control points. Therefore, in custom or batch processes materials management, production control and costing are hypothesized to be more difficult tasks. Accordingly, respondents were asked to classify their site as 1) continuous production, 2) large-batch or semicontinuous production, 3) medium-batch production, 4) small-batch production, or 5) make-to-order or custom production. We assume larger numbers to characterize more-complicated production environments. If more than one category was indicated, the plant was coded as having the most-complicated production process checked.

     b. Production complexity. A key determinant of the production control and costing systems is postulated to be manufacturing complexity. The more complicated the manufacturing setting, the more elaborate the control and costing systems, including the occurrence of frequently issued reports. The research problem becomes one of specifying "manufacturing complexity." As did Karmarkar and Shivdasani (1986), we choose the variance of manufacturing lead times as a measure of manufacturing control complexity. Suppose the plant produces a product with an expected (or normal) lead time of two weeks. A job is released to the plant floor on May 1. If the product is delivered on May 14, then the lead time variance is zero. For all products produced, lead time variance is defined as the mean squared difference between actual lead time and expected lead time. The greater the lead time variance, the more unpredictable are delivery dates. In such plants, the materials control system requires methods for calculating release dates and for expediting work. Also, larger safety stocks and longer lead times are expected, which increases work-in-process inventories. More frequent reporting in production control and accounting systems is required to provide managers with timely data to control the production processes and the constantly changing work-in-process inventories.

     Our concept of complexity—lead time variability—is potentially observable. However, most plants do not maintain the detailed records required to compute this variable. Instead, we use the following proxy measure: the difference between maximum lead time and minimum lead time for the typical product in the plant. This proxy measures both the complexity of the manufacturing process induced by market demands and the complexity induced by the existing production control system. Our proxy variable can have a high value even with a "simple" manufacturing process, if it is operated with a "bad" production control system.

To provide some evidence that the difference between maximum and minimum lead times has some construct validity as a measure of complexity, we test the association between this measure and other variables thought to be associated with complexity (i.e., custom production versus large-batch or semicontinuous production, plant seasonality, number of operations on a typical route sheet, machine reliability). We predict that these variables are positively associated with increasing manufacturing complexity. (For example, with more active lots in production, the lead time variance should increase.)

One would expect that the variance of production lead time can be reduced by more elaborate production control systems, by holding inventories, or by investing in additional production capacity. These activities decrease the complexity of the firm's control problem. Thus, a lack of association between the variable, maximum less minimum lead times, and the other variables thought to be associated with complexity could occur if managers engage in such variance-reducing activities.

c. Number of products. The next physical characteristic of the manufacturing process thought to affect control and costing systems is the number of products produced at the plant. In plants dedicated to a single product, costing and production control are simple tasks. As product mix increases, the resources consumed by each product and the control of the processes become more difficult. When heterogeneous products compete for scarce joint or shared production resources, production control and costing systems must provide data on the consumption of the scarce resources used by the products. A crude proxy for product mix is the number of outputs at the site.

2. Instability of the Production Process

Instability of production can be caused by complexity, but we choose to measure it as the number of engineering changes per year. Plants with numerous engineering changes are expected to have more elaborate control systems than do plants with fewer engineering changes.

3. Relative Importance of Overhead Costs

We expect control and costing systems to become more elaborate as overhead rises relative to direct costs. The importance of cost allocation for decision making (e.g., pricing and control) rises as relative overhead costs rise. If multiple products are produced at a plant, the importance of cost allocations increases with the relative amount of overhead, requiring a more elaborate cost accounting system. The proxy variable used is the ratio of overhead to direct costs.

We also hypothesize that the ratio of indirect to direct costs increases with the refinement of the production control system. In complex production environments, scheduling, tracking, and expediting activities are more important, leading to more elaborate production control activities and, thereby, to higher indirect operating costs. Production environments we might refer to as complex include those that have volatile volumes or mixes of output or those that have multiple products using common resources. The direction of causality between refinement of systems and the ratio of overhead to direct costs runs in both directions.

4. Extent of Competition in the Product Markets

The last independent variable is the extent of competition in the product market. Anecdotal evidence suggests that firms do not upgrade their costing and production control systems unless faced with an external threat or crisis. Such crises often take the form of increased competition in the product market. Khandwalla (1972) finds in a survey of ninety-two firms that output market competition is associated with greater use of management controls, such as standard costing, flexible budgeting, and statistical quality control. Alchian's (1950) survivorship principle predicts that surviving firms will have efficient operating procedures. Firms in monopolistic markets can survive with operating procedures less efficient than those at firms in competitive industries. If these conjectures are correct, then more efficient production and control systems should be found in plants facing competitive markets for their products. Our questionnaire asked plant managers if their products are in competitive markets. The problem becomes one of distinguishing efficient from less efficient production control and costing systems. Following the conventional wisdom, we make the arbitrary assumption that efficient systems are more elaborate and inefficient systems are less elaborate.

Limitations of This Approach

Besides the problems discussed above, at least one other limitation is present in this study. The cross-sectional approach implicitly assumes that there are no significant time lags between changes in the environment (including changes in the production technology and in the production control systems and accounting systems). New technology causes the manufacturing process, production control system, and costing system to change. If new manufacturing processes are introduced that cause the production control system to be modified first and the accounting system to be changed later, then a cross-sectional study at a point in time will report weak associations among the different systems and independent variables. Unless all the systems are adjusted instantaneously, a cross-sectional analysis like that conducted here will not find associations among the variables. But, this is only a problem if technological and system changes are a pervasive phenomenon. This study finds few statistically significant associations among the variables. Our finding is consistent with change being commonplace and with the production and accounting systems adjusting with a lag.

RESEARCH METHOD

We first describe the survey questionnaire. Then, we discuss how the questionnaire is field-tested in five plant visits. Lastly, we describe the random sample of the thirty-nine plants that completed the questionnaire. The next section presents the results of the study. The Appendix presents the five field studies.

Questionnaire

The questionnaire used in this study has two parts. The first part was completed by plant managers, and the second part was completed by plant controllers of the same plants. Plant managers were asked to provide the following data:

1. Inputs and outputs
   a. numbers of inputs and outputs
   b. number of employees
   c. plant size relative to average plant in the industry
   d. competitiveness of the output market (as indicated by the plant manager)

2. Production systems
   a. type of production process (continuous, batch, or custom)
   b. numbers of departments and cells
   c. number of operations on a typical worksheet
   d. type of scheduling system

3. Scheduling production
   a. numbers of active lots, part numbers, and batches
   b. inventory turnover, lead times, processing times
   c. lot tracking

4. Control
   a. seasonality of the plant
   b. equipment utilization and bottlenecks
   c. yield and process problems
   d. machine reliability and frequency of process changes

5. Manufacturing performance measures
   a. type of data collected
   b. level in the firm at which data are collected
   c. use of data in performance evaluation

6. Accounting systems
   a. uses of accounting data
   b. usefulness of accounting data

Plant controllers were asked to provide the following data:

1. General information
   a. percentage of manufacturing volume of 3 largest products
   b. plant profitability relative to typical plant in the industry

2. Cost systems
   a. job order versus process costing
   b. standard costs and variance reporting

    c. frequency of reporting
    d. cost breakdown into materials, labor, overheads
    e. unit-level versus activity-based cost system
    f. breakout of fixed and variable costs
    g. plant treated as a cost or profit center

Field Tests

A nonrandom sample of five plants was selected to field test the questionnaire. Plants were chosen if we knew senior managers in the firm. The sites were selected to cover a range of production technologies: small- and large-batch manufacturing and process manufacturing. After each plant visit, the questionnaire was revised to eliminate confusing terminology and to shorten the survey.

The plant manager's questionnaire, at seven pages, was too long. It required over an hour, on average, for us to complete in a meeting with the plant manager and the manager responsible for scheduling. Part of the reason for the excessive time was that managers frequently did not have data on several questions and had to estimate the numbers. For example, they often did not know minimum and maximum lead times, number of batches per year, and the average number of active production lots. Two or three minutes were required to estimate the percentage of machines utilized 90%, 70%, and 50% of the time, and to estimate the percentage of time work-in-process is spent in processing, moving, and queueing. The plant controller's questionnaire required about 30 minutes for us to complete in meetings with them. They had little difficulty answering the questions.

Random Sample

To construct the random sample of firms used in the pilot study, the following procedures were used.

1. *Marketing Economics Key Plants, 1979–1980* identified the plants. This publication lists 40,000 manufacturing plants in the United States that have 100 or more employees. Using the 1980 edition imparts a survivorship bias into this sample.

2. All plants with 600 employees or more in SIC manufacturing industries 300 to 3999 were randomly sampled: a selection of firms, one firm from every four pages of the alphabetically listed

plants, yielded one hundred and five plants. A research assistant called each plant manager and inquired about willingness to co-operate in the study. Forty-eight plant managers agreed to par-ticipate. Four plants had substantially reduced their work force since 1980, when the listing was published. These firms were retained in the sample.

3. The two-part questionnaire was mailed to the forty-eight plant managers, accompanied by a cover letter and a University of Rochester Simon School sport shirt to encourage their partici-pation. Each plant manager was asked to forward the second questionnaire to the plant controller. The phone number of our research assistant was included for those managers or controllers who required assistance in answering any questions. Follow-up telephone calls were placed, and the plant manager was asked if any assistance was required. Thirty-nine completed question-naires from plant managers and controllers were returned. The final sample of forty-four surveys consists of thirty-nine mail questionnaires and five questionnaires completed during the field study.

Response bias is clearly a concern in this type of study. Without a detailed analysis of the nonrespondents, we cannot conclude that the reported results are generalizable to the population of manufac-turing firms.

FINDINGS

The field studies generally confirm the hypothesis that the design of cost accounting and production control systems depends on the type and stability of the production process and the importance of overheads and competition faced by the firm. The conclusion sec-tion of the Appendix presents a detailed summary and conclusions drawn from the field studies. That discussion points out the compli-cated nature of the relation among market conditions, the production process, and cost systems and the difficulty of measuring important independent and dependent variables. For example, all firms in the field study were "small- to medium-batch" producers. The field stud-ies show that these processes are very different and have different production control and cost accounting requirements. For example, the system required by a steel plant is very different from that re-

Table 12-1   Industry Composition of the Sample

SIC Industry	SIC Code	Number of Firms
Firms		
Industrial chemicals	28	2
Rubber and miscellaneous plastics	30	3
Leather goods	31	1
Stone, clay, glass, and concrete	32	4
Primary metals	33	5
Fabricated metals	34	5
Machinery, except electrical	35	10
Electrical and electronic machinery equipment and supplies	36	5
Transportation equipment	37	4
Instruments	38	3
Miscellaneous manufacturing	39	2
Total number of firms		44

quired by an industrial testing equipment plant (see Appendix). These varying requirements are not captured by our descriptors of the process or by other independent variables. This causes weak statistical association between the process type and the dependent variables.

The sampled firms comprise a broad cross section of manufacturing firms, with the largest concentration being in nonelectrical machinery manufacturing (see Table 12-1). Table 12-2 provides summary statistics on the plants included in the sample. Six results are noted from Table 12-2:

1. The sampled plants are very diverse. Employment ranges from 40 to 3,400 employees. The volumes of the largest three products produced in the plants range from 5% to 100% of the total. The ratios of numbers of inputs to numbers of outputs range from .01 to 6,750. The number of days after the close of the accounting period until the accounting reports are received ranges from 0 to 30. And the number of cost pools varies from 1 to 225. Most of the variables in Table 12-2 exhibit significant cross-sectional variation, as indicated by the 25% and 75% fractiles of the distributions.

2. Many of the variables in Table 12-2 are highly skewed. For example, the number of operations in a typical routing sheet varies between 1 and 1,000, with a mean of 40 and a median of 10.

Table 12-2 Summary Statistics of Plants Included in the Sample

Variable	Median	Mean	Minimum	25%	75%	Maximum	Number
					Percentiles		
1. Inputs and Outputs:							
No. of employees	405	596	40	190	690	3,400	44
Volume of top 3 products (% of total)	71	65	5	31	100	100	41
Ratio of inputs to outputs	1	194	.01	.30	4	6,750	39
2. Production Systems:							
No. of departments in plant	8	11	0	5	15	50	43
No. of cells in plant	14	32	0	6	40	176	37
No. of operations on route sheet	10	40	1	6	15	1,000	42
3. Scheduling Production:							
No. of active lots	400	1,334	6	50	1,200	14,000	42
Inventory turnover	4	6	1.4	3	7	20	39
Inventory in purchased parts (%)	28	29	0	10	45	85	42
Inventory in WIP (%)	30	34	2	13	53	90	42
Inventory in finished goods (%)	0	8	0	0	10	50	42
Lead time of typical product (in days)	28	51	3	14	58	360	40
Complexity (in days)*	42	69	0	15	79	360	37
Total setup-to-run-time (%)	20	84	0	8	25	100	33
Lead time in processing (%)	35	37	0	10	54	95	35
Lead time in moving (%)	10	11	0	5	10	40	34
Lead time in queueing (%)	50	49	0	30	77	95	34
4. Control:							
Equipment utilization (%)	70	70	30	64	80	90	42
No. of significant bottlenecks	3	5.3	0	2	6	40	38
No. of engineering changes/ year	200	737	0	55	813	5,000	35
5. Using Accounting Data:							
Acc. sys.—external reporting**	5	4.4	3	4	5	5	42
Acc. sys.—transfer pricing**	4	3.9	1	3	5	5	37
Acc. sys.—cost control**	4	3.7	2	3	4	5	41
Acc. sys.—evaluate performance**	3.5	3.4	1	3	4	5	42
Acc. sys.—operating decisions**	3	3.4	1	3	4	5	42

Table 12-2   (*Continued*)

Variable	Median	Mean	Minimum	25%	75%	Maximum	Number
			Percentiles				
6. Categorization of Cost Systems:							
No. of variances reported	6	5.8	0	4	7	9	43
Days to receive cost reports	5	7	0	2	10	30	44
Overhead to direct costs (%)	49	59	6	25	68	194	43
No. of overhead cost pools	5.5	23	1	1	30	225	42

*Complexity is maximum minus minimum lead time for the largest-volume product.
**In these statistics, 5 denotes that the accounting system "meets all requirements," 1 denotes that the accounting system is "useless."

The number of engineering changes per year has a mean of 737, a median of 200, and a range of 0 to 5,000.

3. Most production processes are quite complicated: the median number of operations in a routing sheet is 10: the median number of active lots in process is 400; the median difference between maximum and minimum lead times for the typical product (complexity measure) is 42 days; and the median number of overhead cost pools is 5.5.

4. Setup and queueing times are significant. The median setup-to-run-time ratio is 20%. For a typical product, only 35% of lead time is spent in processing, whereas 50% of lead time is spent in queue, and 10% of lead time is spent moving the product.

5. As perceived by the typical plant manager, the accounting system is most useful for external reporting, and its usefulness declines for internal purposes such as performance evaluation and operating decisions (see Section 5 of Table 12-2). Using a t-test, the mean reported usefulness of accounting for external reporting is statistically significantly larger than the mean reported usefulness of the accounting system for operations decision making. These findings are consistent with the Johnson and Kaplan (1987, 13) claim that management accounting systems are dominated by external reporting requirements.

6. Overhead is 49% (median across sites) of direct labor and direct materials.

Table 12-3 provides summary statistics on the dichotomous variables. Eight results are noted:

Table 12-3 Percentage of Firms in the Sample
with Various Characteristics

Variable	Percentage of Respondents	Number of Firms Responding
1. Inputs and Outputs:		
Plant larger than typical in industry	58	44
Plant in competitive industry	83	42
Plant more profitable than others in industry	37	43
2. Production Systems:		
Custom or small batch	63	44
Medium or large batch	27	44
Continuous or flow	21	43
Rate-based, repetitive, or batch flow production	56	43
Plant fully just-in-time	11	44
Plant partially just-in-time	68	44
MRP systems—class A or B user	36	44
MRP systems—class C or D user	25	44
MRP systems—user class unknown	3	44
Not an MRP user	36	44
3. Scheduling Production:		
Tracking lots	68	41
4. Control:		
Shifting or changing bottlenecks	39	38
Problems with yield	55	42
Problems with machine reliability	79	42
5. Data Used to Measure Manufacturing Performance:*		
Direct labor	72	43
Materials	42	43
Scrap or rework	51	43
Process yield	41	43
Defect rates	42	43
Capacity utilization	30	43
System uptime	37	43
Adherence to schedule	44	43
Lead time	19	43
6. Categorization of Cost Systems:		
Job order	37	43
Process	33	43
Hybrid job order and process	30	43
Standard costs used	98	44
Cost reports issued daily	17	41
Cost reports issued weekly	20	41

Table 12-3   (*Continued*)

Variable	Percentage of Respondents	Number of Firms Responding
Cost reports issued monthly	61	41
Single plantwide burden rate	30	44
Multiple burden rates	18	44
Cost pools first accumulate costs then allocate them to products (two-stage process)	52	44
Costs separated into fixed and variable portions	77	43
Plant treated as a cost center	51	43

*Data in Section 5 are collected at the cell level.

1. Fifty-eight percent of the respondents report that their plants are bigger than the average plant in the industry. This number suggests a possible selection bias: only managers in larger plants are in the sample or are responding. Using a minimum number of 600 employees to select the sampled plants is likely to induce the bias.

2. Only 11% of the plants are fully just-in-time and 64% use MRP systems.

3. Seventy-nine percent of the sites report problems with machine reliability; 55% report problems with yield.

4. Direct labor is collected at the cell or work station level in 72% of the firms. Of the various items of data collected, this is the most frequently collected information at the cell level. Lead time data, the least frequently collected, are gathered at the cell level in only 19% of the plants. Other performance data are collected in 30–51% of the plants.

5. Job order cost systems are used in 37% of the plants; 33% report using process cost systems; and the remainder report using hybrid systems. Ninety-eight percent of the plants report using standard costs.

6. Sixty-one percent of the plants report costing data monthly, only 17% report such data daily, and 20% report weekly.

7. Thirty percent of the plants surveyed use a single plantwide overhead rate.

8. Seventy-seven percent of the plants separate costs into fixed and variable portions.

One of our key propositions is that the nature of the production process affects the choice of accounting and control systems. Continuous, batch, and custom production processes are expected to have different types of costing and control systems. Table 12-4 presents contingency tables on the association between production process and five system-choice variables. Because of the small number of observations, categories were combined to increase the number of observations in each cell. Small-, medium-, and large-batch production processes were combined into one group. In the first contingency table, there is no association between production process and lot tracking. However, in the second, MRP systems are more frequently observed in batch production settings. Job order costing tends to be more prevalent in custom production; process and hybrid systems are more prevalent in continuous and batch processes (panel 3). Finally, in panels 4 and 5, the frequency of the accounting system (daily, weekly, or monthly) and accounting system choice (one or many burden rates versus cost pools) are not associated with the production process using classical statistical methods.[9]

Table 12-5 presents the rank order correlations between our complexity measure (difference between maximum-minimum lead time for the largest-volume product) and various variables (e.g., machine utilization, number of active lots) thought to be associated with complexity. Only one of the nine variables (number of active lots) has a statistically significant correlation—.33 one tailed p-value of .03. When all the variables are included in a multiple regression to explain complexity, the resulting F statistic has a p-value of .37. This indicates an insignificant linear statistical relation between complexity and the set of variables thought associated with complexity.

Table 12-6 contains rank order correlations between the dependent variables (MRP, lot tracking, number of cost pools, number of standard cost variances, frequency and lag of accounting reports, number of performance measures accumulated at the cell level) and the independent variables (production process, complexity, number of outputs, number of engineering changes/year, ratio of overhead to direct costs, and whether or not the plant is in a competitive industry). The estimated rank correlations are uniformly small and statistically insignificant. The largest rank order correlation is .43 (ratio of overhead to direct costs and number of performance measures collected at the cell level). Care must be taken in interpreting these rank

Table 12-4 Contingency Tables between Production Process Type and System Choices

Production Process	1. Lot Tracking		2. MRP System	
	Yes	No	A-, B-, C-, D-type User	Unknown or Not MRP
Continuous production	1	2	0	4
Batch production (small, medium, or large)	10	4	12	3
Custom production	17	7	15	10
Chi-Square statistic	1.83		8.57	
P-value*	.40		.01	

Production Process	3. Job/Process Costing		4. Frequency of Accounting Reports	
	Job Order	Process/Hybrid	Daily or Weekly	Monthly or Quarterly
Continuous production	0	4	1	3
Batch production (small, medium, or large)	5	10	3	10
Custom production	11	13	11	13
Chi-Square statistic	3.23		2.14	
P-value*	.20		.34	

Production Process	5. Accounting System	
	One or Many Burden Rates	Cost Pools
Continuous production	1	3
Batch production (small, medium, or large)	6	9
Custom production	14	11
Chi-Square statistic	1.87	
P-value*	.39	

*Because more than 20% of the cells have fewer than 5 expected observations, the significance tests are overstated.

Table 12-5 Spearman Rank Order Correlations between Complexity Measure and Production Process Characteristics
(All correlations are predicted to have positive signs)

Variable	Rank Correlations	P-value (1-tail)	Number
Machine utilization (%)	−.16	.19	35
Number of operations in routing	.22	.11	35
Number of active lots	.33	.03	36
Production continuous (1), medium batch (3), custom (5)	.09	.30	37
Bottlenecks predictable (1) or shifting (2)	.01	.49	33
Yield is a problem (1 = no, 2 = yes)	−.10	.71	35
Machine reliability is a problem (1 = no, 2 = yes)	.15	.19	35
Production is seasonal (1 = yes, 2 = no)	−.13	.23	35
Number of significant bottlenecks	.02	.45	32
F statistic on multiple regression	1.17	.37	28

Note: Complexity is defined as maximum lead time minus minimum lead time for the largest-volume product.

correlations. These are simple correlations, not partial correlations, and do not control for other factors. For example, the number of engineering changes per year is large for firms producing custom or highly diverse products. These firms tend to use small- to medium-batch or custom manufacturing processes. (The rank correlation between engineering changes per year and production process type is 0.44.) Production process type is strongly related (a priori) to the use of MRP systems, yielding a negative correlation between engineering changes per year and the MRP variable. However, the partial correlation between engineering changes per year and MRP after controlling for production process should be zero.

The last two rows in Table 12-6 report the F statistics and the associated p-values of the multiple regression whereby each dependent variable is regressed on all the independent variables. All variables have been converted to ranks and then the multiple regression is estimated on the ranks. This reduces heteroscedacticity in the data. Only two of the seven multiple regressions (number of cost pools and number of standard cost variances reported) are marginally statistically significant (both regressions have p-values of .11).

Table 12-6 Spearman Rank Order Correlations between Independent and Dependent Variables and Multiple Regression

Independent Variables		Dependent Variables					
	MRP	Track Lots	Number of Cost Pools	Number of Variances	Frequency of Accounting Report	Lag in Accounting Report	Report at Cell Level
Production process[a]	−.18	−.11	−.34*	−.25*	−.18	.26*	−.28*
Complexity[b]	−.08	−.17	−.35*	−.23	−.21	.01	.10
No. of outputs	−.05	.10	.34*	.13	.04	.02	.05
No. of engineering changes/yr.	−.16	.22	−.12	.10	.14	.12	.17
Overhead to direct costs	−.02	−.10	.26*	.12	.22	−.22	.43*
Plant in competitive industry[c]	−.16	.01	−.04	−.27*	.19	.11	−.08
F statistic of multiple regression	.72	.74	2.11	2.05	.70	1.02	1.09
P-value of F statistic	.64	.63	.11	.11	.66	.44	.41
Number of observations	25	25	23	25	23	25	25

Note: For the dependent variables

MRP = 1 if MRP is Class-A user, 2 if Class-B user, 3 if Class-C user, 4 if Class-D user, 5 if unknown, 6 if not an MRP user.

Track Lots = 1 if lots are tracked, 2 otherwise.

Number of Cost Pools = number of overhead cost pools in the costing system.

Number of Variances = number of standard cost variances calculated and reported.

Frequency of Accounting Report = 1 if daily, 2 if weekly, 3 if monthly.

Lag in Accounting Report = number of days after close of period to receive accounting reports.

Report at Cell Level = number of performance measures reported at the cell level.

a) Production continuous (1), large (2), medium (3), small batch (4), custom (5).

b) Complexity is maximum minus minimum lead time for the largest-volume product.

c) 1 if plant in competitive industry, 2 if somewhat competitive, 3 if noncompetitive industry.

*Significant at the .10 level (2-tail test)

CONCLUSIONS

The exploratory nature of this study and the small sample-size preclude drawing strong inferences; however, some interesting facts were learned.

1. Plant managers perceive their costing systems to be more useful in satisfying external reporting requirements than in serving internal managerial purposes.

2. MRP systems are more likely used in batch production environments than in continuous production environments.

3. Setup-to-run-time ratios are high (20%) and queueing times are a substantial portion of lead time (50%) at the median plant.

4. Despite the accolades about JIT and lead times in the popular press, few firms are using lead time-related performance measures or "pull" control systems (less than a third). Only 11% of the plants were described as fully JIT. The use of JIT and pull techniques generally require paced or synchronous operations. On the other hand, two-thirds of the firms surveyed were MRP users, and a third considered themselves Class-A or Class-B users.

But, in general, we found few empirical associations among costing and production control systems and the hypothesized independent variables.

Several possible reasons can explain the lack of stronger findings:

1. The survey instrument is noisy. First, some of the questions were not clearly written, leading some respondents to misinterpret the question. Second, although the response rate from managers agreeing to participate was high (39 of 48), some of the questionnaires were completed with a lot less care than others were. Most questionnaires had some unanswered questions. Third, many plants do not contain just one production process or group of homogeneous production processes. Some plants are collections of heterogeneous production processes, using several control and costing systems. Trying to categorize plants with heterogeneous processes and systems together with those that have a single process or system introduces measurement errors in both the dependent and independent variables.

2. Our a priori expectations of relations between dependent and independent variables may be incorrect. Alternative explanations for the choice of accounting and production control systems may be more important than the ones hypothesized here (or, extant systems may have been randomly chosen). This last possibility, while plausible, is inconsistent with empirical regularities found in financial accounting procedure choices (Watts and Zimmerman 1986).

3. The tests are weak. We lack a meaningful set of terminology to classify accounting and control systems and types of production processes. For example, "medium-batch manufacturing processes" is a vague term and means different things in different industries. Likewise, our crude classification of cost systems according to the number of overhead cost pools likely misses important distinctions. As pointed out in the conclusion section of the Appendix, a clear (if negative) conclusion from the study is that the categorizations available for production control systems and accounting systems fall short of the complexity apparent in production processes. This is a symptom of the lack of empirical work in this field. Descriptive categorizations such as "batch flow" or "continuous" are not the most objective, since they are not associated with observable attributes.

The tests are also weak if the production control and accounting systems are slow to adapt to current production modes. As we discussed, one would not observe statistically significant associations between the dependent and independent variables if there are adjustment lags and they are prevalent across industries. Kaplan (1986) in a number of site visits found that costing systems lag behind changes in the manufacturing process. But the rate of change in the accounting system is a management-decision variable. Given enough resources, managers could change accounting systems contemporaneously with production processes. Presumably, the reason that changes in the accounting system lag production process changes is that the incremental benefits of changing the accounting system are less than the incremental costs. The weak associations among the accounting, production control, and manufacturing process variables in our study are consistent with a management view that perceives the benefits not to outweigh the costs of changing the accounting system contemporaneously with changing the manufacturing process.

NOTES

1. The terms "cost accounting system" and "costing system" are used interchangeably.

2. Among the many studies describing hierarchical production control schemes are those by Holt et al. (1960), Hax and Meal (1975), Jaikumar (1974), and Akella, Choong, and Gershwin (1984).

3. Specific features of cost accounting and production control systems likely are complements or substitutes for one another. For example, cost accounting is used to predict and monitor costs. Prediction activities include estimating product costs, department and firm expenses, and how production changes affect costs. Monitoring activities include monitoring the efficiency of the subunits of the production system and managers' performance. Production control systems can be designed to complement or substitute for cost accounting data to predict or to estimate costs. Cost accounting and production control systems design likely is sensitive to the joint benefits and costs of both systems.

4. Activity-based cost systems ignore the externalities involving the cost categories. Karmarkar, Kekre, and Kekre (1985a and 1985b) demonstrate that batch-sizing decisions for one product affect production lead time for all products using common machines. Rummel (1989) illustrates the relation of net present value costs to batching decisions using a simulation. His cost functions are highly nonlinear, reflecting cross-product effects. He also shows that the relation cannot be modeled using a separable cost function of the conventional form with setup (transaction) and holding costs. However, a queueing model of the type used by Karmarkar et al. (1985a) is shown to fit quite well. However, unit-based systems also suffer from the same problem.

5. The survey instrument is available from the authors upon request.

6. Since 98% of the firms in our sample use standard costs, actual cost systems versus standard cost systems is not a dependent variable.

7. Specifically, managers were asked if they are Class-A, -B, -C, or -D MRP users. Generally, Class-A users use both priority and capacity planning at top-management levels. Class-B users are the same as Class-A users, but top management does not give full support. Class-C users have order launch with priority planning only. And, for Class-D users, MRP exists mainly as a data-processing function with informal systems used for order launch. See Anderson et al. (1980).

8. Cost systems are also categorized as using a single factorywide burden rate, multiple burden rates, or cost pools (used first to accumulate costs, which are then allocated to products). The variable "number of cost pools" is highly correlated with the trichotomous variable. Results are insensitive as to which variable is used.

9. The small samples in the contingency tables in Table 12-4 preclude sharp results using classical statistical methods. However, a Bayesian approach to the data is more forgiving of the sample size. For example, consider the conditional distribution of the probability of finding lot tracking (panel 1) given a particular process category (continuous, batch, or custom). If we assume a uniform prior for each con-

ditional probability, described as a Beta distribution with parameters (1,1). Given the observations in the first panel of Table 12-4, the posterior Beta distributions for the conditional probabilities have parameter sets (2,3), (11,5), and (18,8) for the three rows, respectively. The posterior mean conditional probabilities are of course different; furthermore, the distributions are also surprisingly concentrated (i.e., informative). Thus, given the data in the first panel, the probability that lot tracking is used for continuous systems has an expected value 0.4 with a standard deviation of 0.2; while the probability that lot tracking is used in custom shops has an expected value of 0.7 with a standard deviation of 0.07. The distributions for these probabilities have very little overlap. Seen in this light, the probability of encountering lot tracking appears to be clearly higher with custom systems, as the data in the first panel would intuitively suggest. The distinctions are even sharper in panels 2 and 3, comparable in panel 5, and not very sharp in panel 4.

REFERENCES

Akella, R., Y. Choong, and S. B. Gershwin. "Performance of Hierarchical Production Scheduling Policy." *IEEE Transactions on Components, Hybrids and Manufacturing Technology* 7 (1984): 225–240.

Alchian, A. "Uncertainty, Evolution and Economic Theory." *Journal of Political Economy* 58 (June 1950): 211–221.

Anderson, J., and R. Schroeder. "A Survey of MRP Implementation and Practice." In *Proceedings of the MRP Implementation Conference*, 1979: 6–42. Minneapolis: University of Minnesota, 1979.

Anderson, J. C., R. G. Schroeder, S. E. Tupy, and E. M. White. "Materials Requirements Planning Systems: The State of the Art." Unpublished paper, Minneapolis: University of Minnesota, 1980.

Cooper, R. "Cost Classification in Unit-Based and Activity-Based Manufacturing Cost Systems." Unpublished manuscript, Harvard Business School, 1989.

Hax, A. C., and H. Meal. "Hierarchical Integration of Production Planning and Scheduling." In *Studies of Management Sciences*, Vol. 1, *Logistics*, edited by M. A. Geisler. Amsterdam: North Holland Publishing, 1975.

Holt, C. C., F. Modigliani, J. F. Muth, and H. A. Simon. *Planning Production, Inventories and Work Force*. Englewood Cliffs, NJ: Prentice-Hall, 1960.

Horngren, C. T., and G. Foster. *Cost Accounting: A Managerial Emphasis*. Englewood Cliffs, NJ: Prentice-Hall, 1987.

Howell, R. A., J. Brown, S. Soucy, and A. Seed. *Management Accounting in the New Manufacturing Environment*. Montvale, NJ: National Association of Accountants, 1987.

Jaikumar, R. "An Operational Optimization Procedure for Production Scheduling." *Computing & Operations Research* 1 (1974): 191–200.

Johnson, H. T., and R. S. Kaplan. *Relevance Lost: The Rise and Fall of Management Accounting*. Boston: Harvard Business School Press, 1987.

Kaplan, R. S. "Accounting Lag: The Obsolescence of Cost Accounting Systems." *California Management Review* (Winter 1986): 174–199.

Karmarkar, U. S., S. Kekre, and S. Kekre. "Lot-Sizing in Multi-Item, Multi-Machine Job Shops." *IIE Transactions* 17, no. 3 (1985a): 290–298.

———. "Lot-Sizing and Lead Time Performance in a Manufacturing Cell." *Interfaces* 15, no. 2 (1985b): 1–9.

Karmarkar, U. S., and I. M. Shivdasani. "Alternatives for Batch Manufacturing Control." Unpublished working paper, Center for Manufacturing and Operations Management, University of Rochester, 1986.

Khandwalla, P. N. "The Effect of Different Types of Competition on the Use of Management Controls." *Journal of Accounting Research* 10 (Autumn 1972): 275–285.

McClain, J. O., and L. J. Thomas. *Operations Management: Production of Goods and Services.* Englewood Cliffs, NJ: Prentice-Hall, 1985.

Rummel, J. "Cost Models for Batching Decisions." Ph.D. thesis, William E. Simon Graduate School of Business Administration, 1989.

Schmenner, R. W. *Production/Operations Management: Concepts and Situations.* Chicago: Science Research Associates, 1987.

Watts, R., and J. Zimmerman. *Positive Accounting Theory.* Englewood Cliffs, NJ: Prentice-Hall, 1986.

APPENDIX

ORGANIC CHEMICAL PRODUCTION PLANT

Plant Output and Organization

This plant uses 1,800 raw chemical compounds to produce over 900 organic chemicals for a wide variety of applications. The plant's outputs are intermediate products used in other chemical products. Over 200 employees work on 450 machines in three large, interconnected buildings and a smaller building. They are organized into four manufacturing departments and one service department. Each manufacturing department is composed of about three work centers or cells. There are ten to fifteen bays in each work center. A bay consists of three or four reactor vessels. Two bays share filtration equipment (centrifuge). There is roughly one dryer in each department.

Safety and quality are of the utmost concern in the manufacturing process. Cost is of less importance. Manufacturing cells with similar production capability are not physically grouped together but rather are disbursed throughout the plant to assure that, in the unlikely event of an accident, the plant will have remaining production capability to produce the wide range of products.

Manufacturing Process

Organic chemicals are produced in a series of complex chemical reactions. Several raw materials are combined and heated in a reactor (a still). Skilled workers are required to operate the reactions to bring the temperatures up to the right levels at the right times. The output is then filtered to remove impurities and another set of reactions occurs and its output filtered. Then, the product is dried in a dryer. Last, the output is tested and the equipment is cleaned and readied for the next work order. To produce the final (intermediate) product, several series of these processes are combined. The production process is intermittent, batch flow with small- to medium-sized batches. Raw materials and overhead each account for about half of manufacturing costs. Direct labor accounts for a small percentage.

There is considerable variation in process yield and quality across batches because operating the reactors requires substantial operator skill. Small changes in the chemistry of the raw inputs and impurities have large impacts on quality and yield. The chemists are continually making small changes in batch sizes and input mixes to affect yields and quality. There are few process changes but numerous product changes.

At any one time, there are over 200 active work orders in the plant. There is considerable variation in lead times across products. One high-volume product has over a one-year lead time from inventory order to delivery and requires 20 manufacturing steps. For other large-volume products, typical lead time from the issuance of the work order to the delivery of the final product is about two and a half weeks. Thirty-five percent of this time is spent in processing, 10% in moving intermediate production, and 55% in queues waiting for processing and assembling the necessary inputs. About 20% of total processing time is spent on "wrap-up," which includes cleaning the reactors. Plant utilization is very high. Equipment utilization averages 80%. This plant is bigger and more profitable than other plants in the industry.

Manufacturing Control System

The plant uses a computer mainframe-based commercial MRP II system to control production. The new system became operational in February 1988. The system tracks lots. Every time a batch moves to another control point, a transaction is entered into the MRP system. Work orders for jobs are released to the job floor. Kanban or just-in-time control is not used internally or for deliveries. This commercial MRP system was designed for traditional job shop parts manufacturing environments. The plant manager said that substantial time and creativity are required to "fool" the system into treating releases correctly. For example, a series of reactions is often organized as a "campaign," with close coordination between the separate tasks. In the MRP system, the coordination requirements are not automatically recognized.

Measuring Manufacturing Performance

The new MRP system is the principal system measuring manufacturing performance. Direct labor, materials, scrap, and process yield are tracked by job and cell. Performance of personnel at the cell (work station) and department level is not evaluated directly by any one performance measure. Managers are held responsible for quality, safety, and meeting delivery schedules. Plant management is held responsible for costs and schedules, but again this is not a high priority.

Accounting System

The accounting system is a job order cost system based on standard costs. The new MRP system provides basic cost information on a daily basis. Management is planning to use activity-based costs to compute overhead rates for indirect costs. These are the "standards" entered into the MRP system, which costs jobs at standard cost. At the end of each month, all finished jobs are costed at actual, which requires variances to be assigned to the finished jobs. Fixed and variable costs are not used for normal reporting purposes. Plant management believes the accounting system meets requirements for external reporting purposes and partially meets requirements for transfer pricing and cost control. Plant managers rely on other systems to evaluate performance and to provide information for operating decisions.

Observations

1. An activity-based costing analysis revealed that the largest-volume product was consuming very little testing resources. The product's quality control was ensured in other ways. But testing costs were allocated on pounds of product produced. When testing costs were allocated based on actual testing inputs, the reported cost of the high-volume product fell 20%.

2. The accounting system has been in a state of change for several years. The current system is really a number of different systems involving the MRP system, the general ledger, PC-based spreadsheets, and other software on a variety of equipment. The system is scheduled to change again in twelve months when it will be required to "close the books" within one week after the end of the month instead of the current three weeks.

3. All the plant's customers are other internal divisions. They are billed for product at full actual cost. But, because actual costs are not known until the end of the year when all variances can be allocated to the jobs, end users receive statements each month revising the cost of products received earlier in the year. Thus, a customer that received just one delivery from the plant in January would receive statements throughout the year revising the cost of this one delivery. This practice is scheduled to be eliminated. Deliveries will be billed at roughly full standard costs and remaining variances will be allocated to downstream lines of business at the end of the year.

INDUSTRIAL TESTING EQUIPMENT PLANT

Plant Output and Organization

This plant produces testing equipment used by manufacturers, testing laboratories, and researchers. The plant produces 720 different finished products organized into three major product families. The products are assembled from over 6,000 parts, which go into ten major kinds of subassemblies like printed circuit boards and power supplies. The plant has about 60 workers organized into two main sections: component fabrication and assembly. The assembly area is organized physically into three modules, each of which is assigned a certain product family. Recently, the modules were used as the basis for reorganization of the work force into teams (red, white, and blue). Under the reorganization, in addition to direct labor, support and indirect staff (inspection, quality control, engineering, materials handling) are also assigned to teams.

The component fabrication area is less amenable to this type of assignment, since there are common resources shared by all products. These include automatic insertion machines and a wave solder machine. Nevertheless, in order to avoid a fourth organizational group, these machines have been assigned to teams in an arbitrary way. In addition, due to output variation, printed circuit board production is not uniform across the three product families, so that the teams in this area may be assigned work freely from other product groups.

Manufacturing Process

The major part of the fabrication process consists of printed circuit board production. This includes automated insertion of standard components (medium-batch process), manual insertion of other components, and wave solder (semicontinuous). Fabricated and purchased parts and subassemblies are inventoried and drawn as needed for final assembly. Final assembly is a manual serial build in batches. There are four major levels in the bill-of-materials for the average product, although each level may involve several steps.

Direct materials account for 70% of manufacturing costs, direct labor 10%, and indirect costs and overheads 20%. The production process is fairly stable, but there are frequent engineering changes to products (as many as 200 per year). The bottlenecks in the plant, mostly in fabrication, change with mix. Process yield and machine reliability are significant issues, and preventive maintenance is used in most machine centers. The leading product comprises 15% of the total volume of output, as does the second. The remaining products have small shares of the volume.

At any time, there are 400 active orders in the system. The average batch size for a product is a two-week's supply. Lead times do not vary substantially and the average lead time is 60 days from release to finished inventory. However, lead times for purchased components average 12 weeks and may be as long as 30 weeks. Only 30% of shop time is processing time, the remainder being queue, move, and storage.

Manufacturing Control System

The plant uses a minicomputer-based MRP system to control production. Over the last few years, production managers have carried out a substantial restructuring of the production bill-of-materials in order to effect lead time reductions. The plant does not use pull or Kanban methods, or detailed scheduling software.

Measuring Manufacturing Performance

Direct labor is tracked at the cell level, materials at the plant level. Scrap and defect rates are monitored at the department level. Capacity utilization, delivery performance, and lead times are all tracked at the plant level, and there is considerable emphasis placed on lead times and delivery performance. Inventory turn and work-in-process are considered important measures, and inventory is valued at fully burdened cost. Summary reports are primarily produced at the plant level for upper management. In addition, education, training levels, and cooperation with peer groups are used in performance measurement.

Accounting System

The costing system has elements of both a job order and a process costing system, with emphasis on the former. Standard costs are used, and variances are computed for price, labor rate and usage, overhead, and scrap. Plant management and department heads receive variance reports. Product costs are reported monthly; a single plantwide burden rate is used, and allocation of costs is on the basis of standard direct labor hours. The system meets external reporting requirements and is used for transfer pricing (done at full standard cost). It is not widely used for control or operating decisions by production managers.

Observations

The accounting system was not being widely used to develop costs or to provide production managers with information for operating decisions. The controller perceived this as a user problem rather than as a deficiency of the system. He also felt that no concrete incentives were attached to measures such as direct labor and materials, which were in use. Production managers, on their part, expressed a stereotypical lack of confidence with the value of the accounting system. Production used many nonaccounting measures such as lead times and education and training and also used somewhat intangible issues such as reaction to contingencies. Furthermore, there was a growing emphasis on the use of group or team measures of performance.

STEEL PLANT

Plant Output and Organization

This plant has 1,800 workers and uses three basic raw materials (nickel, chromium, and scrap) to produce over 25,000 different intermediate products: specialty steel coils of varying degrees of hardness, widths, gauges, and finishes. The products are sold to end users who produce parts for everything from sinks to nuclear submarines. The plant is organized into seven departments, including a maintenance department. Twenty-four major pieces of equipment comprise the work centers. The highest-volume product accounts for 50% of total manufacturing costs.

Manufacturing Process

The production process consists of melting operations, where slabs are hot-rolled into coils, and finishing operations, where the coils are cold-rolled. Melting and finishing operations are housed on the same site in two large, separate buildings. In melting operations, the three raw materials are first melted in a large electric arc furnace. A continuous caster produces a 50-inch by 8.5-inch slab. In finishing operations, slabs are reheated, cut, and rolled into coils of approximately .14-inch thickness. Finishing operations involve a series of rolling and slitting processes and produce products with various finishes and dimensions. The typical coil goes through about eleven steps in the production process. The metallurgy of the melt operation is critical in producing final coils with the desired hardness and finish. The ability of the product to resist corrosion, for example, depends on the chemistry of the melt operation. The melting of a "heat" is approximately a 4–6-hour process, including refining and casting, and produces 12 coils. Melting takes place three shifts a day, seven days a week. All the coils in a heat must have the same chemistry. Therefore, they have to batch order coils to make a melt. Since the plant is operating at capacity, very little output is for inventory. Currently, there is a 12-week backlog of work. Raw materials account for about 50% of total manufacturing costs. Labor and overhead (including energy) each account for about 25% of manufacturing costs.

Process yield is a significant management problem. Defective coils result when the surface characteristics, for example, do not meet specifications (perhaps because small bubbles or scratches appear). These may be due to a bad melt (wrong input mix or wrong melt temperatures/time) or bad finishing operations. Fixing responsibility for defects requires conferences involving the various department heads. Defects and rework are major considerations.

At any one time, there are 420 active work orders in the plant. Typical lead time from the issuance of the work order to the delivery of the final product is about six weeks. Only 10% of this time is spent in processing and moving intermediate production; 90% is spent in queue waiting for processing. Plant utilization is very high. Ten percent of the equipment is used 90% of the time, and the remainder of the equipment is used about 70% of the time ("time" being the normal operating period of the plant). The scale of this plant is bigger, and the plant is more profitable, than other plants in the industry.

Manufacturing Control System

Detailed production schedules are set weekly by agreement of production supervisors. Careful scheduling allows the production of a large variety of products using relatively few, highly utilized machines. The plant uses the corporate computer to track production and to account for product costs. The system, which tracks lots, took four years to develop and has been in operation for thirteen years. It is constantly being revised. Every time a coil moves to another control point, weight on and off the operation is entered to measure materials loss. Resources used are tracked by coil, so that productivity, yield, quality, and spending variances are assigned to the coils that generate the variance. Daily production reports are issued reporting production in units, units-per-hour, uptime, production yield, scrap, rework, delays and month- and year-to-date figures for every one of the 24 equipment centers (i.e., control points) at the main plant.

Measuring Manufacturing Performance

Manufacturing performance measures are calculated by the production control/cost system. Manufacturing supervisors are evaluated against standards. Day-to-day operations are evaluated against specified production standards, such as uptime of equipment, production yields, and rework. These standards are last year's actuals adjusted for expected price inflation and productivity improvements. Approximately 100,000 different standards are set throughout the entire firm. Meeting last year's performance is insufficient at this firm. Significant efficiency gains are expected. Weekly and monthly statements compare actual performance to standards in dollars. Longer-term objectives (for example, involving process improvements) are set each year for each production supervisor and are considered an important part of the manager's job.

Accounting System

The accounting system is described as a "modified, standard direct cost system." It is a job order cost system that also accumulates costs at production work centers. At the core of the system are standard machine rates for each of the 24 work centers. Costs are first accumulated by each of the 24 work centers. All labor costs, supplies, utilities, and maintenance are budgeted for each center. The total annual budget for the work center is divided by the projected number of hours of uptime operation to derive a rate per machine-hour (i.e., work-center hour). At each work center, costs are applied to output of the center by multiplying actual hours spent on machines times the standard machine rate per hour. For example, crane operators who move coils are costed back to the actual coils moved, using the work center rates discussed above. "Actual" costs are collected by each job and each work center.

The standard cost per hour in a work center is a direct cost-based amount. It does not include depreciation for the equipment in the work center or any general factory overheads, such as engineering, accounting, property taxes, insurance, or salaried people. These later costs, which amount to about 10% of sales, are treated as period costs and are written off. A major capital cost is relining the arc furnaces. These costs are assigned to the melt operation and apportioned to each melt based on the expected number of melts the relining will produce.

All levels of management receive and use the cost data on a daily and weekly basis. The plant, primarily the melt operation, is at maximum capacity. Resource allocation and pricing decisions are based on "variable margins" (selling prices less actual variable costs). Work centers are scheduled so that products with the highest "variable margin" (i.e., contribution margin) per hour of bottleneck work center are emphasized. Managers report that the major function of the cost system is to control operations and to make product-pricing decisions. Least important is its use for external reporting.

Observations

Two interesting observations emerge from our study of this plant. First, the integrated production control and costing systems are a major strategic item in this company's success. These currently separate systems are being merged into a total production-planning system. The CEO designed it and is an outspoken advocate of the importance of accurate cost data. The system is used in four different ways: to evaluate manufacturing performance by operation, to make cost estimates, to schedule equipment to maximize profit margins, and to provide tactical business team managers with variable margins by item, customer, grade, and product. The CEO feels that the performance measures support an incentive system that encourages managers and workers to improve productivity. Productivity arises from the efficient use of available production capacity and of input factors, such as energy, materials, and labor. Second, unlike other steel companies, the system ignores accounting depreciation and other period costs. The company is managed using the contribution margin approach.

CERAMIC PRODUCTS PLANT

Plant Output and Organization

The plant is part of a complex of two plants located at the same site and managed by the same plant manager. The plants use different production processes. Each plant produces several products using shared equipment and processes. A commercial management organization responsible for sales and marketing exists for each product group. One production organization is responsible for managing both plants.

The plant we discuss is the larger of the two. Ninety percent of the plant's sales are high-volume standardized products sold to OEMs. The remainder are low-volume customized products. High-volume products are managed by the OEM commercial organization and low-volume products by the "custom" commercial organization. There are several hundred products produced at the plant, with the top two products comprising 40% of output. The firm is the dominant U.S. producer of OEM products. Custom products are a recent outgrowth of the technology developed for the OEM line.

The plant is a profit center. Output of the plant is sold directly to customers. The plant employs 900 workers over three shifts. The production organization within the plant has five departments, including two line departments and three support departments (maintenance, machine shop, and process management). The two line departments are divided into several subdepartments (cells).

There is a separate engineering organization for the plant, divided into four departments, responsible for engineering projects, raw materials sourcing, process control, and coordination of low-volume custom production with the dominant OEM production. Production scheduling for the two plants is done centrally by the production staff.

Manufacturing Process

OEM products are produced in a large-batch flow process, with two major production stages: forming and finishing. Production involves 230 operations and 13 major pieces of equipment. There are fewer than 10 raw materials used. In forming, a ceramic material is mixed, forced through an extruder, and sent to a dryer. In finishing, the products are fired in a kiln, cut, ground, and packaged. Large batches are fired in the kiln. Process steps after firing are on a synchronous finishing line. Within each stage, careful coordination of process steps minimizes the work-in-process inventories. There are only two places where inventories accumulate. Custom products use some equipment in the forming and finishing departments, but they also use a job shop adjoining the main production area where specialized finishing steps are performed.

At any one time, there are twenty open orders for OEM products. The equipment at the plant is highly utilized; half the equipment is at 90% utilization. Yield is an important problem, and significant resources are expended to improve it. Approximately one-quarter of the OEM parts have engineering changes made to them in the course of the year. Currently, there is a two-month lead time from order to shipment, and a week lead time from the beginning to the end of production. Sixty percent of production time is actual processing time, the remainder is queueing time. Cost of production is over 50% overhead, with labor the next most important cost. Materials only account for 10% of cost.

Manufacturing Control System

The plant uses an MRP system to schedule production. Scrap, yield, defect rates, and adherence to schedules are tracked at the machine (cell) level, while labor, materials, and uptime of machines are tracked at the department level. Work-in-process inventories are tracked at the plant level. The plant information services department publishes a throughput report, reporting scheduled versus actual production and yields for each machine each day. The report is given to cell supervisors daily. Each department also prepares a performance report using its own system, reporting data of local concern.

Measuring Manufacturing Performance

Supervisors of production cells are primarily evaluated on the basis of yield and adherence to schedule. In addition, quality goals and process-loss goals (pounds in versus pounds out) are set. Managers of the production stages are evaluated by those goals and by spending variances, absenteeism, safety, and quality process goals. The plant manager is evaluated by these goals and by work-in-process inventory goals and by responsiveness to new products.

Accounting System

The plant uses a process cost system using standard costs. The production process is divided into four stages: firing, extrusion, finishing, and cutting, and cost data are accumulated and tracked for these stages. Thirty cost pools are used. Each individual account is separated into fixed and variable accounts. Overhead is allocated to each stage-by-stage expense. Overhead is allocated between OEM and custom products at each stage by sales dollars. Costs are allocated to products by scheduled hours at a stage. Depreciation is included in the cost pools. This was not always the case. The change was made to increase manager's cost for production time. The accounting system was designed for high-volume flow production involving OEM products. The custom product line, a relatively new addition to the plant, also uses the standard cost system. The controller feels that the system accurately measures the cost of manufacturing OEM products but not of custom products. A separate, largely manual job order system is used to track costs of custom products. This system uses some data from the main system and some separately maintained cost data. Cost reports are prepared monthly and sent to department supervisors two days after the close of the month. The reports are by process within a stage and do not report product costs.

It is felt that the accounting system meets most requirements for cost control and performance evaluation. The system is judged to be less satisfactory for external reporting since it values inventory at current cost and must be adjusted by corporate staff for LIFO valuation. The plant is highly utilized and managers recognize that the cost data undervalue production costs since the cost of capacity, aside from depreciation, is not priced out.

Observations

The plant's management is continuously involved with improving performance, including process and quality improvement, personnel programs to develop a "partnership with employees," and organizational changes. For example, manufacturing was recently moved from a product focus (organized and managed by product groups) to a manufacturing focus (manufacturing is a separate organization, distinct from commercial product groups). It was felt that the change would give more attention to manufacturing. Although each plant has its focused production group, this organization is different from one using a strict "focused" factory concept. Innovation is also occurring in the accounting system. Unresolved accounting issues include a proper way to value the opportunity cost of production time and ways to improve costing of custom products. A corporate staff/plant group is exploring ideas to improve the accounting system.

CHEMICAL MIXING PLANT

Plant Output and Organization

Although this plant uses 350 raw chemical compounds to produce over 1,500 chemical product-container size combinations, 100 products account for 80% of the output. The chemicals are intermediate products used in other chemical products. The plant's 200 employees work on 55 machines in one building complex. They are organized into four functions: mixing, filling, engineering, and inventory flow. Mixing and filling have 50 work centers or cells (15 mixing lines and 35 filling lines). Most of the output is sold externally.

Manufacturing

Raw materials account for more than half of total manufacturing costs. Direct labor accounts for a small percentage of manufacturing costs and overhead is the remainder of those costs. At any one time, there are 50 active work orders in the plant. This plant has a four-week planning horizon. Production schedules are set at the beginning of each four-week period. Raw materials are delivered two days before production is scheduled. A job is in the plant about one day. As soon as it is packaged, it is shipped. There is no finished goods inventory. All production is made to order. Plant utilization is high. The plant operates two shifts a day, five days a week. One of the 35 filling lines is a bottleneck. The scale of the plant is bigger, and the plant is more profitable, than others in the industry.

Manufacturing Control System

The plant uses a commercial MRP system to control production. This is a new system, which became operational in February 1988. A transaction is entered into the MRP system every time a batch moves to another control point. The plant does not use Kanban. Weekly production reports, by day and shift, are available on Wednesdays of the following week.

Measuring Manufacturing Performance

The new MRP system is the principal system to measure manufacturing performance. Direct labor, materials, process yield, and capacity utilization are tracked to the cell level. Scrap, adherence to schedule, and lead time are tracked to departments. Performance evaluations are based on direct labor and materials, scrap, yield, adherence to schedule, and lead time.

Accounting System

The plant uses a job order cost system. The MRP system feeds the cost accounting system. Standard costs are used and the usual variances (except mix, yield, and scrap) are computed and reported up through plant management levels. The cost system does not separate costs into fixed and variable components. Product costs are reported monthly. Overhead costs are first accumulated into about 100 cost pools representing work stations and are then allocated to jobs using direct labor costs, machine-hours, or testing hours. Product is transferred at actual full cost.

The plant controller believes that low-volume jobs are undercosted because certain overhead items such as purchasing costs do not vary with job size yet are allocated to jobs based on raw materials dollars in the batch. It would be very cumbersome to "fool" the MRP to enable it to track purchasing costs. A "phantom" purchasing work center would have to be created for each job. Although no job would have to go through a purchasing work center, it would be assigned a purchasing work center dollar charge. To implement such a system would require manual transactions to move the job through the phantom purchasing work center and the other phantom work centers necessary to reflect costs that vary at the batch level or process level but not at the unit level. The plant controller stated there already were too many transactions in the system without adding the confusion and extra labor required for the phantom transactions. The current cost system tracks jobs but cannot accumulate costs by mixing or filling lines. The data are in the system, but new software would be needed to sort and report by work center. The company is reluctant to write specialized software for these reports.

Plant management believes the accounting system meets requirements for external reporting purposes and partially meets requirements for transfer pricing and cost control. Plant managers rely on other systems to evaluate performance and to provide information for operating decisions.

Observations

Operations people express the opinion that the accounting system is fine for external reporting, transfer pricing, and managing the operations at a macro level but is not terribly useful in managing the production process on a daily basis. The plant manager believes that the accounting system is adequate for managing the whole operation, but the manufacturing manager (his subordinate) expresses reservations.

FIELD STUDIES: CONCLUSIONS

Evidence from the field studies supports the hypothesis that design of control and costing systems depends on the type and stability of the production process, the relative importance of overheads, and the extent of competition faced by the firm. It is interesting to note that all the plants visited used small- to medium-batch flow systems. However, there was significant variation among plants, batch sizes, and the number and variety of products manufactured.

The steel plant produces thousands of finished products, many of them in small batches using unique routings. The products share many pieces of equipment. Complexity, as we measure it, could be very high unless detailed production schedules are done carefully and production schedules are strictly adhered to. In fact, complexity is low.

At the other extreme of product variety is the ceramic products plant. This facility produces several hundred products, in equal-sized batches that share identical process routings and equipment. The process is paced by fixed cycle times at each production stage, and complexity is low.

The chemical mixing plant and the organic chemical production plant produce a large number of outputs. Routings are standard and batches vary in size. Organic chemical operates in an environment of high complexity. Products travel through the plant visiting processes shared with other products. Chemical mixing operates in an environment of relatively low complexity. Products share production facilities, but processing is accomplished in a single day on dedicated lines.

The industrial testing equipment plant is organized into three product families that have dedicated production facilities, and products have set routings. Batch sizes vary by order requirements. Complexity is low because assembly operations are dedicated to products, and careful scheduling of shared fabrication processes reduces lead time variability.

The plants' markets vary in competitiveness. Steel and industrial testing are judged most competitive, with several competitors producing identical products. Ceramic products is the least competitive, with only one U.S. competitor; the two chemical plants face intermediate competition, producing specialty chemicals for internal use. Notable, too, is that process yield is important for several of the plants: steel, mixing, organic, and ceramic.

The production control and accounting systems for the plants are designed to meet the process/product/market requirements of plants. Steel has the most products, the most shared equipment, and a high overhead cost structure. Maintaining schedules and reducing yield losses are important factors if the high capital resources are to be most profitably used. In addition, steel produces custom orders and requires an effective system to monitor and estimate order costs for control and bidding. Steel employs MRP, lot tracking, detailed scheduling, low-level reporting of cost and performance data, and daily production and cost reports. This is the most elaborate system we studied.

Ceramic products has similar requirements, but a narrower product line that uses an identical process flow. Again, maintaining schedules and reducing yield losses are important factors in achieving profitability on the high capital resources used. However, detailed scheduling is not needed in this balanced flow environment. Lot tracking and daily yield reports are needed for quality control and cost management. Accordingly, the plant uses a less-complicated MRP system, lot tracking, and daily production control reports. Detailed cost accounting data are not really necessary for cost control or required for cost estimation, so that the period of reporting for costs is longer than the period for production. Ceramic's cost and production control systems are less elaborate than steel's are.

The two specialty chemical plants—organic chemical and chemical mixing—operate in environments where many orders must be scheduled and tracked, and both use elaborate MRP scheduling systems. Minimizing yield and scrap are important for maintaining schedules and reducing costs. Both plants track these measures by job and cell, and both use lot tracking to maintain schedules. Manufacturing performance reports are on a monthly cycle. The plants use a job order cost system with a monthly reporting cycle that does not associate costs with the lines that produce them, so that cost reports are not useful for cost control. This is consistent with their missions: to produce specialized, high-quality intermediate products for which cost is not important. Clearly, the cost and production systems are less elaborate. However, one would expect that since organic chemical operates in a more complex environment, it would have more elaborate systems; there is little evidence that it does.

With stable products and demands, and dedicated assembly lines, industrial testing equipment requires a less elaborate production scheduling and control system than those required by the other plants. Production scheduling and control is most important for shared fabrication activities. Assembly lines are worker paced and do not require detailed scheduling. Manufacturing performance is monitored at high levels, compared with other plants. Scrap and rework are tracked at the department level (fabrication or assembly) and lead time and delivery performance at the plant level. Recently, assembly workers have been assigned to teams. One benefit of the reorganization is the ability to assign performance measures to workers and managers in lower-level units, but this has not yet been done. Note that industrial testing equipment serves a competitive market and its production process uses a minimum of shared resources, with low overhead. Given stable products and stable demand, the costing system can be simple. Cost systems are not required for cost control, performance evaluation, or product costing. The system is not elaborate. For example, the plant uses a single burden rate. The production control and cost accounting systems are the least elaborate of those of all the plants we studied.

This analysis demonstrates the complicated nature of the relation among market conditions, the production process, and the cost systems, and the difficulty in measuring important independent and dependent variables. For example, the simplicity of the production process and the stability of products and demand make less elaborate systems desirable for industrial testing, despite the competitiveness of its market. The simplicity of production processes is not well measured by terms such as medium batch or any of the other independent variables. All the firms in the field study assessed themselves to be small- to medium-batch producers. We anticipated that these difficulties would cause weak associations between the dependent and independent variables in statistical analysis.

About the Contributors

HOWARD M. ARMITAGE is an associate professor and area head of management accounting and information systems at the University of Waterloo. He holds a B.Sc. and Ph.D. from Michigan State University. He is a certified management accountant in Canada.

He has numerous publications in the areas of accounting and information systems and is the author of a monograph linking management accounting systems to computer technology. His current research interests include the impact of technology on the management accounting profession and developing innovative productivity and quality costing systems. He has been a consultant and lecturer for numerous companies and programs in North America.

ANTHONY ATKINSON is a professor of accounting in the School of Accountancy at the University of Waterloo. He received a Ph.D. from the Graduate School of Industrial Administration at Carnegie-Mellon University and is a certified management accountant.

Professor Atkinson has published articles in various accounting journals, both academic and professional, relating to the topics of incentive contracting and organization design and has served on the editorial board of seven journals. He has published two monographs containing field studies dealing with issues in transfer pricing and cost allocation. He is currently completing a monograph, with Howard Armitage, dealing with the topic of productivity measurement, and has just begun work on a collection of field studies with Grant Russell relating to activity analysis and activity costing. He co-authored with Robert Kaplan the second edition of *Advanced Management Accounting* (Prentice-Hall) and is the author of the "Exchange" column in *CMA Magazine*.

RAJIV D. BANKER is a professor of accounting and management at Carnegie-Mellon University. He received his bachelor's degree in mathematics and economics at the University of Bombay with top honors, and a doctorate in planning, accounting, and accountability systems at Harvard Business School. He is professionally qualified as a chartered accountant and a cost accountant.

Professor Banker is currently involved in several research projects, including the design of productivity accounting systems, economics of information systems, nonparametric estimation of cost and production functions, evaluation of relative efficiency of organizations, financial analysis of industries, and analysis of managerial decision making. With Professor Datar, he has been commissioned by the American Accounting Association to write a monograph on "Productivity Measurement for Performance Evaluation." His research on "Assessing Factors Affecting Productivity" is funded by the National Science Foundation. Banker is currently co-editor of the *Journal of Productivity Analysis* and is on the editorial boards of several journals.

TIMOTHY BRESNAHAN has been teaching economics at Stanford University since 1979 and visited the Harvard Business School as a Marvin Bower Fellow in

1986–1987. He has a Ph.D. from Princeton University and works primarily in the industrial organization and economics of technology fields. His interests lie in the connections between competition, new technology, and industries' contribution to the long-run growth of the economy.

Bresnahan is the author of numerous studies of competition and technology in specific industries, notably automobiles, brewing, aluminum, computers, and the plain paper photocopy industry. His work is largely focused on the use of careful statistical measurement methods. He has served as an adviser to government agencies responsible for antitrust enforcement and for government statistics; he now chairs the American Economics Association's advisory committee to the Census Bureau.

W. BRUCE CHEW is an assistant professor at the Harvard Business School. Mr. Chew completed his Ph.D. in business economics at the Harvard Graduate School of Arts and Sciences, after being awarded one of Harvard's first Dean's Doctoral Fellowships. He received a B.S. in computer science from the University of Michigan.

Mr. Chew's research focuses on the disruptive impact of change on corporations and the ways in which management shapes that impact. His recent published works include "No-Nonsense Guide to Measuring Productivity," *Harvard Business Review* (January–February 1988), with Kim B. Clark and Takahiro Fujimoto and "Product Development in the World Auto Industry," (*Brookings Papers on Economic Activity*, March 1987).

KIM B. CLARK is a professor at the Harvard Business School. He received his B.A., M.A., and Ph.D. degrees in economics from Harvard University.

He has served on the secretary's staff at the U.S. Department of Labor and was a member of the committee on the Status of High-Technology Ceramics in Japan of the National Materials Advisory Board. Professor Clark was co-chairman of the 75th Anniversary Colloquium on Productivity and Technology at Harvard Business School and is a research associate of the National Bureau of Economic Research.

Professor Clark's research interests are in the areas of technology, productivity, and operations strategy. His current research focuses on product development in the world auto industry. In September 1988, the Free Press published *Dynamic Manufacturing*, Professor Clark's latest book, co-authored with Robert H. Hayes and Steven C. Wheelwright. Some of Professor Clark's publications include *Industrial Renaissance*, with William J. Abernathy and Alan M. Kantrow; "The New Industrial Competition," *Harvard Business Review* (September–October 1981), with W. J. Abernathy and A. M. Kantrow—which won the McKinsey Prize for 1981; *The Uneasy Alliance: Managing the Productivity-Technology Dilemma* (1985, edited with Robert H. Hayes and Christopher Lorenz); and "The Interaction of Design Hierarchies and Market Concepts in Technology Evolution," *Research Policy*.

ROBIN COOPER is an associate professor at the Harvard Business School. Cooper received his M.B.A. with high distinction from Harvard and was named a Baker Scholar. He earned his D.B.A. from Harvard. A native of England, Cooper received his B.S. degree in chemistry with first-class honors from Manchester University in 1972. Before beginning his graduate studies, he worked as an accountant for Coopers & Lybrand in its London and Boston offices from 1972 to 1976.

In his research, Professor Cooper examines how firms determine product costs and how the design of cost systems affects the way firms enact their chosen strategies. Cooper is a regular contributor to the *Journal of Cost Management*, having written a four-part series entitled "The Rise of Activity-Based Costing." He has also published in *Management Accounting* and has had two articles published in the *Harvard Business Review*.

SRIKANT DATAR is an associate professor of accounting and industrial administration at Carnegie-Mellon University. He received his B.A. in mathematics and economics at the University of Bombay and his M.A. in economics and statistics and his Ph.D. in business from Stanford University. He has won several academic honors and is professionally qualified as a chartered accountant and a cost accountant. He also holds an M.B.A. from the Indian Institute of Management at Ahmedabad.

Professor Datar's research interests are in the areas of productivity accounting systems, nonparametric estimation of cost and production functions, accounting for quality and flexibility, strategic cost analysis, economics of information systems, management decision making, information economics, and auditing. He has been commissioned, with Professor Banker, to write a monograph on "Productivity Measurement for Performance Evaluation" for the American Accounting Association.

GEORGE FOSTER is the Paul L. and Phyllis Wattis Professor of Accounting at the Graduate School of Business, Stanford University. He is co-author with Charles T. Horngren of *Cost Accounting: A Managerial Emphasis* (Prentice-Hall, 1987, 6th edition). Other papers he has co-authored in the field-based management accounting area include "Cost Accounting and Cost Management in a JIT Environment"; "Flexible Manufacturing Systems: Cost Management and Cost Accounting Implications"; and "Manufacturing Overhead Cost Driver Analysis." Foster's ongoing research includes activity accounting implementation and cost driver analysis.

Foster is an executive committee member of Computer Aided Manufacturing-International (CAM-I). He recently was awarded honorary doctorate degrees from the University of Ghent, Belgium, and the University of Vaasa, Finland.

ANDERS GRÖNLUND is a doctoral student at the Gothenburg School of Economics and Legal Science in Sweden. His thesis work on management control of local operations provides the empirical basis for the article.

MAHENDRA GUPTA is a Ph.D. student in accounting at the Graduate School of Business, Stanford University. Gupta has an M.S. in industrial administration from the Graduate School of Industrial Administration, Carnegie-Mellon University. He is a member of the National Association of Accountants and the American Accounting Association. His major research interests are in the area of cost management and field-based management accounting. He has co-authored, with George Foster, "Manufacturing Overhead Cost Driver Analysis."

J. MICHAEL HARRISON is the Gregory G. Peterson Professor of Operations Management in the Graduate School of Business, Stanford University. He earned a B.A. in industrial engineering at Lehigh University, an M.A. in industrial engineering at Stanford University, and a Ph.D. in operations research at Stanford, before joining the Stanford faculty in 1970.

Professor Harrison specializes in the modeling and analysis of production, distribution, and service systems. He is an affiliated faculty member of the Stanford Center for Integrated Systems, where he is heavily involved in the analysis of semiconductor manufacturing operations. Professor Harrison is the author of one book and more than thirty articles in leading professional journals.

CHARLES A. HOLLOWAY is the Herbert Hoover Professor of Public and Private Management in the Graduate School of Business, Stanford University. In 1988–1989, he was a visiting professor at the Harvard Business School and MIT. He holds a B.S. from the University of California, Berkeley, and an M.S. and a Ph.D. from the University of California, Los Angeles. At Stanford, he has served as associate dean for academic affairs and is a faculty member in the decision sciences group; he serves on several boards of directors and has lectured widely to academic and executive audiences.

Professor Holloway's current interests are in manufacturing and technology management. He has written numerous articles on scheduling and mathematical programming.

RAMCHANDRAN JAIKUMAR is an associate professor at Harvard Business School, where he teaches a course on the management of advanced manufacturing and technology policy.

He has developed and implemented a number of computer-integrated logistics and manufacturing systems for which he was twice awarded the prestigious Franz Edelman Prize for management science practice. His recent study of flexible manufacturing systems, "Postindustrial Manufacturing," in the *Harvard Business Review* (November–December 1986) developed a new paradigm for manufacturing management.

Professor Jaikumar's research interests are in the areas of technology management and the role of computers in operations strategy and flexible automation. His present research is in developing intelligent systems for design, process control, and coordination in the automotive and steel industries and studying the technological shifts in the textile, semiconductor, and machine tool industries.

H. THOMAS JOHNSON is the Herbert Retzlaff Professor of Cost Management at Portland State University. A graduate in economics from Harvard, he received an M.B.A. in public accounting from Rutgers and a Ph.D. in economic history from Wisconsin.

Dr. Johnson has authored or co-authored four books and over 50 articles and reviews on subjects in accounting, economics, and management. His book *Relevance Lost: The Rise and Fall of Management Accounting* (Boston: Harvard Business School Press, 1987), co-authored with Robert S. Kaplan, received the American Accounting Association's Wildman Award. Other honors he has received for his publications include Harvard Business School's Newcomen Award (1978), the Academy of Accounting Historians' Hourglass Literature Award (1981), and the National Association of Accountants' Lybrand Prize (1987 and 1988). A member of Harvard Business School's First Colloquium on Field Research in Management Accounting, Dr. Johnson serves on the editorial board of the *Journal of Cost Management*.

STEN JÖNSSON is a professor of accounting and finance at the Gothenburg School of Economics and Legal Science in Sweden. He graduated from the University of Gothenburg, majoring in managerial economics, received the licentiate degree in 1968, with a thesis on resource allocation problems in a decentralized organization, and a Ph.D. in 1971, with a thesis on the planning problems of investment development companies.

His research has focused on behavioral and organizational aspects of the use of information in managerial decision making. He has published studies on strategic discontinuities, the need for semiconfusing information systems, planning and budgeting in political organizations, and lately, information supports for the management of responsibility centers. He is the editor of the *Scandinavian Journal of Management*.

ROBERT S. KAPLAN is the Arthur Lowes Dickinson Professor of Accounting at the Harvard Business School and a professor of industrial administration at Carnegie-Mellon University. He served as dean of the Graduate School of Industrial Administration at Carnegie-Mellon University from 1977–1983, where he has been on the faculty since 1968. He received a B.S. and an M.S. in electrical engineering from MIT and a Ph.D. in operations research from Cornell University. He received the 1987 AICPA/AAA Notable Contributions to Accounting Literature Award and the 1988 Outstanding Accounting Educator Award of the American Accounting Association.

His current research interests focus on developing new management accounting systems for the rapidly changing environment of manufacturing and service organizations. The revision of his textbook *Advanced Management Accounting* (with Anthony Atkinson) was published by Prentice-Hall in 1989. His other books include *Relevance Lost: The Rise and Fall of Management Accounting* (co-authored with H. Thomas Johnson) and *Accounting & Management: Field Study Perspectives* (co-edited with William J. Bruns, Jr.). He served on the executive committee of the CAM-I Cost Management System Project, the manufacturing studies board of the National Research Council, and the Financial Accounting Standards Advisory Committee.

UDAY S. KARMARKAR is Xerox Professor of Operations Management and director of the Center for Manufacturing and Operations Management at the William E. Simon Graduate School of Business Administration, University of Rochester. He is the editor of the *Journal of Operations Management* and co-editor of the Harvard Studies in Manufacturing and Technology Management. His research interests are in manufacturing management and operations strategy. His work has been published in *Econometrica, European Journal of Operations Research, Harvard Business Review, IIE Transactions, Management Science, NRLQ, OR Productions and Inventory Control,* and *Organizational Behavior and Human Performance*. He holds a B. Tech. degree in chemical engineering from the Indian Institute of Technology, Bombay, and a Ph.D. in management science from MIT (Sloan).

SUNDER KEKRE is an associate professor of industrial administration at Carnegie-Mellon University. He earned a B. Tech degree in mechanical engineering from the Indian Institute of Technology, New Delhi, and an M.S. and a Ph.D. from the University of Rochester. Dr. Kekre's research is interdisciplinary and deals with production, accounting, and marketing issues in batch manufacturing settings.

Currently he is investigating flexibility and cost of quality in vehicle assembly systems, design for manufacturing, learning effects in cellular manufacturing and strategies for improving field service. He has been involved in several projects with companies such as GM, Eastman Kodak, and H.J. Heinz. His research work has been published in the *Journal of Manufacturing Systems, Operations Research, Interfaces, IIE Transactions*, and the *Journal of Accounting and Economics*.

PHILLIP J. LEDERER is assistant professor of operations management at the University of Rochester, William E. Simon Graduate School of Business Administration. He holds a Ph.D. from Northwestern University in applied mathematics and a B.S. in physics from SUNY at Stony Brook. His research interests focus on the integration of economics and operations management. He has written papers on competitive location and network design and on the organization of financial justification procedures, among others.

TRIDAS MUKHOPADHYAY is an assistant professor of industrial administration at Carnegie-Mellon University. He earned a B. Tech degree in electrical engineering at the Indian Institute of Technology, Kharagpur, an M.B.A. at the Indian Institute of Management, Calcutta, and a Ph.D. at the University of Michigan, with a specialty in computer and information systems. His research and teaching interests include the business value of information systems, measuring productivity of software development, and manufacturing information systems. He is a contributor to several international conferences on information systems, and his publications feature analytic models of information systems effectiveness.

JAMES PATELL is the Kilpatrick Professor of Accounting and associate dean for academic affairs at the Graduate School of Business, Stanford University. Professor Patell earned his B.S. and M.S. in engineering from MIT and a Ph.D. in industrial administration from Carnegie-Mellon University. He has taught at Stanford since 1975 and was a Ford Foundation visiting associate professor at the University of Chicago during 1981–1982. His research has centered on empirical investigations of the effects of financial disclosures on the stock and options markets, and he has published articles in the *Journal of Accounting and Economics, Journal of Accounting Research, Journal of Financial Economics, Journal of Business and Economic Statistics, Journal of Legal Studies*, and the *Accounting Review*.

MICHIHARU SAKURAI is a professor of accounting in the School of Business at Senshu University, Tokyo, Japan. He received a Ph.D. in accounting from Waseda University.

He has published several books, including *Managerial Cost Accounting* (1979), *Study on Management Accounting Standards in the U.S.* (1982), *Cost Accounting* (1983), *Cost Accounting for Software* (1987), and *High-Tech Accounting* (1988). He has published numerous articles in Japanese as well as American journals, such as *Industrial Management* and *Diamond Harvard Business* (Japanese version of *Harvard Business Review*).

He has been an active member of the Japan Accounting Association and the Japan Cost Accounting Association. He was the recipient of the Japan Accounting Association Award for Outstanding Contribution to Accounting Literature in 1979 and the Japanese Certified Public Accounting Association Academic Award in 1982.

He currently serves on numerous Japanese government and industrial committees related to the cost accounting of high-tech, software, communication, and service industries. He also served as a researcher and consultant to the CAM-I Management Systems project.

PETER B. B. TURNEY is the Tektronix Professor of Cost Management at Portland State University. He received a B.A. in economics and accounting from the University of Bristol, England, and an M.S. in accounting and quantitative analysis and a Ph.D. in accounting and information systems from the University of Minnesota.

Dr. Turney's articles on cost management and information systems have appeared in leading management journals. He has co-authored, with Robin Cooper, several Harvard Business School cases on product costing. The second edition of his book *Auditing EDP Systems*, co-authored with Donald Watne, will be published by Prentice-Hall in 1990.

JEROLD L. ZIMMERMAN is Alumni Distinguished Professor at the William E. Simon Graduate School of Business Administration, University of Rochester. He holds a B.S. degree from the University of Colorado and a Ph.D. from the University of California, Berkeley. He won the American Accounting Association 1978 Competitive Manuscript Award for "The Costs and Benefits of Cost Allocations." His two papers, co-authored with Ross Watts, "Toward a Positive Theory of the Determination of Accounting Standards" and "The Demand for and Supply of Accounting Theories: The Market for Excuses," received the American Institute of Certified Public Accountants Notable Contribution to Accounting Literature Award in 1978 and 1979. He and Watts published *Positive Accounting Theory* (Prentice-Hall, 1986), and his articles have appeared in leading academic accounting journals.

Index